G000153447

SAINTS ARE NOT SAD

F. J. SHEED

SAINTS ARE NOT SAD

Short Biographies of Joyful Saints

IGNATIUS PRESS   SAN FRANCISCO

Originally published in 1949, Sheed & Ward, Inc., New York.

NIHIL OBSTAT:
  Eduardus J. Mahoney, S.T.D.
  Censor Deputatus

IMPRIMATUR:
  E. Morrogh Bernard
  Vic. Gen.

Westmonasterii, die 2a Augusti, 1949

Initial capitals by Johannes Troyer

Cover image © Peter Zilei/iStockphoto
Cover design by Roxanne Mei Lum

© 2012 Ignatius Press, San Francisco
All rights reserved
ISBN 978-1-58617-597-9
Library of Congress Control Number 2011 30701
Printed in the United States of America ∞

"A sad saint would be a sorry saint."

— ST. FRANCIS DE SALES

CONTENTS

ASSEMBLER'S NOTE

When Milton wrote:

Avenge, O Lord, Thy slaughtered Saints,

he was not calling down a curse on the writers of saints' lives. Yet many a saint has suffered more from his biographer than from his persecutors. The fathers stone the prophets, and the sons build the monuments: and often the monuments ought to be stoned too. This, if done as an act of reparation to the dead, is a pious act, but it should not be done merely to relieve the feelings. The best thing of all is to ignore the unworthy monument and build a worthy.

The last quarter-century has seen a great number of worthy monuments, almost a rebirth of hagiography, with the accent on reality, the saint allowed to be himself and not forced to fit the writer's notion of what a saint ought to be. Some of the best books of the years between the world wars were saints' lives. There is no point in listing them, they are still in print, still selling and likely to sell.

But as well as the books, there have been shorter sketches of saints, of the same decent reality, appearing here, there and everywhere. Because it is a pity that they should be lost, forty of them are brought together here.

What has the reader to gain from meeting the saints in such large numbers? Two things—relief from monotony, and contact with vitality. First, relief from monotony: men are in their essential personality irreducibly diverse: but sin blots out the distinctions and reduces the diversity: sin drains out the color of the man (which is his own and inimitable) and replaces it with the color of sin which is common property: all sinners look less like themselves and more like one another. Saints are intensely themselves. Second, contact with vitality: sin, being a following of the line of least resistance, inevitably lessens vitality: it takes no more vitality to go with the stream of inclination than with

11

any other stream: but to go against, as the saint does, demands immense vitality. If by chance you think saints are saints because they lack the energy for sin, meet forty of them and see.

F. J. S.

SAINTS ARE NOT SAD

SAINT PAUL

[*d. probably* A.D. *67*]

C. C. Martindale, S.J.

UST BEFORE the coast of Asia Minor swings south toward Palestine, is a small triangle of soil among huge mountains—Cilicia. In it, upon the Cydnus, stands the town Tarsus. For a thousand years before Christ, Greeks, Assyrians, Persians, Syrians, Jews, and, last of all, the Romans, had poured into the land; Julius Caesar himself had fascinated the town and for a while it renamed itself Juliopolis. When he was murdered, Anthony went there to visit his half-of-the-world, and Cleopatra, with purple sails and silver oars, was carried up the Cydnus to visit him. But the town had retained its proud personality and had deserved to do so. To maintain and develop itself, it had literally hurled its river this way and that, the stream that used to run now in driblets, and now torrential and yellow, making the plain a mere marsh horrible with malaria. It had established the shifting coastline with solid quays, huge docks and warehouses; inland, behind the steaming orchards, its merchants had built opulent villas on the foothills; and even through the Taurus range, that rock wall over 4,000 feet high behind them, chisels had carved a carriage road with cliffs sheer 600 feet this side and that, for trade to pass over the bleak uplands with their boulders, salt-crusted lakes, and heaths, and descend once more to the vast emporiums like Ephesus or Smyrna, and set forth, westward, to Greece, to Italy, Spain or Gaul, or Britain. High above even these aristocrats of trade, lived Roman Citizens of Tarsus, proud as princes.

In, then, this town, heiress of so many centuries, a boy was born when our Lord may have been but fifteen years of age. He was named Saul, after the first king of Israel, his family being Jewish, of the tribe of Benjamin. His father, Roman citizen, yet intensely Jewish, sent his son,

aged about thirteen, to Jerusalem to be educated by the famous Rabbi
Gamaliel. The education was traditional, narrowly religious, fiercely
nationalist.

Even though proud of his citizenship and able fully to appreciate
the grandeur and the structure of the Roman Empire, Saul was to
grow up passionately Jewish. He was to be above all, "Hebrew, son of
Hebrews; Pharisee, son of Pharisees: according to the strictest sect of
our religion I lived a Pharisee"; he was "irreproachable" even as to the
ten thousand regulations with which tradition had overlaid the Law of
Moses.

Back in Tarsus during our Lord's brief public life, he never actually
met him: but he was again in Jerusalem just when St. Stephen provoked his listeners to frenzy by proclaiming that the Jesus whom they
had crucified was the Christ, their King; and while they were battering
Stephen into pulp with stones the youth was grimly keeping guard over
the cloaks they had thrown off. He was "approving everything that was
being done"; went straight to the high priest to get leave to exterminate
the new sect; forced his way into private houses and dragged both men
and women to prison; and, says he (when the memory of those days
had become a haunting nightmare), "in my excess of madness I would
pursue them even into distant cities." They fled, in fact to Damascus,
and thither, "breathing out threats and murder", he followed.

The city was already gleaming white amid its orange groves, when
a light shone for him that outdazzled the noon, and from the light, a
vision, and a voice. "Saul, Saul, why persecutest thou me?" "Who art
thou?" "I am Jesus, whom thou art persecuting." "Lord, what wouldst
thou have me do?" "Stand up, enter the city, and it shall be told thee
what thou must do . . ." Blind, led by the hand, he stumbled into
Damascus, was received by the frightened Ananias, and was baptized.

See then here a whole life violently uprooted; a mind turned upside down; a career of flaming publicity, of nationalist ferocity, extinguished; a prospect of meeting with but rage on the part of his one-time
allies, and with, at best, a chill bewilderment on the part of Christians
still bleeding from the wounds that this terrifying convert had inflicted
on them. No wonder he plunged into the hidden deserts of Arabia to
recapture his very wits; to steel his will for the future struggle; to pray
his way into the very heart of the mystery that had been revealed to

him—that *Christ was one with his Christians*—"Why persecutest thou *me?*" that *Christ* was *within himself*—"Christ was revealed *in me*"—and to assimilate the enormous charge that had been laid on him—that he was to be *world*-Apostle. "Thou art like a casket specially chosen, within which my Name is to be carried far—even to the pagans."

Clearly I cannot, in these few minutes, even outline to you this man's further life: his return to Palestine and gradual acceptance by the apostles; his clashes with the Jews as the arch-apostate; his active life, beginning around Tarsus itself; then gradually taking in all Asia Minor; its Romanized towns; its ancient stony villages in the unsophisticated uplands that he liked so much; down then into its feverish coast cities, commercial yet fanatically religious centers like Ephesus, a sort of Shanghai crossed with Mecca; then over into Europe, planting himself, for example, at Philippi, a nerve center of the military and trade life of the Empire, and at Thessalonika, that half of you remember as Salonika. Nor his descent into delicate, cultured Athens, where they politely laughed at him; and into Corinth, city of trade and blatant immorality, which welcomed him far better. Nor of his journey to Rome (his shipwreck off Malta is described with glorious vivacity by St. Luke, his doctor and chronicler); nor can I explain why I think it certain he went afterward to Spain and conceivably even into Britain.

I can't even properly describe his character—his genius for friendship, his quivering sensitiveness, his exquisitely responsible gratitude, his passionate *interest* in everything—why, in athletics! He says he has his race to run, and *runs* it, in no doubt about his goal; he fights, not like a man who is *shadow boxing*—his almost motherly tenderness, his white-hot earnestness of conviction; his attention to smallest details, the sublimity of his ideal; his total disregard of physical pain, of dangers from brigand or from secret assassin, or from official police, or from sea or from fire. I can't even express to you his delightful sense of humor; his perfect courtesy; the obstinate courage required for his monotonous work, first trying (and failing) to persuade his fellow Jews, and then trying to convince the pagan populations (and succeeding), and again, straining to keep his converts loyal to the Faith they had professed. And all this, being a man small, ugly, constantly ill, often feeling horribly frightened, desperately lonely. I say this, not out of my head, but able to prove each word from his own letters.

I will then, single out two points only. One a thing that he did; the other, why he did it.

Across the enormous square surrounding the midmost of the Temple of God in Jerusalem stood a wall; on a marble tablet was engraved the statement that it was death for any non-Jew to penetrate beyond it. Christ, said Paul, has "*broken down* the dividing wall"; God's Fatherhood, Christ's brotherhood, and Saviorhood, are for all men, pagans no less than Jews. That, from the outset, had been the Christian doctrine: the other Apostles had proclaimed it and acted on it. But Paul declared that his personal *vocation* was to preach that truth among the pagans especially. "Nay," he cried out, "there *exists* now no more Jew versus Greek, no more free man versus slave—nay, no more male versus female—you are all One Person in Jesus Christ." "To be circumcised, to be uncircumcised—that is nothing—but, a New Creation!"

And he preaches this (as I said all Saints live their life) *intensely*. "Of this Gospel was I made minister by the free gift of Grace given me according to the energizing of his power. His power that is *on the scale of the Energy of the Might of his Strength* that he made to act in the person of Christ. Ah, to me, the least of all Christians, was given this grace —to announce to the pagans the unfathomable riches of Christ" . . . yes, "for *this* I strain and struggle in the measure of that Energy of his that energizes so mightily in ME."

Strange thought, that but for the energy of this man, itself derived from the power of God in Christ, there would not be this day that great dark dome of St. Paul's that overlooms the Thames. But may St. Paul bequeath to you much more than any dome—domes, after all, some day are bound to fall. What, then, must he supremely give to you?

The source of all that creed, that vitality; simply, Christ. What did he feel about himself? That he was "Bruised, but not broken; dismayed, yet not despairing; hunted, yet not fainting; stoned, but never slain— ever bearing about in our very body the killing of the Lord Jesus, so that the *Life* of *Jesus* may be revealed in this our dying flesh! threedot *Therefore* play we not the coward; but even though our outward man be being worn away, yet from day to day is our inner self made new; for the trivial anguish of the moment works out for us overwhelmingly,

overwhelmingly an eternal weight of glory, for we look—not on things visible, but on things unseen. What we see, endures but for an hour —the Unseen is eternal!" "Oh I reckon the sufferings of the present moment as not worthy to be counted in view of the glory destined to be revealed in our regard. If GOD is for us, who can be against us? Who is going to lay charge against God's Chosen? *God* . . . But God makes us *just*! Who shall condemn us? Christ? But he died—rather, he rose, he is at God's side, interceding for us. Ah—who shall separate us from that love of Christ? Shall affliction, or persecution, or hunger, or nakedness, or dangers, or the sword; (all that can and does separate us poor humans from one another)? . . . But in these *very things* we more than conquer, through him who loved us. Ah, I know well, that neither life nor death, nor angels nor spirits, nor the present nor the future, nor height nor depth nor anything created shall be able to separate us from the Love of God that is in Christ Jesus our Lord."

No wonder, then, that at long last the aged Apostle, left alone in his underground prison at Rome, could look back in perfect peace on all of his life—the packed uproarious cities and the moorland villages, the seas and the foreign lands, right back to his babyhood at Tarsus, with its walled-in waters and hot orchards—yes, and from amid the thronging memories of friends, he needed not to exclude the face of Stephen shining like an angel's through the blood, nor of all those Christian men and women he had sent freezing into death. Now his own time had come.

The half-dozen soldiers hurried him out, down through squalid slums to the Tiber, with his back to the theaters and palaces and temples and all of the golden, rosy Rome of Nero, and then, by the Ostian road, three miles, till they turned off to the left, into a little pinewood where medicinal springs flowed. Old, sick, lonely, very tired, Christ's servant was stripped, for the last time flogged, tied to a pine tree, and beheaded. (You can still kneel there, for the site is ascertained. The place is silent, save for the eucalyptus leaves that whisper above the murmuring waters, and for the voice of prayers.) Friends were allowed to remove the body to a spot somewhat nearer Rome, and in time a different Emperor placed above the tomb the inscription that still is ours—PAUL, APOSTLE, MARTYR. He who had proved that during his earthly years life *was* for him just "Christ"—"I live—no more just *I*—but Christ is living in me"—now lives, according to his favorite phrase of all, "*in Christ*", still praying and still energizing until such time as, throughout creation, Christ shall be "All in all."

SAINTS PERPETUA
AND FELICITY

[d. 203]

*The martyrs Perpetua and Felicity with their companions suffered in the am-
phitheater of Carthage on the seventh of March, A.D. 203. They were natives,
most probably of Carthage itself, perhaps of the neighboring town of Thurburbo;
and were arrested under the edict of Septimius Severus, promulgated in 202.
The third century was not an era of general persecution; for after the first fury
of Nero's reign the emperors, though without abrogating his decrees, had often
refrained from enforcing them. The arrest of Christians was frequent, but it was
irregular; and as the number of the faithful increased, the magistrates gave up
the hope of exterminating the new religion, and endeavored only to check its
course by the sacrifice, for example's sake, of a few from among its multitudes.
The edict of Severus was aimed, it seems, not at families already Christian, but
against new converts from paganism, and even of these many must have been
spared (the Christian mother and brothers of St. Perpetua were not arrested);
but many also were denounced and condemned.*

*Among these the most famous names are those of St. Perpetua and her com-
rades. Herself a young matron of the illustrious family of the Vibii, she was
doubtless chosen on that account as a conspicuous and exalted victim. Perhaps
of her household were the slaves Felicity and Revocatus; of Secundulus and Saturninus we know only that they were of the same group of catechumens; while
Saturus had been the means of their conversion, and of his own will joined the
other prisoners after their arrest.*

By a not uncommon custom the martyrs were first placed in custodia libera
*—that is, they were guarded by sureties in a private house. Thence they were
taken up to the State prison (it was built above the town) where they suffered
not only the common rigors of imprisonment, but also (on one day at least) confinement to the stocks. Here St. Perpetua was visited by her pagan father and
her Christian relatives; her husband, of whom we hear nothing, may have been
a timid Christian and in hiding; more probably, he had died before.*

The sufferings of the martyrs in prison and the visions that consoled them, their trial, condemnation and martyrdom are related in the passion itself with a force and directness which would render vain any repetition of the story here.

～

THE PASSION OF SAINTS PERPETUA AND FELICITY

Translated by Walter Shewring

F ANCIENT EXAMPLES of faith kept, both testifying the grace of God and working the edification of man, have to this end been set out in writing, that by their reading as though by the again showing of the deeds God may be glorified and man strengthened; why should not new witnesses also be so set forth which likewise serve either end? Yea, for these things also shall at some time be ancient and necessary[1] to our sons, though in their own present time (through some reverence of antiquity presumed) they are made of but slight account. But let those take heed who judge the one power of one Holy Spirit according to the succession of times; whereas those things which are later ought for their very lateness to be thought the more eminent, according to the abundance of grace appointed for the last periods of time. For *In the last days*, saith the Lord, *I will pour forth of My Spirit upon all flesh, and their sons and their daughters shall prophesy; and upon My servants and upon My handmaids I will pour forth of My Spirit; and the young men shall see visions, and the old men shall dream dreams*. We also therefore, by whom both the prophecies and the new visions promised are received and honored, and by whom those other wonders of the Holy Spirit are assigned unto the service[2] of the Church, to which also was sent the same Spirit administering all gifts among all men, *according as the Lord hath distributed unto each*—do of necessity both write them and by reading celebrate them to the glory of God; that no weakness or failing of faith may presume that among those of old time only was the grace of divinity present, whether in martyrs or in revelations vouchsafed;

---

[1] Or perhaps "familiar".
[2] Literally "furnishing".

since God ever works that which he has promised, for a witness to
them that believe not and a benefit to them that believe. Wherefore
we too, brethren and dear sons, *declare* to you likewise *that which we
have heard and handled*; that both ye who were present may call to mind
the glory of the Lord, and ye who now know by hearing may have
communion with those holy martyrs, and through them with the Lord
Jesus Christ, to whom is glory and honor for ever and ever. Amen.

2. There were apprehended the young catechumens, Revocatus and
Felicity his fellow servant, Saturninus and Secundulus. With them also
was Vibia Perpetua, nobly born, reared in a liberal manner, wedded
honorably; having a father and mother and two brothers, one of them
a catechumen likewise, and a son, a child at the breast; and she herself
was about twenty-two years of age. What follows here she shall tell
herself; the whole order of her martyrdom as she left it written with
her own hand and in her own words.

3. When, saith she, we were yet with our sureties[3] and my father
was fain to vex me with his words and continually strove to hurt my
faith because of his love: Father, said I, seest thou (for example's sake)
this vessel lying, a pitcher or whatsoever it may be?[4] And he said, I
see it. And I said to him, Can it be called by any other name than that
which it is? And he answered, No. So can I call myself nought other
than which I am, a Christian. Then my father moved with this word
came upon me to tear out my eyes; but he vexed me only, and he
departed vanquished, he and the arguments of the devil. Then because
I was without my father for a few days I gave thanks unto the Lord;
and I was comforted because of his absence. In this same space of a few
days we were baptized, and the Spirit declared to me, I must pray for
nothing else after that water[5] save only endurance of the flesh. A few
days after we were taken into prison, and I was much afraid because
I had never known such darkness. O bitter day! There was a great
heat because of the press, there was cruel handling[6] of the soldiers.

---

[3] See Introduction.

[4] In the symbolism of early Christian art such a vessel was used to signify a Christian's
good works, or sometimes the Christian himself as the "vessel of Christ". St. Perpetua may
have had this in mind.

[5] The *ab aqua* of the Latin most probably means not "from" the water of baptism, but
"after" it; for the moments just afterward were held to be especially apt for the request of
particular graces (Tertullian. *De Baptismo*, c. xx).

[6] Or it may be "extortion".

Lastly I was tormented there by care for the child. Then Tertius and Pomponius, the blessed deacons who ministered to us, obtained with money that for a few hours we should be taken forth to a better part of the prison and be refreshed. Then all of them going out from the dungeon took their pleasure; I suckled my child that was now faint with hunger. And being careful for him, I spoke to my mother and strengthened my brother and commended my son unto them. I pined because I saw they pined for my sake. Such cares I suffered for many days; and I obtained that the child should abide with me in prison; and straightway I became well, and was lightened of my labor and care for the child; and suddenly the prison was made a palace for me, so that I would sooner be there than anywhere else.

4. Then said my brother to me: Lady my sister, thou art now in high honor, even such that thou mightest ask for a vision; and it should be shown thee whether this be a passion or else a deliverance. And I, as knowing that I conversed with the Lord, for Whose sake I had suffered such things, did promise him, nothing doubting; and I said: Tomorrow I will tell thee. And I asked, and this was shown me.

I beheld a ladder of bronze, marvelously great, reaching up to heaven; and it was narrow, so that not more than one might go up at one time. And in the sides of the ladder were planted all manner of things of iron. There were swords there, spears, hooks, and knives; so that if any that went up took not good heed or looked not upward, he would be torn and his flesh cling to the iron. And there was right at the ladder's foot a serpent[7] lying, marvelously great, which lay in wait for those that would go up, and frightened them that they might not go up. Now Saturus went up first (who afterward had of his own will given up himself for our sakes, because it was he who had edified us; and when we were taken he had not been there). And he came to the ladder's head; and he turned and said: Perpetua, I await thee; but see that serpent bite thee not. And I said: It shall not hurt me, in the name of Jesus Christ. And from beneath the ladder, as though it feared me, it softly put forth its head; and as though I trod on the first step I trod on its head. And I went up, and I saw a very great space of garden, and in the midst a man sitting, white-headed, in shepherd's clothing, tall, milking his sheep; and standing around in white were many thousands. And he raised his head and beheld me and said to me: Welcome, child.

---

[7] Or "dragon".

And he cried to me, and from the curd he had from the milk he gave me as it were a morsel; and I took it with joined hands and ate it up; and all that stood around said, Amen. And at the sound of that word I awoke, yet eating I know not what of sweet.

And forthwith I told my brother, and we knew it should be a passion; and we began to have no hope any longer in this world.

5. A few days after, the report went abroad that we were to be tried. Also my father returned from the city spent with weariness; and he came up to me to cast down my faith, saying: Have pity, daughter, on my grey hairs; have pity on thy father, if I am worthy to be called father by thee; if with these hands I have brought thee unto this flower of youth—and I have preferred thee before all thy brothers; give me not over to the reproach of men. Look upon thy brother; look upon thy mother and mother's sister; look upon thy son, who will not endure to live after thee. Forbear thy resolution; destroy us not all together; for none of us will speak openly among men again if thou sufferest aught. Thus he said fatherwise in his love, kissing my hands and groveling at my feet; and with tears he named me, not daughter, but lady. And I was grieved for my father's case because he only would not rejoice at my passion out of all my kin; and I comforted him, saying: That shall be done at this tribunal, whatsoever God shall please; for know that we are not established in our own power, but in God's. And he went from me very sorrowful.

6. Another day as we were at meat we were suddenly snatched away to be tried; and we came to the forum. Therewith a report spread abroad through the parts near to the forum, and a very great multitude gathered together. We went up to the tribunal. The others being asked, confessed. So they came to me. And my father appeared there also, with my son, and would draw me from the step, saying: Sacrifice; have mercy on the child. And Hilarian the procurator—he that after the death of Minucius Timininian the proconsul had received in his room the right and power of the sword—Spare, said he, thy father's grey hairs; spare the infancy of the boy. Make sacrifice for the Emperors'[8] prosperity. And I answered: I am a Christian. And when my father stood by me yet to cast down my faith, he was bidden by Hilarian to be cast down and was smitten with a rod. And I sorrowed

---

[8] These were the associated Emperors Severus and Caracalla.

for my father's harm as though I had been smitten myself; so sorrowed I for his unhappy old age. Then Hilarian passed sentence upon us all and condemned us to the beasts; and cheerfully we went down to the dungeon. Then because my child has been wont to take suck of me and to abide with me in the prison, straightaway I sent Pomponius the deacon to my father, asking for the child. But my father would not give him. And as God willed, neither is he fain to be suckled any more, nor did I take fever; that I might not be tormented by care for the child and by the pain of my breasts.

7. A few days after, while we were all praying, suddenly in the midst of the prayer I uttered a word and named Dinocrates; and I was amazed because he had never come into my mind save then; and I sorrowed, remembering his fate. And straightway I knew that I was worthy, and that I ought to ask for him. And I began to pray for him long, and to groan unto the Lord. Forthwith the same night, this was shown me.

I beheld Dinocrates coming forth from a dark place, where were many others also; being both hot and thirsty, his raiment foul, his color pale; and the wound on his face which he had when he died. This Dinocrates had been my brother in the flesh, seven years old, who being diseased with ulcers of the face had come to a horrible death, so that his death was abominated of all men. For him therefore I had made my prayer; and between him and me was a great gulf, so that either might not go to other. There was moreover, in the same place where Dinocrates was, a font full of water, having its edge higher than was the boy's stature; and Dinocrates stretched up as though to drink. I was sorry that the font had water in it, and yet for the height of the edge he might not drink.

And I awoke, and I knew that my brother was in travail. Yet I was confident I should ease his travail; and I prayed for him every day till we passed over into the camp prison. (For it was in the camp games that we were to fight; and the time was the feast of Geta Caesar.[9]) And I made supplication for him day and night with groans and tears, that he might be given me.

8. On the day when we abode in the stocks, this was shown me.

---

[9] Geta was the younger brother of Caracalla, and had been raised to the rank of Caesar in 198. The word *natale* here has not its strict sense of "birthday" (for according to Spartianus, Geta was born on May 27), but means the feast commemorating his elevation.

I saw that place which I had before seen, and Dinocrates clean of body, finely clothed, in comfort; and where the wound was before, I saw a scar; and the font I had seen before, the edge of it being drawn down to the boy's navel; and he drew water thence which flowed without ceasing. And on the edge was a golden cup full of water; and Dinocrates came up and began to drink therefrom; which cup failed not. And being satisfied he departed away from the water and began to play as children will, joyfully.

And I awoke. Then I understood that he was translated from his pains.

9. Then a few days after, Pudens the adjutant, in whose charge the prison was, who also began to magnify us because he understood that there was much grace in us, let in many to us that both we and they in turn might be comforted. Now when the day of the games drew near, there came in my father unto me, spent with weariness, and began to pluck out his beard and throw it on the ground and to fall upon his face cursing his years and saying such words as might move all creation. I was grieved for his unhappy old age.

10. The day before we fought, I saw in a vision that Pomponius the deacon had come hither to the door of the prison, and knocked hard upon it. And I went out to him and opened to him; he was clothed in a white robe ungirdled, having shoes curiously wrought. And he said to me: Perpetua, we await thee; come. And he took my hand, and we began to go through rugged and winding places. At last with much breathing hard we came to the amphitheater, and he led me into the midst of the arena. And he said to me: Be not afraid; I am here with thee and labor together with thee. And he went away. And I saw many people watching closely. And because I knew that I was condemned to the beasts I marveled that beasts were not sent out against me. And there came out against me a certain ill-favored Egyptian with his helpers, to fight with me. Also there came to me comely young men, my helpers and aiders. And I was stripped, and I became a man. And my helpers began to rub me with oil as their custom is for a contest; and over against me I saw that Egyptian wallowing in the dust. And there came forth a man of very great stature, so that he overpassed the very top of the amphitheater, wearing a robe ungirdled, and beneath it between the two stripes over the breast a robe of purple;[10] having also

---

[10] The interpretation of this difficult passage is probably this: The man wears a white *tunica*,

shoes curiously wrought in gold and silver; bearing a rod like a master of gladiators, and a green branch whereon were golden apples. And he besought silence and said: The Egyptian, if he shall conquer this woman, shall slay her with the sword; and if she shall conquer him, she shall receive this branch. And he went away. And we came nigh to each other, and began to buffet one another. He was fain to trip up my feet, but I with my heels smote upon his face. And I rose up into the air and began so to smite him as though I trod not the earth. But when I saw that there was yet delay, I joined my hands, setting finger against finger of them. And I caught his head, and he fell upon his face; and I trod upon his head. And the people began to shout, and my helpers began to sing. And I went up to the master of gladiators and received the branch. And he kissed me and said to me: Daughter, peace be with thee. And I began to go with glory to the gate called the Gate of Life.

And I awoke; and I understood that I should fight, not with beasts but against the devil; but I knew that mine was the victory.

Thus far have I written this, till the day before the games; but the deed of the games themselves let him write who will.

11. And blessed Saturus too delivered this vision which he himself wrote down.

We had suffered, saith he, and we passed out of the flesh, and we began to be carried toward the east by four angels whose hand touched us not. And we went not as though turned upward upon our backs, but as though we went up an easy hill. And passing over the world's edge we saw a very great light; and I said to Perpetua (for she was at my side): This is that which the Lord promised us; we have received his promise. And while we were being carried by these same four angels, a great space opened before us, as it had been a pleasure garden, having rose-trees and all kinds of flowers. The height of the trees was after the manner of the cypress, and their leaves sang without ceasing. And there in the garden were four other angels, more glorious than the rest; who when they saw us gave us honor and said to the other angels: Lo, here are they, here are they: and marveled. And the four angels who bore us set us down trembling; and we passed on foot by a broad way over a plain. There we found Jocundus and Saturninus and Artaxius

---

purple-edged and open in front (somewhat like a white cope with purple orphreys); beneath it is a purple undergarment, visible between the purple bands of the *tunica*.

who in the same persecution had suffered and had been burned alive; and Quintus, a martyr also, who in prison had departed this life; and we asked of them where were the rest. The other angels said to us: Come first, go in, and salute the Lord.

12. And we came near to a place, of which place the walls were such, they seemed built of light; and before the door of that place stood four angels who clothed us when we went in with white raiment. And we went in, and we heard as it were one voice crying *Sanctus, Sanctus, Sanctus* without any end.[11] And we saw sitting in that same place as it were a man, white-headed, having hair like snow, youthful of countenance; whose feet we saw not. And on his right hand and on his left, four elders; and behind them stood many other elders. And we went in with wonder and stood before the throne; and the four angels raised us up; and we kissed him, and with his hand he passed over our faces.[12] And the other elders said to us: Stand ye. And we stood, and gave the kiss of peace. And the elders said to us: Go ye and play. And I said to Perpetua: Thou hast that which thou desirest. And she said to me: Yea, God be thanked; so that I that was glad in the flesh am now more glad.

13. And we went out, and we saw before the doors, on the right Optatus the bishop, and on the left Aspasius the priest and teacher, being apart and sorrowful. And they cast themselves at our feet and said: Make peace between us, because ye went forth and left us thus. And we said to them: Art not thou our Father, and thou our priest, that ye should throw yourselves at our feet? And we were moved, and embraced them. And Perpetua began to talk with them in Greek; and we set them apart in the pleasure garden beneath a rose-tree. And while we yet spoke with them, the angels said to them: Let these go and be refreshed; and whatsoever dissensions ye have between you, put them away from you each for each. And they made them to be confounded. And they said to Optatus: Correct thy people; for they come to thee as those that return from the games and wrangle concerning the parties there. And it seemed to us as though they would shut the gates. And we began to know many brothers there, martyrs also. And we were

---

[11] I venture to give the liturgical Latin in my English here; for the Latin original gives the liturgical Greek: *Agios, agios, agios.*

[12] "And God shall wipe away all tears from their eyes" (Rev 7:17).

all sustained there with a savor inexpressible which satisfied us. Then in joy I awoke.

14. These were the glorious visions of those martyrs themselves, the most blessed Saturus and Perpetua, which they themselves wrote down. But Secundulus by an earlier end God called from this world while he was yet in prison; not without grace, that he should escape the beasts. Yet if not his soul, his flesh at least knew the sword.[13]

15. As for Felicity, she too received this grace of the Lord. For because she was now gone eight months (being indeed with child when she was taken) she was very sorrowful as the day of the games drew near, fearing lest for this cause she should be kept back (for it is not lawful for women that are with child to be brought forth for torment) and lest she should shed her holy and innocent blood after the rest, among strangers and malefactors. Also her fellow martyrs were much afflicted lest they should leave behind them so good a friend and as it were their fellow traveler on the road of the same hope. Wherefore with joint and united groaning they poured out their prayer to the Lord, three days before the games. Incontinently after their prayer her pains came upon her. And when by reason of the natural difficulty of the eighth month she was oppressed with her travail and made complaint, there said to her one of the servants of the keepers of the door: Thou that thus makest complaint now, what wilt thou do when thou art thrown to the beasts, which thou didst contemn when thou wouldst not sacrifice? And she answered, I myself now suffer that which I suffer, but there another shall be in me who shall suffer for me, because I am to suffer for him. So she was delivered of a daughter, whom a sister reared up to be her own daughter.

16. Since therefore the Holy Spirit has suffered, and suffering has willed, that the order of the games also should be written; though we are unworthy to finish the recounting of so great glory, yet we accomplish the will of the most holy Perpetua, nay rather her sacred trust, adding one testimony more of her own steadfastness and height of spirit. When they were being more cruelly handled by the tribune because through advice of certain most despicable men he feared lest by magic charms they might be withdrawn secretly from the prison-house,

---

[13] The narrator's words are not clear, but seem to mean that Secundulus was beheaded in prison.

Perpetua answered him to his face: Why dost thou not suffer us to take
some comfort, seeing we are victims most noble, namely Caesar's, and
on his feast day we are to fight? Or is it not thy glory that we should
be taken out thither fatter of flesh? The tribune trembled and blushed,
and gave order they should be more gently handled, granting that her
brothers and the rest should come in and rest with them. Also the
adjutant of the prison now believed.

17. Likewise on the day before the games, when at the last feast
which they call Free[14] they made (as far as they might) not a Free
Feast but a Love Feast, with like hardihood they cast these words at
the people; threatening the judgment of the Lord, witnessing to the
felicity of their passion, setting at nought the curiosity of those that ran
together. And Saturus said: Is not tomorrow sufficient for you? Why
do ye favorably behold that which ye hate? Ye are friends today, foes
tomorrow. Yet mark our faces diligently, that ye may know us again
on that day. So they began all to go away thence astonished; of whom
many believed.

18. Now dawned the day of their victory, and they went forth from
the prison into the amphitheater as it were to heaven, cheerful and
bright of countenance; if they trembled at all, it was for joy, not for
fear. Perpetua followed behind, glorious of presence, as a true spouse of
Christ and darling of God; at whose piercing look all cast down their
eyes. Felicity likewise, rejoicing that she had borne a child in safety,
that she might fight with the beasts, came now from blood to blood,
from the midwife to the gladiator, to wash after her travail in a second
baptism. And when they had been brought to the gate and were being
compelled to put on, the men the dress of the priests of Saturn, the
women the dress of the priestesses of Ceres,[15] the noble Perpetua remained of like firmness to the end, and would not.[16] For she said: For
this cause came we willingly unto this, that our liberty might not be
obscured. For this cause have we devoted our lives, that we might do
no such thing as this; this we agreed with you. Injustice acknowledged
justice; the tribune suffered that they should be brought forth as they
were, without more ado. Perpetua began to sing, as already treading on

---

[14] At which ancient, as modern, custom allowed the condemned choice of food and drink.
The martyrs used the occasion for the celebration of the *Agape*.

[15] The Roman names probably represent the Carthaginian deities Baal-Ammon and Tanit.

[16] Literally, "that firmness (of hers), noble to the end, resisted".

the Egyptian's head. Revocatus and Saturninus and Saturus threatened the people as they gazed. Then when they came into Hilarian's sight, they began to say to Hilarian, stretching forth their hands and nodding their heads: Thou judgest us, said they, and God thee. At this the people being enraged besought that they should be vexed with scourges before the line of gladiators (those namely who fought with beasts). Then truly they gave thanks because they had received somewhat of the sufferings of the Lord.

19. But He who had said *Ask, and ye shall receive* gave to them asking that end which each had desired. For whenever they spoke together of their desire in their martyrdom, Saturninus for his part would declare that he wished to be thrown to every kind of beast, that so indeed he might wear the more glorious crown. At the beginning of the spectacle therefore himself with Revocatus first had ado with a leopard and was afterward torn by a bear also upon a raised bridge.[17] Now Saturus detested nothing more than a bear, but was confident already he should die by one bite of a leopard. Therefore when he was being given to a boar, the gladiator instead who had bound him to the boar was torn asunder by the same beast and died after the days of the games; nor was Saturus more than dragged. Moreover when he had been tied on the bridge to be assaulted by a bear, the bear would not come forth from its den. So Saturus was called back unharmed a second time.

20. But for the women the devil had made ready a most savage cow, prepared for this purpose against all custom; for even in this beast he would mock their sex. They were stripped therefore and made to put on nets; and so they were brought forth. The people shuddered, seeing one a tender girl, the other her breasts yet dropping from her late childbearing. So they were called back and clothed in loose robes. Perpetua was first thrown, and fell upon her loins. And when she had sat upright, her robe being rent at the side, she drew it over to cover her thigh, mindful rather of modesty than of pain. Next, looking for a pin, she likewise pinned up her disheveled hair; for it was not meet that a martyr should suffer with hair disheveled, lest she should seem to grieve in her glory. So she stood up, and when she saw Felicity smitten

---

[17] See the title-page of Leclercq, *Les Martyrs*, I, for the reproduction of such a scene from a second-century lamp. The "bridge" in the next sentence is distinct from that in this; it probably crossed the ditch or moat at the edge of the arena.

down, she went up and gave her her hand and raised her up. And both of them stood up together and (the hardness of the people being now subdued) were called back to the Gate of Life. There Perpetua being received by one named Rusticus, then a catechumen, who stood close at her side, and as now awakening from sleep (so much was she in the Spirit and in ecstasy) began first to look about her; and then (which amazed all there), When forsooth, quoth she, are we to be thrown to the cow? And when she heard that this had been done already, she would not believe till she perceived some marks of mauling on her body and on her dress. Thereupon she called her brother to her, and that catechumen, and spoke to them, saying: Stand fast in the faith, and love ye all one another; and be not offended because of our passion.

21. Saturus also at another gate exhorted Pudens the soldier, saying: So then indeed, as I trusted and foretold, I have felt no assault of beasts until now. And now believe with all thy heart. Behold, I go out thither and shall perish by one bite of the leopard. And forthwith at the end of the spectacle, the leopard being released, with one bite of his he was covered with so much blood that the people (in witness to his second baptism) cried out to him returning: Well washed, well washed. Truly it was well with him who had washed in this wise. Then said he to Pudens the soldier: Farewell; remember the faith and me; and let not these things trouble thee, but strengthen thee. And therewith he took from Pudens' finger a little ring, and dipping it in his wound gave it him back again for an heirloom, leaving him a pledge and memorial of his blood.[18] Then as the breath left him he was cast down with the rest in the accustomed place for his throat to be cut. And when the people besought that they should be brought forward, that when the sword pierced through their bodies their eyes might be joined thereto as witnesses to the slaughter, they rose of themselves and moved whither the people willed them, first kissing one another, that they might accomplish their martyrdom with the rites of peace. The rest not moving and in silence received the sword; Saturus much earlier gave up the ghost; for he had gone up earlier also, and now he waited for Perpetua likewise. But Perpetua, that she might have some taste of pain, was pierced between the bones and shrieked out;

---

[18] The end of the soldier's story will be found by those who wish it in the entry of April 29 in the ancient calendar of the Church in Carthage: *Pudens Martyr*.

and when the swordsman's hand wandered still (for he was a novice), herself set it upon her own neck. Perchance so great a woman could not else have been slain (being feared of the unclean spirit) had she not herself so willed it.

O most valiant and blessed martyrs! O truly called and elected unto the glory of Our Lord Jesus Christ! Which glory he that magnifies, honors and adores, ought to read these witnesses likewise, as being no less than the old, unto the Church's edification; that these new wonders also may testify that one and the same Holy Spirit works ever until now, and with Him God the Father Almighty, and His Son Jesus Christ Our Lord, to Whom is glory and power unending for ever and ever. Amen.

SAINT ANTHONY OF EGYPT

[251–356]

C. C. Martindale, S.J.

HEN SPEAKING of St. Paul, I suggested that part of his work consisted in keeping his converts loyal. The Church of Christ never was, and never professed to be, a sort of pious clique. Our Lord himself pictured it as a field containing weeds as well as wheat; a net, having in it fish both pure and poisonous. The Church does not exist for men who are already good; but to help men to become good: her Sacraments are not prizes for the perfect, but much rather, medicines and tonics for the spiritually sick or weakly. Yet the Church is not a mere hospital for the morally diseased, or for religious casualties, or spiritual convalescents. The generous heart, the strong worker, the vivid imagination, the triumphant will—all these are catered for by her and called to live within her. Still, Christians are a mixed lot, and most men themselves are mixtures, as our own conscience tells us all too clearly; and I like to think, on the whole, of the Church as consisting of men who are *trying*, probably failing quite often, getting mauled and floored, but getting up again—and indeed, what can't happen in the ring, getting *helped* up again. We shall present ourselves to our Judge with plenty of black eyes and rainbow-colored bruises administered by World, by Flesh, or by Devil momentarily successful; but he won't mind that: he will say: "Well—anyway—you've *won!*"

I say all this because after two hundred and fifty years of Christianity, the level of the early enthusiasm, the standard of holiness, had sunk a good deal. No wonder. By that time, Christianity was becoming popular; and the net began to envelop people wholesale, and so contained a higher percentage of queer fish than it had done. Also, important persons of all sorts—politicians, officials, courtiers—were becoming Christians, and it is none too easy to find an *undiluted* character among these, or a behavior that can always rhyme with conviction. They think they have to compromise, to be reticent, to consider the careers of their relatives, and so forth. And meanwhile, in enormous cities like Egyptian Alexandria, worldliness and vice among the pagan generality rose to a pitch that there was no public opinion about it at all, and the worst parts of, say, Port Said are respectable compared to what the effrontery of a large Egyptian city was then.

However, persecution could still occur. It broke out, under the emperor Decius. Christians fled to the deserts, and after a while stayed there by preference. The vile life of those cities stank in their memories. The towns had been too hateful, or too seductive. Just then, Anthony was born. He was well-to-do, and at eighteen inherited his parents' three hundred acres of rich Egyptian soil, and their fortune. But Christ's words: "Go, sell what thou hast, and give it to the poor", struck home to him. He handed over his land to the poor of his village; got rid of his capital; and went to seek, in the desert communities of Christians, for some experienced old man who should control his wayward, impressionable temperament which, he knew, he could not govern all alone. For fifteen years he lived a life of study in the great Egyptian solitudes till he found even these insufficient, and retired further to a dismantled fort on the Nile, where he lived on a load of bread brought to him every six months, and dates off the local palms. His friends visited him periodically, and found him always well.

You might suggest that this was a running away. Why didn't he stop in the towns, help his fellow Christians, and, as they say, "do good", or anyhow something practical? Mooning among tombs! Shunting the rough-and-tumble of life off on to those who had pluck to cope with it! Well, I return to that in a moment. I will just say that anything destined to be strong and efficacious in *action* needs a drastic preparation of *character*. When Anthony knew himself, and could *govern* his most vigorous self, "keep himself" thoroughly "in order", as they say, he would do all that exterior work too. Hasty self-production, self-advertisement, talk, rushing around—this never gets a man far, and the results don't last. And meanwhile, his reputation for shrewd spirituality and true knowledge of the world grew so fast that men simply flocked to him and made a colony around him; and, when persecution broke out afresh, he *did* leave his solitude and visit his suffering fellow Christians at Alexandria and in the Sudan mines where they were imprisoned; such was the awe in which people already stood of his overwhelming personality, that he was never himself arrested, and could disregard the persecuting police with a nerve that never deserted him. After five or six years he went back, even deeper into solitude, across the Nile to a cliff that fronted the Red Sea. It says something for the *permanence* of his work that both his earlier monastery and this second one are still, after more than one thousand years and six centuries, existing and inhabited.

Here, then, he settled, cultivating enough ground around his cell to support himself. Below him, in the plains, thousands of monks had established themselves, and he went regularly down to visit, examine and advise them. Troops of people journeyed long distances to seek similar advice and had a hostel of their own; but, if they stayed any time, they had to work, on weekdays, like the monks, at baking, weaving, and so on.

Here is, condensed, an anecdote that will show you the fashion of men's thoughts, in those days; and also, Anthony's method of dealing with people.

Elogios, "struck by a passion for eternal things", deserted the world's hubbub. But he grew lonely; met a cripple, and promised God that he would look after him till he died. The cripple, after fifteen years, fell sick. Elogios bathed, fed and cured him. With convalescence, came temper. The cripple raved at his benefactor, crying: "Put me in the marketplace. I want meat!" Elogios gave him meat. "No—I want the crowds! Put me back where you found me!" Elogios was puzzled. "Am I to cast him forth? But God and I have entered into compact. Am I to keep him? But to me he gives bad days and nights. . . ." His friends said: "Both of you go to Anthony." So they went. Now when people called on Anthony he had them announced as from "Jerusalem" or from "Egypt", according as their quest was sincere or frivolous. "Which are these?" he asked. "A mixture", said his secretary. Elogios entered first. Anthony said gravely: "Thou wouldst cast this man forth? But he who made him does not cast him out. Thou wouldst cast him forth? But God raised up the Fairer One than thou art, to gather him. . . ." Then to the other, he said: "Crooked and crippled soul! cease thy fight with God! Knewest thou not that it was *Christ* who served thee? For *Christ*'s sake it was that Elogios made himself thy servant." He bade them farewell affectionately; they went home friends, and died within three days of one another.

Besides this, Anthony's influence began to exert itself like a radiating force in other countries too—thus St. Hilarion visited him about 310, and inaugurated monasteries in Palestine; Mar Agwin did so in 325 in Mesopotamia; St. Pachomius, nearer home, in 318. Anthony had two qualities proper to great men—he was able (such was the force of his personality) to leave almost complete freedom and initiative to the men under his immediate influence: and he did not grumble if others imitated but also modified his system—thus Pachomius started a much more centralized, highly organized monasticism, with carefully planned departments concerned with every sort of handicraft—gardening, carpentry, iron work, tanning, dyeing, cobbling, writing—a whole hive of useful industry *not* carried on for gain.

It was this sort of monasticism that was destined to spread in the West. Not only did the Christian Emperors come to value the civilizing as well as the spiritual genius of Anthony, and what *they* said naturally traveled far, but that intellectual giant, Athanasius of Alexandria, who knew and loved St. Anthony, wrote his *Life*, and that traveled farther still, and influenced, at a crisis, the life of St. Augustine himself, of whom I hope to speak next time,[1] and Augustine has influenced every century in this our West until our own. And away in Southern Italy, further off still in Gaul, further still in Ireland, types of monastic life were set up in direct descent from Anthony's. Nay, St. Benedict, 480–543, utilized, while he adapted, the kind of life taught by the Egyptian Saint, and thereby, I say deliberately, created one of the three forces that made Europe so much as possible. Why do I say that? Because when the Barbarians, the Huns, Goths, Franks, Vandals, swept into the western half of the Empire, they crashed up against three immovable facts—the Papacy, the Bishops with their cathedral churches and their schools, and the monasteries. A chaotic mind is always awestruck by an orderly one; violence is impotent before fearlessness; moral or social anarchy very soon yields to a Will firmly set toward what is right, a way of life that tends steadily toward men's betterment. And the monasteries were centers of grim study, steadfast instruction, development of agriculture, of ever-improving handicraft, of respect for authority, of orderliness of mind, of discipline of the will. You never can begin to calculate what Europe, and England herself, owe to the monks. When Henry VIII, in desperate need of money, destroyed the monasteries, and handed over their lands and revenues to his favorites, he did what

---

[1] In the broadcasting series in which all the sketches contributed to this book by Father Martindale were first delivered.

by itself would have sufficed to create the problem of poverty and un-
employment even had there been no Industrial Revolution. Yet did he
not destroy, even in this land, monasticism; not only would the best
in our public school system, I think, have been impossible without
the Benedictine tradition; there are more monks, we are told, now
in England than before the religious revolution; the great educational
houses—Ampleforth, Douay, Downside, and smaller ones, Ramsgate,
Ealing, Belmont in Herefordshire; that positive magnet for visitors,
Buckfast Abbey in Devon—built wholly by the hands of monks—are
governed by Benedictine monks, sons of St. Benedict, who was the
heir of Anthony.

Anthony died in 356, aged a hundred and five years, his sight and
hearing unimpaired, and all his teeth sound in his head. His was a personality sublime, yet sane: commanding, colossal yet simple, shrewd,
drily humorous, and affectionate, even tender; able to converse with
politicians and philosophers, judges and generals, yet to make friends
with the average man of marketplace and shop. His willpower was
tremendous, yet *controlled*, and never bursting forth into mere tyranny;
his intelligence, accurate; his vision, sublime; yet never wild, never
fanatical. This *hermit* was the most "sociable", most "clubbable", of
men. What, then, is self-advertisement? He used none of it, and yet
seems as familiar to me as any aged man that I honor has been. And
what is money? He got rid of his, yet built a memorial as lasting as
the pyramids, more meaningful than they. For who is grateful to, who
does homage to, the builders of those colossal excrescences of stone?
What is position, social or political? He sought neither—and which
of the politicians or even emperors of his day, let alone the financiers,
means anything to *us*—is *doing* anything now? But Anthony is *active*.

And when I have been sailing through the Red Sea, and have watched
the sun rise upon the westward mountains, and seen them change from
grey to lavender, from lilac into daffodil and crocus, into rose red and
carnation, when have I not thought of the dawn of St. Anthony upon
our world, and the warmth and splendor and vitality that he has left
upon it and within it? Why, it is really because of him, and by no means
because of Anthony—friend, then foe, of Caesar, and Cleopatra's lover
—that any of you, named Anthony, is so called!

SAINT AUGUSTINE OF HIPPO

[354-430]

Alban Goodier, S.J.

EN APPROACH St. Augustine with mixed feelings. So high does he tower above those of his generation, perhaps above those of every generation, that they look up to him with a certain awe, almost with fear. The very sight of his works, more, probably, than those of any other writer of the past, frightens us and puts us off; someone has seriously said that merely to read what Augustine has written would take an ordinary man a lifetime. Nevertheless, to one who will have courage and come near, it is strange how human, and even how little in his greatness, Augustine is found to be. "I liked to play": *delectabat ludere*, he said of himself in his childhood; and there is something of that same delight to be found in him to the very end of his days.

Augustine was born in Tagaste, a Roman town in Numidia, North Africa. It was a free town, and also a market town, set at a place where many Roman roads converged; to it the caravans from east and west brought their merchandise, in it the luxury of Rome was repeated, with the added freedom of Africa. He was the eldest son of one Patricius, a well-to-do citizen of the place, a pagan but not a fanatic, whose ideal of life was to get the most out of it he could, without being too particular as to the means. Patricius, at the age of forty, had married Monica, a girl of seventeen, a Christian on both her father's and her mother's side. This marriage alone would seem to imply a certain laxity of faith in the family; the fact that Monica owed most of her religious and moral training to an old nurse confirms it.

It cannot be said that the marriage was a happy one. Perhaps it was not intended to be; it was a marriage of convenience and no more. For the pagan Patricius it meant life with a woman who, the older she became, and the more difficult her situation, clung the more to her own religion, and would have nothing to do with his free and easy ways, to call them by no worse name. For Monica it meant a life of constant self-suppression; of abuse even to blows, for Patricius had fits of violent temper; of slander on the part of those who were only too anxious to pander to Patricius, or were jealous of the influence her meek disposition had upon him. Three children were born to them, Augustine the first, but none of them were baptized. In those days a middle course was found. As children were born they were inscribed as catechumens; the baptism might come later, perhaps whenever there was danger of death.

Augustine grew up among pagan children, apparently in a pagan school, and his morals from the first were no better than theirs. He could steal, he could cheat, he could lie with the best of them; to do these things cleverly and successfully was a mark of talent rather than of vice. He went to school, and he hated it, both its restraint, and the things he had to learn. He was thrashed repeatedly, and when he came home received little commiseration, even from his own mother. His boyhood, from his own description, was an unhappy time; it tended to make him all the more bitter and reckless. But he was a precociously clever child, and in spite of his thrashings, which only made him more obstinate, and his own idleness, he learned more than his companions. Both his father and his mother became ambitious for him; they decided to give him a better education than could be given him in Tagaste. He was sent to Madaura, a prosperous city thirty miles away.

But thirty miles, in those days, and for a boy such as Augustine, was a great, separating distance. Here at last he was his own master; the longing he had always had to do just what he liked, without let or hindrance from anyone, was allowed free scope. He studied the pagan classics, for he loved to read and read; he studied not only their literature, but also their ideals and their life. These were exemplified all around him, and he could take part in them as much as he pleased; the pursuit of pleasure at all costs, the wild orgies of the carnivals of Bacchus, the worship of the decadent Roman ideal, smart, sensual, excusing, boldly daring, laughing with approval at every excess of sinful love. Such was the atmosphere the clever, imaginative, craving, reckless Augustine was made to breathe in the city of Apuleius at the age of fifteen; and to face it he had nothing but the flattering encouragement of a pagan father, the timid fear of a Christian mother whose religion he had already learned to despise. He soon became simply a pagan, a non-moral pagan at the most critical time of his life.

The consequences were inevitable. Augustine came home from Madaura addicted to the lowest vices. What was worse, he seemed to have no conscience left; worse still, he had a father who looked upon the same excess as a proof of manhood, the sowing of wild oats now which gave promise of great things later. Only one chain held him, the love he had for his mother. He laughed at her pious ways, he deliberately defied and hurt her, but underneath, though he tried not to own it to himself, his respect and admiration and affection for her had steadily increased. It was the same on her side, which made the bond all the stronger. Monica's life with her husband had been unhappy and loveless, and the love she longed to give was poured out on her favorite yet reckless son. The more she loved him, the more she was appalled at the life he was already living, and at the future to which it must inevitably lead. She blamed herself for having been partially the cause of his downfall. She had encouraged the plan of his going to Madaura; she had given him little to protect him while he was there; she would do all she could to win him back, though it was to be the struggle of a lifetime. This made her strive all the more for her own perfection; if she was to influence him at all she must herself be true. Since she could say little to him, she would pray for him; she watched him, but it could only be from a distance. And Augustine, though he made nothing of it at the time, though he often took delight in hurting her by his boast of wickedness, knew nevertheless that she prayed, and watched, and loved; and he returned that love, and it grew.

The next step in Augustine's career was to Carthage. It was the center of learning and pleasure in North Africa, and Augustine craved for both. There he lived, from the age of seventeen, learning and loving as he wished, for there was no one to check or guide him. "I went to Carthage", he wrote later, "where shameful love bubbled round me like boiling oil". But he was wise enough to know that this was the opportunity of his life; in the midst of his evil living he worked hard. At this point his father died, a Christian at the last, which cannot but have had an effect on the son; and the pinch of poverty, in consequence of the death, made him work all the harder. He soon became known as the gayest, the most gifted, the most sensual scholar in the University of Carthage; a threefold triumph, of each of which he was proud.

In the schools of Rhetoric his declamations were proposed to other students as models; outside the schools he was admired and courted as the reckless votary of love.

But the ways of God are strange. One day, in the midst of this thoughtless life, he was studying Cicero. He lighted on the following passage:

> If man has a soul, as the greatest philosophers maintain, and if that soul is immortal and divine, then must it needs be that the more it has been steeped in reason, and true love, and the pursuit of truth, and the less it has been stained by vice and passion, so much the more surely it will rise above this—earth and ascend into the skies.

This sentence, suddenly come upon, was, he tells us, the beginning of light. It made him restless; his eyes continually went back to it; he began to ask himself whether, after all, he was as happy as he affected. He looked for a solution elsewhere, whether a confirmation of the teaching, or a quieting of his conscience, he did not care. He paid more attention to the other pagan philosophers, but they did not lead him far. He took to the Bible, and for a time it held him; but soon that, too, became insipid, and he put it away. He knew something about the Manicheans, with their doctrine of a good and an evil spirit. They claimed to have a solution for all such problems; above all they pretended to solve them without too much surrender of the good things of this world. Sin could not be resisted, passion was a necessity; the doctrine suited Augustine very well as a check to this new thing, conscience, and he accepted it. Augustine became a Manichean.

We may now leap over some years. Augustine returned to Tagaste, and there set up a school; his restless soul soon tired of it, the provincialism of the place stifled him, and he went once more to Carthage. There he opened another school of Rhetoric; it was a great success, but being a youth of little over twenty he had need to supplement his knowledge with further reading. Nothing came amiss to this voracious mind; he read anything and everything that came in his way, the classics, the occult sciences, astrology, the fine arts. Meanwhile, more as a practice in dialectic than from any sense of conviction, he set himself to the task of converting his friends to Manichaeism, and in part succeeded. At last, again grown restless, and devoured with an ambition for which Carthage had grown too small, he decided to seek his fortune in Rome, the center and capital of the whole world. In spite of his mother's appeals, in spite of remonstrance from the woman he had ruined but who had been faithful to him, he eluded them both and slipped away, to make a name for himself as a conjuror in words in the heart of the Empire.

But the design of God was very different. Augustine's sojourn in Rome was anything but the success he had anticipated. Scarcely had he arrived when he fell ill, and had to depend on the charity of condescending friends till he recovered, a fact which galled him exceedingly. As soon as he was well, he set about drawing pupils round him; this, in self-occupied, bustling Rome, was a more difficult matter than it had been in Carthage or Tagaste. Moreover, the climate and the life of the place began to tell upon him. He could not endure its stifling air, its cobbled and uneven streets, while the coarseness of its manners disgusted this man of the world who, though steeped in vice as much as any Roman, still insisted on refinement. The gluttony and drunkenness he saw everywhere about him, the coarse outcries raised from time to time, in the theaters and elsewhere, against all foreign immigrants, the lack of interest in things intellectual even among those who claimed to be most cultured, the childish imitation, among the rich and so-called upper classes, of eastern splendor and extravagance, the multitudinous temples of all kinds of gods, disgorging every day their besotted votaries—the heart of Rome being eaten out by the serpent of Asia—the contempt for human life, above all for the life of a slave or a captured foe, all these things, in spite of his own depravity, began to tell upon his mind. He was more alone now, and was forced to reflect; his life was in the making and he had to look into the future; if he continued to sin, to his own disgust he found that he did so, not because it satisfied any desire, or because it gave him any pleasure, but because he could not help it. He knew that he was its slave, whatever he might appear, however he might boast of liberty. Long since had Manichaeism lost its hold upon him; as he had once used his dialectic in its favor, so now it amused him to tear it to tatters. He clung to it still, for it provided him with a convenient cloak with which to cover and excuse the life which he was at present powerless to check; but in his heart he did not believe in its tenets any longer.

Then another force came into his life. Augustine had kept his school open in Rome with no little difficulty, not because he was not successful, but because his pupils would often go away leaving him unpaid. From sheer and undeserved poverty, it seemed he would have to return to Africa. Suddenly a professor's chair at Milan was offered for competition, and Milan, for many reasons, had come to mean more to Augustine than Rome itself. Milan, not Rome, was now the city of the Emperor and his court; Milan was the center of culture and fashion; above all, it was the home of Ambrose, and Ambrose was a name that was ever on the lips of any master of rhetoric. Augustine competed for the post, and with the help of sundry friends obtained it. He went to Milan; he sought out Ambrose, first to criticize and judge as a master of letters, later to discover a friend. It was not long before, to his own surprise, he was pouring out his now miserable soul into the bishop's ear.

Still that did not come all at once. It would seem that the plain straightforward Roman, though a better scholar, in many ways, than Augustine, never quite understood the eager, melancholy, sensitive and sensuous African, who, nevertheless, was by this time straining for a guide to lead him to the truth. The days passed on into years. The young and ambitious rhetorician had found solid ground at last, and Milan took him to its heart. Great men and wealthy noticed him, invited him to their mansions; Augustine began to tell himself that he could wish for nothing better than to be as one of them. He would settle down, content with that goal; he would marry and become respectable, according to the standard of these men of the world; he would put away the woman he had wronged, and the rest would easily be condoned. He made a first step—and he failed; the ending of one fascination did but open the way to another. He told himself that he could not help but sin; it was part of his nature, his manner of life had made it a necessity. Then why trouble any more? One day, as he came home from a triumphant speech delivered before the Emperor, drunk with the praises showered on him, an intoxicated man lurched across his path, reveling in coarse merriment. Why should he not live as that man lived? Not, it was true, in the same brutish way; but there was a drunkenness that would suit him, which would let him live for the day, without giving the rest a moment's reflection.

Nevertheless, as all this self-questioning showed, a new thing had awakened in him, and he could not make it sleep. He listened to Ambrose when he preached, ostensibly to study him as a rhetorician; he came away forgetting the rhetoric, but with a burning arrow in his heart. More and more he saw what he must do, if he would be even what his own ideal of himself pictured to him; he saw it, but to do it was quite another thing. He listened to the Church's liturgy; he watched the people at their prayers in full contentment all around him; he longed even to tears that he might be one with them. Still he could not bring himself to pay the price. Let us listen to him here as he tells the story of his conflict at this time. Thus he writes:

> O my God, let me with a thankful heart remember and confess to thee thy mercies on me. Let my very bones be steeped in thy love, and let them cry out: Who is like to thee, O Lord? (Ps 35:10) Thou hast broken my bonds asunder; I will offer to thee the sacrifice of thanksgiving (Ps 116:16, 17). How thou hast broken them openly I will declare; and all who adore thee, when they hear my tale, shall say: Blessed is the Lord, in heaven and on earth; great and glorious is his name.

> The enemy held my will captive; therefore he kept me, chained down and bound. For out of a froward will lust had sprung; and lust pampered had become custom; and custom indulged had become necessity. These were the links of the chain; this was the bondage in which I was bound, and that new will which was already born in me, freely to serve thee, wholly to enjoy thee, O God, the only true joy, was not yet able to subdue my former wilfulness, strengthened by the wantonness of years. So did my two wills, one new, the other old, one spiritual, the other carnal, fight within me, and by their discord undo my soul.

More and more the truth grew upon him, yet Augustine could not bring himself to act. In a succession of passages he dwells upon his hesitation; they are among the most tragically dramatic pages that he ever wrote. Let us hear some of them.

> Thou didst on all sides shew me that what thou didst say was true, and by the truth I was convicted. I had nothing at all to answer but those dull and dreary words: Anon, anon; or Presently; or, Leave me alone but a little while. But my Presently, presently, came to no present, and my Little while lasted long.

> What words did I not use against myself! With scourges of condemnation I lashed my soul, to force it to follow me in my effort to go after thee.

Yet it drew back; it refused to follow, and without a word of excuse. Its arguments were confuted, its self-defense was spent. There remained no more than mute shrinking; it feared, as it would death itself, to have that disease of habit healed whereby it was wasting to death.

Thus I lay, soul-sick and tormented, chiding myself more vehemently than ever, rolling and writhing in my bondage, longing for the fetter to be wholly broken which alone now held me, but yet did hold me secure. And thou, O Lord, didst harry me within with thy merciless mercy; thou didst multiply the lashes of fear and shame, lest I should again give way, and lest I should fail to break this last remaining bond, and it should recover strength, and bind me down the faster. I said within myself: Let it be done at once, let it be done now; and even as I spoke I all but did it. I all but did it, but I did it not. Still I sank back to my former place; I stood where I was and took breath again. Once more I tried, and wanted somewhat less to make me succeed, and again somewhat less, and I all but touched and laid hold of the object of my longing; yet again I came not at it, nor touched it, nor laid hold of it. I still recoiled; I would not die to death that I might live to life.

These petty toys of toys, these vanities of vanities, my longtime fascinations, still held me. They plucked at the garment of my flesh, and murmured caressingly: Dost thou cast us off? From this moment are we to be with thee no more for ever? From this moment shall this delight or that be no more lawful for thee for ever?

The time came when I scarcely heard them. For now they did not openly appear, they did not contradict me; instead they stood as it were behind my back, and muttered their lament, and pulled furtively at my cloak, and begged me, as I stood to go, but to look back on them once more. Thus did their shackles hinder me, and I shrank from shaking myself free from them, that I might burst my bonds and leap forward whither I was called. At the last some habit would whisper in my ear: Dost thou think that thou canst live without these things?

But the liberation came at last. Monica, his mother, had prayed on; she had long since come to Milan to be near her son. She had shared his successes with him, and had even joined in the congratulations; but most of her time had been spent in the church, so much so that she had won the attention of Ambrose the Bishop. One day, on meeting Augustine, he congratulated him on having such a mother. That chance word, it would seem, was the beginning of the last act in the drama.

Augustine was flattered with a worthy flattering; he was glad for his mother's sake and his own, and the love within began to take on a new warmth. On such little things may great destinies depend. And in the meantime, Augustine himself, though continually beaten, did not give up the struggle. If he could not face the hardest ordeal, at least he could do something. One by one he pushed the shackles away; first the bondage that compelled him to live in sin, then that of his false philosophy. Next he ceased to be even by profession a Manichean. Last of all he laid aside his office as municipal orator; it is a proof of the refining process through which he had by this time gone when he tells us that he had grown ashamed of the lies he had to tell for the sake of beautiful language.

At length the final grace came, and Augustine received it. "I was tired of devouring time and of being devoured by it", he writes; he must decide one way or the other. He had come to Milan a skeptic; he had by this time left that far behind. The evidence of a loving and a patient God, the truth of Jesus Christ, the peace and contentment of those who received him and lived by him, the summing up of all the philosophers had to say in the teaching of the Bible, the example of great men before him, who had suffered as he now suffered, had seen as he was now beginning to see, had made the leap and had found rest and peace, all these things crowded in upon him, and he knew what he should do. On the other hand was the surrender, the tearing away from all those things, good and evil, which hitherto had made life sweet, or at least as sweet as one like him could ever hope to find it. He could not do it. He despised himself for his hesitation but he could not move. He despised the Roman world which he now knew so well but he could not leave it. Besides, by this time he was ill; he was not himself. To make a change under these conditions was imprudent; when he was well again, he would never be able to persevere, and to fall back, once he had repented, would be only to make his second state worse than the first. He could not decide; even if he decided, it seemed to him that he could not make himself act. He must get someone to help him. He could not go to Ambrose; Ambrose had done for him all he was able and yet so far had failed. There was an old man, Simplicianus; he had been the confessor of Ambrose. In desperation he would go to him.

And Simplicianus received him, and humored him; humored him

even in his pride, pointing out to him the nobility of truth and sacrifice. There were set before Augustine pictures of St. Antony in the
desert and his followers, the hermits of Egypt, who at that time were
the talk of Christian Rome. They had surrendered all; yet they were
simple men with not much learning. Augustine was in his garden; he
thought he was alone. He lay down beneath a tree; his tears wet the
ground.

"How long?" he cried, "How long shall this be?. It is always tomorrow and tomorrow? Why not this hour an end to all my meanness?"

As he spoke a little child in a house close by was singing some kind
of nursery rhyme, and the refrain was this: "Take up and read, take up
and read." Mechanically Augustine stretched out his hand to a book he
had brought with him. It was *St. Paul's Epistles*. He took it up, opened
it at random, and read:

> Put ye on the Lord Jesus Christ, and make not provision for the flesh to
> fulfill the lusts thereof.

Suddenly all was quiet. He knew his decision had been made, and
that he had the power to execute it. There was no more trouble. Augustine rose from where he lay, went into his mother's room, and
there at her feet surrendered his past for ever. Soon he was at the feet
of Ambrose; he had been lost and now at last he had found himself. He
was at the time just thirty-three years of age. He celebrates his victory
in the following passage:

> O Lord, I am thy servant; I am thy servant and the son of thy handmaid.
> Thou hast broken my bonds asunder; I will offer to thee the sacrifice
> of praise (Ps 116:16, 17). Let my heart and my tongue praise thee; yea,
> let all my bones say: O Lord, who is like to thee? Let them proclaim
> it; and do thou in return answer me, and say unto my soul: I am thy
> salvation (Ps 35:10). Who am I, and what am I? What an evil thing have
> been my deeds, or if not my deeds my words, or if not my words my
> will? But thou, O Lord, art good and merciful, and thy right hand hath
> reached down into the abysmal blackness of my death, and from the
> bottom of my heart hath emptied out its deep of corruption. And thy
> gift was this, no longer to will what I willed, but to will what thou didst
> will. How came it that after all those years, after it was lost in that deep
> and darksome labyrinth, my free will was called forth in a moment to
> submit my neck to thy easy yoke, and my shoulders to thy light burden,

O Christ Jesus, my Helper and my Redeemer (Ps 19:4)? How sweet did
it at once become to me to be without the sweetness of those baubles!
What I feared to be parted from, it was now a joy to part with. For
thou didst cast them from me, thou the true and richest sweetness. Thou
didst cast them forth, and in their place didst substitute thyself, sweeter
than all delight, though not to flesh and blood, brighter than all light,
but more hidden than the lowest deep, higher than all honor, but not to
them that are high in their own conceits. Now my soul was free; . . . and
my infant tongue spoke to thee freely, my light, my riches, my health,
the Lord my God.

For the purposes of this study we do not need to follow Augustine
too closely through the rest of his career. He was still, to the world
about him, the brilliant professor of Milan; only a few of his friends
knew of the change that had taken place. He would continue his lectures; there should be no sensation about him. But his health, never
strong, had been shaken by the ordeal; it gave him a reason to retire
to the villa of a friend at Cassicium, and there for a time he took up
his abode. It was a blessed interval.

During that period of rest the longing for solitude came over him; a
longing which he never lost during all the remainder of his active days.
He was still Augustine, the half-pagan; the saint was yet to be formed.
The love of argument still delighted him, and that in surroundings that
made life on earth most sweet; the comforts of ease, the pleasure of
congenial companions, the delight in everything that his eyes could
gaze upon. If he laid aside his lectures in Milan, none the less he went
on teaching in his new home; but his lessons were drawn from the good
things about him, the light in the sky at dawn, the noise of running
waters, the goodly warmth of the sun in his veins. By means such as
these the natural man was clarified, prepared for the great things that
were yet to come.

That he might begin again he must leave Milan and Rome, and return
to his native Tagaste. On the way his party stopped at Ostia; there took
place the memorable scene which he shared with his mother, Monica,
when, as he tells us, her conversation led him up to a vision of God
he had never known before; there, too, his mother died, and the loss
almost broke his heart.

He returned to Carthage and thence quickly made his way to Tagaste.
Now he could begin in real earnest; and he began as he had learned

others had begun before him. His inheritance, now that his mother was dead, he distributed to the poor; for himself, he would turn his house into a monastery, and, with his friends, would live a life of prayer, and study, and retirement. But this was not to be. Already he was famous in Tagaste; and there came a day when, as was the manner of those times, the people would have him for their priest and he was ordained. As a priest he was sent to Hippo, and there his new career began. He lived a monastic life, but his learning and preaching, first to his own people, then against the heretics about him, made it impossible that he should be hid; soon the cry was raised that he should be the bishop.

The rest of his story need not concern us; the rout of the Donatists, who then threatened to dominate northern Africa, the rebuilding of the Church in true poverty of spirit, along with care for the poor, and what we would call the working classes, the administration of the law which fell upon his shoulders, the incessant preaching and writing, the quantity of which at this time appalls us. We are told that he preached every day, sometimes more than once, often enough, as the words of his sermons indicate, his audience would have him continue till he had to dismiss them for their meals. What concerns us more is the inner soul of the man in the midst of all these labors.

For Augustine could never forget what he had been, and the fear never forsook him that with very little he might be the same again. At the time of his consecration as bishop he asked himself with anxiety whether, with his past, and with the scars from that past still upon him, he could face the burden. From time to time old visions would revive and the passions in his soul would leap toward them; even in his old age he trembled to think that some day they might get the better of him. To suppress temptation he would work without ceasing; he would allow himself no respite. When he was not preaching, or helping other souls, he would write; when he was not writing he would pray. When prayer became blank from utter weariness of age still he would pray with a pen in his hand; the only rest he would allow himself was reading, for that, he confesses, was still his delight. By means such as these he kept his other nature down. When we look at the volumes of his works we may assure ourselves that one at least of the motives which produced them was the determination in Augustine's soul to keep his lower nature in control by incessant labors.

Nevertheless labor alone would never have saved or made the Augustine that we know. Living as he was as archbishop in a time of violence, when knives were easily drawn to solve the problems of theology, he had himself often to act with severity. Still the heart of Augustine was an affectionate heart; if in the old days it had led him far astray, in his later life it led him no less to sanctity. While he mercilessly hammered the Donatists about him, at the same time he could address his fellow priests in words like these:

> Keep this in mind, my brothers; practice it and preach it with meekness that shall never fail. Love the men you fight; kill only their lie. Rest on truth in all humility; defend it but with no cruelty. Pray for those whom you oppose; pray for them while you correct them.

Yet more than that was his ever increasing hunger after God. In the time of his conversion he shows us how this hunger proved his salvation; then he uttered the memorable sentence by which he is best known:

> Thou hast made us, O Lord, for thyself, and our heart shall find no rest till it rest in thee.

As the years went on, and as he grew in understanding of this goal of all affection, the hunger was only the more intensified. There is a pathetic scene recorded in his later life, when he gathered his people about him and complained to them that they would not leave him time to pray. With the simplicity of a child he reminded them that this had been part of the bargain when he had become their bishop; it was their part of the bargain and they had not kept it. He asked them, now that he was growing old, to renew their engagement; to permit him to have some days in the week when he might be alone; then they might do with him what they would. They promised; but again the promise was not kept. Circumstances were against him and them; he was living in an age when the old order was being shaken to its foundations, and there was need of a man to build a new world on its ruins. That man was Augustine, and while his eyes and his heart strained after heaven, his intellect and preaching had perforce to attend to the raising of the City of God.

But it was just for this purpose that Augustine had been made. He knew the pagan world and depicted it as no man has done from his time till now; the picture he draws is as true today as it was then. And

equally true and efficacious is his antidote. As he himself had to grope
through his own darkness till he came to God, and then, and then only,
saw all in its right perspective, so he told mankind that they would
find no solution of their problems in so-called peace, in shirking all
restraint, in substituting law for morality, in stifling every voice that
ventured to denounce evildoing, in finding equivocal phrases which
seemed to condone all sin. They would find it only where alone it
could be found; the world would find no rest till it found it in God.

Augustine did not live to see so much as the dawn of the new day
which he heralded; on the contrary, his sun went down, and there
came over Africa and Hippo the blackest night. As the old man sat
in his palace the news was brought to him of the wanton destruction
carried out by the Arian Vandals. Nothing was being spared; to this
day Northern Africa has not recovered from the scourge. The word
vandalism passed into the language of Europe at that time, and has never
since been superseded. He heard it all, he appealed to the Roman ruler
to defend the right; he was listened to, and then he was betrayed. Still
he did not move. With energy he called on his priests to stay with
their flocks, and if need be to die with them. At length came the turn
for Hippo to be besieged by land and sea. In the third month of the
siege Augustine fell ill, probably of one of the fevers which a siege
engenders. He grew worse; he knew he was dying; he made a general
confession and then, at last, asked that he might be left alone with
God. Lying on his bed he heard the din of battle in the distance, and
as his mind began to wander he asked himself whether the end of the
world had come. But he quickly recovered. No; it was not that. Had
not Christ said: "I am with you always, even to the end of the world"?
Some day, somehow, the world would be saved. "Non tollit Gothus
quod custodit Christus", he told himself, and with this certain hope
for mankind he went away to the home he had once described as the
place "where we are at rest, where we see as we are seen, where we
love and are loved." It was the fifth day of the Calends of September,
August 28, 430.

SAINT PATRICK

[389-461]

Alice Curtayne

 AINT PATRICK'S own account of his parentage is the simplest imaginable and would apply to nearly half the population of Ireland today: he tells us in his *Confession* that his father, one of several sons, owned a small farm and lived in a village. A detail or two, less familiar, should be added. Patrick's father was a decurion, that is, member of the municipal council of a Roman town, and both he and his father before him appear to have been clerics. Concerning this, Bury hazards the suggestion that the decayed dignity of decurion had become so burdensome, attempts were frequently made to escape it by taking minor Orders.

Patrick further tells us that he was born in Banavem Taberniae. The identification of this place-name has perplexed the centuries. Modern scholarship appears to have settled down firmly to the opinion that it was in Monmouthshire, somewhere near the mouth of the Severn, rather than near Dumbarton in Scotland, although this conclusion is most repugnant to Scottish opinion. For a personal appreciation of the Saint, it is all one whether he was born in Monmouth or Dumbarton. His Roman citizenship is what counts. He was thoroughly Romanized. All through life he displayed the typically Roman qualities of simplicity and endurance. And this it is that lends his life such marvelous unity: the pattern emerges exact.

Moreover, Banavem Taberniae, wherever it was, ceased early in life to have much significance for Patrick. When he was sixteen years old, that village was the scene of a great pirate raid. Patrick was captured

This personal study is based chiefly on the *Confession*. The quotations given are from Dr. J. D. Newport White's Translation. Acknowledgment is also due to the works of Drs. Todd, Healy, Gwynn, Bury and Helena Concannon.

near his father's villa and carried overseas, one of thousands of prisoners, who formed the best part of the pirates' booty. Landing on the coast of Antrim, his captors sold him to the petty king of the district, in exchange for a few kine. The boy's head was shaved as a sign of his status: he was given a slave's garb—a sheepskin tunic descending to the knees and leather sandals laced with thongs. He had to do the menial work of four Pagan households. One of his chief occupations was the herding of swine on the slopes of Mount Slemish.

It was a searing experience. The change of life was radical, drastic, and apparently final. Flung utterly helpless into the hands of heathen masters who held him in rigorous slavery, this son of a Roman decurion was shocked into a precocious gravity. His new life was so hard as to be a sort of daily castigation, as testified by the reminiscent shudder with which, in his old age, he described it: "I was chastened exceedingly and humbled every day in hunger and nakedness." Referring to the fate of those captives from Banavem Taberniae, he says briefly: "The Lord poured upon us the fury of his anger."

Before this occurred, Patrick tells us that "he knew not the true God"; that "he was ignorant of the living God"—perplexing phrases, since he was obviously the child of Christian parents and mentions priests as tutors of his childhood. The phrases can imply that he was an average, careless youth (in his own estimation) to whom religion had no vital meaning, at least until he had completed his fifteenth year. Then, in his destitution, he turned to God and began for the first time to know him with personal experimental knowledge:

> And there the Lord opened the understanding of my unbelief that, even though late . . . I might turn with all my heart to the Lord my God, who regarded my low estate, and pitied the youth of my ignorance, and kept me before I knew him, and before I had discernment. . . . Now, after I came to Ireland, tending flocks was my daily occupation; and constantly I used to pray in the daytime. Love of God and the fear of him increased more and more, and faith grew, and the spirit was moved. . . .

I do not think that Patrick, in his terrified "conversion" on Slemish, formed the purpose of returning to Ireland as a Christian missionary, for in his old age he referred to that enterprise as a "great grace . . . that formerly, in my youth, I never hoped for nor thought of." But he received a divine, very personal and very precious, initiation in his loneliness, and his response was a resolution to serve God perfectly.

This became "the fixed purpose of his soul", from which he never afterward swerved. The divine plan in his regard, the method of that service, was but gradually unfolded to him. Every time a part of the road was disclosed, he saw an obstacle confronting him, each appearing more formidable than the last. These barriers were six in number: servitude, ignorance, the hostility of superiors, the forbidding magnitude of the task suggested to his mind, the treachery of a friend, temptation to despair. He displayed utter singlemindedness in his efforts to coerce exterior circumstances into conforming with inner divine direction. That is the whole story of his long life. It could be shown symbolically as a drama of six scenes.

Patrick as a slave boy was utterly powerless to accomplish any good. His master being a Druid, the youth was hemmed in by the inhibitions of a strong Pagan creed, of unquestioned ascendancy throughout the land. Probably, to his awakening religiousness, the core of his destitution was in his complete severance from the sacramental life of the Church, from all communion with his kind. It is unnecessary to enter into the material rigors of his life. Slaves, in the Ireland of his day, were hardly accorded human rights. Fiacc tells us that Patrick, in captivity, never ate human food. In a land where no money appears to have been coined, a slave was the unit of barter. One slavegirl was reckoned the equivalent of three cows. As an indication of the absolute ownership exercised, a master could send his slave even to kill a man and the slave was bound to obey. A glimpse of the treatment meted out to this class of the community is found in that episode in Patrick's later life: he met some slaves cutting down yew trees with such blunt instruments that the palms of their hands were bleeding freely. Intimately interested, he questioned them, and they told him they were not allowed to sharpen their irons on the flagstone, as that would make their work too easy.

In short, Patrick felt himself morally bound to find a way out. But six years passed before he attempted his escape. Then it was in response to divine guidance and from no exterior suggestion that he made his dash for liberty. He was told the direction to take in order to find a ship. By this time a man of twenty-two, he disappeared unobserved from his master's household and walked two hundred miles through unknown country, terrors encompassing him, the fear of pursuit and recapture behind him. During all that way he says he met with nothing to alarm him.

When he reached the port, the ship that his inner voice had told him of was casting its moorings, but the captain indignantly refused to allow the exhausted slave to board her. After a discussion with his crew, however, he changed his mind and recalling Patrick, who had already taken refuge in prayer, he allowed him to clamber on. The runaway had not the least notion of his destination, but he cast himself into the hands of God Almighty, having learned, as he said, "that he can be utterly trusted."

There began an Odyssey in which hardship was the chief note. Patrick, in this passage, is like an athlete engaged in physical combat with an adversary, with such awful persistence did slavery fetter him. He soon found that he had changed one form of servitude for another of a more disagreeable sort. To the human eye, that state threatened to engulf him; his name seemed about to be obliterated from the world of doers. Writing of it in his old age, he becomes confused in his recital of those strange vicissitudes. After three days at sea, they disembarked on some unknown coast and then journeyed for twenty-eight days through a desert, where food failed them and they were on the verge of death by starvation. The heathen crew taunted the Christian youth that his almighty God had forsaken him, because they were not likely to see a human being again. Patrick affirmed his unshaken confidence and then a herd of swine appeared and the wanderers had food in abundance. What occurred subsequently is uncertain, but it seems that after another fourteen days, during which they always found food and fire and dry quarters in which to sleep, the company reached the habitations of men and shortly afterward Patrick escaped, having spent two months with his new masters. He found out his kindred in Britain, who received him as a son and gave sympathetic ear to the tale of his tribulations. He had overcome the first obstacle to his perfect service of God, the helplessness of servitude. But immediately the second barrier arose before him: his ignorance.

With that fixed purpose of his soul no other way of life was possible save a dedicated one. Patrick resolved to be a priest. Now the swineherd of twenty-two had had a valuable moral training on Slemish, but from the academic point of view, his incompetence was disastrous. His studies having ceased when he was fifteen, he was wholly uneducated. Nevertheless, with ardor and patience, he immediately began making up for his deficiency.

Despite the most painstaking research, the twenty-year interval between Patrick's escape from Ireland and his voluntary return is still
darkly mysterious. In his *Confession* he says no word about that interval. Four names are mentioned as the centers of his training: Marmoutier, near Tours, Lérins, Arles, Auxerre. The monastic foundations of Marmoutier, Lérins and Arles were of European fame and
their pupils considered privileged. Four saints are mentioned among
Patrick's exemplars or preceptors: St. Martin of Tours, St. Honoratus,
St. Amator, St. Germanus. These men were not notable for piety only:
they were among the foremost scholars and ecclesiastical organizers of
the day. If they contributed to the formation of Patrick, then he lacked
no external stimulus to cast off the impediment of ignorance.

Even a fleeting acquaintance with St. Germanus of Auxerre would
have a deep effect on Patrick. Educated in Rome for law, he joined
the army instead and later became a priest. He was an officer in the
army up to the very day of his ordination. A character of outstanding
originality, he was sent to Britain by the Pope in 429 to combat the
heresy of Pelagius. That combat was not fought by preaching only,
but on at least one occasion by actual physical combat, during which
the military prowess of Germanus reasserted itself and ended in his
winning what is known as the "Alleluia" victory. It is often asserted
that Patrick accompanied Germanus on that mission to Britain, though
the primal authority for the statement is slight.

Regarding Patrick's training, there is certainty in two aspects. He was
happy during that period, because he longed unutterably in later life
to revisit the places known to him in Gaul. In that congenial monastic
atmosphere, the soul of the crushed and despised swineherd expanded
in gracious tranquility. He emerged profoundly versed in at least one
branch of study—Scripture—which appeared afterward as though woven into the texture of his thought, so that he habitually expressed himself in the language of Holy Writ. He developed other gifts too that
are rarer, because inborn: one of these was construction and another,
administration.

In that period when he was thus laboriously overcoming the barrier
of ignorance, he began to have dreams of a sharp-cut distinctness in
one of which a courier appeared with countless letters, one of these he
gave to Patrick. The missive was superscribed with the words, "The
Voice of the Irish." As the student was wonderingly unfolding it to

read, he heard the voices of many, crying to him as with one mouth, "We beseech thee to come and walk once more among us." He heard that plea so often that it became very familiar in his ears. He even knew the very people who thus called to him, theirs was "the voice of those who live beside the Wood of Foclut which is nigh unto the western sea." And in his dreams that cry to Patrick possessed a quality of such urgency that it seemed to break his heart. His awakenings were confounded with the mystery of it. He began to understand that his work as a priest was to be missionary, and the field, Ireland.

The moment Patrick understood it, the third barrier arose in the opposition of his superiors. They thought such an enterprise at once too hazardous and too responsible for him, beyond his capacity. His statement of the position is clear:

> The Lord showed mercy upon me thousands of times, because he saw in me that I was ready, but that I did not know through these (revelations) what I should do about my position, because many were forbidding this embassage. Moreover, they used to talk among themselves behind my back and say "Why does this fellow thrust himself into danger among hostile people who know not God?" They did not say this out of malice, but it did not seem meet in their eyes, on account of my illiteracy, as I myself witness that I have understood.

Yet he must have urged the evangelization of Ireland with unabated persistence. The question of raising him to a bishopric was finally mooted, in order to permit him to embark on the mission of his choice, and then the opposition that broke out was even fierce in its nature. Patrick tells us that a friend of his "fought" for him in his absence. Opponents must have even imputed to him unworthy motives to account for his persistent determination to go to Ireland. This is evident from his protestation:

> I testify in truth and in exultation of heart before God and his holy angels, that I never had any cause except the Gospel and his promises for ever returning to that nation from whence previously I scarcely escaped.

But at length Patrick overcame the opposition of his superiors sufficiently to enable him to proceed. As a consecrated bishop, he returned to Ireland in the year 432.

Immediately the fourth barrier presented itself in the sheer magnitude of the work he had undertaken. When Patrick leaped ashore at that inlet of Strangford Lough, he must have seen himself infinitesimally dwarfed in comparison with the enormous complexity of his task. We do not know who his companions were, but they were few in number. He had not come to savage tribes, but to a country with a highly organized religion which had become fused with a strongly developed native culture. There were in Ireland only a tiny number of scattered knots of Christians, whom Palladius had either baptized or brought with him. They were completely disorganized. Patrick had practically to begin at the beginning. He had no native power whatsoever on his side, nor even any access to its goodwill. In fact, the moment he disembarked the authority with which he was invested fell from him in the eyes of a people who did not comprehend it, and he reassumed the status of a fugitive slave. Patrick's first attempt at a solution was *activity*. In the way he set to work, he was like a Titan released.

His methods were characterized by boldness. He did not try to work by quiet diffusion, by peaceful propaganda. He lighted an enormous bonfire on the top of Slane in defiance of the royal edict and then had to appear before the High King to give an account of himself. Thus he joined issue at once. Everyone knows the story of that paschal fire lighted by Patrick on the first Easter of his mission. But Tirechan in the telling of it has a wonderfully expressive phrase. He says Patrick kindled the fire "in the nostrils of King Laoghaire." So strong was the tribal sentiment in Ireland and so accurate the missionary's memory, he knew it was useless to try to work upward from the people. He attacked the chieftains, and when he won, the tribes followed. But Patrick's was no timidly proffered apologetic. He flung Christianity in the face of Druidism.

His preaching and his baptizing were on a superhuman scale. It is related that he once preached for three days and three nights without pause. The old accounts add piously that to his audience the time seemed but as one hour, to all save one of his hearers at least, a girl— St. Brigid—who fell asleep. The delightful detail is added that when Patrick noticed her slumbers, he would not allow her to be awakened. He baptized hundreds of thousands with his own hands and signed the chrism of confirmation on their brow. In his old age, he liked to ruminate on those companies of the newly baptized who had passed through his hands. With unabated energy year after year, he labored on from tribe to tribe and left them in every case as a people reborn:

I am a debtor exceedingly to God, who granted me such great grace that many peoples through me should be regenerated to God and afterward confirmed, and that clergy should everywhere be ordained from them for a people newly come to belief. . . .

In truth the rapid ordination of a strong corps of native clergy proved, as was to be expected, a most powerful factor in promoting the confidence of the people. Even he himself was amazed at it. He never underestimated the magnitude of his work, but he humbly ascribed it directly to God:

Wherefore then in Ireland they who never had the knowledge of God, but until now only worshipped idols and abominations—how has there been lately prepared a people of the Lord, and they are called children of God? Sons and daughters of Scottic chieftains are seen to become monks and virgins of Christ. . . . Their number increases more and more—and as for those of our race who are born there, we know not the number of them. . . .

This latter fruit of his work, the blossoming monasticism, was as striking as the emergence of a native clergy, and was like a divine guarantee of stability.

The conversion of Ireland to Christianity is a golden page in history. But the tendency in Patrician literature has been to exaggerate somewhat the ease of that conversion. True there was not the slightest attempt at organized persecution of the Church, but there was plenty of sporadic, isolated hostility. One instance is the plot to assassinate Patrick, which resulted in the death of his devoted charioteer. We know of at least one attempt made to poison him. Once he and his companions were stoned. His own account of the hardships of his mission shows that physical courage played a large part in his work:

On occasion, I used to give presents to the kings, besides the hire that I gave to their sons who accompanied me; and nevertheless they seized me with my companions. And on that day they most eagerly desired to kill me; but my time had not yet come. And everything they found with us they plundered, and me myself they bound with irons. And on the fourteenth day the Lord delivered me from their power. . . . Daily I expect either slaughter, or to be defrauded, or reduced to slavery, or an unfair attack of some kind. . . .

There is even more kinship between this Apostle of an agricultural country and the laborer in the fields than is derived from rural birth and farmer parentage. Notice how readily intelligible to such a one is Patrick's simile describing the grace of his mission:

> I was like a stone lying in the deep mire; and he that is mighty came, and in his mercy lifted me up, and verily raised me aloft and placed me on the top of the wall. . . .

Moreover, Patrick was a toiler. Every plowman is a symbol of him, and the more stubborn the glebe to be broken, the more profuse the sweat, the more perfect the symbol. *Toil* is the keynote of his mission. He himself described it as "my laborious episcopate", "labor which I had learned from Christ my Lord". He worked like a man possessed. Afterward, when he tried to describe it, he shrank from the hugeness of the recital; "It would be a tedious task to explain it all in detail, or even in part. . . ."

The old "lives" are full of numerical evidence of the sheer laboriousness of Patrick's work. The founding of a new church is a favorite episcopal dream, but what of a bishop who founds *seven hundred* places of worship, ordains five thousand priests, gives minor orders to an unnumbered host of clerks, and consecrates three hundred and seventy bishops? Those are the figures given in the Tripartite Life. Dr. Todd has discussed exhaustively the ecclesiastical machinery that allowed room for so many bishops over so small an area. I need not dwell upon that here. Suffice it to say that at least every tribe had to have its bishop.

To appreciate his labor, it must be borne in mind, too, that when Patrick founded a church, the act was something very much more strenuous than blessing a foundation stone. He did not go about his missionary work with a companion or two, in the later Franciscan manner. You must see him with his traveling "household" ranged around him. This household comprised an assistant bishop; a chaplain; a brehon or judge, to advise him in legal matters; a "champion" or "strong man", for bodyguard; a psalmist; a chamberlain; a bell-ringer; a cook; a brewer; a sacristan; two table attendants; a driver; a firewoodman; a cowherd; three smiths; three artisans; three embroideresses; three masons. This household was modeled on those of the petty kings, an instance of how Patrick adapted himself to native customs, and maintained his dignity. In his ceaseless missionary travels, he and his company were like a small township on the move. They thundered up to a chieftain's dun, with their train of chariots, wagons, tents, baggage, equipment. The churches were mostly built of timber, or wattle and

clay, and when Patrick founded one, he nearly always assisted with
his own hands in the building of it. His household then provided the
furnishings. His coppersmiths made altars, chalices, patens and quad-
rangular book covers. His smiths made the nails used in the building,
the door hinges and handles, the bells. His embroideresses made the
vestments and altar cloths.

Patrick was the first hedge-schoolmaster in Ireland. In addition to
the retinue detailed above, there traveled always with him in his journeys his "school"; a group of likely Irish boys, suitable candidates for
the priesthood, whom he trained in practical missionary work, while
he taught them the psalter, missal and ritual in preparation for the con-
ferring of Holy Orders. When he founded a church center, he nearly
always had one member of this "family" ready to take charge of it.

Results best proclaim him. He came to Ireland in the year 432, and
before ten years had passed he had the Irish Hierarchy established under the primacy of Armagh! In the firmament of the Church, he had
made Ireland a bright star. Already, in that brief span of years, he saw
the whole country linked up, even to its remotest parts, with churches
and monastic foundations, to which a great tide of conversions was
flowing steadily, with a strong native clergy in possession. The thing
was accounted miraculous and the eyes of Christendom were turned
on his work. Impressed by the mission organization in that northern
island, Rome had raised it to the status of an ecclesiastical province,
making Patrick its Metropolitan, with his seat at Armagh. And when
Patrick wrote in his old age from his retirement at Saul, he had the
gratification of seeing a native bishop his Metropolitan successor—
Benignus, whom he had trained from boyhood.

But before these things came to pass, Patrick had passed through
the last trial of his vocation—the treachery of a friend—and the most
grievous temptation of his life—a temptation to despair. It seems that,
in his superiors' view, Patrick had never wholly made up the defect of
ignorance. Since that ignorance was of a special kind, namely, an inability to converse and write with ease in classical Latin, it had better
be designated by the less offensive term, *rusticitas*. A deep awareness
of this, for the deficiency had almost disqualified him for the mission,
made Patrick sorrowfully self-conscious about it to the end of his life.
In his *Confession*, written when he was an old man, he emphasizes his
rusticitas with almost wearisome reiteration:

I am the most illiterate and the least of all the faithful, and contemptible in the eyes of very many . . . a fool . . . the abhorred of this world. . . . I had long since thought of writing; but I hesitated until now, for I feared lest I should fall under the censure of men's tongues, and because I have not studied as have others, who in the most approved fashion have drunk in both law and the Holy Scriptures alike, and have never changed their speech from their infancy, but rather have been always rendering it more perfect. For my speech and language is translated into a tongue not my own, as can be easily proved from the savor of my writing, in what fashion I have been taught and am learned in speech. . . . Now in mine old age, I earnestly desire that which in youth I did not acquire. . . . When a youth, nay, almost a boy, I went into captivity in language (as well as in person) before I knew what I should earnestly desire, or what I ought to shun. And so today I blush and am exceedingly afraid to lay bare my lack of education; because I am unable to make my meaning plain in a few words to the learned. . . . Perchance it seems to not a few that I am thrusting myself forward in this matter with my want of knowledge and my slow tongue. . . .

It must be remembered about Patrick that he was bilingual and his "slowness of tongue" can have applied only to his converse in Latin. During his captivity in Ireland, he had to learn the Gaelic speech of his masters, and this acquirement was of enormous benefit to him when he returned as missionary. He preached to the people in the language of their homes. His feats as a preacher must be offset against his protestations of *rusticitas*. One recalls that sermon of three days and nights during which the time seemed to his audience to be but one hour. That does not argue a lack of fluency or intelligibility. The only conclusion is that Patrick was perfectly at home with his Irish converts, so much so that he became gradually less at home when communicating in Latin, whether by tongue or pen, with his ecclesiastical colleagues.

His *rusticitas* must also be considered in conjunction with his extraordinary zeal for the promotion of learning. An illustration of his method is seen in the story of the conversion of Ernaisc and his son Loarn. These having signified their readiness to hear of the new faith, Patrick immediately sat down with them under a tree and proceeded to teach them what is called in the "Lives" the alphabet, but what was in reality a written compendium of Christian doctrine. That picture of master and pupils under a tree illustrates every stage of his missionary progress. He not only taught orally, but he taught the written word too, and with extreme diligence he taught his pupils how to write the Gospel. There is another extraordinary picture one likes to hold in mind. On one occasion the pagan inhabitants of a district through which Patrick and his band were passing showed the greatest alarm, believing that the Christians had descended upon them with arms for aggressive purposes. But what the Christians were carrying in their hands were, not weapons, but wooden boards, rather like the Irish short sword in shape and size. On these harmless staves the "alphabet" was inscribed and the pupils were learning as they marched along the road! Patrick had literally armed his converts with the doctrine of Christ.

Yet when the success of his mission was admittedly phenomenal, Patrick was still far from winning the unanimous approval of his colleagues and superiors. Before he became Metropolitan, an enquiry was actually instituted into his fitness to be head of the Church in Ireland. Now among those appointed to "try" Patrick was his best friend, unnamed in the *Confession*, but concerning whose loyalty he never previously had any doubts. The Unnamed had been his friend in student days, even before Patrick had been made a deacon. To him, Patrick, before his ordination, had confided a secret. It concerned some error into which he had lapsed, or imagined he had lapsed, before he was fifteen. The Unnamed had strongly supported Patrick for the bishopric, had urged his merits against all opponents. Then came the astounding reversal. At that "trial" of Patrick, this friend suddenly turned against him, and even betrayed the secret—that ancient confidence of some thirty years' standing—and urged it as a reason for Patrick's removal from office.

Here is the saint's own account of the unhappy episode:

> After the lapse of thirty years they found, as an occasion against me, a matter which I had confessed before I was a deacon. Because of anxiety, with sorrowful mind, I disclosed to my dearest friend things that I had done in my youth one day, nay, in one hour, because I had not yet overcome. I cannot tell, God knoweth, if I was then fifteen years old. . . .

He writes of it in his old age, perhaps twenty years after the occurrence, and it is clear that the wound he then sustained was not yet healed. That blasting disillusionment in friendship had filled him with a bewilderment which the passage of years had not cleared from his mind:

I am grieved for my dearest friend . . . a man to whom I had entrusted
my soul! . . . How did it occur to him (or, how could he bring himself)
to put me to shame publicly before everyone? . . .

The arraignment resulted in Patrick's deposition from office. As he
phrased it, he was "rejected". He was even superseded for a brief period. This was the supreme crisis of his life. It occurred in the full tide
of his success; he had just brought the organization of the Church in
Ireland to the point where he could press for the establishment of a hierarchy. When the unjust sentence smote him, he was fearfully tempted
to acquiesce, to abandon his life's work; this to him was a counsel of
despair. He believed afterward that if he had yielded to the formidable
pressure then exercised upon him, he would have jeopardized his soul's
salvation. He referred with a kind of dread to that anguish of indeci-
sion; with dread and gratitude, as in speaking of a horrible abyss from
which a friendly hand had at the last minute restrained him:

Certainly on that day I was sore thrust at that I might fall both here and
in eternity. But the Lord graciously spared the stranger and sojourner for
his name's sake; and he helped me exceedingly when I was thus trampled
on, so that I did not come badly into disgrace and reproach. . . . Hence,
therefore, I render unwearied thanks to my God who kept me faithful
in the day of my temptation. . . .

Instead of submitting therefore, it would seem that he forced himself to go to Rome, where he was reinstated in office. He immediately
returned and resumed his labors for the conversion of Ireland.

St. Patrick was advanced in years by the time he had overcome those
six obstacles to his free service. Henceforth he walked in liberty, but
he had not far to go. The long level rays of sunset were already shining
on his road. He died at peace in the midst of his adopted people. It
is characteristic of him that his grave is unknown. Disputes about its
location arose not very long after his burial and the uncertainty persists
to the present day. In the annals of Christian history, he is an example
of the prophet who was not stoned. In the history of the country he
evangelized, his name shines out as the one patriot who was Unde-
feated.

The legends woven around Patrick are the most sheerly poetic and
the most beautiful in Christian hagiography. The mind that elabo-
rated those stories was beautiful: a glad, utterly guileless mind, always

grateful for the vision. It is the mind Patrick bequeathed to Ireland. Both legend and authentic record show that, despite his great constructive gifts and volcanic energy, he was a man of the easiest approach, who inspired intense love and loyalty. The shining simplicity of his life must have been reflected in an abiding tranquility of expression, which won the world to him. When the chieftain Dichu heard of his landing, he sallied forth in battle-array to bar his passage, but "when he saw the face of Patrick, he loved him." After the seasoned old warlord, it is a child who joins him. As he was mounting his chariot, taking leave of the parents of Benignus, the child clung to his foot in such a passion of grief that Patrick was forced to take him too. A delightful legend tells of another boy going to him in tears and the great missionary, gravely arresting those tears with his finger on the boy's cheek, turned them into gems. The two princesses, Ethne and Fedelm, trust him at sight and converse with him without a shadow of restraint.

His humble and cheerful comradeship with all classes once saved his life. The charioteer, Odran, overhearing a druidical plot to assassinate him, did not reveal it to his master but suggested instead that they should change places: in other words, Patrick would drive and Odran would recline at ease behind. Patrick at once assented, though the request must have seemed to him extraordinary. The result was that Odran was killed by a spear thrust and the saint escaped. The stories of Bishop MacCartan and Trea illustrate the same characteristic. When MacCartan had been serving Patrick for fourteen years, he thought it was time he had a rest. Being the saint's champion, his work was to assist him over the fords of rivers, over difficult roads, and in general to act as bodyguard and defense. Patrick was attached to him, and therefore it did not occur to him to give MacCartan promotion to easier work. But MacCartan conveyed the position by uttering the most dismal groans every time his services were required. "What's the matter with you?" said Patrick. "Age and infirmity", replied the other. "And all my comrades are now in churches whereas I am still on the road." "True", replied Patrick after a pause, and he immediately gave him a church.

When Trea came to be baptized, her veil was down over her face. It would seem that the angels had arranged it like that. The usual fashion was back over the head, and when Patrick reached her, he instinctively raised his hand to adjust the veil. "Is it not good that it should remain as it is?" said the maiden a trifle pertly. "It is good", said the Bishop submissively.

Patrick identified himself so closely with his converts that the world has almost come to regard him as an Irishman. But he was in exile among a people whom his compatriots in Empire regarded as barbarian. And frequently his state of exile pressed bleakly in upon him. He had recurrent attacks of homesickness in which the thought of revisiting his own people in Britain and Gaul rose with irresistible allurement before his mind:

> Wherefore, then, even if I should wish to part from them, proceeding thus to Britain—and glad and ready was I to do so—as to my fatherland and kindred, and not only that, but to go as far as Gaul in order to visit the brethren and to behold the face of the saints of my Lord—God knoweth that I used to desire it exceedingly.

His peaceful conquest of Ireland was never touched with the least suggestion of exploitation. He must have drawn heavily upon some missionary funds upon the continent, for he seems to have personally financed the whole enterprise in order to win the people's confidence. He accepted nothing from them, not even the "laborer's hire". He had a horror of receiving any material reward for his work. He tells us himself that when pious women gave him gifts to express their recognition, he returned them. He returned them even when those gifts were cast upon the altar, preferring to cause a little transient hurt than to permit the initiation of a doubtful practice. He served his newly ordained clergy without accepting from them, as he phrases it himself, "even the price of my shoe". "I did this so as to keep myself warily in all things . . . and that I should not, even in the smallest matter, give occasion to the unbelievers to defame or disparage." His entire independence in all matters of material benefit made a profound impression on the pagans, as is illustrated in that amusing story of Daire and his cauldron. This unswerving attitude was one of the sources of Patrick's power.

Probably the greatest tribute ever paid to St. Patrick occurs in Fiacc's Hymn, where such emphasis is laid on his power of overcoming by example where he had failed to convert by the spoken word. The greatest sermon he ever preached was his own life. That Hymn has preserved a remarkable picture of a man, who was "not deterred by cold, not possessed by hunger or thirst, sleeping on a bare stone, with a wet cloak around him, a rock for his pillow . . . enduring great toil."

SAINT BRENDAN

[483–577]

Donal O'Cahill

HE BIRTH of Brendan was not without presage. Patrick, standing on a Limerick hill and stirred by the grandeur of Kerry, had foretold it. Cara, Brendan's mother, had had a vision in which her bosom was bright with heavenly radiance and her breasts shone like snow. Erc, her bishop, had explained it saying she should bear a son great in power and rich with grace of the Holy Spirit. Airde, a wealthy neighbor, had invited St. Becc Mac De to prophesy some important event and he had answered: "There shall be born this night, between you and the sea, your true and worthy king whom kings and princes will honor, and whom he shall guide to heaven."

That night, in the year 483, the district north of Tralee was full of strange portent. A wondrous light blazed over Barra, near Fenit, illuminating the minds of men even as it struck the sea or lit the hills. For Brendan, son of Finnlugha and predestined patron of Kerry and Clonfert, was born. . . . Early next morning Erc and Airde came, like the eastern kings five centuries before, to do homage to the promised child. Taking him in his arms, the bishop blessed him and claimed him as fosterling. Airde, rejoicing, made an alms of thirty cows with their thirty calves and offered his protection forever. Then the infant was taken to Ardfert and baptized at Wethers' Well, a place still honored by seasonal pilgrimage. Mobhi was the name first given him, but a mantle of white mist (broen finn) was seen to descend until it veiled all Fenit, and henceforth he who was white in soul and body was called Broenfinn or Brendan.

The Ireland into which Brendan had been thus ushered was fraught with great change. War's terrible intoxication was losing its attraction for the Irish, who were everywhere accepting the doctrines of Christ.

The descendants of warriors who had harried the Romans to the Alps had yielded to the pleadings of Patrick and were even then raising throughout their land the foundations of a Spiritual Empire that was to last to the end of time.

When Brendan was a year old, Erc, complying with custom and desirous of keeping him within his own jurisdiction, had him sent to a fosterage in Killeedy, County Limerick. There but a few years before, St. Ita—the youthful Brigid of Munster—had founded her convent and gathered a number of women whose austerities and ministrations won the esteem of many saints. The nun whose mortifications inspired St. Cummian's writings naturally exercised a profound influence over Brendan. Her special interest in him is perhaps proof of the promise given even by his earliest years. He returned her affection by a devotedness that deepened with time and drew him back to her in later life for sympathy and counsel in all his undertakings.

After five years Brendan returned home and was placed under the care of Erc. In the early ages of the Church the duty of educating youthful aspirants to Holy Orders usually devolved on the bishops themselves. Thus it was with St. Augustine in Hippo, with St. Ambrose in Milan, and the same system obtained in the early instruction of the Irish saints. To this preceptorship amid native surroundings we must turn if we would trace the growth of that fervour and love of perilous emprise which were to fructify so marvelously in the manhood of the saint. Erc—the boy's patron and earliest bishop of whom there is record in Kerry—has been identified with the "sweet-voiced" brehon who fearlessly acclaimed Patrick at the court of King Laoghaire. Years before, on the withdrawal of Benignus to Connaught, he had come from Slane to continue the mission among the tribes of West Munster. None more fitted, Erc fired the boy's imagination with stories of Patrick's achievement and stirred the childish soul with a longing for emulation. Here, too, Brendan's wanderings by the sea bred a familiarity with its moods that mitigated its terrors, and its eternal thunderings sowed in his consciousness the seeds of a wanderlust not merely daring but divine. Of those years of pupilage in Kerry—and they continued for fourteen years—only the most meager accounts have come down. These, however, convey an impression of Brendan's great application to study and of a character unusually strong.

The old legends linger upon those early days. Contrasting with the paucity of authentic record, they tell with much detail of his providential protection in times of danger and of his sustenance in need. In the drought of summer fresh springs burst forth for him, birds flew to his succor, and a doe came each morning from the upland of Luchra to yield him her milk. Once when ten years old, he accompanied Erc on a visit of ceremony. While the bishop was preaching, the boy,—who had been left waiting in a chariot—proceeded to recite the psalms. A little girl, attracted by the sweetness of his voice, jumped in beside him and asked him to play. But Brendan, considering his dignity slighted, gave her a sound thrashing and regretted it immediately. He confessed his guilt to the bishop and received the stiff penance of spending that night in a cave. There the young penitent passed the time in prayer or in chanting the psalms, and his voice was so powerful even then, it was heard at a distance of a thousand paces. Erc was both pleased at the prompt obedience and amazed at the boy's courage. In Brendan's ready, almost gay compliance with the bishop's command there is evident not only the early development of his humility but the first proof of that fearlessness so striking in later years. Of this period of his life, and indeed of the subsequent ten years, but one fact is known: that he had the occasional companionship of his sister Briga. Perhaps this may be the reason for assuming that she too received her early training under Erc.

Having completed his preliminary studies at home, Brendan, at the age of twenty, went northward to the theological school of Clonfoish. While on the way he encountered the heathen warrior Colman MacLenin. If the hardened soldier was not impressed by the student's bearing he was certainly fascinated by the imperiousness of his mission. For Brendan bade him forsake the ignoble calling of war and invited his service under the captaincy of the Universal King. He kindled the warrior's imagination with his story of a banner tattered, maybe, but unsullied and above surrender, and promised him a place in the Christian Army whose legions were to rise on the edges of the earth and whose glory should endure forever. The warrior yielded to the student. Together they traveled into Connaught, and MacLenin, kneeling before the aged Jarlath, became Brendan's first convert. He it was who founded Cloyne, became its first bishop, and is now venerated under the name of St. Colman.

Under the presidency of Jarlath the seminary of Clonfoish, near Tuam, had won a great reputation for the teaching of Scripture and it was to pursue such study that Brendan had enrolled. That his demeanor and application soon attracted notice is shown by the friendship that sprang up between master and pupil despite the disparity in their ages. Indeed Jarlath's removal of the See to Tuam—the seat of the present Archdiocese—was due to Brendan's suggestion when leaving.

Before Brendan's ecclesiastical studies were completed a large number of his kinsmen had settled at Magh Enna in Mayo. So large was that migration, the district chosen became known as "Upper Kerry". Thither Brendan next turned, probably at his kinsfolk's request and with a disciplinary eye to the more intractable members of the tribe. But subsequent events give the journey an even deeper significance. It is said that an angel appeared to him and dictated the Rule by which he was to govern his life and the lives of the multitudes later subject to him. Although the original is no longer extant, similar rules have come down from the immediate successors of St. Patrick who were the pioneers of Irish monastic discipline. Of these early codes the most important is that of St. Ailbe of Emly which is said to resemble in a general way the Rule of St. Brendan. It enjoined absolute obedience and the observance of silence each day until the hour of one o'clock, for "two-thirds of piety consist in silence". The monks had to subsist on the most meager fare and sleep on the floors of their cells, dressed in their habits, and with little covering. Hospitality was stressed but no lay person was allowed to enter the monastery enclosure. This rule of Ailbe's runs into sixty-nine strophes enumerating the minutest details of community life and shows a severity without parallel save in the records of Egyptian asceticism.

During Brendan's stay in Magh Enna there occurred an event which shattered the quietude of his visit. A young man had died and Brendan met the funeral cortege on the way. Filled with sorrow, he bade the relatives have faith and prayed over the corpse. The incredible happened —the dead man was restored, to the joy of an amazed throng. This stupendous news spread like wildfire and Brendan had to flee from the importunities of the people and from the inducements of the king who wished him to remain in their midst. But a wider conquest than that of the plains of Magh Enna was luring Brendan.

He returned home in the year 513 and being thirty years old—the age required by the canons of the early Church—he was ordained by his old preceptor, Erc. His gravity of purpose from the beginning is proved by his self-imposed abstinence. For he never afterward partook of food that had had the breath of life although he imposed no such law upon his disciples. Immediately after ordination he set about stimulating in his native county that monastic spirit he had seen practiced so imposingly elsewhere in Ireland. There can be little doubt that his labors were greatly facilitated by the influence of his family who were of noble lineage and several of whom became saints. It is probable that he was helped in no small degree too by those tribal whisperings of the miraculous powers he had exercised in the west. In a short time many followers gathered to his Rule and the growth of cells, oratories, and churches was a natural sequence. Though no date is ascribed to the foundation of Ardfert it is generally considered to have been his first. Barrow, Rathoo, Kilfenora, and a cell on Brandon Hill followed in quick succession. Thus there grew up, always under his guidance and not seldom built by his own hands, those various villages of huts with their common refectories and churches, and self-sustaining communities who devoted themselves to the monastic life.

The spontaneity of the response astonished Brendan. In the steady stream of disciples he saw proof of the enduring strength of Irish monasticism, and doubtless this initial success brought home to his mind the ultimate limitations of insular endeavor. He saw growing up throughout the land many institutions like those of Clonfoish and Clonard. Men and women, inspired by the same ideal, were thronging to them until Ireland, loud with psalms, became a gigantic hive of religion whose members' chief need was fresh fields to which they might bear their honeyed faith. It was a reversal of the Gospel state of things: harvesters were not lacking; the need was a new terrain where souls might be garnered for God. The situation did not leave Brendan unaffected for long. His practical mind probed the problem; it was appropriate that he should find a solution in the sun. Ever since childhood he had seen it blaze a path of glory over the wastes to the unknown west. Since the world began that sight had stirred even the least imaginative among men and, inevitably, it filled with dreams of discovery the missionary soul of Brendan. There, to the west, might be the haven he was hoping for—a possible outlet for that surging tide of the missionary Gael. "Everyone who hath left father, or mother, or sister, or lands, shall receive an hundredfold." The words of the Gospel rose to his mind and thus, after something like twenty years' labors at home, Brendan thought of other lands.

Popular imagination has for long represented Brendan as an aimless wanderer, a sort of vagabond of the sea. Conventional accounts needed but a few judicious touches to portray him as a soft but successful pirate who had, somehow or other in a blanket of mist, captured a place in the Christian Calendar. No conception could be more remote from reality. In an age that was practical enough to produce multitudes of saints, Brendan was supremely practical. Even as a child he had shown signs of it in those odd moments of leisure snatched for study, and on the morning of his ordination too by those self-imposed rigors. He is Saint precisely because he was a navigator with the highest possible purpose, because he was in fact a conquistador for Christ.

A voyage of exploration had many attractions for one of Brendan's mold. It appealed to that spirit of daring he had shown even as a child in the cave, and it held too the alluring prospect of that perfect contemplation possible in a ship at sea. But even stronger reasons impelled him. The early Celtic peoples had an immemorial belief in the existence of an Elysium set beyond the rim of the western ocean. Bearing a variety of names this island shone in the amberlight of romance, reflecting the desires of the different races. Even in Christian times there was a tradition current along the western seaboard of Ireland that the "Land of Promise" could be seen every seventh year. Brendan could not remain wholly indifferent to such tales. It seems however that his greatest incentive came from a brother monk, Barinthus, who was a navigator credited with western voyages. Having heard this monk's account of his travels, Brendan withdrew to his cell on Brandon Hill. There, for three days, he fasted and prayed for guidance—alone, with the ocean beneath him rolling outward to the alluring west.

At the end of the vigil Brendan announced his decision to sail and ordered three boats to be built. The crew of sixty were selected, provisions were gathered, and the day named. Then, with a courage that equaled his faith, he sailed from the Kerry bay that still bears his name and disappeared into romance and mist.

For periods varying between two and seven years Brendan is said to have explored the western ocean. Although the traditional accounts of his adventure are made grotesque by fable there is evidence that he reached a delightful land. Some accounts place his landing in New-foundland and others mention the Virginian Capes. While these are not authoritative, there is said to be proof in indigenous remains that Irishmen had settled in America centuries before the Spanish sighted its shore. It is said too the Darien Indians spoke a language akin to that of the primitive Irish, and that an eighth-century people in Florida were speaking the Irish tongue. Furthermore, the early Mexicans were un-doubtedly acquainted with Christianity's central truths. When Cortez and his six hundred landed there in 1519 they were amazed to find their arrival hailed as the fulfillment of a native tradition, strong as it was cer-tainly old. They were told that, many centuries before, one whom the natives called Quetzalcoatl—*the Precious*—had come from some "holy island" of the northeast, in a boat with "wings" or sails. According to their centuried tradition he was a tall white man, advanced in years, with broad forehead, black hair and beard, and he wore a long garment, over which hung a mantle marked with crosses. For several years he remained in their country teaching the divine faith. So greatly was he venerated by the people, they attributed his subsequent departure to the workings of some malign influence and were comforted only by his promise to return or to send some of his disciples instead.

This man was certainly a Christian missionary from Europe and it seems probable he labored among these Toltecs some time between the sixth and eighth centuries. At that period there was great missionary activity among the nations of Europe, and those familiar with eccle-siastical history know that Ireland—"Insula Sanctorum"—was fore-most, aflame with apostolic zeal, her sons shrinking from no peril, by land or sea, in their labor for the salvation of souls. If Quetzalcoatl was not Brendan—and the assumption that he was involves no serious inconsistency—then it seems fruitless to seek his identity. Nor is there lacking external evidence of Ireland's early maritime enterprise in the west. Icelandic sagas of great antiquity chronicled the western voyag-ing of Irish monks, and the Scandinavians knew the elusive island as *Irland it Mikla* or Ireland the Great. In many ancient maps St. Bren-dan's Island, under various denominations, was marked in the western sea and to some extent influenced Columbus. So recently as 1634 the French geographer, Tassiu, drew a map in which he placed the island of Hy Brazil to the west of Ireland.

Of the actual land discovered by St. Brendan nothing authentic is known. An old legend, after picturesquely enumerating the perils of the voyage, tells of a lovely land with extensive meads decked with flowers and laved by many rivers, of thickly-set trees, fruit-laden, swaying before scented winds in a light that always shone. Brendan explored the country in every direction and at last came to a great river which he was unable to cross. Here a heavenly messenger appeared to him and, telling him that the land would be made manifest to his successors, bade him depart.

Brendan's return home was the signal for great rejoicings. Crowds flocked to welcome the Christian Ulysses whose reappearance had the air of a return from the dead. Even the wonted calm of monastic life was broken by tales of marvelous exploits: how Brendan's ships laden with plants, seeds, and provisions had struggled against raging seas; of the islands seen and the wonders worked; of the monks' arrival and stay in the long-sought land, and of the angelic voice bidding them return. The heroic deeds thus related flew through the schools of Ireland, to Britain and the Continent until the name of Brendan became talismanic throughout Europe. It was inevitable that tales told with such impetus, and by nature of their very appeal, should develop into diverse and fantastic legends. Recited in Irish, sung in Norman-French, and read in an increasing number of languages during the eleventh century, Brendan's adventures fascinated the medieval mind and later influenced, among others, the poet Dante.

The Saint's fame brought religious thronging to his Rule. Providence was aiding him and he lost no time in turning to good account the material that lay at hand. He began with Kerry. In a sequence not determined he raised foundations at Kilmalehedar, Gallerus, and in the Blasket Islands, as though in response to that insistent call of the sea. Perhaps there was too in that choice a certain prescience of the trend of the later Gael. To Iveragh also it is thought he turned and built in the Glen Parish, near Caherciveen. With unabated zest he traveled constantly between the different communities, superintending, teaching, gathering neophytes, until Kerry was girdled with religious settlements and he was again seized with that divine unrest.

The Rule thus strengthened and his spiritual sway at home secured left Brendan still unsatisfied. He seemed hypnotized by conquest, he had an insatiable thirst for souls. Having appointed a successor, he left his native county and again his course is vague. The versatility of the man can be gathered from the fact that subsequently he occupied a chair at the school of Ross and founded a monastery at Inishdadrum, on the Shannon, where he worked several miracles. It is a matter of conjecture whether at this period he turned to Ireland's most famous school, Clonard. That he studied there at some time is certain, and the native love of learning in those days is sufficient to counter the possible objection of old age.

The fame of Clonard attracted crowds of students of all ages not only from Ireland but from abroad. Founded by St. Finnian in 520, this college on the Boyne grew from a hermitage of wattles to an immense monastic establishment like a translated town of the Thebaid. There under the canopy of heaven, in those fields by the river, could be seen the amazing spectacle of three thousand scholars, freely fed and freely taught, acquiring the Classics, Philosophy, and Scriptures, and giving homage to God before Augustine had yet seen the heathen hordes of England.

It is impossible to determine how long Brendan remained at Clonard. When we next meet him, however, he is again trimming his sails for the sea. This second voyage is said to have been advised by St. Ita and undertaken about the year 530 in penance for some rash act. But a more likely supposition is that his decision was influenced by the sojourn at Clonard. Finnian had labored for many years among the Britons in Wales and it is very probable he urged Brendan to a similar mission. So once more, impelled by the old impulse, Brendan spread sail and this time turned his prow to the east. There ensued a ten years' absence from Ireland which, despite the vagueness of his itinerary, stamps him as worthy of a place among the most indefatigable missionaries of our race.

Restless as the sea he loved or the winds he bent to his will, he followed his calling with the superb abandon of one who acknowledged it eternal and bounded only by the commandments of God. His was a sustained whirlwind campaign. One might light on his tracks anywhere from the Azores to the Arctic, or from Avilion to the littorals of the Holy Land. In Caledonia, considered unconquerable even by the Romans, he walked as if with royal license. There particularly he seems to have spent considerable time. Perhaps the secret of that protracted stay lies in the call of his exiled kin! At any rate his ubiquity there is commemorated by a variety of churches, shrines, and patrons, and by numerous hills, rivers, and sounds bearing his name. With the sea-roving Cormac he visited Iona and brought to the Orkneys and Shetland the light of faith. Nor is it unlikely that he voyaged at this time to St. Kilda, the Faroes, or even to the Ultima Thule of the north. That these islands were visited by Irish monks in the early centuries of Christianity is undisputed history. Irish bells, books, and croziers were found in Iceland by Gardar the Dane in 863, and by Ingulf eleven years later when the Norwegians colonized it.

When he had spent three years in the north Brendan appeared in Wales, astonishing the people by his miracles. While there he visited that famous alumnus of Armagh—Gildas the Wise. We find Brendan with St. Cadoc at the monastery of Lancarvan, and then building a hermitage, as might be expected, on the banks of the Severn. Still later he labored with his friend of the Atlantic voyage, St. Malo, in Brittany. There he founded Alyth—Alectum—and lent his name to several spots along that shattered coast. A shrine to St. Brendan in Tenerife may not be unconnected with his voyage to Palestine.

Brendan's return about the year 540 is invested with the mystery that surrounded his departure. From the conflicting accounts there emerges, however, one fact: that he brought with him many disciples, one of whom bore princely rank. It is stated that Brendan visited St. Brigid after his return, but as her death occurred twenty-five years earlier this chronology is manifestly wrong. Whatever the date of his visit, its purpose is interesting. During his travels abroad Brendan had heard St. Brigid's help invoked with astonishing success. Greatly edified, he composed a hymn in her honor and on returning home he visited the Saint. Being asked the reason of her great power, she replied that never for a moment was her attention diverted from God. Whereupon Brendan, no doubt magnifying his peccadilloes, confessed his remissness and was sweetly reproved. The meeting is important because it shows the great humility which ran as a leitmotif through the lives of all the Irish Saints. Brendan's life was a prolonged striving after perfection; it is not wholly figurative to say he hid from ecclesiastical honors or knelt in penance before a nun.

It was probably after his return from this voyage that he built at Clonemery and carried on those labors that gave his name to a hill by the Nore. After this the ring of his evangel is heard once again in Connaught, but that thundering voice is on the wane. There on the Corrib, with his nephew, Moennen, he founded the monastery of Inchiquin —first in the west—in the year 552. A little later and in the same vicinity he raised for his sister, Briga, and her community the nunnery of Anaghdown. That divine urge was still his driving force, but one has now the impression that he was fighting against time. He went northward to Mayo and established himself in the solitude of Inish-Gloria—an island off the coast. There he must have given himself up to contemplation. . . . The years were crowding in upon him even as the billowing seas around his island home. Since his boyhood the world had grown larger, in the sphere of exploration he himself had played an honorable part. He recalled those voyages eastward and northward, the clamant heathen hosts. He looked to the west and remembered. There was challenge in what he saw: the infinite possibilities of the mission, the urgency of this warfare for souls. And relieved against all was the stark inadequacy of human endeavor.

Brendan's response was typical. He went south into Galway and there by the Shannon, in the year 560, founded the missionary school of Clonfert. He threw into the work all his remaining energy for it was the culmination of his labors and the last great venture of his life. Clonfert's rapid growth to the forefront of Ireland's numerous academies is a tribute to his influence and fame. Under the guidance of his nephew, Bishop Moennen, it attracted the intellect of Europe, and had illustrious names on its roll. Renowned warriors become students might have been met there, or white-cowled mendicants who could have worn crowns. On the authority of Senan we have it that no less than six boat-loads of foreign students, bound for the school, came up the Shannon on one day. Thus the school flourished for many centuries, fed on the produce of its own pastures, weaving its own wool, served by its own fleet, and numbering by the thousand those students whose heaven-fired enthusiasm sped the Faith to every land in Europe.

The organization of so important a settlement as Clonfert was heavy work for Brendan. But frequently, too, he was forced to absent himself. He responded to those urgent calls from his scattered communities, he attended Chapters, made visitations, arbitrated feuds. For about twenty years he toiled ceaselessly up and down the country, never slackening in his regard for the disciples of his Rule. But the work was wearing him and he was withering with the years. During those last visits to Kerry there was a longing in his heart and the brethren saw sadness in his looks at the sea.

In the year 577 he went to his sister's convent at Anaghdown. There on Sunday the 16th of May, having celebrated Mass, he turned to the community and told them that his end was near. An old Life, recording the dialogue between the Saint and his sister, recreates that pathetic scene and echoes, however faintly, their tremulous tones:

BRENDAN: Commend to God in your prayers my departure from this life.

BRIGA: Dear father, what have you to fear?

BRENDAN: I fear as I pass away all alone, and as the journey is darksome, I fear the unknown region, the presence of the King, the sentence of the Judge.

Then Brendan, at the age of ninety-four, having given final direction for his burial, blessed the community and passed to his reward.

Great multitudes, hearing the news, flocked to the convent and clamored for the privilege of having his body buried in their midst. But the Saint had foreseen this difficulty and had provided. In the dead of night and by stratagem his remains were taken in a wagon from Anaghdown, on the three days' journey to the place of his choice—Clonfert. There, in all honor, Brendan—Saint and Navigator—was laid to rest while psalms were chanted, canticles sung, and may be the winds and the waves were still.

SAINT COLUMCILLE

[521-597]

Raymond O'Flynn

HERE IS A CHAPTER in the *Imitation* on the "different motions of nature and of grace"; a complementary one might be added on their conformities. For it is not the effect of grace to destroy or to supersede nature, but to uphold and elevate it. Grace is essentially positive—an affirmation of all truth, a desire of all goodness, a delight in all loveliness; it is the assertion of the will to live.

No doubt, so long as the flesh lusts against the spirit, the negative aspects of asceticism will be prominent, and it is chiefly self-reproof and self-correction that are stressed by the older hagiology. But there is a newer, and perhaps a better way: which is, to exhibit the lives of the saints in accordance with their psychology; to show how this special character resulted in this special holiness.

In the case of the Irish saints this procedure is even obvious. For in no other people has the fusion of blood and religion been so natural or so complete. Some close affinities must have existed between the old Gaedhlic stock and the Gospel engrafted on it, when it burgeoned spontaneously into such luxuriant holiness. Already in the lifetime of their National Apostle, "the sons and daughters of the Scots were becoming monks and virgins of Christ" in numbers unprecedented. That vivid Celtic imagination, which had peopled the countryside with preternatural agencies enabled them all but to visualize the unseen things of Faith. That dissatisfaction of soul which betrayed itself in wistful yearnings for the Land of the Ever-Young was readily transformed into Christian unworldliness. That ardent temperament—the *perfervidum ingenium Scotorum*, as it came to be called—speedily generated an army of intrepid apostles. That strange, almost mysterious influence, which made all who came into contact with them "more Irish than the Irish themselves", bade fair to fill Europe with their spirit. And generally the work of grace in them looked less like a new creation than a new direction.

But, among "the hosts of the Saints of Eire" there is one who represents in an eminent degree the national character sublimated by grace, and who, on that account has been canonized in the supreme Triad of Ireland's sainthood by a people meticulous even as to the distinctions of sanctity. There were brave men, it has been said, before Agamemnon, and they were lost in oblivion, *sacro quia carent vate*—because they lacked an inspired bard. More fortunate in that respect than Patrick or Brigid, Columba was celebrated by the chief poet of his nation in a Song of Praise—the extant *Amhra Choluim Chille*. And fittingly. For it was he—himself a "harp without a base chord", as witness his Latin and Irish verses—who "stayed the poets", when they were threatened with banishment for their troublesomeness. But, what is of greater import still, he has been made the subject of a biography which Montalembert describes as "one of the most living, most attractive and most authentic monuments of Christian history."

According to its author's "Preface", based on "what was committed to writing before our time, or what we, diligently inquiring, have learned by hearing from certain experienced and faithful ancients", the "Life" by Adamnan, Abbot of Iona, is vivid and graceful portraiture indeed. To be sure, it is frank hagiography, and abounds in miracles and celestial apparitions which bespeak an age of greater Faith than ours. But why demur?—the modern world gapes even at the actualities of Lourdes; while we, who know how intimately interfused are nature and grace, feel as little misgiving when we read that the Saint changed water into wine for the Sacred Mysteries, or was visited by angels, as when we are told he transcribed the Psalter, or scaled the Grampians and urged his curragh through Loch Ness.

Whatever of the aura that surrounds the saint, even the unbeliever must acknowledge the greatness of the man and the splendor of his achievement. Columba has left no such literary monument as his younger contemporary Columbanus, nor did he occupy a like position in the ample field of Continental affairs. Yet has he made an impression on the imagination and exercised a spell over the heart more like the heroes of legend than the characters of history. To proud lineage, noble physique and fine culture, he united the lofty aspiration and splendid daring of the Ireland of his day; and fulfilled his vast enterprise in romantic conditions that would have enhanced the exploits of Cuchulain or Fionn. He was "the high saint and high sage, the arch-presbyter of the island of the Gaedhal, the brand of battle set forth with the divers talents and gifts of the Holy Ghost." "There was not born of the Gaedhal", adds an old biographer, "a being more illustrious, or wise, or of better family than Columcille, nor did there come of them another who was more modest, more humble, or more lowly."

Such the personality that forms the background to the prophecies, miracles, and visions which are the explicit theme of Adamnan. But it is a personality expressed with photographic distinctness. Certain events may be obscure; but the man himself, "angelic of aspect, clean in speech, holy in work, great in council"; the "Island Soldier of Christ who could not pass the space even of a single hour without applying himself to prayer, or reading, or writing, or some manual labor"; the founder of churches and the friend of saints and kings, "dear to all, ever showing a pleasant, holy countenance", is more intimately known to us than any personage of his epoch.

"Noble in sooth", says the Life given in the *Leabhar Breac*, "was Columcille's kindred, for of the kindred of Conaill son of Niall was he." The child was born on December 7, 521, at Gartan, County Donegal, his father Fedhlimidh being Prince of Tyrconnel, and his mother Ethne eleventh in descent from Cathair Mor, progenitor of the Kings of Leinster. According to custom, he was given in fosterage to the priest who had baptized him Colum (Dove), and from a cell where he was used to pray he early gained the addition by which he has since been distinguished. "Has our little Colum", the children of the place would ask, "come today from the cell in Tir Lughdech in Cinnel Conaill?"

His education was continued in the Ecclesiastical School of St. Finnian at Moville, County Down, and after a further period of secular instruction by Gemman, an aged Bard of Leinster, he passed to the great institution of Clonard. There he had for preceptor another St. Finnian, "the Wise Tutor of Eire's Saints", and for associates the group who, with Ciaran the founder of Clonmacnoise and himself, were to become renowned as "the Twelve Apostles of Erin". Being ordained priest by Bishop Etchen, he prosecuted his studies in the institute of St. Mobhi at Glasnevin near Dublin, where he remained until the students were dispersed by the Yellow Plague which devastated many parts of Europe in 544.

Incidentally, it is for those who talk of an "independent" Scottish Church to ask themselves if the pupil of St. Finnian, who had himself

frequented Candida Casa (Whitherne) founded by the Papal Missionary St. Ninian, and who had stayed three months with Pope Pelagius
learning "apostolical customs", was less likely to be a "Roman" Catholic than his master, even supposing Columcille could have derived his
Christianity from any other source than the "Roman" Church of St.
Patrick.

Columcille was only twenty-five, when he opened his first church
and school amid the "Oak Trees of Calgaich", and in sight of "the salt
main on which the seagulls cry"—"my Derry, my little Oak Grove",
as he affectionately remembered it; and his subsequent career in Ireland
was that of a monastic founder and scholar, until he "set up his everlasting rest in Iona" in 563. "A hundred churches which the wave fre-
quents he has on the margin", says the *Leabhar Breac*. But there were
others. Thirty-seven have been identified; and, significantly, two of
them—Durrow and Kells—are associated with precious manuscripts.
So richly and exquisitely illuminated is the Book of Kells, Cambrensis
thought it must be the work of angels. Plausibly enough, tradition once
ascribed it to Columcille himself, for he was a lover of fine art and a
tremendous bibliophile. The Lismore Life credits him with the writing of three hundred books; and though this may be merely a round
number, no notice is so frequent in Adamnan as that which shows him
engaged in writing. For instance: "On another day, about the same
hour, a shout was raised on the other side of the strait; and the Saint,
sitting in his little hut which rested on a wooden floor, says to Diarmuid: The man who is shouting beyond the strait is not a man of
refined sentiment, for today he will upset and spill my inkhorn!"

In fact, according to an inveterate tradition, it was violation of the
law of copyright that led to his exile. Was the original the Psalter of
St. Jerome recently brought from Rome by St. Finnian? Was the copy,
transcribed in a "neat but hurried hand", that known as "the Cathach"
or "Battle", which the O'Donnells carried before their array for more
than a thousand years, and which is now in the Library of the Royal
Irish Academy? Was Columcille really responsible for mustering his
kinsmen against the Ard Righ at Culdreimhne? Was he sentenced to
perpetual exile for the bloodshed? (Ominously, his name is connected
with two other battles—Coleraine in 577 and Culfedha near Clonard
ten years later—and he was certainly a stout clansman.) Whatever
be the truth of the matter, some crisis occurred, when he was at the
height of his success, to induce him to quit the land he loved. Adamnan

suggests that his venture was a voluntary *peregrinatio pro Christo*. And we can well believe that the spirit of high adventure which sped his victorious ancestor Niall through Britain to the Loire, and in pursuit of which King Dathi died at the foot of the Alps, was urgent in the blood of the Christian priest. At any rate, in company of twelve others (the Irish, as a rule, conformed to the Apostolic pattern) he directed his course to "Alba of the ravens"—the leader of that intrepid army of *peregrini* who, with staff and satchel of books, clad in white woolen tunic, and having strange frontal tonsure from ear to ear, and eyelids tinted blue, were to make Europe resound for five centuries to the *militiae Christi*—the warfare of Christ.

There is an old Celtic poem with the inscription "Columkille fecit", reminiscent of his Irish home—"the song of the wonderful birds"; the "level sparkling strand"; "the thunder of the crowding waves upon the rocks". But more often quoted are the lines from his "Song of Farewell":

> There is a grey eye
> That looks back upon Erin:
> It shall not see during life
> The men of Erin, nor their wives.
> My vision o'er the brine I stretch
> From the ample oaken planks;
> Large is the tear of my soft grey eye
> When I look back upon Erin.

In point of fact, he revisited Ireland more than once; certainly in 575 when he took part in the Convention of Druim Ceatt, and again before his death, when all Clonmacnoise, monks and populace, thronged to meet him, "as if", says Adamnan, "he were an angel of the Lord". Still, for thirty-four years the Islet of Iona was his permanent abode. There is a legend that he navigated from one island to another until he finally ran his curragh into the little bay since known as Port-na-Curraich. From the hill above—Carn-cul-ri-Erin, the Cairn of the Back turned to Ireland—he was satisfied he could no longer descry his native shores, and there amid the silence of the seas he built his monastery.

We can easily imagine it from Adamnan—the oaken church, where were celebrated the "Sacred Mysteries of the Eucharist"; the "monasterium rotundum", probably a round tower; the guest chamber with its fireplace and vessels of water; the wattled cells of the monks; the farmstead; the mill for grinding corn; and, not least remarkable, below in the harbor the fleets of boats with "sailyards in the form of a cross" plying to and fro with their cargoes of oak and pinewood. It was a veritable hive of industry, for the Columban rule, with its Penitential Discipline, suffered no drones and, apart from the short hours of sleep, the time not given to prayer was spent in a variety of manual industries and—a distinctive feature of Irish foundations—in the writing of books.

Unlike the homes of St. Benedict, an Irish monastery was never a mere asylum from the tumult of the world. Rather it was a citadel, a base of operations from which the "soldier of Christ" (Adamnan's expression) could conduct his campaign in the surrounding territory. According to this native conception, Iona was meant to be a strategic point to preserve the Faith among the Scots of Dalriada, and to carry it to the utmost confines of the Picts. Columcille himself headed the expedition which had for objective King Brude in his northern fastness near Inverness. He pushed his way by land and water through the series of glens and lochs, now linked by the Caledonian Canal, but in those days presenting difficulties which had deterred the legionaries of Agricola. The effort met with success; and from that onward we read of journeys of hundreds of miles on foot, and still more perilous voyages on uncharted seas, until not only the whole of Pictland, but the Hebrides, the Orkneys, the Shetlands, and even the Faroe Isles and Iceland were brought into the "obedience of Christ". So energetically, in fact, was the work carried on, that, already in the lifetime of its Founder, Iona was able to dispatch missionaries to Northumbria, and the Isle of Man, and Southern Britain.

With the incessant coming and going, the "watch" on Torr Abb must needs keep a strict lookout. When it was not some of the brethren rounding the northern side from a missionary outpost in the Isles, or strangers from distant Istria approaching on the south, it was a visitor from Ireland hailing across the Sound, or kindling the beacon fire at night. Then must the little ferryboat put out and row him across the mile of water. For Irish hospitality was even a point of Rule at Iona; and "many", the Scriptures said, "doing hospitality, have entertained angels unawares". If it chanced to be a bishop, like Cronan from Munster, he was received with "the veneration due to him", and "bidden by the Saint to consecrate Christ's Body according to custom", and "in the episcopal rite". If it were an old friend and distinguished—Comgall of Bangor, or Caennech of Ossory, or Brendan of Clonfert—the ordinary fast was dispensed, and there was what Adamnan calls a "joyful day" in the community. When it was none of these, it was sure to be Cormac—a monkish Ulysses more in his element "seeking a solitude in the pathless sea" than poring over Greek manuscripts beneath the oak trees of Durrow. No one could tell when that restless adventurer might turn up. Columcille expostulated with him: "Two years and a month to this night is the time thou hast been wandering from port to port, from wave to wave." Yet he loved the man—he was interesting, and could tell of a voyage of fourteen days and nights to the Arctic ice, and of encounters with strange monsters that threatened the vessel's side, and loathsome creatures "like frogs" that swarmed over the blades of the oars. The solicitous Abbot even used his influence with the Chieftain of the Orkneys to obtain for him safe conduct, and on one occasion summoned the brethren by bell to "pray with all fervor for Cormac; for voyaging too far he has ventured beyond the bounds of human enterprise."

But Columcille was one of those whose sympathy extends to the meanest thing that breathes, and when the expected visitor was merely a crane—"a certain guest", he calls him—"who will arrive very weary and fatigued after the ninth hour of the day and, its strength almost exhausted, will fall on the shore"—even so, the sacred laws of hospitality were not to be neglected. "Thou must keep a lookout", he orders, "on the western part of the isle, sitting on the seashore; and thou shalt lift it up kindly, and carry it to a neighboring house, and attend it for three days and three nights." "At the end of three days" (the delicacy of sentiment is remarkable) "refreshed and unwilling to sojourn longer with us, it will return to the pleasant region of Ireland whence it came. And I thus earnestly commend it to thee for that it came from the place of our own fatherland."

For such "minor occurrences" one may well be content to forego a volume of historic lore. But there were episodes of greater social concern too, as when the Abbot "ordained" Aedhan king of the Scots of Dalriada, or journeyed with that monarch to Ireland, and secured political autonomy for the subject colony in Alba. It may be remarked by the way that the inauguration of the Scottish sovereign is the "earliest recorded instance of a royal coronation in Great Britain", and that part of the ceremonies then used survives in the corresponding service at Westminster. Normally, however, the life at Iona was that which has been outlined. It was a life of homely occupations, diversified by much landfaring and seafaring, and hallowed by supernatural incidents more fit to be "a spectacle for angels than for men."

But "there remaineth a day of rest for the people of God". The time was to come when the "Soldier of Christ" should cease from his labors. No more should he embark in his corracle, or mount his chariot, or penetrate the dense forest with no other help than his staff, and no other defense than the "Prayer of God". No longer should he be seen "reciting the *Three Fifties* on the sand of the shore before sunrise", or "carrying his portion of corn on his back to the mill". No longer should he celebrate the "Mysteries of the Sacred Oblation", or lift up his voice praised for its "sweetness above all clerics". Even the period was to be affixed to the verse of the Psalm he was transcribing. "Here I must stop at the foot of this page," he said, "let Baithin write what follows."

Appropriately, it was on the *Die Sabbato* of the ecclesiastical week, he and the faithful Diarmuid went to inspect and bless the granary for the last time. "Greatly", he said "do I congratulate the monks of my household that this year also you will have enough for the year without stint." And then: "This day is truly a Sabbath day for me, because it is for me the last day of this present laborious life, and at midnight, when begins the solemn Day of the Lord, I shall go the way of my fathers." Whereupon Diarmuid began to "weep bitterly". "And the saint tried to console him as well as he could."

Half way back to the monastery, being "weary with age" he sat down to rest by the roadside when "behold, the white horse, the one which used to carry the milk pails to and fro between the byre and the monastery, coming up to the Saint, lays his head against his breast, and began to whinny and shed copious tears, while foaming at the mouth." Seeing this, Diarmuid began to drive away the "weeping mourner". But the Saint forbade him—"Let him alone, let him alone, for he loves me. To this brute beast the Creator himself has in some way revealed that his master is about to depart." And so saying, he "blessed his servant the horse as it sadly turned to go away from him."

True soldier to the end, he was in his place with the rest at the Vespers of the vigil of the Lord's Day and, "as soon as this is over, he returns to his cell and sits up through the night on his bed, where he had the bare rock for mattress and a stone for pillow." But when the bell rang for Matins, rising quickly, he hastened to the church before the others. Diarmuid, who followed closely, saw the place flooded with heavenly brightness, but on his entering all was dark. "Where art thou, Father?" he called in a voice choked with tears; and "the lamps of the brethren not yet being brought, groping in the dark, he found the Saint lying before the altar. Sitting beside him, and raising him up a little, he lays the holy head on his bosom. Meanwhile the monks, running up with lights, began to weep at the sight of their dying Father. And, as we have learned from some who were present, the Saint, with eyes upturned, looked round with wonderful cheerfulness and joy of countenance, seeing the holy Angels coming to meet him. Diarmuid then lifts up the holy right hand to bless the choir of monks. But the venerable Father himself moved his hand as much as he was able. And after thus signifying his holy benediction he breathed forth his spirit. The countenance remained so long gladdened by the vision of the Angels, that it seemed not to be that of one dead, but of one living and sleeping." It was the Sunday, June 9, in the year 597.

So passed away one of the most majestic personalities in the history of the Christian Church. For three days after his death, "a great tempest without rain lashed the billowy waters", and prevented anyone crossing from the mainland, so that his obsequies were carried out with "melodious psalmody" by his spiritual children alone. The body "wrapped in a fair shroud" remained in the tomb at Iona until the Danish invasions; and it was then translated to Ireland, where it rests "under the flagstone under which are Patrick and Brigid".

Meet burial ground for the man who loved the green hills, and the broad plains, and the winding shores, but most of all the churches of Holy Ireland. Three places, according to the *Leabhar Breac*, make up his "full habitation". To Iona from which he "preached the word of God to the men of Alba, and to the Britons, and to the Saxons" he gave his "grace without stain"; to Derry, "full of white angels from one end to the other" his soul and where else should his body be bestowed but in that old Barn of Dichu at Saul in which Patrick said his first Mass on Irish soil?

Fisherfolk in the Hebrides still invoke Columcille in their Shieling Hymn, and his name is engraved imperishably on the "fleshy tablets" of countless Irish hearts; but he is almost unknown in a land which owes its Christianity, and in great part its civilization, chiefly to him and his disciples. Even Catholics hear mention of him in England only in a prayer which enumerates "Our Fathers in the Faith". And yet, without his far-flung apostolate, there would hardly have been a Christian foundation among the Anglo-Saxons. After Augustine's death, the semi-converted tribes relapsed for the most part into heathenism, with little hope of recovery in the welter of barbarism and internecine warfare now dignified as the Heptarchy. But when the Hibernicized Oswald of Northumbria appealed to the monks of Iona, he introduced the force which definitely established Christianity through the whole extent of Anglo-Saxon occupation. Bishop Lightfoot summed up the situation when he wrote: "Augustine was the apostle of Kent, but Aidan was the apostle of England." Aidan was the spear-head of the Celtic invasion which was launched from Iona only thirty-eight years after the arrival of the Roman missionaries, and which continued supreme in the island until the coming of the Norman-French. Then another foreign influence began to mold the Anglo-Saxon races. But if they got their political organization and "Parliament" from the French, they got their Religion and Church from the Irish. It is true Columcille was in his grave when a mission on a national scale was projected for England. But his memory was still recent in Iona, and it was his spirit that became the tradition of his successors. Courage, scholarship, humanism were vividly present in the monks of St. Columcille, and no more pleasing amity ever sprang up between two peoples, nor one more prolific of the fruits of Religion and Culture than that which subsisted from first to last between the pupil Saxon and the tutelary Gaedhal.

It was the triumph of the "Irish Way" in the sphere of missionary enterprise. And that "Irish Way" had been pointed out by the greatest of their apostles—the devoted, affectionate, and scholarly Columba; the man who effected a more enduring conquest of Britain than Caesar, and brought a greater blessing than any comprised under the "Roman Peace". Iona is desolate, and Canterbury a mere simulacrum. But when Englishmen are recalled to a true sense of their past, it is of Iona they will think with affectionate reverence, as the cradle of their ancient Religion and the fount of their purest civilization.

SAINT COLUMBANUS

[530?-615]

Vincent McNabb, O.P.

BANGOR . . . *there had been a very celebrated monastery under the first Abbot Comgall which produced many thousands of monks, and was the head of many monasteries. A truly holy place it was, and prolific of saints.* . . . *Into foreign lands these swarms of saints poured as though a flood had risen; of whom one, St. Columbanus, came to our Gallic parts and built the monastery of Luxeuil and there made a great people. Indeed so great a people was it, we are told, that the choirs succeeding one another in turn, the solemnities of the Divine Office went on unceasingly, so that not a day or night was empty of praise.* (St. Bernard: Life of St. Malachy.)

The Abbey of Luxeuil was recognized as the monastic capital of all the countries under Frank Government. (Montalembert: The Monks of the West, Vol. II, Bk. 7.)

FTER FOURTEEN CENTURIES the most illustrious Frenchmen are still grateful to the Irish Saint who once dwelt in their midst. Such *Laus perennis* from the gratitude of France could be justified only by a character too great for the skill of any biographer. My readers will, therefore, understand that they are being offered merely an outline sketch which may serve to send them on a voyage of discovery amidst the manuscripts of monastic Ireland.

These manuscripts though outnumbering those of most of his contemporaries are hardly more than the droppings from a banquet table. Yet their scarcity has one compensation. Their very fewness leaves such gaps in the recorded doings of the saint that what is recorded tends to present a series of dramatic incidents which demand that indispensable element in all dramatic art—"the creative onlooker".

The only quite certain date in the Saint's life is the date of his death, November 23, 615. Perhaps there is a touch of divine poetry in the fact that a soul so dedicated to the timeless principles of the spirit should enter history only by the way he entered eternity. All historians agree that he came of a noble Leinster family. But they disagree about the year of his birth, some placing it as late as A.D. 543; some as early as A.D. 530.

According to the Abbot Jonas who wrote his life some thirty years after the saint's death, Columbanus was trained in *"Liberalium litterarum doctrinis et grammaticorum studiis"*. In other words the young Leinster aristocrat received the highest classical education. It would be natural for the Leinster youth to go to Clonard the great motherschool of Ireland which the Leinster St. Finnian had founded with a rare Gaelic blending of sanctity and scholarship. No doubt Columbanus like the rest of the youth athirst for Greek and Latin culture built himself a wattle hut.

We are in touch with the realities of his university life in listening to Abbot Jonas telling us how Columbanus was *formae elegantis praesertim corporis candore*—of handsome appearance, especially of fair complexion. The olive skinned southerner remembers the fair Gaelic "skin" of the Saint.

It was inevitable that a young Leinster aristocrat of no less talent than good looks should soon cross swords with the devil of the flesh. Jonas represents the matter as an attack made on the virtue of the youth by *"lascivae puellae"*, wanton girls. Light is thrown on the matter by the fact that somewhere about this time the king of Cualann sent his daughter to St. Finnian at Clonard to read her Psalter in Latin. It would hardly be beyond the evidence to say that Clonard housed some girl students under conditions somewhat akin to our modern Universities.

A fundamental quality of the saint's soul is shown in his way of meeting the battle now set up within him. But the Abbot Jonas must tell it in his own words:

Whilst he was turning these things over within him he came to the cell of a religious woman dedicated to God. After having greeted her with lowly voice, he made as bold as he could to seek her counsel with the forwardness of youth:

When she saw him in the budding strength of youth, she said: "I going forward with all my strength began the battle. For twelve years I have had no home. Since I sought this place of exile—Christ being my leader —I have never followed the world; having set my hand to the plow I have never looked back. Had I not been of the weaker sex I would have crossed the seas and sought an even more hidden place of pilgrimage.

You are aflame with the fires of youth, yet you dwell in the land of your birth. You lend your ear willy nilly to weak voices, your own weakness bending you. Yet you think you can freely avoid women. Do you remember Eve coaxing, Adam yielding, Samson weakened by Delilah, David lured from his old righteousness by Bathsheba's beauty, Solomon the Wise deceived by the love of women?"

"Go," she said, "go, child, and turn aside from the ruin into which so many have fallen. Leave the path that leads to the gates of hell." Affrighted by these words and—beyond what you would believe of a youth terror-stricken—he returns thanks to his chastener, and bidding farewell to his companions he sets out. His mother beseeches him not to leave her. . . . Casting herself on the ground she refuses him leave to go. But he crossing the threshold and his mother, implores her not to be broken with grief, saying that she shall see him no more in this life, but that whither soever lies the path of holiness, there will he go.

Leaving aside from this moving story what may or may not be due to the imagination of the historian we find the Columbanus who never once went back but always went on and on. We miss the hot-headed somewhat self-opinionated Celt so dear to modern historians. We have the picture of a handsome clever aristocrat at issue with his first battle, yet so self-mistrustful that he timidly seeks counsel where counsel can best be had.

Later on, when he had left his beloved land of birth and was the spiritual father of a family of monks, Columbanus wrote a Rule, which is almost a spiritual autobiography. In it we find a chapter with the now misleading title "On Mortification". It speaks of taking counsel and of obeying counsel taken. How far are we from the headstrong Celt in words like these: "Nothing is sweeter than calm of conscience, nothing safer than purity of soul, which yet no one can bestow on himself because it is properly the gift of another."

The words of this religious woman meant that Columbanus is next to be found with a holy man, once a student at Clonard, who dwelt on one of the hundred islands of Loch Erne. The young Leinster lad had withdrawn from the field of battle. But his withdrawal, far from being accepted defeat was accepted battle. The counsel he had received from the holy woman did not mean that he should decline battle with his enemy but that he should decline to do battle on the enemy's own battlefield. Like his Master he accepted battle on the field chosen for him by the spirit of God.

One only fact of this quiet sojourn on the island has come down to history. We are told that he became so versed in the Sacred Scriptures that he wrote an explanation of David's Psalter. Imagination compels us to wonder if he had been one of a class at Clonard, including the daughter of the King of Cualann whom St. Finnian instructed in the Psalter. No doubt the sob of self-conscious though repented sin vibrating everywhere in these psalms of Sion seemed the fit prayer of this young fugitive from himself.

Our next sight of Columbanus is amidst the wattle-huts of the newly founded monastery at Bangor on the southern shores of Belfast Lough. About the time when Columbanus was with Sinnel on the island of Cluan, another saint, Comgall, was preparing for his life's work by living the life of an anchorite on one of the neighboring islands. Whether the two saints met is a matter of surmise. But the surmise strengthens on learning that soon after Comgall began the monastic life at Bangor one of his first monks was his former neighbor amidst the islands of Loch Erne.

A phrase of Abbot Jonas covers the life of Columbanus amidst the brethren whom he loved, and in a spot as romantically beautiful as any to be found on the coastline of his beloved country:

> The cycles of many years being now fulfilled in the monastery he began yearning to be a pilgrim, mindful of the divine word to Abraham. "Go forth from thy birthland, and from thy kindred, and from thy father's house and go into the land I will show thee." (Gen 12)

His old self-mistrust and his duty of obedience made him broach his desire to his Abbot St. Comgall. No doubt it was a willing obedience that heard his Abbot's refusal. He obeyed the human authority even against what seemed a divine impulse until at last the human authority recognized in this obedience the mark of a divine call.

Bangor could hardly help pricking his soul to pilgrimage. Once or twice during his stay at Bangor he must have seen a boat coming southward from Iona to Bangor Bay, with his fellow countryman St. Columba.

Again, Bangor was within that part of Ireland so hallowed by the coming, and labors and death and burial of Ireland's apostle, as to be called "St. Patrick's Country". Downpatrick where St. Patrick lay buried was some twenty miles to the south.

Saints touch history at its vital points. When Columbanus, remembering the nun's challenge to pilgrimage, saw the place where the runaway slave lay buried far from his homeland and amidst his old slavemasters, even a monastery by one of his country's fairest coasts became unendurable.

A letter which the Saint sent from exile to his monks at Luxeuil will suggest that other motives may have driven him from the consolations of Bangor. He there speaks to the one whom he had left in charge, of the dangers of being loved too much! Columbanus was not a soul that revealed himself easily even to himself. Yet for this reason among others he drew men to his love. But when affection was given him— and it rarely failed to be given—he fled from it; not as if it, but as if he, was sinful.

When the day came for Columbanus to leave his birthland for ever it was a group of thirteen monks that embarked at Bangor. A few years earlier another group of thirteen monks under Columba had embarked perhaps at the same monastic jetty on Belfast Lough. The traditions Columbanus had learned at Clonard and Bangor led him to Wales where his teaching masters had sought sound learning from the Britons, David, Gildas, and Cadoc. The Celtic saint in flight from the love of his own birthland so won upon the monks of Wales that some of them went with him into willing exile.

If Columbanus was born in 530 and his flight from Ireland was 590 he was then in his sixtieth year. According to some historians it was the age of St. Patrick when he came back as Apostle to Ireland. We note these resemblances because more lies within them than secular history may detect. It is undeniable that St. Patrick became, as indeed he has still remained, not only the national apostle but equally the national hero of Ireland. The very details of his life were an inspiration to the Island of Saints.

We do not know and cannot guess the motives why the group of Irish monks asked and found a place of exile in Burgundy then ruled by King Gontran, a grandson of Clovis. We only know that it offered the saint the two things he sought above all else—quiet contemplation of God and work among souls. The dark mountain forests with their darker caves gave him constant isolation from the world which God's love was teaching him to fly. The simple untaught pagans or clansmen of these forests needed his teaching of the faith.

For some time, we are not told how long, the band of monks dwelt in a ruined castle hamlet at Annegray in Haute-Saône. He and his monks seem to have been content to bivouac among the ruins. Yet even in these uninviting conditions the saint's personality had gathered round him such a throng of Burgundians athirst for the monastic life that a new home had to be sought some miles distant at Luxeuil. There was built from the stones of a ruined Roman bath and temple a monastery which has made Luxeuil a place name famous not only in France but throughout the Church and the world.

Though classically minded Abbot Jonas has a charming verbosity in recording the seemingly miraculous everyday life of the saint, yet he lets us see that life in its sometimes stark reality. He tells us how the holy Father Abbot and the community prayed for the wife of a man and she was instantly cured though she had been ill over a year. But he incidentally tells us how this man had brought a wagon of bread and vegetables most opportunely because the community were so poor that they could give a brother stricken with fever nothing but roots and bark!

There is a wonderful story of what befell the Saint as he was one day walking in the dark woods of Haute-Saone. A phrase of Jonas is almost untranslatable . . . "Librum humero ferens de Scripturis Sacris secum disputaret." "Bearing on his shoulder" (no doubt in a Celtic leathern satchel) "the Holy Scriptures and discussing with himself." A saint's dialogues with himself are seldom wanting in interest. St. Columbanus, no doubt stimulated by the wisdom borne on his shoulders, was thinking whether he would prefer to fall in with wild beasts or wicked men. He answered his own question by going forward into the forest where he might meet with the beasts, who, unlike men, had never sinned.[1] The story ends dramatically by his meeting a pack of twelve wolves whom he drove off with a prayer—of how the wolves were followed by a band of Suevi robbers who though close to him

---

[1] An Irish Innocent whom I had the honor to tend in Leicester Jail once said to me: "St. Patrick druv the sarpents out of Ireland. But what was the good of drivin' out the sarpents when he left men—worse than sarpents!"

did not see him—and how diving further into the forest he saw to his ascetic delight a dark cave which he made his own only by instantly taming a fierce bear to whom it belonged.

This bear cave plays a major part in the drama of the Saint whom history has, perhaps, largely misrepresented.

The authentic sources of his life give no reason for representing him as what we might fairly call "the stage Celt"—a man of violent and somewhat uncontrolled zeal. Everywhere he is shown us as a shy blending of scholar and saint whose chief and difficult concern is to find out the Will of God and do it. When the love he always enkindled by his gifts of soul and even of body was obvious even to himself he fled to his bear cave to be *solus cum Solo*.

There is a charming story of how through divine revelation given him in his cave he knew that many of his beloved monks were ill. At once he hastened home. He bade the sick brethren use and thrash the corn in the threshing floor. Needless to say, our beloved Jonas tells us that the obedient brethren were instantly cured; the disobedient stayed ill for the best part of a year and came near dying.

Another story reminds us of the brewer who has found honorable mention among the "company" of St. Patrick. One day before the monks' dinner the cellarer was drawing beer from the hogshead into the large tankard when he was summoned elsewhere by Columbanus. In the hurry of the moment he forgot to put the cork back in the hogshead. It is needless to say that on his return to the cellar the cellarer found not one drop spilled! Whereupon the Abbot Jonas writes: —"O how great was the merit of him who commanded; and how great the obedience of him who did as he was bid."

Tales like these even when garnished by the religious imagination of a home-historian make two things clear—how lovable was the monk whom they idealize; and how realistic were the monks whose life was not only in their house of prayer but in the fields and in the forests. In making these two things clear cloistered chroniclers have created an atmosphere as romantic as the West gave us in Robinson Crusoe or the East in the Arabian Nights.

The growth of the monastery at Luxeuil is witnessed by the foundation of a second monastery at Fountains. With this growth in numbers and influence there came inevitable opposition. As this opposition ended by King Theoderic exiling Columbanus and all monks not of French blood, the matter is seen to be a quarrel between the new religious revival centerd in the monasteries and the half-savage, half-Roman imperialism of the Merovingian monarchs.

The short account of the quarrel given us by Jonas has the merit of being substantially verified by authentic history. The young king of Burgundy, Theoderic (Thierry) II, had given shelter to his grandmother Queen Brunhilda when she was driven out of her own kingdom of Austrasia by the Austrasian nobles. This expulsion from her own kingdom by a very decisive ballot on her character, is corroborated by Jonas.

Inevitably the Abbot of Luxeuil began to attract the confidence of the young king. But a king, with Merovingian ideas of morality, and an Abbot, who was in self-exile for chastity's sake, could be related only on condition that either the king or the Saint uprooted his soul. There was another alternative: that the relationship should end violently as indeed it did.

Pope Gregory's letters to Queen Brunhilda and her grandsons on the need of stamping out simony especially from the episcopate allow us to think that the bishops of the two kingdoms of Burgundy and Austrasia were not the men to correct Merovingian morals. If things came to breaking point between Luxeuil and loose-living Theoderic these prelates might be expected to find their conscience coincide with the king's.

The account given by Jonas of the inevitable collision between the Court and Luxeuil seems true to human nature. Theoderic, though unmarried, was already the father of four children. There is nothing incompatible with the moral atmosphere of a Merovingian court that one day Queen Brunhilda asked Columbanus to bless these four royal children. It may not have surprised but it angered Brunhilda that this foreign Abbot of Luxeuil refused to bless the spurious offspring. When Columbanus the foreigner proved himself more Burgundian than this Spanish Queen by boldly asking for a legitimate offspring to inherit the throne, the break between the monastery and the Court became inevitable.

But the break with such a man as the widely-reverenced Columbanus demanded diplomacy. A favorable opening seemed to be in the question of the keeping of Easter. It was and still is a question so obscure that some writers have accused the British and Irish Churches of being

"Quartodecimans", by keeping Easter as the Jews keep their Pasch, on a day determined by the full moon, even if that day were not a Sunday.

Yet little is known of how the British and Irish Churches computed their Easter. Only one thing is quite certain, that they kept the Easter as first taught them by Rome. It was for him as for St. Paul when St. Peter refused to eat with gentile converts. St. Paul's astonishment was great when a policy toward the gentiles inaugurated by St. Peter seemed to be set aside by—St. Peter. For both Saints it was a crisis of bewildered loyalty. No wonder that in the letters wrung from each by the crisis their bewilderment seems to express itself in phrases almost overshadowing their loyalty.

A Synod of Merovingian Bishops was summoned, as it would seem, on the advice of Pope Gregory, but by order of the Merovingian King, Theoderic. Pope Gregory's reiterated demands that the King (or Queen Brunhilda) should summon a Synod, made mention of several matters needing reform; but there was no mention of the Easter difficulty. When, then, the Episcopal Synod made it their chief concern to indict Luxeuil for its Easter observance the Abbot did two things: (1) he wrote a plain letter to the Synod, and (2) he wrote an equally plain letter to Pope Gregory. In other words he followed his national Saint and hero St. Patrick, who met a kindred difficulty by appealing to the Pope.

Both letters have been unfortunate in their commentators. Few if any of these commentators have been capable of judging the letters *in vacuo* as the pleading of an Abbot for retaining in his Monastery a chronological observance initiated by Rome. They have seemed to think that the nationality of this self-exiled Irishman was the determining factor in the letters. Yet the present writer has sought in vain to find in these letters any trace of the stage-Irishman so beloved by even the Catholic historians of the incident.

In the letter to "My Lord and Fathers and Brothers in Christ, Bishops, Priests and other orders of the Church", Columban the sinner and the scholar (and the Leinster aristocrat) never forget his courteousness of sanctity, even when the Celtic humor might easily have soured into gall. He most humbly thanks God that they, who should have assembled twice a year to correct public morals which were so corrupt, should at last assemble on his account to deliberate on the matter of Easter which has been so often discussed. There is a tone of weariness but

not of anger when he deals with this matter; as if Bishops who were
contentedly living under a king ruled by concubines might well discuss
something more vital than the Calendar!

The old master of classical phrases has a passage which ranks him
with even the Latin masters of eloquence. He beseeches but one thing
from them that in their holiness they would have peace with him and
charity and would "Let him be quiet in these woods[2] and live near
the dust of our seventeen dead brethren as indeed you have let us live
in your midst these twelve years so that we might pray for you as we
have prayed—and, indeed, as was our duty."

He even pleads—alas! unsuccessfully for his aging fellow exiles with
these court clerics: "Take heed, O holy Fathers, to these poor veter-
ans and aged exiles, whom to my mind you should console rather than
disturb."

The saintly Abbot had gauged the situation with the realism of a
contemplative. This Synod was not an assembly of delicately orthodox
Bishops who could not bear a different ritual or even a different Calendar: they were a group of perhaps court-cowed prelates who were
made the cat's paw of a Merovingian Court, enraged at Columbanus
and his monks sitting in silent Mardochai condemnation at their gates.
The result of the Synod's and the Court's deliberations was inevitable.
Columbanus the exile who had proved himself a more patriotic Burgundian than their hierarchy or their king was driven from the silence
of the woods, and the seventeen graves of his dead brothers into exile.

A letter of the Saint to the reigning Pope St. Gregory the Great has
found immortality among the topics of controversy. It must always
be borne in mind that if St. Columbanus has left us more written remains than most of his contemporaries there is not one line of merely
self-defense; but many precious lines in defense of others. To himself
he was always Columbanus the sinner, who since his exile from his
birthplace and then from his birthland had never slackened his flight
from himself. But as often happens to men of God, these souls who
are so shrinking and voiceless in self-praise or self-defense, these lambs
of self-diffidence become lions when they have to defend some old
"veterani" against the fury of a king.

---

[2] *Ut mihi liceat cum vestra pace et charitate in his silvis silere*—a phrase so perfect with its wealth
of sibilants that we can almost overhear the rustling of the forest leaves.

We do not know whether this letter from St. Columbanus to St. Gregory was written before or after the Synod. But it seems certain that it sprang from the circumstances that called the Synod together. That the Abbot of Luxeuil addresses the Bishop of Rome to end a controversy, not on a matter of faith or even of ritual but only of observance, is a sign of that instinct for Rome which St. Patrick had implanted in the Church of his apostolate. Those who see in the letter a proof that St. Columbanus was in effect a pre-protestant of the seventh century lay stress on words that would make a pre-protestant of St. Paul for his letter to the Galatians and of St. Irenaeus for his letter (on the Easter question) to St. Victor.

A picturesque pun has done much service to this theory of Columbanus, the pre-protestant. Those who differed from the Luxeuil monks on the Easter date quoted St. Leo the Great. But St. Columbanus with whimsical childlikeness suggests that in this matter St. Leo's decision could be set aside by Gregory—for "is not a live dog better than a dead lion (Leo)". Far from depreciating the great "Chair of Peter", as he styles it, the man who uses this phrase is making a profession of faith that the present occupant of this chair can reverse the disciplinary enactments of a former occupant whose name still resounded through West and East as the Defender of the Faith in Jesus Christ.

It is regrettable that this letter and another sent to St. Gregory seem never to have reached their destination. Perhaps it was asking too much of Merovingian broadmindedness to permit such letters to pass out of the country. Had the letter reached St. Gregory the difficulty felt by Columbanus in giving up, on the authority of the Gallic Church, what he and his fathers had received from the authority of Rome, would have been met by all the broadmindedness of St. Gregory's letters to St. Augustine on the difficulties in England.

In the end St. Columbanus seems to have recognized that Rome of the Popes had spoken and the matter was ended, save for his obedience. As all mention of the difficulty passes from his correspondence and from the further annals of Luxeuil he and his monks seem to have been obedient.

In order to appreciate the state of things against which the peace-loving saint and scholar Columbanus battled, only to find himself in exile, we must realize the following plain facts about the Merovingian sovereigns:

1. Chilperic, king of Neustria, at the instigation of his concubine Fredegonde, murders his wife Galeswinde.

2. Chilperic's brother, King Sigebert of Austrasia, is likewise murdered by Chilperic and Fredegonde, concubine of Chilperic.

3. Queen Brunhilda, sister of the murdered Queen Galeswinde and wife of the murdered King Sigebert immediately marries Merovee, son of King Chilperic the murderer.

4. The day after Merovee's marriage with Queen Brunhilda, King Chilperic imprisons his son Merovee. Soon afterward it is given out that Merovee has committed suicide!

5. Chilperic is murdered presumably by either Fredegonde his concubine or Brunhilda his sister-in-law. This murder leaves Fredegonde acting queen at Neustria, during the minority of her son Clotaire.

6. King Childebert, son of Queen Brunhilda, dies a sudden and apparently natural death. This death leaves Brunhilda acting queen of Burgundy and Austrasia during the minority of her sons Theoderic and Theodebert.

7. Theoderic becomes king of Burgundy—is notoriously profligate—is advised to marry by St. Didier, Bishop of Vienne—marries Queen Brunehault—within a year divorces his wife and murders St. Didier.

8. King Theodebert, brother of Theoderic and grandson of Queen Brunhilda, marries Bilichild; and then murders her.

9. Theodebert is murdered by his brother Theoderic or by his grandmother Brunhilda.

10. King Clotaire of Neustria murders his cousin Theoderic, and the five illegitimate sons of Theoderic and his aunt Queen Brunhilda. This brings a lull of peace to France.

This is a plain unvarnished statement of some of the authentic facts about the atmosphere in which the quiet peace-loving contemplatives of Luxeuil found themselves. It is therefore to the credit of Luxeuil and its monks that their Abbot and all the monks that were not Franks were forced to leave the kingdom ruled over by Theoderic.

The spirit in which this champion of justice met exile is summed up in one incident.

On the day when Theoderic defeated and captured Theodebert at Tolbiac, Columbanus, exiled at Bregentz, was seated on a fallen trunk with a noble young French monk Cagnoald whose father was in high position under Theodebert. In a vision he saw the battle, and the bloodshed. He awoke in grief. Cagnoald having found out the cause of his master's grief besought him to pray for Theodebert and against Theoderic. But the old saint, incapable of personal hatred, answered: "Your counsel is foolish and unholy. Nor is it the will of God, who bade us pray for our enemies."

The little group of monks with Columbanus at their head were escorted down the Loire through Orleans and Tours to the port of Nantes. While awaiting the hour of his forced departure for Ireland the Saint dictated a letter of which another noble soul has said: "It contains some of the finest and noblest words that Christian genius has ever produced."[3] But as we deem it almost sacrilege to mutilate a masterpiece we will not quote it here.

One thing only must be said, in defense of a Saint who sometimes needs defending against his fellow Catholics.

From its first word of peace to its last anguish-laden word of fatherly love and prophecy there is not even a shadow's shadow of anger. Indeed the Saint contrives to suggest that instead of being soldier-driven from the delights of Luxeuil he is flying from its burden, "*Ego fugio*". Yet true to himself, he implies that the burden he is flying is only the burden and danger of their too great love.

There are certain noble words of this half-willing exile which must be given to our readers as the faithful Jonas has given them to us. One day when the king's messengers, Bertarius and Bedulius, found Columbanus in choir they asked him in the king's name to leave the kingdom and go back whence he came. The undaunted follower of St. Patrick replied: "*Non enim reor placere Conditori, semel natali solo relicto, denuo repetere*." (I do not count it pleasing to the Creator that having once left my birth-land, I should again return.)

In the face of such supreme desire for exile we are not surprised to read that the Irish bark, which was to make Columbanus break his troth was driven upon the rocks where it lay stranded for three days. How far this was due to the Saint's prayers with God or with the captain we have no means of knowing. This much we know, that if the stranding of the bark was not a supernatural doing of God's love for the Saint it was a deliberate doing of the Saint's supernatural love for

---

[3] Montalembert. *The Monks of the West.* Bk. vii.

God. In all these obscure matters one thing is clear. The Saint had his way. He did not go back whence he came!

But the old Saint did not mean to stay out of his birth-land only to "be quiet in the woods". In a delicately tuned mood of self-accusation he confessed that his desire of "preaching the Gospel" had somewhat cooled. He determined to go eastward where there were still many pagans. Theodebert of Austrasia was able to give him a place of prayer and preaching at Bregentz on Lake Constance amid the ruins of a Roman town. Some three years were spent amid dangers from famine and men. The pagans were so hostile to these Westerns that two of the monks were slain. Yet the little group of monks left their ruins only when their old enemy Theoderic by defeating and murdering Theodebert had become King of Austrasia. The King's hatred could not spare the Saint; and Columbanus with only one companion was again driven forth to his place of exile and death.

Some years before in the quiet woods of Luxeuil he had penned these immortal words of a soul homesick for heaven:

And thou, O Life, how many hast thou played false; how many misled; how many made blind?

Nought thou art in thy flight; a shadow to our sight; cloud-smoke in thy height.

Daily thou comest; and daily goest—one in thy beginning; many in thine end—sweet to the foolish; bitter to the wise.

Who love thee, know thee not; who look down on thee, understand thee. Thus art thou not truthful but deceitful—thou makest thyself true; and showest thyself false.

What then art thou, O life of men? Man's life thou art not; but a way to life.

Sin is thy beginning; death, thy end. Thou wouldst have been true had not man's sinful trespass maimed thee; now thou art faltering and mortal since all who go thy way are appointed unto death.

A way unto life thou art, not life; for thou art not true—a way, but not straight—to some long, to some short—to some broad, to some narrow —to some glad, to some sad—to all alike, swiftly passing and beyond recall.

Thus art thou to be questioned; not trusted, not defended—traversed, not dwelt in, O unhappy life of man! since on the way a man dwelleth not but walketh; and he who in the way walketh in the homeland dwelleth.

It was an old man of three score years and ten—or, according to others, it was an old man of four score—who set out to cross the Alps in his last pilgrimage. His mind was more than ever filled with the thoughts of life's swift passage to the *patria* of his soul. If ever his own song on "Life but the way to life" reflected his outer circumstances it was when he turned his exiled face southward toward death.

Something like a reward of peace was given to this peace lover in this short nightfall of his life. The province of Lombardy, which he entered when he had crossed the Alps, was ruled by Agilulph, an Arian. His wife was the wise, noble, saintly Theodolinda, to whom St. Gregory had dedicated his Dialogues. The fame of Columbanus seems to have already reached the Lombard court. King Agilulph, who a few years before was besieging Rome and creating the desert of the Campagna, welcomed the exiled saint almost as a national asset. Within the Apennines, at a spot now famous under the name of Bobbio, there was a ruined basilica dedicated to St. Peter. If, as is not unlikely, the ruins were the handiwork of these ruthless Arian Lombards, there was a quality of penance and restitution in Agilulph the Arian's gift to Columbanus.

One incident throws a last light on the undaunted worker so soon to be called into the night where no man can work. To restore the basilica the little group of monks cut and dragged timber from the neighboring wood. Sometimes the great trees were felled where no timber-wain could go. The monks were forced to carry the great beams on their shoulders. Yet God seemed so manifestly to help these men to help themselves that heavy logs which, on the word of Jonas, thirty or forty men could barely have carried over level ground, were carried over rocks on the shoulders of Columbanus and two or three monks. With a touch of poetry Jonas adds that the Abbot and his two or three monks carried their load "with such unfaltering feet as if moving in play and with joy".

For the last time we ask our readers of a century which has heard the heresy of the "Leisure State" to watch the old monk of some four score years helping to carry great beams on his shoulders. This man and his little group of monk-woodmen are, for the moment, the most vital center of education in the West. But what further conclusion should be drawn from this Nazareth poverty our readers themselves must draw.

Queen Theodolinda's prayer and plan for the conversion of her Arian husband and the Lombards received sudden reinforcement by the illustrious exile from Luxeuil. The anger of one Queen—Brunhilda—was the opportunity for a greater. Although ten years had elapsed since Agilulph had begun a friendship with St. Gregory which might soon have fruited in the King's conversion, Gregory's death had withdrawn the main clerical influence over the King's Arian mind. With the coming of Columbanus Theodolinda saw the possibility of Gregory's influence being renewed.

But in Lombardy Columbanus met for the first time the subtle atmosphere of the two great Eastern heresies: the King and most of his Lombard subjects were Arians. Of the rest of his subjects many, even among the clergy, were Nestorians, immeshed in the famous controversy of the Three Chapters. Columbanus could find his peace-nurtured believing mind only bewildered by these Oriental disputations and phrase weavings—historians wrong both him and the original sources of his history when they see descending the slopes of the Alps only a dogmatic sleuthhound yearning for controversial blood.

But Queen Theodolinda saw that this undaunted lover of truth and peace was God-sent to bring peace to her King and people through the truth. Though his life was now measured only by months he could not stint himself when from the Lombard court itself came a royal request for help in bringing Arian and Nestorian Lombardy to faith guaranteed by the See of Rome.

A letter written by the Saint to the reigning Pope Boniface IV on the need of summoning a Synod to bring dogmatic peace throws a last ray of light upon the soul of the Saint. We will set down some of its main features.

1. He writes this letter to the Pope:

I am asked by the King that I should put before your kindly ears in detail the matter that is grieving him; for the schism of the people is a grief to him on account of the Queen and her son and perhaps for his own sake too; seeing that he is believed to have said that if he knew the truth he would believe. . . .

[Again:] "a pagan Lombard King requests a dull-witted Irish stranger to write . . ."

[Again:] "The King asks you, the Queen asks you, all ask you, that all things may become one as soon as possible, so that as there is peace in the father-land there may be peace in the *faith* and the whole flock of

Christ may henceforth be one. Rex regum! tu Petrum, te tota sequetur ecclesia. (O King of Kings, follow thou Peter, and the whole Church will follow thee.)"

2. An attempt was made to separate him from Communion with Rome: "Almost the first moment of my crossing the frontiers of the country a certain person gave me a letter giving me to understand that you were to be shunned as having fallen into the sect of the Nestorians." This anonymous "certain person" was probably a Bishop of some importance in Northern Italy.

3. Thereupon he wrote a defense of Rome and of the orthodox faith. . . . "Thereupon I made such reply as I could . . . for I believe that the Pillar of the Church is always unmoved in Rome."

The Abbot Jonas assures us that, no doubt by the wish of King Agilulph and Queen Theodolinda, he took up his abode near Milan, and that "by the weapon of the Scriptures he might rend and destroy the deceits of the heretics, that is, of the Arian heresy, against whom he wrote a book of fine scholarship."

4. His loyalty to Rome was so great that he sent this book to the Pope for approval or condemnation. It is the same Columbanus who appealed to Pope Gregory for a ruling on the Easter question.

"This (book) I have sent to you that you may read it and correct it where it is contrary to the truth; for I dare not count myself to be beyond correction."

5. He witnesses that the Irish Church acknowledges the authority of the Roman Pontiff, not because of Rome but because of St. Peter:

All we Irish dwelling on the edge of the world are disciples of Saints Peter and Paul and of the disciples who, under the Holy Spirit, wrote the Sacred Canon. We accept nothing outside this evangelical and apostolic teaching. There was no heretic, no Jew, no schismatic, but the Catholic Faith, as first delivered to us by you, the successor of the apostles, is kept unshaken. . . . We, indeed, are, as I have said, chained to the Chair of St. Peter; for although Rome is great and known afar, it is great and honored with us only by this Chair.

In writing this last witness of an Irish Saint, Columbanus was refuting beforehand the argument current since the sixteenth century, that the See of Rome set up by St. Peter obtained its supremacy not because of Peter but because of Rome. Two Churches, Persia and Ireland, by their witness to the Chair of Peter, are the refutation of this argument; because Persia in the East and Ireland in the West were unconquered by Rome.

The sequel of this effort of the Saint to further the designs of Agilulph and Theodolinda was the conversion not only of Agilulph, who had but a few months to live, but of the Lombard people. In founding Bobbio so near Milan, the emporium of so many Eastern heresies, this exile from the further West had set up a blockhouse of the faith where it was most effective. For centuries it was a citadel of scientific defense which owed its existence to the man who united culture and sanctity in one mind and heart. When ruin overtook it after centuries of life the gathered treasures of its library enriched the libraries that still enrich the scholarship of the world.

Before we part from our patient readers, we would remind them that the Church has to thank St. Columbanus for two contributions of great worth—his Rule and his Penitential.

In his Rule he does not seem to have set down much that was original, but merely to have embodied the stern asceticism of his fellow countrymen and especially of his fellow monks at Bangor. In the end it was found that the less exacting Rule of St. Benedict was more acceptable to the would-be monks of the West. Yet although the sterner rule everywhere yielded to the milder, every movement toward a reform of the Rule of St. Benedict has been a movement toward the ideal, and even the toil-ideal of St. Columbanus.

But the Rule of St. Columbanus has not rendered to the Church a greater service than his Penitential. A recent writer has said:

> The fact of outstanding importance with respect to the *Penitential* of Columbanus is that while it corresponds to no existing practice to be found anywhere in force from former times on the continent of Europe, it reproduces all the main features of the peculiar system which has been seen at work in the Keltic Churches. . . . As in the British and Irish Systems, the penance and the reconciliation are alike private.[4]

It is not a little remarkable that by the end of the seventh century the Rule of St. Columbanus, for whatsoever reason, practically disappears, and the Rule of St. Benedict becomes supreme. But his Penitential system not only survived in the monasteries which were now being founded, but

---

[4] *A History of Penance.* By Oscar D. Watkins, (Longmans Green, 1920), p. 615.

was destined in time, after the later English influence, to become the general penitential system of Western Europe.[5]

Few customs are so characteristic of "the Latin Church" which is officially distinguished from "the Eastern Church" as the very frequent and humble practice of Confession. It is to the credit of sinful human nature that this Sacrament, which our Redeemer made not so much an obligation as a privilege, should yet be frequented almost as an obligation. Perhaps we are close to the motive of this humble practice in thinking of its connection, by way of cleansing, with the great Banquet of the Body and the Blood. One of the chief glories of the fellow countrymen of Columbanus will be that to him more than to any other individual in the Church this lowly practice seems due.

The last literary testament left by St. Columbanus during his few months at Bobbio is this letter to Pope Boniface IV. Were it the only clue to the soul of the saint during his approach to death, we might so misread it as to look upon its writer as a born and unwearied warrior for the faith—the Tertullian of his age. But we have other clues to his character. When three score years and more—and as he says: "*Morbis oppressus acerbis*" (bowed with heavy ailments) he wrote to his young friend Fedolius a charming poem in Adonic verse. Its student touch, its wealth of classical allusion, its preciosity, if proof of any thing, are proof that its writer, far from being the Tertullian, was the Nazianzen and the Prudentius of his distraught age.

We are not told how, but only when he died. It is the one certain date in his life; for on that day, the twenty-first day of November, the year of Our Lord six hundred and fifteen, Columbanus the exile was welcomed home by his Father who is in heaven.

And the heavenly Father has been so generous toward the tireless fugitive from himself that throughout the centuries that have scattered holy things to the winds the body of Columbanus has been untouched in its last resting place in the heart of the Apennines.

---

[5] Ibid., p. 124.

SAINT BEDE

[672–735]

Gervase Mathew, O.P.

I Bede, a servant of God and a priest of the monastery of the blessed apostles Peter and Paul, which is at Wearmouth and Jarrow, being born in the territory of the same monastery, was given by kinsfolk at seven years of age to be educated by the most reverend Abbot Benedict and afterward by Ceolfrid; spending all the remainder of my life in that monastery, I wholly applied myself to the study of scripture. Amid the observances of the rule and the daily charge of singing in the church I ever took delight in learning and teaching and writing. In the nineteenth year of my age I received the diaconate and in the thirtieth the priesthood, both of them at the hands of the most reverend Bishop John and at the bidding of Abbot Ceolfrid. From the time of my admission to the priesthood until my fifty-ninth year I have endeavored for my own use and for that of my brethren to make brief notes upon the holy Scriptures, either out of the works of the Venerable Fathers or in conformity with their meaning and their interpretation. (Historia Ecclesiastica Gentis Anglorum. Lib. V, Cap. XXIV.)

HEN BEDE lay dying in his cell at Jarrow on the vigil of Ascension day 735 his disciples noted the same serene aloofness which we can still trace in so much that he has written. It was already darkening, and the last of the light barely defined the skin coverlets and the little chest and the worn writing tablets. Small as was his cell, the white walls seemed high against the darkness as he lay stretched on the stone flooring with his two disciples bent above him.

He had lain ill since before Easter, and now he knew that it would soon be time to die, for he had finished with his book of extracts from the Blessed Isidore and his translation of St. John was almost ended. The treasures in his casket—the spice and incense and embroidered linen—had been distributed among the Mass priests of his house. As he lay there he murmured ceaselessly—antiphons from the office for *quinquagesima*, uncouth Northumbrian verses on man's destiny and the need for prudence, and aphorisms culled for his pupils' sake. Again and again his mind would wander back to Paulinus' life of Ambrose, and he would repeat the saying of the dying bishop: "I have not so lived that I am ashamed to live among you, yet neither do I fear to die, for we have a loving Lord."

For nearly sixty years he had lived in his Northumbrian abbey, years spent in the round of choral duty and in untiring industry for the sake of his disciples. "I would not that my children should learn a lie." We can still trace the course of ceaseless study; that laborious handbook the *De Arte Metrica*, written while he was yet a deacon; the treatises on Orthography and on Tropes; the *De Temporibus*, and then those happier years spent "pasturing in the flowery meadows of the fathers." He had written of the nature of the rainbow and of the color of the Red Sea; of clouds and of frost and of the River Nile; of the astrolabe and of blood letting; of the seven wonders of the world, and of the seven stars that hang between the earth and sky. He had learned so much, he had written so much, he had been interested in so little.

He had taken the habit at a time when the worship of the old gods still lingered in the country places and when many of the wandering leaders of the northern Church followed the Celtic rites. He had witnessed the return of Roman order, the dioceses of the Roman pattern, the victory of the Benedictine Rule. It was an age in which these changes bred a sudden and unjustified self-confidence in those whose lives were passed within the framework of religious custom. The monastic system whose bare outline seemed so imposing in a society where institutions were still incoherent had not yet been put to proof. Something of the old pagan wonder at the magic runes still stirred the mind of the Northumbrians as their slow thoughts brooded on the holy house. The golden chalices and the worked heavy jewels were but the inmost wonder of such shrines. An element of wizard strength still hung about the fine cut wood of these high new abbeys, the thrones of a priesthood of more subtle power than that which once served their fathers' gods. Yet the wonder which the Christianized herdsmen could but half express would change to a stronger passion as the tale of the rich treasure chests spread eastward. It was an essential limitation of the monastic outlook that the heathen world did not concern them, save as a field for the preaching of Christ's Gospel. How trivial and remote

the chaffering of the Norse traders seemed to them—an occasional galley storm-beached, the rapid bargaining talk. In the background of the
life of Jarrow and Monkwearmouth, behind the careful chanting and
religious custom, there passed unperceived the northern movements.
Threatening the whole new system, bringing in time destruction and
the sword, there moved the friendless sea.

Again, so far as the country was present to them in the runes for
fertility and for protection, the monks could not but feel the quick
contempt bred of their prized and recent learning. They could understand the herd rearing and appreciate each danger of the fells, but the
peasant gatherings roused scorn as the ceorls stood through the warm
nights in summer with the linden wood shields upon their shoulders
and the scramasax hafts tapping their cross-garters, while they gazed
with an innocent and heavy wonder at the kindling of the Midsummer
Fire.

But the monks could see with such clear pleasure the tide of the
Anglian Renaissance, the new sculpture on the High Crosses, the fresh
illumination—the rood of Bewcastle, the Gospel of Lindisfarne; the
coming of the Byzantine art *motifs* to the north, the twisted foliage
and the vine and the acanthus leaf, the old gold and the vermilion, the
cloisonné and the green of patined bronze.

Through all his life Bede had lived remote in serene appraisement.
He had no share in the inverted classicism, half Greek half Latin, of
the school of Canterbury, or in the growth of the Christ saga in the
north. He had had his training in the old rhetorical tradition of the
last years of the Empire, and he could appreciate Aldhelm's intricacy
or Aethelwald's; the cadencies of their clause rhythm, the allusive obscurity of epithet, the changing color of the simile. He writes of the
shining luster of the new style. It had had no influence upon his own.
He was still less affected by the literary movement in Northumbria,
which was to culminate a lifetime later with the poems of the Vercelli
book. He prized such verses, since they witnessed to a talent bestowed
by God and used to his Glory, and it would seem that he had himself
received the gift of facile improvisation. But such a gift, the *dulcis canor*
of Richard Rolle, often accompanied the strong affective mysticism
of the northern contemplatives, and those of his verses which remain
to us harbor no echoes of the new Christian epic in the North. He
had learned his quantities from Ausonius and his metaphors from the

Cathemerinon, and while the gleemen in the great hall at Bamborough sang to the glory of Christ victorious and of his chosen war band of apostles, godlike heroes, twelve high descended leaders of the hosting, Bede wrote in his laborious hexameters of leaf-laden boughs and of flower-strewn fields and of the Four Last Things.

There was nothing unnatural in such detachment from the interests of his time. The quick play of Bede's imagination was haunted by phantasms of the coming judgment, when the skies should open and the stars fall and each Christian learn his eternal destiny. To him each Catholic was an exile homesick for paradise—*non hic habemus manentem civitatem*. Through all his work the same conceptions, often the same phrases, are recurrent: *Peregrini in huic saeculo, in patria, in via, in itinere huius exilii*, and at last *a carnis ergastulo soluti coeleste regnuni intramus. A carnis ergastulo*, a whole philosophy lies implicit. Man's body the slave's prison of his soul.

Though St. Bede's three references to Plato would seem to have been drawn from some *catena aurea* of the sayings of the wise he was none the less the first of the English Platonists as he studied the shadow world in which he lived preoccupied by the world it shadowed. Such an attitude is nowhere plainer than in his fourteen works in exegesis, for as he "bruised the precious spices of the word of God" he knew that the literal meaning is to the allegorical as water is to wine. His mind rose upward from the sea that typified the world of sense and the spittle that signified man's wisdom to the golden lily of Resurrection and the silver of God's word.

The long years of contemplation, while it enhanced his consciousness of an unseen world around him, yet freed him from that sense of multiplicity which is the nemesis of the Platonist mood. The overwhelming consciousness of the fair harmony of creation, the sacramental concord of created things—*pulchra rerum concordia, mira concordia sacramenti*—which characterized the later years of his labor, was the expression of a mysticism rather than of a philosophy. This is true also of a doctrine of number which led him to see in the world of phenomena a notation of God's music. He came to prize the numeric value of each letter in the Holy Name. The ten which represents the I in *Iesu* was the dearest to him of all the numbers, for it signifies the reward of Heaven, since it is the multiple of five and two, that is of man's five senses multiplied by the love of his neighbor and of God.

Such vision seems fantastic to us, for it is impossible of attainment, yet it had formed the natural counterpoise to a neo-Platonism derived through those fathers who had learned the *Enneads* before the quick darkness of the early Middle Ages had settled. For it led him to seek not for absorption, but union—complete union of intention and will and desire, a following of Christ even to the exact placing of footsteps. His work had been hampered by the ill-equipped scriptorium of his house and by the need of books; he had been sickly from boyhood; he had always had his detractors; even his orthodoxy had been denied, but his serenity was undisturbed, for to him the perfection of the Christian life lay not in renunciation but in acceptance.

Yet in so far as his mysticism linked him with a great body of solitaries who waited in a silence of the faculties unbroken by study it led to an increasing alienation from that Celtic tradition of learning which was already one of the most vital elements in the Catholic scholarship of his time. There was so vivid a contrast between the quiet years of study at Jarrow—*sequens vestigia magnorum tractatorum*—and the eager and clamorous life of the Irish schoolmen among the bandying of dispute. For Bede was content to teach his pupils "out of the works of the venerable fathers or in conformity to their interpretation." He had no zest for new discovery, and he was conscious that he was the heir of a great tradition, a tradition that it was his life work to perpetuate in the north.

It is true that he held the "Scotti" to be holy men skilled in both learnings, the sacred and profane, and eager to impart them to others. His own master, Trumhere, had been their disciple, and much of the material detail of monastic scholarship had been affected by their influence. But their spirit remained alien to his own as he wrote in delicate half-uncials of the Irish script that Prudence is the mother and the nurse of the virtues.

The increasing contact of his later years can only have emphasized a wide divergence. He must have felt all the Benedictine distaste for gyrovagues as he listened to the wandering scholars in the hospice at Jarrow, long haired monks with painted eyelids, disputing on the sixteen colors of the four winds of the sky. Yet there is no trace of this in his writings, and such vagaries lie hidden in the wide charity of his reticence. It was left to St. Aldhelm of Sherborne to express the Anglo-Roman attitude to Celtic learning; the Irish, he noted, gave suck from wisdom's udder, but in dispute they snarled their syllogisms like molossian hounds.

Such a judgment was necessarily superficial. The eighth century in the lands of Celtic culture was the seeding time of a harvest that had not yet been garnered. The hampered thought and clumsy perverted Latin of the Irish scholars foreshadowed the clear glory of Erigena, and in their delight in dialectic as dialectic they were the precursors of those great schoolmen of the thirteenth century who were to see in every syllogism a theophany of the Incarnate Word.

The growing divergence between the traditions of the Celtic and Northumbrian schools was a cardinal misfortune of that age. St. Bede himself has suffered from it, for it led him to spend his life away from the quicker current of Catholic thought, seeking for truth not in the judgment but in the concept. He was never to be freed from a certain scorn for that imperfection of intellect, the reason. To him the one road to the knowledge of God was the road to Calvary, a journey beyond abstract reasoning and judgment, the ripening of a field which in this life was never to be fully garnered.

Though he had taught for many years since it was God's will that he should be master in Jarrow school, his wide patristic knowledge had been chiefly motivated by his strong love for the fourfold sense of Scripture—"the fountain of gardens, the well of living waters which run with a strong stream of Libanus". But for the great commentators that might have remained for him a garden enclosed, a fountain sealed up. He had had no will to tread the winepress of God's word alone. It was the Fathers who had led him in *Regis cellaria*, and reading them he pastured among lilies.

But if his learning had been inspired by his devotion to God's word his devotion to God's word resulted from his devotion to the Word made flesh—the devotion that is so apparent in the most self-revealing of his books, the commentary upon the song of songs, to the golden blossom Christ and the Church his body. Bede's words as he lay dying: "My soul desires to see Christ my king in his beauty", serve both to summarize and to explain his teaching. For it was his realization of the Incarnation as a present fact that led to his strong loyalty to the Catholic Unity: *indivisa in se, a aliis vero divisa*—in antithesis to the city of hell, the impregnable city of God.

"For we being many are one bread, one body." The Pauline conception of the Church remains apparent throughout the Christocentric trend of all Bede's thought. It is this that explains so much by which his work is differentiated, a sense of the individual significance of each human life and a formal courtesy of style alien to the literary convention of his age. For he knew that the men of whom he wrote were the threads from which Christ's seamless coat was woven, temples of the Holy Spirit and the vine branches, the Resurrection and the Life. And it was this that brought him when already old to the study of the history of the Church, for to him Church history was the Fifth Gospel. Even "the Ecclesiastical History of the English nation" may be regarded as yet another essay in exegesis, a somewhat elaborate commentary on a sentence from the Epistles: "Who hath called you out of darkness into his marvelous light who in time past were not a people, but are now the people of God."

Such an attitude to history is not without disadvantage, yet it has served to enhance St. Bede's value and repute as an historian, for the methods of his exegesis, the careful naming of authority and the slow weighing of contrary opinion, was to bring him fame as one of the multitudinous fathers of historical criticism. While since the years of contemplation had freed him from the bias of party prejudice, it was a sequel to his detachment that he should write objectively. And this is made more evident by his love of right order; all that he has written is marked by the sober restraint of the Benedictine tradition. Yet though writing in a clean and simple Latin he shows something of that sense of texture which characterises so much of Anglo-Saxon prose, linking it to the *opus anglicanum* of the tapestries. Akin to the limited perspective of such woven shadows the historical horizon of the *Historia* seems also rigid and near, and, when the deafness of his perception is admitted, his figures from the past stand as if tapestried, angular, a little hard and flat.

This same rigidity of terrestrial outlook had led him to view the future unsuspecting the rending of his pictured figures in the burning of the monasteries and the glare of Norse sea raids. The lay magnates in his countryside may not have shared the sense of his security; the years of his religious life had witnessed the fading power of the Northumbrian kingship and the Scandinavian ferment. But pasturing in the meadows of the fathers he had no thought for the Eorlcund-men without the gates and their harsh clamor. He had no concern for the

crude apprehensions of "scarlet-clad spear leaders" or Hordaland and
Rogir and the wild "hersir" culture. Such matters were not fit subjects
for meditation for those who had risen to follow the authority of the
monastic elders and the rule of the prudent Father Benedict.

In the spring Bede died, he was still serenely unconscious of ruin
impending. There were no longships in sight in that stormy season as
he looked out on the green following seas running southward from
the coast where the "horse-whales" lay on the cold foreshore. A father
had said of the northern region that from thence the waters of the earth
pass down. This was a fact worthy of all credence, and in the monastery
they kept as ornament the finely-polished bones of horse-whales' teeth.
But for the rest he knew little of the Hyperboreans or of the customs
of the north.

Living on the far limit of the Roman world, Rome was to him *Ca-
put et Domina Orbis*, the Holy See. An ever-conscious membership of
a visible society, united by a common rule and a common worship, a
worship that was ordered to God's glory and a rule that was a manifes-
tation of his power, had brought with it a new stability in that world
of change. To Bede, living under the protection of the lord abbot of
"the monastery of the Holiest Apostle St. Peter in Saxony", the passing kings had signified so little. "The most glorious" King Ceolwulf,
and "the ferocious" Egefrid were only shadows half reflected in the
repeated epithet of cloistered talk. But his abbots had been the support
and protection of the liberty and peace of the spirit, the oracles of God's
will. They had fostered his patristic learning and had shared with him
his quiet pleasures—the religious anagrams and the rhymed acrostics,
the riddles on the sacred mysteries and the tales of holy death. "God
has ordained the youth Hwaetbert to the leadership of souls and to a
spiritual dukedom", St. Bede writes of a new abbot, "who by love and
zeal for the pieties has long won for himself the name Eusebius. The
blessing conferred by the ministry, dearest bishop, has confirmed the
election of the brethren, so there returns to me the delight of searching carefully and with my whole soul for the wonders of the sacred
scriptures. Therefore, aided by thy prayers, most beloved of pontiffs, I
begin the fourth book of my Allegorical Exposition of Samuel, and I
will endeavor to communicate to my readers all that I can of mysteries,
if he will but unlock them who holds the key of David." How well
that passage expresses the ordered power of a serene theocracy in its
relation to the central duty of St. Bede's study.

Yet there must have been much even within the brotherhood of the twin monasteries of the two apostles from which Bede stayed remote, an imprudent neglect of the midday sleep and the unwise fasting of the overzealous or the field sports and the crude jesting of some younger monks. He has no share in that preoccupation with the body which marks so much of the asceticism of his time. He had none of the zest for loud color and contrast of the school of St. Aldhelm or their innocent delight in a sophistry. The traditional love for the classics reminded him of the parable of the prodigal son: the Christian scholars had gone into a far country and the pagan verses they were fain of were the husks the swine did eat. Yet in an age when the literary vocabulary was singularly rich in invective and the studies of his contemporaries seamed by their feuds, we can find no trace in Bede's writings of any personal enmity. The failings of his companions were forgotten in the quiet charity that has made his *Historia* the chronicle of a Golden Age, and no divergence between him and them disturbed his tolerance. He had learned that in his Father's house there were many mansions. And in Britain, as he notes, "there are found many excellent pearls of all colors—red and purple and violet and green and white".

All his life he was to retain this spirit of unchanging tranquility. He knew, for he had read it in St. Isidore, that he was living in the sixth age of the world. He knew, as he wrote to Bishop Egbert, that evil men abounded on the earth. But he seemed to be at the last rebirth of better things. The return of the old civilization to Northumbria had been reflected even in the trivial surroundings of his life of prayer, as he thought of the fine new glazing on the lanterns in the choir he could remember the days of his monastic childhood and the smoke upon the horn. His memory must have been checkered by such contrast; the old arch priest of Coldingham, the rude clumsy gestures with which he unhooked his traveling spear and the present prior speaking with a certain nicety of phrase and prudent diction of the holy abbot in his new sarcophagus beneath the turf. He had no presage of the coming ruin as he dreamt of the final victory of Roman order, of the columns reerected, and of the broken wall cleared of the moss, and of the end-less colonnade.

His life had been spent among the treasures amassed by the great abbots of his house *Religiosi Emptores*—the silk hangings embroidered in the *rotellae* with winged dragons, the silver arm-reliquaries and the cups of onyx. The life in the scattered steadings and in the rush-strewn halls of the chiefs must have seemed very far away. The quiet of the monastery was hardly broken by the coming and going of the poor at the abbey gate, or by the visit of some benefactress upon pilgrimage, the leathern curtains shrouding her as the great ill-made wheels of the royal cart jolted on the rock-strewn northern way. There would be ale at the hospitium for the nobles of the retinue while her household priest brought tidings of the Royal Curia, the princesses and their praised virginity and the virtue of the queen.

It was not seemly that the horse-thegns of the retinue should discuss such matter on the ale-bench, nor would it be needful for them to hold communion with any of the monkfolk vowed from childhood to God's service. For the ordered security of a life of prayer had been sufficiently safeguarded by the strength of Rome; there was among the precious muniments of the house "a thing by no means to be despised, a letter of privilege from the lord Pope Agatho, by which the abbey was rendered safe and secure for ever from any foreign invasion." All in that great community were conscious of the protection of a central power, of the wealth of the abbey treasure, of the high tradition of their learning and of the sacrosanct immunity of their lives.

Yet how remote was such knowledge from the same conceptions mirrored in the imaginings of the thegns, themselves gesithcund-men and "dearly born", they were well aware of the blood-price of each monk and knew there were no stronger rune-binders this side the Wendel sea. They had heard of the red twisted gold in the sacrist's keeping and of the embroidered coverlets from Greekland of the worth of many hides. They even shared in some memory of Roman strength, for they had heard the gleemen sing of it. "With the Greeks I was, with the Finns and with Caesar, he who had rule over towns and feasting, riches and joys and the realm of Welsh land." But they could remember other echoes from the chanting: "a broken shield of linden and bronze inset", "the tarred oars foam besprinkled and the driving of the wave". And for two years now they had taken note of the omens, they had seen the moon blood-pitted and the sun hanging a dark shield in the sky.

But even if Bede had foreseen the end of so much effort, flames from Jarrow and Monkwearmouth and a half-quenched civilization beyond Humber, it is unlikely that it would have influenced his life's work or disturbed the tenor of his years of study. For his life's purpose had been the fulfillment of God's will, and this, implying an overwhelming trust in Providence, involved an entire acceptance of the future. While though he did not conceive of so natural a disaster as a viking raid, he was not unprepared for sudden cataclysm. For nearly sixty years he had awaited the advent of the Lord. And he could remember the Yellow Death when he was a child in the abbey and the nights after so many burials when he had stood alone with Ceolfrid in the great high-fashioned nave, the old man in the abbot's stall with his lips moving ceaselessly. The light had fallen on the veins of the statues' breakage and the merovingian ivory. There had been winged lions on the chancel imposts and writhing basilisks carved upon the frieze, and in the darkness beneath the rafter the rood whose wood seemed almost living. But he had been conscious then of another presence and of the angels chanting in the choir.

There was no one now left in the abbey to share that memory, but it was to stay with him till he died. Years after he was to say to his disciples: "I know that angels visit the canonical hours and the congregations of the brethren. What if they do not find me among them? Will they not say where is Bede? Why comes he not to the prescribed devotions?"

The presence of an unseen world around him and the duty of the prescribed devotions had been the motifs of Bede's life.

∼

SAINT BONIFACE

[680–755]

Aelfric Manson, O.P.

HE CHARACTERISTICS which distinguish a nation are difficult to determine: we tend to hypostatize the virtues in the form of our own nationality, and are surprised when we meet them elsewhere. What is an Englishman? What is that type of mental outlook and behavior which, through the centuries, marks him out? The problem is complicated by the various influences that the dwellers on this island have experienced. It is not just the question of the continuity of a race living for generations on its own soil. The Norman Conquest, for example, meant the coming of a new people into the old stock; and a new consciousness. Will a man before that Conquest manifest the same traits as a man after it? Is each of them the genuine unalterable Englishman? So we may reflect when dealing with this English saint who lived three hundred years before the Norman came. For Boniface impresses us with an almost fantastic resemblance to what would now be considered as typically English greatness. He combined the love of travel and adventure of an Elizabethan with a genius for statesmanship and administration. He was a man, we might say, using an imperial ability for the extension of the Kingdom of God. It would have been a great interest to have known what he looked like. But there is nothing approaching a contemporary portrait: in the eighth century there were no portrait painters, or even cameras. Many of his letters remain, and these are of great importance for the events of his career and the general life of his period. But he was not a great writer; his style is the common style of the age, and although we can draw general observations about him from his letters—his affection for his friends and his fidelity to them, his love of books in general and of the Scriptures in particular, his profound dependence upon intercessory prayer—we miss those

personal indications which make us intimate with a man, like Lamb,
for instance, who can convey his individuality through words.

There is, however, one delightful exception. Boniface himself was,
rigidly, a total abstainer; and he imposed the practice in the monasteries
he founded. Not that he had a puritanical dislike of wine or beer; it
was because he considered drunkenness the most common failing of
his countrymen. And far from wishing to impose a universal taboo, he
recognized that wine was meant expressly to make joyful the heart of
man. In a letter to his friend Egbert, Archbishop of York, after asking
him to send Bede's commentaries on the Scriptures which will be useful for the sermons of the missionaries, and having sought his advice
on a disciplinary matter, he concludes: "Lastly, we have sent across
to your grace with the bearer of this letter, two measures of wine as a
proof of affection, that, at our loving entreaty, you may use it to spend a
happy day with your brethren." This provision for an episcopal "happy
day" surely reveals a pleasant and humorous aspect of the austere exile
who, at that moment, bore the burden of an entire new province of the
Church upon his shoulders. But it is a glimpse only; for the most part
he remains a hidden figure. He was, in fact, one of those men whose
personality is best understood by their achievement, whose character
and ideals remain expressed in the work they left behind them. What
Boniface created was what Boniface was: in it there lies incarnate all
he stood for, his dreams and ambitions, his vision, his very essence.

He lived over eleven hundred years ago. But the interest he provokes
is not simply that of a great missionary and a great saint. He was certainly both of these. He is also an exceedingly actual figure, for he was
one of the makers of the unity of Europe, that shattered unity which
today we are trying to rebuild. Most people would admit that Germany
is at the center of this problem: it was her defection at the Reformation
that made definite the long-threatened cleavage in the West: it is her
renascent nationalism that seems to menace the formation of a new
international order. The matter is urgent, and it is of extreme importance to recall that Germany's entrance into Christendom and civilization was made possible by an Englishman for whom his nation's riches
were not a hoard for private and exclusive possession, but a divine gift
to be shared, to be used for the common good. Boniface is rightly
called the Apostle of Germany, because, as a member of the Body of
Christ, he was supremely conscious of his responsibility in building

up that Body; his was a self-giving life spent in *aedificationem corporis Christi*. This was the principle that made the unity of Europe possible, a principle that in no way denies the rights and functions of individual nations but, on the contrary, fulfills them by making them contributing members of a great community, incorporated into Christ. It is the divine life which flows into the world through the Risen Christ that alone provides a sufficient force to unify the multitude of minds and wills either of the nations of Europe or of all mankind. Thus it was in the beginning of our civilization: thus it will have to be if our modern attempts are to succeed.

In the seventh century the Roman Empire, which had been for several centuries the mainstay of at least political and legal unity in Western Europe, was no longer a reality. No man living could remember it: the ruins of its cities and its roads alone survived as visible witnesses of past magnificence. The empire had retired to the East, and Constantinople had become and was to remain for generations the outpost and bulwark of civilization. Only in a few cities of Italy did the Imperial authority still strive to uphold its name in the West: in vain, for the latest horde of barbarians, the Lombards, proved irresistible. The barbarians: these were the tribes who had swept down from the north into Gaul, into Spain, into Italy, across the sea to Africa, across the northern sea to England: these were the new people, as yet a chaotic mass, who had broken down the old order, and who constituted the elements from which Western Christendom was to be fashioned. That process had begun; the passing of the empire had not been altogether a loss, for it allowed the chief instrument of the new order to develop in freedom. As the Dark Ages changed into the Middle Ages the creative role of the Papacy became more and more evident. Already it was the one great missionary force of the West. In 596 St. Gregory the Great had sent forth Augustine and his band of fellow Benedictines to convert the pagan Anglo-Saxons of Britain. That mission had been successful; in a hundred years the Christian Church was flourishing in every part of the island. Its progress inspired and stimulated civilization, and Anglo-Saxon England, the England of Bede, became the center of learning in the West. It was from this mature and vigorous society that Boniface went forth to be the agent of another Gregory in the conquest of further realms for the unity of Christ.

He was born about 680, probably at Crediton in Devonshire, then in the kingdom of Wessex, the last of the Anglo-Saxon kingdoms to receive the faith. His parents were Christians of noble rank. As a child he seems soon to have shown his desire to become a monk, and he was accepted as an oblate of the abbey of Exeter. There he remained until adolescence, when he was sent to complete his studies at the abbey of Nursling; in the diocese of Winchester. Both his new abbot, Winbrecht, who was also his master, and the bishop, Daniel, were to remain his friends for life. His studies were primarily Scriptural, and it was here that he acquired that profound love and knowledge of the Bible which is so evident in all his letters as a missionary. He must have learned also some at least of the seven liberal arts; verse making, at any rate, he never forgot—it was a favorite Anglo-Saxon elegance, and both his letters and those of his friends often conclude with a few lines of somewhat barbaric elegiacs. He probably owed this literary formation to the renowned teacher St. Aldhelm.

His proficiency was soon noticed and he was made the master of the abbey school. But he was a destined apostle, and we are told that he managed to combine this work with preaching to the people outside. When he was thirty (about 710) he received the priesthood; monasteries were still mainly lay communities, so this may be taken as a sign of the consideration in which he was held. Details of this early period do not abound, nevertheless it is clear that he stood every chance of becoming a distinguished ecclesiastic in his native church. He was even chosen (between 710 and 716) by the synod of Wessex to convey the synodal decrees to Brihtwald, the Archbishop of Canterbury, probably with the intention of linking the Wessex clergy more closely with the primatial see. It was a tribute to his statesmanlike qualities. Everything was pointing to a tranquil, successful career. But Boniface had seen a vision; his talents were to be used in a wider field and for a more adventurous purpose. His career at home came to a sudden close.

It was, as we have seen, a missionary age. Even from a natural point of view the great movement must have appealed to the spirit of youth eager for the conquest of the world. In his own island the subject must have been vivid: there was the story of his people's conversion, not so long ago; missionaries from Ireland; missionaries from Rome. There were the tales of still more recent heroes, the exploits of the men of his own race impatient to hand on the Good News they had received. Willibrord had been working among the pagans in Frisia

(Holland) since 692 and, it was said, had done wonders. And there were others. . . . He was caught into the current. He had to go. But where? His thoughts turned to those heathen who were his ancestors, the Saxons remaining in Germany. This was his first ideal, and though he never achieved it, he never lost it. He would take the Gospel to the Saxons. But he was inexperienced. He must learn something about missionary technique. He would therefore make a preliminary survey of Willibrord's work in Holland and thus gain the necessary experience. So, in 716, having wrung permission from his reluctant abbot, he set sail with three companions from the port of London.

Events on his arrival were not encouraging. The local duke, Radbod, was at war with the Franks; Willibrord had had to retire, and his life's work seemed ruined. Boniface, however, made his way to the ducal court at Utrecht and received permission to remain and preach. He did not remain very long; having gained an idea of the life, he returned to England and his abbey. Meanwhile abbot Winbrecht had died, and the monks decided to elect Boniface as his successor. But Boniface had other ideas. He managed to dissuade them, and in 718 set out again, this time for Rome. He carried with him two commendatory letters from Bishop Daniel, one for the spiritual and lay authorities whose dominions he would pass through on his way, the other for the Pope. He did not wish to be a mere spiritual adventurer. He had a sense of order. He wanted the sanction of the highest authority of the Catholic Church. He was going to Rome to offer his services to the Vicar of Christ.

He picked up many companions on the journey—the Anglo-Saxons had a passion for Pilgrimages to Rome—and, though the winter was severe, they reached the city safely, and offered their thanks at St. Peter's tomb. Then, a few days later, came the audience with the Pope, St. Gregory II. He was a welcome visitor, for this pope had long had plans for Germany, and had already sent his legate to reform the Church in Bavaria. It was the first of many interviews, and the Pope retained him until May 719. We have no details of those conversations, we only know their result. The historic significance of that result indicates their importance. They represent Boniface's initiation to the Apostolate; the Pope was equipping the young man for his first great test. It was to be a difficult experiment, and he must accordingly be well instructed. The Roman emperors had sent forth their legions to add new territories to the empire by force of arms. The Emperors had gone from Rome, and now Gregory the servant of the Ruler of the World was quietly planning for a more enduring kingdom, the pacific conquest of lands the legions never reached.

Boniface went back to Frisia. He was armed with a formal papal letter, authoritatively assigning him as a missionary to the heathen, making him the Pope's collaborator in the spreading of the Word of God. He was to conform to the Roman liturgy in the administration of the Sacraments—and Boniface's work proved to be one of the great influences that secured the general acceptance of that liturgy in the West. He was to refer all difficult cases to the decision of the Holy See— here also his work did much to make effective the appellate jurisdiction of the Roman Court. Finally, to emphasize his special adoption as a missionary of the Pope, Gregory changed his name from Winfrith— the Anglo-Saxon name he had hitherto borne—into that of Boniface. It was as though he was given a new identity as the Pope's man.

He assisted Willibrord for three years, converting the heathen, destroying their idols and building churches. But he had not come to stay, and when Willibrord, in 722, wished to consecrate him bishop as his successor, he pleaded that his mission was not to a single diocese but to the heathen at large, and that, in any case, he had not reached fifty, the canonical age. He won his point, and departed for central Germany. He began in Hesse and Thuringia, a densely wooded and mountainous territory. Irish missionaries had been there before him, but they had failed to organize their conquests. The Christian faith had not developed, and the people remained half pagan. The priests themselves had degenerated, some of them even shared in the worship and banquets of Thor. So Boniface could expect no help from them. He was alone. His only encouragement came from the letters he received from his friends, especially the nuns, across the sea. He wrote for advice as to how he should proceed to bishop Daniel at Winchester. Daniel counseled him not to begin by denouncing the errors of the pagans and the genealogies of their gods. He should first convince them, by discreet and gentle questioning, that the existence of their gods was insufficient to explain either their own origin or that of the world; then show the pointlessness of their sacrifices, compare their myths with Christian doctrines, make them appreciate the imposing *fact* of Christianity, and tell them the story of its triumph in the pagan world. A wise apologetic in the spirit of St. Gregory the Great, Boniface found it successful, and he sent a report of results together with some difficulties for solution, to the Pope. The return letter answered his difficulties and invited him to Rome.

Gregory was satisfied: his experiment had turned out well. The young apostle had had over three years' trial and had proved his genius. He was to be rewarded by receiving a higher command. When Boniface arrived the Pope began by questioning him as to the faith he had been teaching. "Apostolic father", he answered, "as a foreigner I find it hard to understand your speech; give me but time, and I will set forth my faith in writing." The delay was granted and he sent in his profession of faith. Then the Pope gave him another interview in the Lateran which lasted most of the day. At the end he told him that he intended to make him a bishop. This time there could be no refusal: it was the command of Christ's Vicar. He was to be a bishop, but the Bishop of Germany, of all Germany across the Rhine. He was not to be the subject of any metropolitan, but was to be attached directly to Rome. Boniface acquiesced, and his consecration took place on St. Andrew's Day, November 30, 722. He took the ancient oath used by the bishops of Italy, of fidelity to St. Peter and his successor. Then the Pope gave him a collection of the canons of councils to direct him in his ministry, and letters to Charles Martel, the powerful leader of the Franks, asking for his protection, and to the various peoples he was about to evangelize.

He thus left Rome for the second time with increased prestige as a member of the Catholic hierarchy and a legate of the Roman Pontiff. He was welcomed by Charles Martel, who agreed to afford his mission the protection of his power. Charles was by no means the ideal pious prince. He was still very much of a barbarian and preeminently a warrior. But he stood for the preservation of Christianity in the West. The old Merovingian monarchy of the Franks had become senile: Charles reorganized it—just in time to meet the menace of Islam. For the soldiers of Muhammad, having devastated Christian Africa and mastered Spain, were threatening to complete their work by subjugating the lands beyond the Pyrenees. Ten years after his meeting with Boniface, Charles saved our civilization at the great battle of Poitiers (732) and checked their advance for ever. Protection by such a man was of the greatest help to Boniface; not that he had any belief in forcible conversions, but because freedom from aggression and a peaceful environment were the essential preliminaries of the work he had to do. He was conscious of his debt; in after years he wrote to bishop Daniel: "Without the protection of the king of the Franks I can neither rule the people of the Church nor defend the priests and clergy, the monks and nuns of God; nor can I avail to check even the heathen rites and the worship of idols in Germany without his mandate and the fear of him." We are reminded that it was upon no fancy mission that the apostle was engaged; without the awe inspired by the great Frank's name an effective slaughter would have speedily terminated the rising Church of Germany.

All was well when he returned; his converts were flourishing, and his first act was to hold a confirmation. Then he decided upon a bold project. The worship of sacred trees is to be found in many of the "primitive" religions of mankind, and among the Germans the tree was the most impressive symbol of their belief. It seemed to them to possess a living personality, to concentrate within itself the forces that directed the mysterious life of nature. The dark gods possessed it as their presence chamber. On a mountain at Geismar in Hesse there was one of these trees, a venerable and massive oak dedicated to Thor, so ancient that it seemed coeval with time. It stood there, a mighty witness to the reality of the god, a central shrine, a holy place. Season after season it put forth majestic evidence of its vigor, and as long as it remained the confidence of the people in their myths could not be troubled. This Boniface realized, and he determined to cut it down. It was a spectacular occasion. Crowds gathered to see the conflict between the new religion and the old. Surely Thor would not permit this terrible sacrilege. The onlookers waited in silence, waited for a sign. But the Thunderer gave no sign, and the Christian bishop advanced calmly to do his dreadful work. Ringing sounds of the hatchet; persistent; on and on. The people watched petrified. It was unbelievable. Then, as the deadly noise continued undisturbed, fear gripped them. The certainties of their faith were shaken, the convictions of their lives unanchored, chaos in their minds: the gods were impotent. Suddenly an ominous cracking, then a fearful crash; the oak of Thor had fallen.

It was a potent lesson and brought respect for Christianity. Boniface built a chapel on the spot. He found much of the resistance gone, his work prospered and the Christian community grew. At Amöneburg he dedicated a chapel to St. Michael which was later to become a monastery and a missionary center. The next year he passed on into Thuringia and remained there for seven years (724–731). Here also the Church was only a survival. He at once began energetically to rebuild and organize. He secured the cooperation of some of the nobles, preached everywhere, put up numerous churches for the faithful, and started the monastery of St. Michael at Ohrdruff, near Gotha. To have a monastery was to have a power house: it was not only an imposing house of prayer and worship, it was also the source of the apostolate and of civilization. From the monastery a succession of men went forth to convert and instruct, and by the monastic activity, artistic, literary, agricultural, the barbarians learned the elements of a humane order. But monasteries must have monks, and Boniface's helpers were very few. He turned unhesitatingly to his native land and sent an appeal for more. He had been absent over fifteen years, and it would have been natural enough if he had been almost forgotten. Time dims the closest friendships, and a missionary exiled in an unknown land is not a public figure. It is therefore a most remarkable testimony to the force and attraction of his character, that his appeal was answered at once and abundantly. A veritable monastic exodus began. Wessex gave him all he needed, monks, priests, nuns, schoolmasters, in plenty. He welcomed them; they ensured the permanence of his work, they gave him the means for every development. The chapel at Amöneburg became a monastery, and another sprang up at Fritzlar near where the oak had been. Ohrdruff received a solid establishment. Three convents of women soon balanced these three foundations for men. The great missionary had reason for legitimate pride; his labors had not been in vain, the harvest he had prepared was being gathered. His success, however, did not make him forget that he was primarily the servant of the Pope. He kept in close touch with Rome and duly sent his pastoral difficulties for the Pope's decision. A letter from Gregory II, November, 726, in answer to one of his, gives us some idea of what those difficulties were. Among people who only recently were pagan the Church's marriage law naturally raised many problems. The Pope tells him that the canonical rules about impediments to marriage are not to be pushed to extremes. It is doubtless best if they are respected by all those who know that they are united by blood relationship, but one must remember that they are barbarians, and it will suffice if marriage is forbidden to the fourth degree inclusively. A passage in this letter has been quoted as sanctioning divorce and remarriage in the case of the husband of a sick wife. Boniface's letter no longer exists and we can only conjecture the precise nature of the case in question. Gregory then goes on to other matters. He uses St. Paul's principles to solve the question of meat consecrated to idols. Lepers may receive communion, but separated from the faithful. A priest who is accused without decisive testimony may be absolved by his oath alone. Oblates once given to God may not return to the world. Sacraments have an objective value which is not diminished by the unworthiness of the minister; hence there can be no rebaptism of those baptized by an unworthy priest, though it may be conferred on children taken from their parents and who cannot remember whether they received it or not. Confirmation may not be administered twice. Religious should not leave their house in time of infectious diseases—as if they could escape from the hand of God. Not two or three but only one chalice is to be placed on the altar for Mass, as Christ did when he instituted the Eucharist. In spite of the fact that Boniface had sworn in his consecration oath not to communicate with evil priests, he was not to refuse to eat with them—providing they were not formal heretics—but to try to convert them by example and word. . . . This list of replies well illustrates both the complexities of the missionary's daily life and the prudent moderation of his superior. It was his last letter from the Pope for Gregory died in February, 731. With the new pontificate came a new stage in the construction of the Church in Germany. Gregory III, in answer to Boniface's congratulations on his accession, sent him a letter and the pallium. The letter contained certain decisions which were more rigorous than those of his predecessor—marriage, for example, was excluded to the seventh degree. The pallium made him an archbishop. It meant that Germany, which had hitherto been a diocese, was now to become a province; it would have to be divided into dioceses with bishops instituted by Boniface, who was now the metropolitan. He himself was to have no fixed see, in order to preserve his freedom of general supervision. He was to be careful when selecting bishoprics only to choose cities of sufficient importance to befit the episcopal dignity.

Thus those statesmanlike qualities which we noted in his youth were now given their full chance. And he proved himself worthy; it is magnificent to watch the gradual realization of his plans, the unfolding of that achievement which still lasts. He turned first to Bavaria, a country which then comprised upper Austria, the region round Salzburg, the Tyrol and a part of Styria. It had long been Christian but was failing in vigor from the lack of that corporate expression and discipline which is given by councils; these were not held because there was no metropolitan, a deficiency which also entailed the slackening of the bond with Rome. Boniface spent nine years in the work of organization (732–741) but his main activity began after his return from his third and final visit to Rome in 738.

It was sixteen years since he last left the city, and he had many things to discuss with the Pope. Among other matters he was dissatisfied with the rigor of the Pontiff's decisions mentioned above, for though he was obedient he was never servile. He came with a crowd of disciples, was made very welcome by Gregory, and stayed for the best part of a year. The probable reason for this delay was his desire to attend a council and hear its decrees. When he left Rome—for ever—in the spring of 739 he took with him several letters from the Pope. One of them was addressed to the bishops of Bavaria; it presented the legate and reminded them that synods must be held twice every year. Immediately on his return Boniface proceeded with his work. There were already several diocesan sees in Bavaria—Salzburg, Frising, Ratisbon, and Passau—but they were all vacant except the last, and their respective territories were not delimited. He filled the sees and marked out the territories. Then he had to summon a national council of Bavaria. No documents of this council remain, but that it was assembled cannot be doubted, otherwise the strong movement for ecclesiastical reform which began in Bavaria about this time would have no source of origin. The legate's work was completed by the foundation of many monasteries.

He went on at once to Hesse and Thuringia. His task was more difficult here. Bavaria had been Christian for generations and it had been a part of the Roman civilization. There was a tradition of order; there were cities. Here the people had scarcely emerged from barbarism and there were few towns. How was he to obey the Pope's command not to erect bishoprics in insignificant localities? He did what he could. In Hesse he made Buraberg the episcopal see; it was not an important town but it lay between the two monasteries of Fritzlar and Amöneburg and was thus central for the rising Christian community. He appointed as its bishop Wittan, one of the Anglo-Saxons who had answered his appeal from England. In Thuringia which was naturally divided by a great forest he created two dioceses: Erfurt near his monastery of Ohrdruff in the north, and Würzburg on the Mein, a rising town and the ducal residence, in the south. This organization was completed and confirmed by the Pope in 742. Boniface had been a faithful servant; he had made the Church of central Germany in twenty years. He had been laboring now for a quarter of a century. He was getting old. He was worn out. His friends were passing away. Gregory II had long been gone; in October, 741, Charles Martel died; in November Gregory III followed him. It was time for Boniface to retire.

He did not retire: he took upon himself a task equal in magnitude to the former—the reform of the Frankish Church. That church had indeed fallen from its high estate. Boniface's letters bear witness to a terrible decadence. No councils had been held for eighty years. The metropolitan hierarchy had ceased to exist. Some of the episcopal sees had been vacant for years; others were in the hands of laymen or corrupt clerics. Bishops lived in concubinage, hunted and went to war. The inferior clergy were grossly ignorant and taught strange and superstitious doctrines. And to crown all, bands of Irish priests, admitting no ecclesiastical control, wandered from diocese to diocese, teaching what they liked, living as they pleased and irritating everyone with their peculiar Celtic customs. Boniface saw that the restoration of synods was the essential remedy. He gained Carloman, Charles Martel's son, to the project, and received encouragement from the new Pope Zachary. Four great councils were held between 742 and 744, and through them Boniface, who presided over them as papal legate, drew the Frankish Church out of chaos. The metropolitan hierarchy was reestablished: there were to be archbishops at Reims, Sens and Rouen. A council must be held every year. Rigid prescriptions were laid down for the reform of the clergy. Superstition was to be rooted out from the faithful. All these reforms were confirmed at a great council of the Frankish Empire in 747 with Boniface at its head. The council fathers promised lifelong obedience to the Pope, unity with the Roman Church and obedience to the canons. This profession of faith was sent to Rome and placed on the tomb of St. Peter, an expression of the unity between the Churches of France and Germany and the Roman See. After thirty years Boniface's work was done. This great assembly had given a solemn consecration to his life's program. The organization he had striven for was achieved: the bishop at the head of his diocese gathering his clergy round him each year at the diocesan synod; the metropolitan, with his pallium from the Pope, at the head of his province, gathering his bishops round him each year at the provincial synod, and acting as the link with Rome. Truly the Popes had been wise in choosing their servant. Boniface sent the decrees of the Council to Cuthbert, the Archbishop of Canterbury, and suggested that he should reform his Church in like manner. The advice was taken. The Council of Cliff inaugurated reforms identical, sometimes even in words, with those of the Frankish Council.

While he had been pursuing his work among the Franks Boniface had founded, through the agency of his disciple Sturmi, a monastery in the forest of Buchenau between Hesse and Bavaria. It was an adventurous affair for Sturmi and his companions, and they had many difficulties in the dense forest before they found a suitable site. Finally they discovered the marvelous locality where the abbey of Fulda was eventually built, a vast circular valley cut across by the River Fulda, protected by the Rhône mountains. They cleared the forest and in 744 began to build. Boniface came himself, bringing a number of helpers, and a stone church dedicated to St. Savior was put up. Gradually the great abbey arose, and whenever he could the archbishop would come to watch its progress. He initiated the monks in the Rule of St. Benedict and in the Scriptures, and he introduced total abstinence. Then he sent Sturmi to study Benedictine observance in the principal religious centers of Italy, especially in Rome and Monte Cassino. After a year Sturmi returned and was made abbot, and he raised Fulda to rank among the most famous abbeys of Christendom. In his own lifetime it housed over 400 monks. It became a center of German civilization. Boniface loved it: he meant it to continue his work after his death. That is why he secured its exemption from all other authority save that of the Pope. It was situated, he told Pope Zachary, "in the midst of the nations I have evangelized". He wanted to be buried there when he died.

The reform of the Frankish Church had restored the metropolitan jurisdiction, and yet Germany was without a metropolis. In the early days Boniface had had no fixed see in order that he might have freedom to control the entire country. But now that the episcopal organization was completed there seemed no reason why it should not receive its final complement. Boniface had thought the matter over and it had been discussed at the Frankish councils. Cologne was the most obvious situation. It was the largest town in Germany; it was a convenient center for apostolic operations in Frisia and Saxony. Pope Zachary agreed to this. But the moment was unpropitious, for the corrupt group in the Frankish clergy, furious at the reforming decrees, made a violent opposition, and succeeded in preventing his enthronement. Not only this; they also succeeded in temporarily ruining the metropolitan organization in Gaul. The Pope had sent the pallium to the three sees, but the Archbishops of Sens and Reims had disappeared. Only the metropolitan of Rouen remained. It was a severe blow to Boniface. But he made the best of things and chose Mainz as his see. There he found fresh trials. The Saxons, whom from his youth he had hoped to evangelize, burnt down thirty of his churches and slaughtered the faithful. His work was now confined to his diocese, though as papal legate he consecrated King Pepin at Soissons when that prince, by the Pope's decision, superseded the senile Merovingian dynasty. He was now growing very old, and obtained Zachary's reluctant permission to consecrate his faithful disciple Lull to be chorepiscopus and later his successor. Pope Zachary died in March, 752, and was succeeded by Stephen III. Boniface sent a letter of filial devotion in 753. When the Pope crossed the Alps in the winter of 753 to secure the aid of the Franks against the Lombards, Boniface was too feeble to go to greet him, and he took this as a sign of his approaching end. He put his affairs in order, committed his diocese to the protection of Pepin, held his last diocesan council, and bade his dearest friends farewell.

It was a strange farewell. This venerable man of over seventy, with a great life's work behind him, was not preparing for a peaceful death in bed. He was a missionary: that had been the dynamic force in all his life: and he was going to die a missionary. He was saying farewell because he was departing, for the last time, to the mission field. Saxony was impossible, so he would go to Frisia where his work had first begun. He embarked on the Rhine with about fifty followers. They came first to Utrecht, where Eoban, Boniface's friend, was bishop. Then they went on into the marshy land beyond. Here were the pagans, and Boniface began his work. He was successful, and converted many. He arranged to hold a confirmation at Dokkum, near the sea, and waited with his followers for the arrival of the neophytes. But in their place there came a band of heathen bent on slaughter. One or two of Boniface's men were armed, but he restrained them. The end was brief. When they rushed at him the saint raised the book he was reading to protect his head. The sword slashed through both book and head, and that great life was over. His body was taken back in triumph to Fulda, and he lies among the nations he evangelized.

~

SAINT EDWARD

[*1003–1066*]

C. C. Martindale, S.J.

FIRST THOUGHT of speaking of him one Sunday when I had to go straight from Westminster Cathedral, close to the abbey that we owe to Edward, to a church in Chiswick, also dedicated in his honor and packed out with people observing his feast day. When I reread all I could find about St. Edward I half regretted my choice, for not much that is picturesque is recorded about his character. On third thoughts, I decided that after all there was something worth saying just because it would not be so very dramatic. And when I remembered the names of much fiercer, more spectacular, men who surrounded him—it amused me once more to doubt whether even one in those churches was called Sweyn, Thurkill, let alone Hardicanute, whereas there must have been dozens of Edward, Neds or Teds, present; and all our kings named Edward have inherited their name from that distant monarch who, till forty, lived in exile.

I am certainly not going to make a history lecture here. Suffice it to say that after the splendid reign of Alfred you might have thought that this country would have thriven. He died in 901, bequeathing freedom in his very Will. "For God's love, and for the benefit of my soul, I will that they be masters of their own freedom and of their own choice; and in the name of the Living God, I entreat that no man disturb them by extraction of money or in any other way, but that they may be left free to serve any lord they may choose." As a matter of fact, the land went back to misery. The rivalries of great personages or families, and nationalistic greed, Saxon, Angle, Swede, Dane, at one another's throats, brought our island into a state of ravage and burnings, of murder, hamstringing, blinding, scalping which have been described as "hardly paralleled in the annals of American (Indian) ferocity", and,

I might add, to incests and allied horrors *not* to be paralleled among just savages. You hardly wonder that force, indeed, extreme severity, were *demanded* from those who cared or were responsible for justice; and the critics who half-sneer at Edward for his gentleness ought at least not to abuse kings, judges or bishops if, to repress the paroxysms of outrage, they used stern methods that he did not. Yet, after all . . . his is the personality that survives!

When the Danish Canute was acknowledged in 1017 to be King of all England, which thereupon became part of the Scandinavian empire, he sent away the infant sons of the previous king, Edmund Ironside, to Hungary. King Stephen in Hungary was himself a saint; and of his work, enduring till our own period and the treaty of Versailles, and destined to be revived, I should have liked to speak. Edmund's half-brothers, Alfred and Edward, had been taken away to Normandy. But at Canute's death, his two sons, Harold and Hardicanute, again tore the land in half; the former died after four years; the latter, after two years' reign, had a fit during an orgy and died too. It was 1042. Some-one had to be king, and so Edward was sent for, because he was the only survivor of the exiled brothers—Alfred had previously made an attempt to regain his crown, but Harold had caught him, massacred his followers and sent the wretched prince, tied naked to a horse, ex-hibited like a monstrosity through the villages, to Ely, where his eyes were put out and he died.

Now reflect that Edward had grown up a quiet man, robust and ruddy-faced, but with hair and beard early enough quite white, lik-ing the hunt and hawking, but also a home-lover; English by descent, no doubt, but convinced (no wonder) of the immense superiority of Norman culture; and take note that an exceptional amount of agri-cultural and atmospheric depression distressed much of his reign, and that there were actually earthquakes causing much alarm at, for exam-ple, Derby and Worcester; while the great lords at home and threats from overseas kept the horizon seemingly as black as ever—you might have thought that such a man in such circumstances would never have emerged into the light of history at all. Yet he, more than any of them, *did*. The real point is, that even if official historians glorified his reign, partly because it was an *English* one between the Danish tyranny and the Norman invasion and conquest, *public opinion* seldom goes simultaneously wrong about *Character*; *public affection* is not lightly given, or at least, if lightly given, does not last. But when Edward died, his people simply worshipped him, and it was to the "laws and customs of the good king Edward" that they constantly and successfully appealed, thereafter, against Norman oppression. Why was this? I consider, wholly because of the man's character, formed, not by self-indulgence—that *forms* nothing—but by deliberate unselfishness. He was a true king, precisely because he lived, not for himself, but for his people. No doubt he might have kept some of the great earls in order at the expense of massacring others, but he did not adopt this policy. He could, perhaps, have yielded to foreign petitions to enter into wars of aggrandizement; but into one only foreign war did he enter—a war of justice, on behalf of Malcolm, son of the Scottish Duncan, whom Macbeth in 1039 had murdered. And again, how strange it seems that we remember Edward, not because of this war, but in spite of it; and not one of us might so much as have heard of Macbeth, had not Shakespeare been inspired to enshrine some shreds of his story in a work of superb imagination. Millions must have read "Macbeth" without feeling—without so much as dreaming—that the tragic king was ever a real person. But Edward stands out so solid, so brilliant, so alive![1]

In that age when extortion and bribery played so massive a part, Edward seemed indifferent to money—he remitted the whole of the Dane-geld that had been exacted during thirty-eight years from the people and formed a great part of his personal revenue; when his nobles, anxious for his favor, had squeezed from their vassals a large sum and offered it to him, he refused it, and ordered it to be restored to those who had paid it in. Edward was, I should suppose, often enough cheated by men whom he trusted too much; but his ideal was ever *Justice*, national and personal. Thus when Pope Leo IX in 1049 consecrated the cathedral of Rheims and held a council there, Edward sent a Bishop and two Abbots to bring back his decrees "for the welfare of Christendom", and again sent two Bishops to the larger council in Rome, as representing the Anglo-Saxon hierarchy and as his own petitioners. The results have been curious and endure. Not only did they bring back stringent enactments concerning men who, by means of bribes, should seek to obtain bishoprics or abbacies, but, an answer

---

[1] Not everyone agrees with this estimate of Macbeth. We can safely say that the little war could not but seem just to Edward.

to an anxiety of Edward's private conscience. In those times of united Christendom, all eyes turned naturally to Rome. Edward had made a vow to go there. When he became king his nobles dreaded his leaving the kingdom to the probability of renewed civil strife in his absence. The Pope understood this; dispensed him from his vow; but asked that anything Edward had collected for his journey should be given to the poor, and that he should found, or restore, an abbey dedicated to St. Peter. Thenceforward, Edward annually set aside one-tenth of the revenues of his manors, and finally rebuilt, or rather built, Westminster Abbey. Later kings, and very ill-inspired architects, have since then added pieces to that edifice (like the two poor little towers); but the main glory of the work is due to Edward and Pope Leo. It is pathetic that in 1065 he went to London on purpose to witness its dedication; on Christmas Eve he was attacked by fever; with his habitual self-control he tried to remain as cheerful as ever, presided at all functions, instructed his wife Edith to see to the due decoration of the church. But on December 28th she had to represent him at the actual ceremony in the place for which Aeldred, Archbishop of York, when visiting Rome for the Archbishop's pallium, in 1063, had obtained so many privileges and whither papal legates had come to confirm them. Edward died on January 5, 1066, and because of our fantastic habit of beginning to learn English history from the latter part, only, of that year, Edward, with so much more, has subsided into being a mere "pre-conquest" monarch. He was buried in the abbey. The eleventh century Bayeux tapestry depicts the scene; his shrine, having survived later attacks upon it, was once more enriched by King Edward VII and other members of the present royal family, and is still surrounded by kneeling pilgrims on October 13, the day when St. Thomas à Becket, in the presence of King Henry II, solemnly removed St. Edward's body to the shrine itself.

The Christian, as you know, is not committed by his Christianity to any special system of government, be it by king or cabinet or president. But as St. Paul bequeathed more to England and to the world than a cathedral and its dome, so Edward left better behind him than his abbey. He enshrined in himself and exhibited to the world the two essential elements of right authority—the truths that all authority descends ultimately from God; and that all government exists for the wellbeing of the governed, not of itself. Christianity commits the Christian to no form of government as essentially better than any other—monarchy, presidency, dictatorship, cabinet government, popular government, or any other sort; the Christian, objecting as indeed he must to anarchy, demands *government*, but not (save by reason of purely personal preference) this sort or that. On the other hand, he knows that political life, like social, artistic, moral, familiar—every kind or department of life, has to recognize GOD as sole ultimate source of Power, and the Christian must be able to be obeying God when obeying the mandates of his prince. To fail to remember this is to begin to offer to Caesar what belongs to God, and to worship the Beast and his Image, to adore what is fain to set itself up (as the Scriptures so often say) in the Holy Place itself above all that can *deserve* the Name of God. No State, no Government, is Absolute over Conscience. And all authority whether in the home, or in shop or firm, business or trading concern, regional, national, racial matters, exists by no manner of means for the sake of those who are the possessors and wielders of that authority. No boss has the right to exploit one single man, whether yellow, white or black. Yet every age, our own included, has tended to produce its own version of tyranny, and of slave trade. Government must rule, but never may be Tyrant; the governed must obey, but must never be enslaved. May those principles of obedience to God, and so, of Justice toward man, which made Edward into a king who also was a saint, remain. His palaces have perished; not so his abbey. May what it symbolized survive, be intensified among us, and where need be, restored, else lost for us will be that righteous rule which is an image upon earth of God's own kingdom. May that Kingdom come, fully and lastingly.

~

SAINT MALACHY

[1095–1148]

Vincent McNabb, O.P.

SAINT WHOSE LIFE was passed between the years 1095 and 1148, and in Ireland, could hardly fail to provide matter for picturesque and even dramatic biography. It is to the credit of St. Malachy's contemporaries that one of them, perhaps the most illustrious of them, St. Bernard, saw in this son of a wild western island a man worthy to be a model even to saints.

Some notion of the Ireland of St. Malachy is needed by anyone who wishes to have a true notion of the Saint. Yet, even for men and women born within its borders the Ireland of St. Patrick is almost as elusive as a will-o'-the-wisp. If we took at its face value St. Bernard's Gallic judgment on our people, they would appear as a race of partly-Christianized barbarians whose very language was hardly a betterment of animal cries. Perhaps Ireland of the Brehon laws, the bards, the metal-craftsmen, the foreign-going seamen, is a problem that may have only an ascetical solution. If something that St. Bernard and the Latins looked upon as culture had never found a footing—as the Roman legions never found a footing—in Ireland, it may have been that the Irish either by necessity or choice had anticipated the first of the Beatitudes: "Blessed are the poor in spirit for theirs is the Kingdom of heaven."

County Down, which may have been the birthplace and was largely the life-place of St. Malachy, introduced the Saint to all the strong currents of contemporary Irish life. The hamlet of Saul had seen the first as well as the last Mass of St. Patrick. At Downpatrick lay the bodies of St. Patrick, St. Brigid and St. Columcille. A few miles from the grave of these Saints on Island Magee could be seen the handiwork of Danish invaders in the fire-blackened ruins of the school of St. Nendrum founded, perhaps, before St. Patrick's School at Armagh.

At the head of Loch Cuan—called Strang-fiord by the Danes!—the school of Moville was another proof that Danish warcraft had as its war cry, "Destroy! Destroy!" Again a few miles north of Moville, on the southeastern shores of Belfast Lough, was all that successive Danish raids had left of the world-famous monastic school of Bangor. Light is thrown on the strange Irish world of our Saint's day by the fact that in his twenty-eighth year the young priest Malachy found himself Abbot of Bangor with its vast possessions, by the will and resignation of his uncle—a layman!

The latest biographer of St. Malachy sketches the state of things into which the Saint was born. After stating that Armagh had been plundered and burned nine times by the Danes before their final defeat at Clontarf on Good Friday, 1014, he writes:

> The victory brought, no doubt, freedom from foreign oppression, but it did not bring peace. The period separating the defeat of the Danes from the advent of the Normans (1168) was occupied by a fierce contest between three families, the O'Briens of Munster, the MacLoughlins of Ulster and the O'Connors of Connacht—for the dignity of Ard Ri. This war of Gael against Gael was marked by sacrileges and atrocities quite equal to the worst attributed to the Norsemen. . . . The great wonder was that anything survived of the old Christianity and culture.[1]

If the Ireland of St. Malachy's troubled days is too elusive for even the insight of those who love it, the dim historic figure of the Saint himself is an equal problem of elusiveness. A key to this problem may be found, perhaps, in his love for the great St. Patrick who gave up the dignity of the See of Armagh for the hidden life and death at Saul. The two Saints separated from each other by some seven centuries are brothers in their unslaked desire to be hidden, and in their irresistible power of enkindling even a human love which has given them a human immortality.

Malachy O'More (Maolmhadhog Ua Morgair), was the son of Mugron O'More.

His mother's name is unknown. Both parents gave him noble blood. By his father he was given the traditions of Donegal; by his mother he was a child of Down. No better blending of blood could be given even in the Island of Saints.

---

[1] *Life of St. Malachy.* By Ailbe J. Luddy, O.Cist., M. H. Gill & Son, 1930, p. xv, xvi.

His father, who died when Malachy was only seven years old, could have bestowed on the child little beyond his nobility of rank and his gifts of mind and soul. Mugron O'More, like so many of the Irish nobility, was a scholar of such distinction that at the school of Armagh, the most famous in Ireland, he held the most important professor's chair.

Perhaps some matter of scholarship had summoned him from Armagh when death overtook him at Mungret, Limerick, in 1102. The coming of death, perhaps sudden death, into the little family could not fail to influence the sensitive soul of the young Malachy. Even at such an age the sight of a mother's weeping for the death of her children's father can give a new insight into the true value of human life. Indeed sorrow of such weight at an age of such tenderness may end by overshadowing the young mind.

St. Bernard is probably introducing us into the reality of the Saint's next few years by his praise of this nameless woman who was the Saint's mother. A widow with a child-saint in her keeping has done her work well to deserve from the Abbot of Clairvaux such praise as the following:

> His parents, however, were great both by descent and in power, *like unto the name of the great men that are in the earth.* (2 Sam 7:9.) Moreover his mother, more noble in mind than in blood, took pains at the very beginning of his way to show her child the ways of life; esteeming this knowledge of more value to him than the empty knowledge of the learning of this world. For both, however, he had aptitude in proportion to his age. . . .[2]

St. Malachy's childhood was thus passed at Armagh, where a boy's schooling was easily to be had. It would seem that one of his teachers, as so often happens, took delight in the companionship of his boy pupil. Often he would make the boy his companion in those walks which every home of learning treasures as a tradition. The boy's studies were so exacting that, in default of praying in church, he had taught himself to mingle prayer with his work; and even with his country walks. But when he was walking with his own teacher, who may not have been a priest, the boy could find his prayer only by something like a boyish

---

[2] St. Bernard of Clairvaux's *Life of St. Malachy.* H. J. Lawlor, D.D. (S.P.C.K., 1920), p. 7.

prank. Like the average boy sauntering along a country road he would seem to lag behind. Then when he knew he was not seen he would stretch out his arms and send a dart of prayer to be seen and heard not by his teacher on the road but by his Father in heaven.

Somewhere about this time death again came under his roof to take away the one who had given him consolation on death's first visit. At the Saint's age the passing away of an only parent would seem like the passing away of a world. For Malachy, his brother Gillachrist (Christian) and their sister it must have meant the end of their family life.

If ever Malachy had hesitated about his career in life the death of his mother would be the end of these hesitations. His beloved country needed nothing quite so urgently as good priests who might shepherd the people. Everything in Malachy's soul and life—his strength and weakness—urged him to the priesthood.

A step of seeming unwontedness was taken when Malachy placed himself under the spiritual direction of a man whose influence over Malachy was probably the most decisive of his future career. This was Imar O'Hagan, once an Abbot, and now an anchoret in a cell near the great Church of Armagh. St. Bernard's account of the matter is full of the suggestion that St. Malachy's withdrawal from the world was not just an enthusiasm of youth for the ideal, but was opening manhood's strategy of defense against the enemy called the flesh. A family without father and mother *is* open to attack on all sides. Perhaps at the time when, in his teens, he disappointed his family by withdrawing from the world he was withdrawing from a tangle of temptations which soon caught and held his beloved sister. St. Bernard's words are a drama in the making. "The Saint abhorred her carnal life, and with such intensity that he vowed he would never see her again." The dramatic element in this meager outline is not the strong words from the pen of the French orator but the still stronger action from the man whom this biographer has described almost as the meekest of men. The vow never to see his sister must have meant, what was all too common in those wild ages, some adulterous relation of the powerful, shamelessly maintained, to the scandal of the simple and against the laws of God.

As so often happens, the lead given by a nobleman found followers. Soon around the cells of Imar O'Hagan and his young follower were seen a group of Irish youth adventuring all for God.

Some years of this quiet life with God have left only silence with his biographers. But when next these biographers show him to us—as an ordained deacon of some two and twenty years—the quiet life of God is seen to have wrought a work in his soul. His devotion to the poor which aroused the anger and reproaches of his sister must have touched the grateful hearts of the people who could not forget what was remembered three and thirty years afterward when the great St. Bernard told the world how this young Irish nobleman would himself bury the dead poor.

It was not nobility of blood but fitness of learning and holiness of soul that moved Archbishop Cellach of Armagh to ordain St. Malachy to the priesthood in his twenty-fifth year.

This Archbishop Cellach is a man to be studied. Like St. Charles Borromeo he is a proof that an evil state of things, even of ecclesiastical things, need not be all evil. At the age of six and twenty Cellach found himself—we can hardly use a fitter expression—found himself Lord Abbot and Archbishop of Armagh, by right of blood.

But the blood within Cellach's veins was so generous that the young Archbishop, from the first moment of his consecration, was on the side of the Saints. His whole policy from that day till the day of his death was to strengthen the bond between Ireland and its Mother-in-God, the see of Rome.

Cellach was but nine and thirty years old when he saw the Saint so clearly in the young deacon Malachy that overlooking his want of years, he ordained him priest. Within a few months the newly ordained priest was governing the See of Armagh while its Archbishop was carrying out the duties of Metropolitan of Ireland in other parts of Ireland. All that we read of this young priest, now acting head of the chief See of Ireland, is a proof that he was a true priest of the people. Among the people he restored the great sacramental life of the Church—Confession, Holy Communion, Confirmation, and marriage according to the rites of the Church. Among his brother priests he introduced the saying of the Divine Office according to the Roman use. We are told that he had learned singing—St. Bernard, no mean judge of Church song, is explicit on the fact—and that he spread the love of sacred song—the Gregorian plain-song (?)—among his brother priests.

The two saints seem to have understood and loved each other without a shadow of misunderstanding or mistrust till death came to part them for a few years. They shared a great love of their motherland, once the Island of Saints and Scholars. But their love was not blind to the fact that neither sanctity nor scholarship is transmitted by birth; even by gentle birth. It was their common desire to study these two qualities of heart and mind that prompted St. Cellach, on his return to Armagh, to send St. Malachy to Malchus, Bishop of Waterford and Lismore. Malchus, then in his seventy-fourth year, was well qualified to introduce the young priest of Armagh to the sources of the best scholarship and highest sanctity of his age. He had left his Irish home in youth to be a monk in the monastery at Winchester, where the new continental movements in asceticism were fostered. When St. Anselm consecrated Malchus Bishop in 1096 the Irish monk of Winchester came into vital relation with one of the most acute intellects not only of Italy, his native land, but of the Church, not only of his century, but of all time. For three years, under Malchus, the young priest Malachy completed that training of his mind and heart that was fitting him to be looked upon by some historians as St. Patrick's most illustrious successor.

St. Bernard has recalled but one incident of these three years of quiet study with Malchus on the wooded banks of the Blackwater at Lismore. So sinful a life was his sister living that, as we have seen, this young priest, who was all gentleness and mercy, made a vow never to visit her while she lived in sin. Death came to her while her brother was at Lismore. St. Bernard's words are in that master of words' most poignant manner:

For the Saint indeed abhorred her carnal life; and with such intensity that he vowed he would never see her alive in the flesh.

But now that her flesh was destroyed his vow was also destroyed; and he began to see in spirit her whom in the body he would not see.

On hearing of her death he had offered up the Holy Mass for her. Some thirty days after having ceased to offer up the Holy Sacrifice for her:

He heard in a dream by night the voice of one saying to him that his sister was standing outside in the courtyard, having tasted nothing for thirty days. On awakening he soon realized the kind of food for want of which she was pining away.

His prayers and Masses for her soul continued. Soon he saw her at the threshold of the church; but clad in black. Later on he saw her clad

in grey; within the church, but not allowed to the altar. At last she was
seen a third time, with the throng of the white-robed and in apparel
that shone.

This public sin of his sister, with his vow never to see her while her
sin lasted, may have helped him to quit Armagh for Lismore. At any
rate her death, with seemingly her known repentance, made it easier
for him to return in a position of authority.

The summons to return came to him in 1123, when his mother's
brother, a layman, had been elected, by the law of Tanistry, to be Abbot
of Bangor. This layman determined to break the unhappy tradition of
centuries, resigned the Abbey with its rich lands to his priest nephew,
Malachy. But the same Nazareth spirit of poverty was alike in nephew
and uncle.

St. Bernard's account of what took place throws light on the soul of
the young Abbot of Bangor:

> Vast were the possessions of that place. But Malachy, contented with the
> holy place alone, resigned all the possessions and lands to another. . . .
> And though many urged him not to alienate the possessions but to keep
> them all for himself, this lover of poverty did not consent, but caused
> one to be elected, according to custom, to hold them; the place itself
> being kept for Malachy and his followers.

St. Bernard's praise of Bangor, of which an excerpt has already been
quoted, is couched in noble prose:

> Truly was it a holy place, bringing forth most abundant fruit in God,
> so that one of the sons of that holy brotherhood, Lugaid by name, is
> said to have been himself alone the founder of a hundred monasteries.
> This I narrate that those who read may know from this one instance
> what a countless number of others there were. Indeed, its shoots did so
> fill Ireland and Scotland, that these verses of David seem to have sung
> beforehand especially of these times:
>
> > Thou visitest the earth and blessest it,
> >   Thou makest it very plenteous
> > The river of God is full of water.
> >   Thou preparest their corn;
> > For so Thou providest for the earth.
> >   Blessing its rivers,
> > Multiplying its shoots,
> >   With its drops of rain shall it rejoice while
> >   it groweth.

With ten brethren from St. Imar's monastery at Armagh, St. Malachy
began to rebuild the abbey and the monastic life at Bangor. St. Bernard,
accustomed to the noble stone buildings of France, says: "The church
was finished in a few days. It was made of smoothed planks, but closely
and strongly fastened together—a Scotia work, not devoid of beauty."

It is to the credit of those who controlled the Irish Church in those
days that a priest so fit to be Bishop was soon appointed to the Bishopric at Down and Connor (Antrim).

It was in 1124, when the Saint was not quite thirty years old, that
the same great soul, St. Cellach of Armagh, who had made him deacon
and priest, crowned these orders and his own long standing desires by
consecrating St. Malachy Bishop. It is the last time that history records
the meeting of these two great men.

It was to no place of ease that St. Cellach's consecration sent the
young Bishop of Down and Connor. St. Bernard's dark picture of
the state of Christianity that met St. Malachy has stimulated countless
attempts at defense. Perhaps the most dexterous defense against the
French Saint's denunciation of this Irish diocese is a kindred and almost equally dark denunciation of the Church in Southern France and
in Rome. But we venture to suggest that the context of St. Bernard's
words might well refer to Connor alone, which St. Malachy had not
yet visited; and not to Down, which he had known from childhood.

Of far more importance and perhaps accuracy than St. Bernard's denunciation of the good folk of Connor (and Down?) whom he calls
"not men but beasts", is his description of the young Bishop's way
of dealing with them. Fortunately St. Malachy recognized that in the
people of Down and Connor he had to deal with men; of a rugged
stamp, perhaps; but men who knew and would follow a good leader
when they found one. That they had found one in their new Bishop
—a sapling of their own soil—is clear from St. Bernard's words:

> He recognized that he was a shepherd and not a hireling. He made up his
> mind to stand and not to flee; and even to give his life for his sheep . . .
> He chid in public, he argued in secret, he wept now with one and now
> with another. To some he spoke sharply; to some, gently; as he saw what
> befitted each. And when all these stratagems failed he offered for them a
> "broken and bruised heart." How often did he spend whole nights in a
> wake, holding out his hands in prayer. And when they would not come
> to the church he went to meet the unwilling ones in the ways, and going
> round about the city he eagerly sought whom he might gain for Christ.

Often did he go into country parts and villages with that holy band of
disciples who never left his side.

Nor did he ride on a horse, but went on foot, thus showing himself an
apostolic man. How often was he faint with hunger, how often afflicted
with cold and nakedness. . . . At last, all things were so changed for the
better that today the word which the Lord speaks by the prophet may
be spoken of this nation:—Those who before were not my people, are
now my people.

In 1128, some northern king, perhaps Conor O'Loughlin, invaded
Connor and Down. St. Bernard's dark description of St. Malachy's fellow countrymen receives corroboration when we read that this northern king destroyed the monastery of Bangor and drove off the monks.
But their Abbot and Bishop Malachy knowing that his diocese needed
these, his fellow laborers, found a home for his hundred and twenty
monks at Iveragh in Kerry. The site was the gift of Cormac Mac Carthy,
King of Desmond, whom St. Malachy had befriended when King Cormac was a fugitive at Lismore. St. Malachy's genius for friendship was
again seen when the king not only gave him the site and means to
build the monastery but gave his hands and shoulders to the work of
building. Once again the Abbot of Clairvaux becomes lyrical as he
praises his friend the dead Archbishop:

> And these as it were beginning anew, the burden of law and discipline
> which he laid on others he bore with greater zeal himself, their bishop
> and teacher. He himself in the order of his course, did duty as cook;
> he himself served his brethren while they took their food. Among the
> brethren who succeeded one another in chanting or reading in church he
> would not be passed over, but strenuously took his part as one of them.
> And in the life of holy poverty, he not only shared but took the lead;
> being zealous for it more than they all.

On April 1, 1129, St. Cellach, then in his fiftieth year died at Ard-
patrick in the county of Limerick. His death was another landmark in
the life of his friend Malachy. Students of psychical research will find
it of interest to read in St. Bernard's life how in a vision St. Malachy
saw a woman of great stature and reverent mien who, on being asked,
said she was the Bride of Cellach. Then she gave to Malachy a bishop's
staff and disappeared. A few days later St. Malachy received from the
dying Cellach a letter naming him Archbishop of Armagh and sending
the bishop's staff which St. Malachy recognized as the staff given to

him in the vision. In the Ireland of those days the Staff of St. Patrick and the nomination by a successor of St. Patrick did not make a *de facto* Archbishop of Armagh.

The kinsmen of the dead Archbishop used their hereditary right to name as successor his first cousin, Murtough. There was nothing glaringly wrong or even illegal in this application of the clan system to the ecclesiastical hierarchy. Even later centuries have seen royal nomination to bishoprics tolerated by the Church.

As Malachy, who was already a Bishop, held out for three years in his refusal to accept the Archbishopric it is evident that Archbishop Murtough was hardly the wicked intruder of St. Bernard's Gallic invective.

It was only in 1132 that St. Malachy allowed himself to be nominated to the See of Armagh. It is significant that the two Bishops who finally broke down his opposition were Malchus of Lismore, and Gilbert of Limerick, the Papal Legate. It would almost seem that the final authority to compel obedience was the Holy See of which Gilbert was Legate. Three years would give time to lay the matter before the successor of St. Peter. Unfortunately the successor of St. Peter, Innocent II, found the See of Rome, like the See of Armagh, claimed by another —Anacletus—who, after being elected—by a group of Cardinals, had been crowned in St. Peter's on the same day that Innocent II was crowned in another Church in Rome. Something of the still more distracted state of the Church at large may have been reflected in the Church of Ireland. If it was five years before St. Malachy took possession of his archiepiscopal chair in Armagh, it was eight years before Pope Innocent II took possession of his Papal Chair in Rome. In each case the final step was taken by the help of the secular arm. Yet for two years preceding the death of Murtough, St. Malachy "did not enter the city" of Armagh, "lest by such an act it should happen that any of those should die to whom he came rather to administer life."

When St. Malachy finally agreed to accept the Archbishopric of Armagh, St. Bernard reports him as saying:

> You are leading me to death, but I obey in the hope of martyrdom; yet on this condition that if the enterprise succeeds and God frees his heritage from those who are destroying it—all being then completed, and the Church at peace, I may be allowed to go back to my former bride and friend, poverty, and to put another in my place!

It is hardly possible that St. Malachy was not thinking of the beloved apostle of his country, whose memory was in every townland of Down! St. Patrick, the boy who ran away from slavery, was never greater than when in his old age he became a runaway from honor. Saints are often pursued by the example of brother saints. All the holy men who had such an influence on St. Malachy copied St. Patrick's master stroke of resigning honors. Imar O'Hagan resigned the Abbotship of St. Peter and St. Paul at Armagh to become a hermit and to die in Rome, 1134. Malchus had resigned the Archbishopric of Cashel to return to his first diocese of Lismore and Waterford. Gilbert, the Papal Legate, in 1139 resigned his legatine commission and his Bishopric. It was two years after St. Malachy had resigned Armagh for the quiet and poverty of Down. We question whether any Church in Christendom was setting a higher example of flight from ecclesiastical honors than the Church in Ireland.

Once back in his beloved Down, St. Malachy began again to organize a community of men amidst the charred ruins of Bangor. His thoughts, never set on the world, were more and more fixed on God. His brother, Christian, Bishop of Clogher, had gone to God June 12, 1138, with such repute of holiness that St. Bernard wrote of him: "He was a good man, full of grace and virtue. In the mind of the people he ranked second only to his brother, whom he perhaps equaled in zeal for justice and in sanctity of life."

When a man who is a saint, like Malachy, sees his life's work nearing completion, he redoubles his energy lest death overtake him, and the night come in which no man can work. A greater than any saint, after spending thirty years in silence and thirty months in daily preaching, at length when his work was nearing its close, set his face and hastened toward Jerusalem.

None of the great men—Cellach, Imar, Malchus, Gilbert, Malachy —may have known that, under the guidance of God, they were organizing a spiritual building in their beloved country that was to take the stress of eight centuries of political subjugation and four centuries of religious persecution. It was not foresight but insight that guided these men when they built better than they knew. They only knew that no building of theirs would stand when Satan's storms buffeted it, unless they built upon the successor of the man who was made a

Rock. St. Patrick had left them the command "to be Christians, be Romans". That word, faithfully kept, has been the keeping of Ireland's faith.

Instinctively St. Malachy felt that the organization of the Irish Church, so patiently made by Cellach and his friends, would not stand or last if it had not the knowledge and approval of the Pope. It was a Catholic's homing instinct that sent St. Malachy to Rome late in 1139 or early in 1140. This instinct was all the more praiseworthy because for some nine years Rome had welcomed an anti-pope, Anacletus, and had made the rightful Pope, Innocent II, little less than a wanderer in Germany and France.

The Saint's way of traveling was on foot, with only three pack-horses to carry the baggage. Allowing for a month in Rome, the party covered some 3,000 miles in nine months!

The most important incident in the Saint's journey to Rome was his going aside from his direct route to visit St. Bernard at Clairvaux. No doubt, during his stay at York, he had heard of, perhaps visited, the Cistercian monastery of Rievaulx, founded by monks of Clairvaux itself. If so, he would see a state of things recalling his own beloved country—a sparsely peopled, largely untilled countryside being gradually tilled and peopled by groups of peasant families that clustered round an agricultural community of contemplative monks. When St. Stephen Harding, and later on St. Bernard, used the Rule of St. Benedict to form communities of contemplative monks working on the land, they may not have foreseen how this challenge to the Catholic youth of Europe-in-ruins would be romantically accepted. Even the enthusiasm that met the mendicant challenge of Francis and Dominic was hardly greater. In England alone, between the years 1128 and 1152 the Cistercian houses numbered fifty. The community at Rievaulx, shortly after St. Malachy's visit, numbered three hundred, and included the young monk St. Aelred.

It was thus that even on his way to the city of his desire, and to the authority of his obedience, St. Malachy caught sight of what seemed to him the necessary supplement of all ecclesiastical organization. Throughout his life he had sought it without knowing clearly what he sought. He had sought it as a lad when he put himself under the roof and the care of Imar O'Hagan. Even as a young Bishop of

Down and Connor, he had sought it at Bangor. Driven from Bangor he had not been driven from his desire, but had sought it again at Iveragh. Driven from Iveragh to be the successor of St. Patrick at Armagh he sought it with such increasing keenness that he resigned his Metropolitan See to seek it again as Bishop of Down, in his beloved home at Bangor.

It would be an oversight not to detect in St. Malachy a rare genius for what is most practical. He had the even rarer genius to know that practical matters are best taught, not by lessons, but by practice. He never asked others to undertake a burden that he himself had not already undertaken, or was preparing to undertake. The stones and timbers of his monasteries were authentic witness.

When, therefore, he saw Cistercian monasticism civilizing the countrysides of France and Northern Italy he determined to ask his superior, Pope Innocent II, for leave to become a Cistercian. Yet he was not drawn to this merely or primarily by the desire of his heart for contemplative union with God. Knowing that he could not love God, whom he did not see, if he did not love his neighbor whom he did see, he desired to lead others into the Cistercian life by himself preceding them. But his desire to see himself and them working in Cistercian fields or chanting in Cistercian choirs, included a desire to give to his beloved Irish people something of the life that redeemed the world in the highland hamlet of Nazareth.

It is to the credit of Pope Innocent II that he gave St. Malachy every desire of his heart except one. Yet—to use a fine epigram of St. Augustine—"in refusing the desire of his heart he did not refuse the heart of his desire". While sanctioning the creation of the new Archbishopric of Cashel, making Armagh Metropolitan of Ireland, and consenting to give the pall to the two Sees of Armagh and Cashel, Innocent II refused to let St. Malachy become a monk at Clairvaux. In the end this refusal meant that, instead of Clairvaux receiving there and then one Irish monk, Ireland received later on a community of monks firmly settled at Mellifont by the authority of St. Malachy, the legate of the Pope!

Pope Innocent had been for too many years a fugitive from his See not to feel grateful to this saint and bishop, who brought him reverence and obedience from the Island of Saints. He showed his insight into character and his gratitude for loyal obedience by making St. Malachy

his legate in Ireland. St. Bernard records details of a personal kind
that show how St. Malachy's invincible charm had won the Bishop of
Rome as it had won the Abbot of Clairvaux.

> Then the Pope took his mitre from his own head and placed it on
> Malachy's head; nay more, he gave him the stole and maniple he was
> wont to wear at Mass. Then he gave him the kiss of peace and bade him
> farewell strengthened with the Apostolic Blessing and authority.

When St. Malachy revisited Clairvaux on his way home he left four
of his companions with St. Bernard to be his proxies in the monastic
life. In time they came back to him when he founded the first Cistercian abbey in Ireland.

The eight years of life now remaining to St. Malachy have left little
record in his biographies. Three activities may sum up his last years:
1. His foundation of the Cistercian Abbey at Mellifont in County
Louth. 2. His journeyings throughout Ireland as Papal Legate. 3. His
presiding over a National Council.

Four Irish monks and some eight French monks began the first Cistercian Abbey at Mellifont in 1142. Fr. Luddy, speaking with the au-
thoritativeness of a Cistercian, suggests that the disagreement between
the Irish and French monks may have been partly occasioned by the
French monks' building plans! *Sit omen.* The Irish monastic tradition
of extreme architectural poverty did not easily fit in with Gallic views.
In the end the French views prevailed. Fr. Luddy adds: "All the buildings, of course, were of stone; and of such proportions as must have
astonished the simple-minded Celts." Abbeys were founded in the little island so thickly that there were some forty-six at the time of the
Dissolution when the population of the country was not so great as
London or New York. But it is still a moot point whether the Gallic
or the Gaelic view of architectural poverty should have prevailed.

An itinerary of St. Malachy's legatine journeys in Ireland would
probably give us the names of every considerable town in the island.
Of greater importance than this geographical aspect of the Saint's journeyings is St. Bernard's account of the legate's manner of life as he
journeyed.

> From the first day of his conversion to the last of his life he lived without
> personal possessions.

He had neither manservants nor maidservants; nor villages nor hamlets; nor, in fact, any revenues, ecclesiastical or secular, even when he was a bishop.

There was nothing whatever assigned for his episcopal upkeep, for he had not a house of his own. But he was always going about all the parishes, preaching the Gospel and living by the Gospel. . . . When he went out to preach he was accompanied by others on foot; bishop and legate that he was he too went on foot. That was the apostolic rule; and it is the more to be admired in Malachy because it is too rare in others. The true successor of the apostles assuredly is he who does such things. But it is to be observed how be divides his inheritance with his brothers, who are equally descendants of the apostles.

They lord it over the clergy—he made himself the servant of all.

They either do not preach the Gospel and yet eat; or preach the Gospel in order to eat—Malachy imitating Paul, eats that he may preach the Gospel.

They suppose that arrogance and gain are godliness—Malachy claims for himself by right only toil and a burden.

They count themselves happy if they enlarge their borders—Malachy glories in enlarging charity.

They gather into barns and fill the wine jars that they may load their tables—Malachy forgathers men into deserts and solitudes that he may fill heaven.

They though they receive tithes and firstfruits and oblations besides customs and tribute by the gift of Caesar and countless other revenues, nevertheless take counsel as to what they may eat and drink—Malachy having nothing enriches many out of the storehouses of faith.

Of their desire and anxiety there is no end—Malachy, desiring nothing, knows not how to be solicitous for tomorrow.

They exact from the poor that they may give to the rich—Malachy implores the rich to provide for the poor.

They empty the purses of their subjects—he for their sins loads altars with vows and peace offerings.

They build lofty palaces, raise towers and ramparts to the skies—Malachy, not having whereon to lay his head, does the work of an evangelist.

They ride on horses with a throng of men who eat bread for nought, and that is not theirs—Malachy girt around by a throng of holy brethren goes on foot bearing the bread of angels.

They do not even know their congregations—he instructs them.

They honor powerful men and tyrants—he punishes them.

O apostolic man! whom so many and such striking signs of apostleship adorn. What wonder that he has wrought such wonder, being so great a wonder himself.

When the first Cistercian Pope, Eugenius III, asked his old Abbot St. Bernard for guidance as the Supreme Bishop of the Visible Church, the holy Doctor answered in effect: "Study the life and follow the example of St. Malachy; and all will be well." Had St. Bernard's words been more widely read and more faithfully copied all would not be ill as it is today.

Some of the wonders wrought by St. Malachy are narrated by St. Bernard. We are not sure that the evidence for their supernatural character would be accepted by a modern Congregation of Rites. But the narrative is almost a substitute for the Legate's wide itinerary. At *Coleraine* he drove the demon first out of one woman and then out of a second into whom he had entered; in *Ulster* a sick man was at once cured by lying in the Saint's bed; at *Lismore* a demoniac was cured; in *Leinster* he instantly cured a sick babe; in *Saul, County Down,* a woman, whose madness was so great that she was tearing her limbs with her teeth, was cured when he prayed and laid his hands on her; at *Antrim* a dying man recovered the use of his tongue and his speech on receiving the Holy Viaticum; at *Cloyne* when a nobleman besought his aid for his wife, in danger of death through childbirth, the Saint sent her a cup he had blessed and her child was happily born; at *Cashel* he cured a paralyzed boy; on the *borders of Munster* a cripple boy was cured; at *Cork* he raised from a sick bed one whom he named bishop of the city; in another unnamed place a notorious scold was cured when she made her first confession to the Saint (here St. Bernard not, perhaps, very chivalrously observes that this is a greater miracle then raising the dead!); an *island (Rathlin?)* long famous for fishermen had suffered from lack of fish which came back when the Saint knelt down on the shore and prayed.

The following incident deserves a place of honor in a biography of the saint, inspired by the first Eucharistic Congress held in the Saint's native land. It must be told in St. Bernard's own words:

> In Lismore there was a cleric of better life (it was said) than faith. A scholar in his own eyes he dared to say that in the Eucharist there was only the sacrament and not the reality of the sacrament; in other words, only the hallowing and not the truth of the Body.
>
> On this matter, having been often summoned by Malachy secretly but

in vain, he was bidden to a council, yet apart from the laity, so that, if possible, he might be healed without being put to shame. In this council, therefore, there was given the man opportunity of explaining his opinion.

When, with all his cleverness, which was not a little, he had explained and defended his opinion, Malachy himself took up the discussion and answered him. Whereupon being condemned by a unanimous judgment he went out of the meeting, ashamed but not convinced. He said he had not been overcome by argument but compelled by the authority of the Bishop. He added: "And you," Malachy, "have this day put me to shame, speaking against the truth and your own conscience."

Malachy saddened by the hardness of the man, but grieving still more for the hurt to faith and dreading the danger, summons the church, publicly corrects the erring one, publicly warns him to retract. When he would not agree to this, even after the bishops and clergy had urged him, they pronounce anathema upon him as contumacious and declare him a heretic.

Yet did he not awake, but said: "It is the man you all seek; and not the truth. But I will not follow the man and leave the truth." At this word the saint being deeply moved said: "May the Lord make you confess the truth of necessity." To which the other said "Amen." Then the council was brought to an end.

Branded with this mark, he planned to flee, being unable to be accounted disgraced and dishonored. Gathering his belongings together he soon set out. But lo! seized with sudden illness, he stood still, and in sheer weakness threw himself down on the ground breathless and weak.

By chance a wandering simpleton coming to the spot stumbled upon the man and asked him where he was going. He answered that he was taken with weakness and could neither go on nor go back. Whereupon the other said: "Your weakness is nothing else but—death!" This he did not say of himself; for the Lord very fitly corrected by a simpleton one who would not hearken to the same counsels of the wise. Then he added: "Go back home. I will help you."

Thereupon with his help he went back to the town; indeed he went back to his heart and to the mercy of the Lord. At once the Bishop is summoned, the truth is acknowledged, the error is rejected. He confesses his sin and is absolved—he asks for Viaticum—is reconciled, and almost at the same moment his unfaith is disowned by his mouth and dissolved by his death.

St. Bernard's pen has here given us a very finished picture not only of an Irish Saint, but of the Irish Church and people. Lismore, where this "sciolus" was spreading false doctrine about the Blessed Sacrament, might well be called the Maynooth of its day. It held so high a place in the ecclesiastical world that the priest Malachy, although trained in the school of Armagh, had sought further learning from the school of Lismore.

So many cherished memories linked Lismore with St. Malachy that it must have been a heartbreak to find its hallowed schools darkened by heresy. Yet truth, and especially the truth of faith, was always more to the Saint than the most hallowed memory.

We are grateful to St. Bernard for recording how this Legate of the Holy See had such compassion for a brother priest that *often* and *in secret* he sought to win him back to truth. Only when these secret frequent talks were unavailing did he take steps publicly to counter an evil which was publicly endangering the faith of the Irish Church. Biographers of the Saint have not yet, perhaps, seen the full significance of this first council summoned by the papal legate. At that council the Bishops and priests of Ireland uttered their traditional faith in the Real Presence of Jesus in the Holy Eucharist.

Let us here bestow on our readers a spray of Irish Fioretti as fair and fragrant as any of its Tuscan kindred. St. Bernard must say it in his own way:

> A man who in the world's sight was honorable, and in God's sight holy, came to Malachy. He sorrowed concerning the barrenness of his soul; and besought him to obtain from Almighty God the grace of tears.
>
> Then Malachy smiling because he was pleased there should be spiritual desire in a man of the world laid his own cheek on the cheek of the other as though caressing him and said: "Be it done unto you as you have besought."
>
> From that time rivers of water ran down his eyes, so full and so almost unceasing that the word of Holy Writ might seem applicable to him: A garden fount—a well of living waters.

Once on being asked where he would choose to die, he replied: "If I die here, I should do so nowhere more gladly than whence I may rise together with our apostle" (St. Patrick); "but if I must go abroad, then with God's leave I have chosen Clairvaux." On being further asked the day, he named All Souls'.

The man and the saint spoke in these desires. St. Patrick had been from childhood the hero by whose deeds he had shaped his life. He was shaping even his death and burial place after the manner of Ireland's apostle, for whom the grave in Downpatrick is burial in a foreign land.

Clairvaux, with its band of contemplative monks redeeming the soil and thereby redeeming their souls by divinely appointed toil, had appealed to him with the power of a crusade. His own ideal of Nazareth poverty—which anticipated the Poverello of Assisi—saw in Clairvaux something like realization.

And All Souls' Day—the Day of the Dead—bespoke the Western Gael who even as a young deacon had loved the dead with the lowly services of the burial spade!

Nothing was now left for the Saint but to set in order a few things of duty, and then answer his Master's summons of death.

Early in 1148 St. Malachy summoned a National Council at Patrick's Island, Skerries. Innocent II had promised that if such a Council asked for the palls to be given to the Sees of Armagh and Cashel they would be given. Although the Roman See was now occupied by Eugenius III, the promise of Innocent II was not likely to be unfulfilled. Eugenius III, a Cistercian and pupil of St. Bernard, had to flee from Rome and dwell in France, where he presided over a General Chapter of Cistercians at Clairvaux itself.

St. Malachy set out with the request of the National Council that the Sees of Armagh and Cashel should receive the archiepiscopal pall.

Two of the brethren were mouthpieces of the Bangor monks in making the Bishop promise he would once more return to Ireland. Though the promise was wrung from his affectionate heart under compulsion, God gave him to keep it. The boat he embarked in for Scotland was driven by wind and current to Blackcauseway, Strangford Lough. Close by was the chapel of Ballyculter, belonging to the monastery at Saul. It was holy ground. St. Patrick had landed there some seven centuries before; and there had died. God had arranged that the Saint of Down's last night in his beloved Ireland was spent where his mind was filled with hallowed memories of the apostle he loved in life and death. That night the two saints were nearer than men knew.

Through delays in England, where King Stephen was forbidding communications with France, St. Malachy was some months in reaching Clairvaux, where with God's courteous leave he had chosen to die.

St. Bernard's account of how St. Malachy came into their midst and died belongs to the classics not only of divine but of human love! Some day, perhaps in the near future, the scholars in the schools of Down will know it by heart in the sweetness of its original Burgundian Latin:

Though coming from the West he was received by us as the Day Star from on high that visited us. O how greatly did that shining sun fill our Clairvaux with added splendor. How gladsome was the festal day that opened upon us at his coming.

How swiftly and lightly I at once ran to him, though trembling and weak. How joyfully I showered kisses.[3] With what glad arms I embraced this dear one sent from God! With what eager look and soul, O my father, did I lead thee to the home of my mother and into the room of her that bore me!

What happy days I spent with thee, though few! and he with us? To all of us our guest showed himself always gay, always kindly: yea lovable to all beyond belief. . . .

Four or five days of this our feast had gone by when on the solemn day of St. Luke, Evangelist,[4] he had celebrated the Holy Mass before the community with great devotion, being taken with a fever he laid himself down; and we were with him.

Though the fever seemed to the brethren but light, the Saint told them smilingly that it was the beginning of the end!

He asked to be anointed. But when the brethren proposed to bring the Last Sacraments he rose from his sick bed in a far-off cell at the top of the house and walked unhelped to the church. Then having received the Last Sacraments he again walked back unhelped. It was the last journey of one who had worn himself out on foot in the service of his Master.

He assured us that death was at the threshold. Who would believe him a dying man? Only himself and God could have known it. His face seemed no paler nor thinner, his brow unfurrowed, his eyes not sunken, his nostrils not sharpened, his lips not contracted. Such was his fair body and his gracious countenance which even death did not destroy.

Toward evening on All Saints' Day all are around the bedside of the dying Saint. He thanks God who has heard his request to die where he is dying.

He sweetly consoled us, saying:

"Bear me in mind; I, if allowed, will not forget you. It will be allowed. I have believed God, and all is possible to him who believes. I have loved God; I have loved you; and charity never falleth away."

---

[3] Catullus has hardly a more daring phrase, "*Quam laetus in oscula rui.*"

[4] Oct. 18, 1148.

Then laying his hands on the head of each, he blessed them and bade them rest, "for his hour was not yet come". It was the ritual of death in Christ.

His hour came at midnight when All Saints' Day passes into All Souls'; and a shaft of light passes from the Church in bliss to the Church in pain:

> The house was filled—all the brethren—many Abbots who come hither.
>   With psalms and hymns and spiritual canticles we bear our friend company on his homeward way.[5]
>   In the fifty-fourth year of his age, at the time and place he had forechosen and foretold, MALACHY, BISHOP AND LEGATE OF THE HOLY APOSTOLIC SEE, as if an angel snatched from our hands, blissfully slept in the Lord.

St. Bernard's love for his dead friend expressed itself in his own poetic way. While the monks were washing the sacred body he changed St. Malachy's tunic for one of his own. Later on he wore this tunic of his dead friend whenever he chanted Mass on great feasts.

He himself sang the Requiem for St. Malachy. But for some reason which no question ever succeeded in unveiling he changed the Postcommunion prayer for the dead into the prayer for a Confessor Bishop: "O God, who has made the blessed Bishop Malachy equal in merits to thy saints, grant, we beseech thee, that we who celebrate the feast of his holy death may copy the example of his life. Amen." When he had finished the Mass, he went and kissed the feet of his dead friend! It was the canonization of a saint by a saint!

Another slender incident may well find a place among the Fioretti of St. Malachy. At some distance from the body of St. Malachy St. Bernard noticed a boy whose arm hung dead by his side.

"I beckoned him to draw near. The dead hand I applied to the hand of the Bishop, and he gave life to it. The boy had come from afar, and the arm he brought hanging he took back sound to his homeland." Between two Saints the boy's chance of cure was not a minimum!

A glimpse of St. Malachy's Celtic love of Our Lady is given in St. Bernard's simple words:

> And now when all had been rightly done Malachy was given unto burial
> in the chapel of the holy Mother of God, Mary, wherein he took such

---

[5] "*Prosequimur amicum repatriantem.*" The Doctor Mellifluus has a store of such phrases.

joy; the year of the Incarnation of the Lord, one thousand, one hundred and forty-eight, the second day of November.

Five years later St. Bernard, clad in the habit of his dead friend, was laid to rest in the same chapel of their beloved mother. Thus by God's good will, not only are the names of Bernard and Malachy one for all time, but through the befallings of time their very dust is indistinguishably one in a common tomb.

SAINT THOMAS
OF CANTERBURY

[*1118–1170*]

Hilaire Belloc

HE LIFE AND DEATH of Thomas à Becket, Archbishop of Canterbury, may be put in the phrase "Constancy and its Fruit". Now the fruit of constancy is not what the constant agent himself immediately desired. This is because man is a subordinate. He cannot fashion the future to his will; he is used by God.

Men are used. The purposes of God, which guide the universe, cannot be the purposes of one man. But if that one man's purpose is humble and direct, open and good (which means in unison with God's purpose), then he would rejoice at the fruit of his constancy. Though it should not be that which he had desired, it will be consonant with what he had desired. It will be found larger than what he had desired. It will be found more permanent than what he had desired. He will serve God in a sense unwittingly, though wittingly in purpose. But he will glorify God in the result.

Each man who has achieved, has achieved something other than he intended. Each man who has achieved, has achieved something in the same axis with, along the same direction, as his intention was—in proportion as his intention was good.

In the history of Western Europe the episode of the martyrdom at Canterbury is a capital example of constancy. It stands out the more vividly because, in that very place, in that very See, the purpose for which St. Thomas died has been conspicuously denied, ridiculed, frustrated, and (locally) destroyed.

The principle for which St. Thomas suffered martyrdom was this: That the Church of God is a visible single universal society, with powers superior to those of this world, and therefore of right, *autonomous*.

That principle is the negation of the opposite, of the base, ephemeral, thing already passing from Christian life, sometimes called pedantically "Erastianism"; the principle that the divine and permanent is subject to the human and passing power. St. Thomas died for the doctrine, the truth, that the link with eternal things must never be broken under the pressure of ephemeral desires, that the control of eternal things cannot, in morals, be subjected to the ephemeral arrangements of men.

But note this—that his constancy was exercised for a particular form in which that truth applied to the society of his own time. The specific detailed formula for which he laid down his life, later lost its meaning because in the perpetual flux of human arrangements words and conditions changed. The ultimate principle remained unchanged. He fought against an attempt of the civil power in his time to subject the Church of God to its jurisdiction in a particular fashion which since then has ceased to be of meaning. On which account it might be asked whether it were worth while for him to have fought at all. But he gained a victory for the essential principle, so that in his image one man after another arose (and shall in future arise) who have and will —God granting them grace—maintain that same principle: that the things of God are not subject to the judgment of men.

St. Thomas fought against what was in his time a certain innovation, but an innovation apparently so slight, certainly so subtle, and above all so convenient to the general spirit of the time, that it seemed—though an innovation—a piece of common sense which only an obdurate, fanatical man would resist: someone anchored in the past or wedded to a dead ancient formula. He fought against an innovation put forward in sixteen articles, called "The Constitutions of Clarendon"; of which sixteen articles many were tolerable enough, and all arguable, and every one which in one form or another has lapsed from the area of conflict into that of agreed things. The two conspicuous points upon which he resisted were: (1) the judgment by the civil courts of clerics of whatever rank when first accused of a crime—a privilege still existing in Canon Law but in practice everywhere abolished, and (2) the rule that there should be no appeals in spiritual matters to the sovereign pontiff without leave of the king. On this second point the position has been turned by the fact that the non-Christian modern governments (whatever may be true of the future) do not recognize the Supreme Pontiff, nor indeed any such thing as a spiritual court. So our appeals may go forward merrily enough, only Caesar does not admit any jurisdiction in the final court to which they are preferred—nor, as a rule, any matter for appeal. If I desire my marriage to be declared null I may appeal to Rome without leave of the state, because the state does not admit as yet in modern countries that Rome has jurisdiction in such affairs. And though Rome declare my marriage null I am, under Caesar's modern law, bigamous if I marry again, or (what is much more probable) if Rome declares me bound to my wife, I am no adulterer in Caesar's eyes if under Caesar's law I marry another.

How then can it be true that St. Thomas—having apparently technically succeeded by his constancy upon two points which even in his own time seemed to many dubious, and these points having in practice become devoid of any practical meaning today—achieved, and that his constancy bore fruit? In this way. That his heroic resistance prevented the assault of the temporal power against the eternal from being fatal at the moment when, precisely, it might have been fatal.

To put it bluntly, he saved the Church. He came, he was raised up, he was murdered for God, just at the moment which might have been the turn of the tide toward secularization. He checked it for four hundred years. The tide flowed on, but not to the complete destruction of Christian unity. The great intellectual and therefore skeptical movement of the twelfth century was prevented from disrupting Christendom; the tide flowed on, then slackened. The organization of the Church grew old, the arteries of its human organization hardened, by the end of the fifteenth century, more than 300 years after the killing of that man at Canterbury Cathedral, the time was ripe for a greater assault, and the assault was delivered. In part it conquered, but not *wholly*, as, but for St. Thomas, it might have done far earlier.

Fools or provincials would say that the last assault conquered altogether. It certainly has not done so. The extent of its conquest is still debatable. But had not St. Thomas died, even the occasion of this modern debate would not have arisen, for already, at the beginning of the great medieval spring, the Church would have failed.

That, in saving the Church, he saved society itself, was instinctively felt by the common people, through whose spontaneous piety Almighty God achieves his purposes more widely than through any other channel, save perhaps through the channel of individual holiness and courage. The common people, not the clergy (though it was to their interest) in a burst of enthusiasm imposed the worship of the martyr upon Christendom. They felt in their bones (and they were right) that if the laical state—the seeds of which were being sown—should once rise to maturity and complete power they would be what they have become today, half-way to slavery. The independence of the Church was the guarantee of their customs and of that spirit whereby Christian men grope toward, in part always enjoy, and necessarily and always proclaim, freedom. It required the imbecility of modern Dons to wonder why St. Thomas should have so suddenly become a popular saint—why Canterbury should have become one of the great shrines of Christendom and to decide that it was due to some odd mechanical conspiracy on the part of the priests! It was one of the most unplanned things that ever happened in history. It rose like a spring out of the earth exactly as, in a quite different field of spiritual appeal, there sprang in our own day the recognition of St. Thérèse of Lisieux: a young woman high among the Saints of God.

There is another major consideration in the matter of this great saint. Is it better to be direct or subtle? I mean, is it better for the purposes of God to be direct or subtle? Which is the better for one's own soul there can be no doubt. But is it better to be direct or subtle for the achievement of the Kingdom?

Now to that unending doubt there are, as to all unending doubts, two answers equally valid. For there are conditions under which to be subtle is essential, when, without subtlety, there is nothing but disaster, even in the matters of the soul; and there are also conditions under which (and this is more easily forgotten by the tortuous and fallen spirit of man) for the achievement of the Kingdom it is better to be direct and to challenge.

Were not the first method admissible human affairs, and therefore the affairs of God on earth, would be a chaos and would fail. But for those who ridicule the second method as something impossible or, what is worse to the intelligence, grossly insufficient, St. Thomas provides an example. it happened to be his business, it happened to be his duty, it happened to be his triumph, to be direct. As against the multiple, to be single; as against the diverse, to be absolute; as against maneuver, to charge.

There is yet another question arising from this great story. It is the

most searching question of all. "What about pride?" All challengers
suffer, of necessity, the temptation of pride. They are of the breed of
certitude and of simplicity; being simple and certain they will brook
no contradiction; they are as it were blindly convinced of the right
—and the right is their right. Now to make certain that you are always right is to put yourself in the position of God, and in so far as
you put yourself in the position of God you are suffering from the
weakness and nastiness of pride. These protagonists have always been
accused of that fatal flaw in themselves. What is much more important
for the comprehension of their very selves, they have always been at
least *tempted* to it: now a permanent temptation is part of character, but
by the Grace of God it is not necessarily a mastering part.

It is true, then, that all the great protagonists have had pride for a
companion. To yield to it is their temptation, but it is a constitutional
tendency and not a motive of their energy. They are sure. None shall
deflect them. Yet their object being something outside themselves, they
have in them a solvent of the evil thing; and I will believe that those
who appear before the throne of God after heavy battles in the right
cause, yet clouded with too much opinion, will have it easily forgiven
them; especially if they have been defeated in the battles of the Lord.

Yet let this also be noted: that the instruments which are chosen for
work of this kind, those of the Tertullian spirit, cannot but be of that
human sort which is imperfect through aggression and assertiveness
and edge. They are sent out to dig like chisels; they must of necessity offend on that against which they act; for every permanent work
is done in hard material and against the grain. Were they not what
they are, nothing would be achieved for the Kingdom—or, at least, all
would be only half done.

If these things be so (and they are so) let us consider the process
whereby this great saint came to his glory.

What we today call England, a certain unmistakable unit, a nation,
was created by the success of the Bastard William of Falaise, called
"The Conqueror", when he confirmed by arms his claim to rule the
country. (The word "conquest" is deceptive. There was in his day no
modern idea of the violent unjust rape of one territory by the people
of another—but to discuss all that would take too long.) What we call
England was made, grew from, began, upon a Sussex hill in 1066. Not
that the blood which we call English began then and (God knows) not

the landscape nor the deep things which inhabit the native soul. All these are immemorial; the English imagination, the English humor, the English Englishry is from the beginning of recorded time. The pirate invasions from the "Angulus" or Bight of Denmark, their few colonies on the eastern coast, never profoundly affected this island. Nor is language a guide. But just when Europe was turning to a crystalization of nations out of that circling cauldron of the Dark Ages, England also was crystalized; and it was the Norman influence which precipitated her thus from a boiling into a crystalization. The process had not gone on a lifetime when St. Thomas was born.

We do not know the exact date of his birth. It was almost certainly between fifty and fifty-five years after the decisive battle which put the Bastard of Normandy, William, upon the throne of Westminster. It is thought that the year 1118 may be the most probable guess. St. Thomas was born in London, in Cheapside, at the end of December, the son of a London merchant, who had begun business upon the other side of the channel in Rouen, and had there secured wealth. It was a time when, for now nearly a hundred years past, the directing classes of England had been more and more mixed with the Continent and in which they had more and more come to be French-speaking—as must have been St. Thomas himself and all his people. The distinction between the gentry and merchants had not rearisen (it is the nature of society, and crops up period after period). His father was of gentle blood in the sense that the family had been territorial in Normandy, nor did St. Thomas ever feel himself to be other than the equal of those with whom he mixed. He was a huge powerful young man, good at every bodily exercise, a fighter on horseback; he certainly had ambition, and he was helped therein by those through whom he rose. He was of a world alive and eager, and after his first advancements, partly perhaps through the wealth of his father, much through the recognition of his abilities, and more from the protection of the first man in the kingdom, the Archbishop of Canterbury, who promoted him, he rose. He took the Plantagenet side in the days when the young Plantagenet heir who was to be Henry II, at least ten years younger than himself, came by certain accidents to be the King of England. This Henry II of England sprang from the famous house of Anjou; packed with vitality, showing sparse red hair, intense, violent, exact; and the two men of similar energy became closely bound together.

Now this Henry II of England, this new king of the new Angevin stock, great-grandson of William the Conqueror, married the divorced wife of the King of France. She was the heiress of all the West and the South, and her young husband became not only King of England but, under a sort of feudal homage, real ruler beyond Normandy (which he had inherited on the English side), also of all the South and West of the French kingdom. He was thus in his active and battling youth possessed of a greater recruiting field and a greater revenue than the French King, his Sovereign; and upon his will the future of Europe would largely depend. Therefore St. Thomas as his bosom friend and fellow-in-arms stood out also before Christendom. Thomas fought for his junior, the king, during the expedition into Southern France in 1159, seven years after Henry's accession; he became glorious through a single combat with another man, saddle to saddle; he was the soldier of his day. His young master and friend determined to make him his all-sufficient minister, the title of such in that day being "Chancellor".[1] That young determined king of so much, and lord of half the West, did more for him. Henry being thirty years of age and St. Thomas about or over forty, the king determined to make him Archbishop of Canterbury, and thereby to make him also the first man in the kingdom.

It is essential to understand what this meant. In theory the monks of Canterbury could elect their Archbishop; in practice for centuries, the king really nominated him.

The Church throughout the West was one body; the English province of the Church—or rather the two provinces of the Church in England, York and Canterbury—had been but part, for four hundred years at least, of Western Christendom. The unity of the Church had survived an anxious disruptive period after the death of Charlemagne more than three hundred years before, when, for the better part of two centuries, all manner of disturbances and quarrels had threatened to overwhelm Christendom. In that interlude—that interregnum as it were of our civilization—all manner of disruptive forces threatened us. The Muslims who had swept over half Christendom perpetually attacked in the South; Mongol and Slav Pagans from the East; Scandi-

---

[1] The term, though preserved, has of course nothing in common with the modern title of Lord Chancellor, which applies to some chance lawyer or other who has worked his way through Parliament.

navians from the North; the great landowners made themselves masters over their districts, and there survived of the imperial authority almost nothing, of local royal authority very little. The revenues of the Church, fixed in ancient endowments of land, fell in part a prey to the great families. But the structure of society held fast; the Mass, the Liturgy, the hierarchy, the framework—clerical and lay—stood.

About a hundred years before St. Thomas' birth the energies of Christendom began to raise a new dawn; and for that century those energies proceeded to a rapid extension of architecture and letters and learning. We have the vast adventure of the Crusades; we have the revivified powers of the Papacy, always admitted and always in the very nature of society, but now to be fully exercised. With all this there went a new discipline throughout the Church; the enforcement of the long lapse in the matter of celibacy and an increasing clarity in the organization which would bind Christendom together. But at the same time there came necessarily, with greater wealth and clearer thinking and more eager ambitions, the growth of power in the Princes—of whom Henry II of England was among the very first.

It was in such a conjuncture, with the power of the Pope now well and consciously organized, with all Christendom knowing that on it, and the full society of the Church in hierarchy below it, the future would depend—for that civilization was at stake in a rising quarrel between the independent universal Church and the local magnates—it was just at such a crisis that "Thomas of London" as he signed himself, was, on the insistence of his companion-in-arms and deep friend, the young man Henry, put into the See of Canterbury.

He was consecrated on Sunday, June 3, 1162, to the See which his old patron had occupied and which had been vacant for a year. It was a Sunday which St. Thomas in memory of the event turned into that Feast of the Trinity, the name of which has been preserved ever since. We must never forget that it was from Canterbury that the Feast of the Trinity proceeded, as did that other solemn Catholic custom, the Elevation of the Host after consecration at Mass.[2]

---

[2] Landfranc, St. Thomas' chief predecessor and first Archbishop of Canterbury in the new England, was the great defender of the Real Presence, when the first doubts began to be cast upon it in France during his youth, and in reparation, or by way of especial homage, he would hold the Host reverently in his hands after consecration, lifting it somewhat in front of his face, and it seems that it was from this gesture that the full Elevation developed.

Immediately upon St. Thomas' elevation to the throne of Canterbury the inevitable clash between his strong character and the strong character of his junior, his close friend, his king appeared. For St. Thomas, authoritative, determined and always laying upon himself a clear course and always holding a clear definition both of his rights, but still more of his duty, was now the unquestioned head of the Church in England, and the Church was not a part of the State, was not indeed a *part* of Christendom; it was the *soul* of Christendom, superior to any local government and independent of any temporal government, not only in all that concerned doctrine but in all that concerned its own discipline and personnel.

With the awakening of a new and greater civilization in this twelfth century and with the revival of the old doctrines of imperial right under the lay imperial code of the Roman Empire this superior, intangible, autonomous character of the Church was challenged. An effort could not but arise on the part of the lay power to make the Church within that power more and more subordinate to the earthly monarch of the realm. England, the best organized state of the time, and Henry its King, now lord of Normandy and all Western France as well, Henry, who was upon the whole the strongest monarch in Christendom, still young (little over thirty) and of a fiery energy, could not but move as he did. He began an attempted control over that part of the universal Church which lay within his frontiers. Had he at once and wholly succeeded the disaster, which was as a fact postponed for four hundred years, would have begun in the twelfth instead of the sixteenth century and—what is much more important than a mere postponement—it would have been universal, it would have affected the whole structure of the Church and condemned that structure to decay; it would not have been a mere division of Christendom, leaving a Catholic portion saved and sound, but a sapping of the vital principle of Christendom throughout Europe.

The moment for the revolutionary change proposed by this first Plantagenet was after a fashion inevitable, for it corresponded to another change which had come upon the Church itself. The main body of the Church officials, the "clerics", from its earliest days to the close of the dark ages, was composed of the hierarchy: priests and bishops. Less than the priests, but usually on their way to becoming priests, were the deacons and subdeacons. There were also many who were in lesser orders and were still called "clerics", though not, properly speaking, of the sacred hierarchy. The general tone was given by the priest, he was the *typical* cleric; the lesser clerics were only a fringe. The determining number which gave its color and tone to the mass of ecclesiastics, those who would be generally recognized under the term "clergy", were the fully qualified priests who alone could consecrate and offer up the sacrifice of the Mass. The great bulk of them were settled as parish priests, though there was also a large number who were unattached, candidates for endowment who had not yet received it and might never receive it.

Now at the end of the Dark Ages and the first stirrings of the high Medieval civilization, that is, with those last years of the tenth century when it was clear that Europe had saved herself from barbarian and Muslim pressure and the great siege was at an end; when one reform after another, each more thorough than the last, was leading up through more than a lifetime of effort to the Cluniac movement and at last to the glorious achievement of St. Gregory VII, when the origins of the Crusades had appeared in Spain, when a new culture was beginning in the schools and an administration more and more developed in the local courts, the clerical members were vastly increased.

They were so increased *not* by the addition of a great number of new priests, but by a great number of new men whose activities were secular, though they were tonsured and affiliated to the clerical body. These kept the accounts, they studied and systematized the old and new laws, they were the writers, the negotiators and the calculators; they filled the growing mass of minor posts which the new civilization had produced; they fulfilled nearly all the duties which could not be fulfilled either by the fighting class or by those who cultivated the soil, or by the artisans. It is from this great mass of non-priestly but clerical men that there has been derived our word "clerk", and in general the identification of the word "clerical" with the whole business of writing. Those who taught were clerics, most of those who negotiated between princes were clerics, those who looked after papers of public or private wealth were clerics.

The consequence was that the State was now—by 1162—newly faced with the presence of a new vast clerical body, fulfilling the functions and liable to the temptations and accidents of the layman. It was newly faced with thousands of individuals who were technically part of the clerical—that is to say, the Church—organization, and therefore amenable only to the Church law and the Church courts, and yet in daily avocation what today we should call laymen.

This state of affairs was not only the excuse, but in part the cause of the king's novel attempt: but he made no distinction between the various parts of the clerical body, and if his policy had won, any priest, however exalted his position, would have fallen (as he has fallen in modern times) under the lay power. The medieval autonomy of the Church would have disappeared, and with it, soon, religion and the unity of Christendom.

In the first year after the new Archbishop had been enthroned the great quarrel broke out. At Woodstock, in that royal manor on the land which was later made over to Marlborough as a reward for Blenheim, the king published "The Constitutions of Clarendon". Here we must note very carefully what these were and—a very different thing—what they purported to be.

The document purported to be "a record of recognition" of his grandfather's (Henry I) *customs* in Church matters, the *accepted* Church law of the realm. It is of the first importance to mark that. There was no admitted innovation. Such an idea would have been abhorrent to the time. The only test of right was custom; and to effect this beginning of revolution a pretense had to be made that it was an old custom which was being claimed and which furnished the moral basis for the action which the king proposed to take. But the thing was a falsehood. Although the document includes in its sixteen clauses not a few customs which had indeed tradition behind them, it also contains two of the utmost moment, both of which were revolutionary. These two clauses were the third and the eighth, and it is interesting to note the subtlety with which those who served the king attempted to give to a novelty (and subversive novelty at the time) an excuse.

The eighth clause lays it down that no ecclesiastical appeal could be carried beyond the king's court (that is, to Rome) without leave of the king. Appeal could be made from the archdeacon to the bishop, from the bishop to the archbishop, and from the archbishop to the king, but the further appeal to Rome was declared to be against custom and right save when it was especially permitted by the Crown. Observe here this question of the old custom and right, at any rate since the Conquest. The Crown had claimed, the Church had never admitted, the right to prevent *recorded pronouncements* passing into or out of the kingdom without the royal leave. Thus a Papal Bull could not be introduced into England after the Conquest save by leave of the king; but it had never been admitted, I say, as a moral right by the Church: it could not be so, for to admit it would be to make the unity of the Church dependent upon the will of a local sovereign. It had been a custom of force and not of agreement between the two separate powers. But this new eighth clause in the Constitutions of Clarendon said something quite different. It said that there was no constitutional right of appeal from English ecclesiastical courts to Rome; they laid it down that *custom* so deemed; and so to lay down the custom was a falsehood.

Much more important in practice (because in practice appeals would have constantly been allowed anyway) was the third clause of the sixteen, which was the one round which in reality all the battle was to rage. By this clause the personnel of the Church, the members of that international and supernational body coincident with the Papal authority and with all Western Christendom, was to be treated—in this realm at least—as the laymen were treated, and to be regarded in the administration as subjects of the king, and not as officers of a universal church. Hitherto any cleric accused of a crime could be tried by his ecclesiastical superiors only. They could for a grave crime degrade him, were he to offend again he would then be tried of course as a layman, his privilege of clergy had gone. But the principle was clear and universal, that while he was still a cleric he was amenable to clerical jurisdiction alone.

The introduction of this capital revolution was effected, as I have said, with great subtlety of phrase. "Clerics accused in any matter" (it ran) "being summoned by the king's justice and the Ecclesiastical Court, it may be seen what matter should be replied to in that Court . . . so that the king's justice shall send into the Court of Holy Church to see for what reason the matter is being dealt with there. And if the cleric be convicted or shall confess, he should not further be protected by the Church."

This is on the face of it much more tentative and much more of a compromise than we are usually told in our textbooks, where we are informed that the king proposed purely and simply to take jurisdiction out of the Church's hands. The form of words was such that a well-meaning ecclesiastical authority might be deceived and that men too timid to resist might salve their consciences.

It was clear that the intention was—it would at any rate soon be made the effect of such a clause—that clerics accused of a crime should in practice be withdrawn from ecclesiastical jurisdiction and treated as laymen. But it might be argued from the form of words that all that was going to happen was a courteous discussion between the lay and ecclesiastical power as to what the man was had up for, and whether it really did concern the Church, etc., etc. It is of capital importance to remember this in the story of what follows.

This document containing these revolutionary proposals, the Constitutions of Clarendon (it is a short thing, less than 2,000 words in length) is drawn up in the form in which it had been assented to by the magnates of the kingdom, including the bishops, and at the head of the list of those who assented was the name and title of Thomas, Archbishop of Canterbury, the first man in the realm and the head of the English province of the Church Universal. *The Constitutions were accepted.* The lay lords accepted them of course, but so did the bishops, and (possibly under a verbal misunderstanding) the Pope.

St. Thomas himself accepted them, but he had already grasped the core of the matter; he accepted grievously and with grave reluctance after a delay of three days, saying that he must obey the Pope, but that such obedience was compelling him to perjury—meaning presumably that he never could in practice agree to the changes proposed. All had begun in the summer of the year after St. Thomas' enthronement as Archbishop, in the month of July, 1163. In October a Council at Westminster confirmed the Constitutions. But the resistance of St. Thomas was beginning. When the bishops agreed, they had only agreed (presumably under St. Thomas' influence) with the clause added, "saving our order". The bishops in their turn had influenced St. Thomas in his agreement as late as January of the next year, 1164, when all the great of the realm were again summoned to Clarendon.

But St. Thomas believed that he had acted like St. Peter; his conscience would not let him rest, and Henry knew that it would soon be open war between them.

He saw the Archbishop twice, he understood what resistance he was to be prepared for, and he summoned for the October of that year (1164) another great council at Northampton. Instead of sending a special summons to the first man of the realm—the Archbishop and Primate—he sent for him by orders to the officers of the County of

Kent, a planned belittling, and an insult to one whom he now regarded as an enemy.

St. Thomas came to that great meeting, and was there an isolated man. He appeared in the outer hall, with his huge figure standing out above them all, grasping his Cross in his own hand instead of having it borne before him, as though for a symbol that he alone, Thomas the individual soul, was standing out with none to befriend him or support him.

The bishops of England, some of whom were his personal enemies, but most of whom at heart knew that he was doing right, begged him to yield. He retorted by solemnly telling them that it was *their* duty to obey *his* authority.

The quarrel grew fiercer, Henry forbade an appeal to Rome, and told the council to denounce the saint for a traitor. The king's attitude was modified for a moment through the hesitation of the bishops, when they saw how grave the matter had become; he allowed the appeal to Rome, but he carried out a policy of violent financial persecution, demanding huge sums from the See of Canterbury upon various pleas of chicanery; and on All Souls' Day of that year (1164) St. Thomas secretly sailed from Sandwich to take refuge upon the Continent, to see the supreme Pontiff of Christendom in person and to be free from the peril of direct constraint. Before the end of November he had seen Pope Alexander III at Sens. He laid at the feet of the Papal authority two things; the text of the Constitutions against which he was holding out, and his archiepiscopal ring—tender of which meant that he was willing, or rather anxious, to resign his See and so leave the decision to his successor, and the Pope free.

At this point we must particularly regard the attitude taken by Alexander III, the Pope of the day. It can be too much excused, but it can also be maligned.

Alexander III was one of the great political Popes who have, in the Providence of God, been preservative of Catholic political power in the world. He was engaged in a struggle against the greatest of the Emperors, Barbarossa, and was defending not only the liberties of Rome and the Church, but of the Italian cities. The Emperor and his Germans had set up against him an anti-pope, and Alexander was at this moment in France because he was virtually exiled from Italy by the strength of his opponent. It was of the highest moment that so powerful a king

as Henry should not join forces with the new German schism. Anyhow, whether he is to be praised upon the whole or blamed, the Pope,
deliberately considering all the circumstances, chose to temporise. He
would not allow St. Thomas to resign; he said that the Constitutions
of Clarendon were not to be accepted as a whole, but that six of them
were acceptable—"tolerable" was the word—that is, to be accepted
if necessary. In general his support of St. Thomas was lukewarm. He
aimed at a reconciliation, and what is more, it seems that he still thought
the issue to be only a verbal one, a question of formulation, of interpretation. If that were so, he was wrong and St. Thomas was right;
it was not a verbal matter but a matter of vital principle, as the event
would certainly show if ever the proposed changes were accepted.

There followed for years a swaying struggle, in which at moments
St. Thomas was nearly reconciled to Henry—on condition of course
that he was not made to accept the obnoxious thing—in the course
of which Henry nearly yielded twice, but also in the course of which
there were moments of acute tension and almost of violence. Thus,
when St. Thomas took refuge with the Cistercians at Pontigny, Henry
threatened in revenge to expel all the Cistercians from England. Toward the end of those uncertain years of St. Thomas' exile Henry went
so far as to have his young son crowned by St. Thomas' especial enemy, the Archbishop of York, Roger de Pont l'Eveque—although the
Primate alone had the right to crown the kings or heirs of England. To
meet the threats that were taking place against ecclesiastical property
and the usurpations of his enemies in his absence St. Thomas began
to issue excommunications. He had even threatened that if Henry did
not amend before Candlemas of the year 1170 he would be put under
an interdict. It was in the June of that year that Henry committed the
blunder and the outrage of having his young son crowned by Roger of
York, though not only St. Thomas but the Pope himself had forbidden
such action. The king feared he had gone too far, and began to go
back. A few weeks later, at Frétéval, he was so far reconciled that he
promised to be guided by the Archbishop's counsel, and to keep silent
upon the whole revolutionary policy of ecclesiastical jurisdiction. He
even openly proposed to return to England in the company of St.
Thomas. But he delayed, and made shifts for further delay, until at the
end of the year, in the November of 1170, St. Thomas proceeded to
the final actions which culminated in his martyrdom.

It was proposed to send the saint back to his See, the property of which was to be restored and the administration put again into his hands; but as a sort of warder over him during the journey was set John of Oxford, a notorious enemy with whom he would not have been safe, and he learned that Roger of York and the Bishops of London and Salisbury, who were also especially opposed to him, were plotting to prevent his landing. St. Thomas had obtained from the Pope letters inhibiting and conditionally excommunicating those who opposed the Primate. He sent these letters across the Channel in advance of himself, dispatching them on Sunday, November 29, while he sailed on Monday, November 30, from Wyssant—the little port between Calais and Boulogne then often used—and on the next day, Tuesday, December 1, he landed at Sandwich and proceeded to his palace and cathedral at Canterbury. He there reiterated his position again fully and awaited whatever results might follow from his firmness. Those against whom he had moved the Pope to act demanded unconditional absolution. He replied that he must await the Pope's further letters. And they proceeded to the king in order to lodge their appeal. Meanwhile, the property of the See was not restored, as had been promised, and to the burning indignation of the Archbishop, the immediate lands of the archbishopric were in the hands of robbers and despoilers, notably a lawless brigand of a fellow, De Broc, who had seized one of the archiepiscopal castles, Saltwood, and was making it a nest of robbers.

On Friday, Christmas Day, St. Thomas excommunicated De Broc, and four days later—Tuesday, December 29—appeared those four knights who had acted upon the king's passionate words, and were ready to slay. They bade St. Thomas absolve the bishops. He was steadfast, and refused. It was the afternoon of that winter day, and the sun was already sinking, when they came back armed and with them De Broc, determined to save his booty and to that end to extract his own absolution by force. In the presence of these five men, now armed, the monks dragged their great master with them into the cathedral, through the cloisters by the north door. They would have barred the door, but St. Thomas forbade them to do so. The light was now failing and the great church was half in darkness when the armed murderers burst in by that north door. All fled save one Grim, who stood by his master, holding the Archbishop's Cross in his hand. The swords were drawn, and with one of them the Archbishop's cap was struck off.

He knelt upon the stone floor of the North Transept, not far from
the corner pillar thereof where one turned into the Ambulatory round
the Choir. So kneeling he covered his face with his hands. He was
no longer throwing back angrily into the teeth of his opponents the
insults they had given him: he saw that death was upon him. And as
he so knelt, with his hands before his face, he murmured, "To God
and Blessed Mary, to the patron Saints of this Church and St. Denis
I commend myself and the cause of the Faith." He bowed his head
and awaited the blow. The first that struck was Fitzurse; Grim put up
his hand to shield his master, but his arm was broken and the sword
gashed that master's head. Another blow followed, and he fell. A third
cut off the crown of the skull and with the sword's point the brains
were scattered upon the stones. Then, having done these things, they
left the body where it lay and fled out into the now dark winter air.

Those few moments of tragedy in the North Transept of Canterbury
had done what so many years of effort had so far failed to do. The
whole movement against the autonomy of the Church was stopped
dead. The tide ran rapidly backward—within an hour St. Thomas was
a martyr, within a month the champion not only of religion but of
the common people, who obscurely but firmly knew that the independence of the Church was their safeguard. A tale of miracles began,
and within a year the name of St. Thomas of Canterbury was standing
permanently above and throughout Christendom. Everywhere there
were chapels and churches raised to his name, and then came the great
uninterrupted pilgrimages to his shrine year after year, till it rivaled St.
James of Compostella, becoming the second great center in the West
and loaded with gems and gold and endowment.

~

SAINT LAURENCE O'TOOLE

[*1128–1180*]

C. P. Curran

 N 1128 when Lorcan O Tuathail was born scarcely more than a day's march from Dublin, the seat of his future See was to him and his people an almost foreign city. It had been a Norse town for nearly three hundred years. It had grown to be the convenient center of a maritime Norse state which stretched from the Orkneys to Waterford exercising sovereignty at times over Northumbria and Man. Olafs and Sitrics minted their own coins there with the title "High King of the Northmen of Ireland and England". The eleventh century city of "gold, silver, hangings and all precious things" grew steadily in wealth during the twelfth century but was shrinking in political importance. Its dream of a Norse hegemony was over; its kings had dwindled to ruling jarls who were beginning to adopt Gaelic patronymics and to own the real or nominal overlordship of Ard Ri, or Leinster King as the central sovereignty waxed or waned. In this see-saw of power where also the fortunes of the saint's family fluctuated, the city was gradually falling into the national rhythm but in many essentials its people were still a Norse and not an Irish community; a seafaring, trading folk living within walls with their ships lying up along the Stein, meeting in assembly at the Thing-mote, ruled by bishops who looked to Canterbury and not to Armagh, worshipping in Christ Church founded by Sitric beside which Hasculf the Jarl had his stone mansion, or in churches dedicated to overseas saints, St. Mary's of the Ostmen, St. Olaf's or St. Michan's.

The bishops, as we have said, looked to Lanfranc, Anselm or Ralph rather than to the successors of St. Patrick. The Norse of Dublin owed their Christianity to the Anglo-Saxons. They saw England a great Christian and Danish Monarchy under Canute. When the Conqueror landed

they recognized the Northman cousinship and so grew up an orientation of which Lanfranc and his successors were not slow to take advantage in the interest of Church reform and enlarged jurisdiction.

Thirty miles south of this city of conflicting tendencies Glendalough
lay in the heart of the Wicklow mountains, the "quiet habitation of
sanctity and literature" to use Dr. Johnson's phrase, though in truth it
had been plundered and burnt by Norse or by accident already some
thirteen times. Across the hills to the west lay the plains of Kildare
where—probably near Castledermot—Lorcan was born. His mother
was an O'Byrne, his father O Tuathail, on both sides a princely stock.
To be the descendant of kings is in Ireland to be in the way of humorous commonplace. None the less the vitality of some of these old
stocks is worth observing. The Ui Neill, for example, maintained an
independent principality for fifteen hundred years down to the flight of
the Great Earl in 1607 throwing out repeatedly and indeed in our own
day foremost men in the State. So also we find a recurring outcrop of
notable names in the family of St. Lorcan to the present occupant of
his See. It is not to be supposed that the vigor of such a stock counted
for nothing in the shaping of a saint.

When he was born his family had been ousted from their ancient
throne and Dermot MacMurrough was the representative of the usurp-
ing line. Giraldus has painted the portrait of this great-limbed, violent
man whose voice was hoarse with much shouting in battle, an enemy
of his own people and hated by strangers, whose hand was against every
man and every man's hand against his. Between Dermot and Lorcan's
father there was that brooding hostility which seeks guarantees. The
king's hand fell heavy on the son who was sent to him, a ten-year-old
hostage, to Ferns. Less ill used than his sister who was later given to
the king in marriage, Lorcan was sent in bonds away from the king's
house to a "stony and barren region" where first he practiced by necessity those austerities which were later his by choice. There he passed
two years in sordid misery until rescued from the king's hands by his
father's threats of speedy reprisals. The Bishop of Glendalough was the
mediator and the young Lorcan was sent across the hills to him who
first introduced him in St. Kevin's sanctuary to the quiet recollected-
ness of Christian life and studies. His father arriving in a few days
and, proposing to dedicate one of his sons to the service of God and
St. Kevin, the saint's biographer relates how he desired the Bishop to

cast lots between his sons to this end. *Laurentius risisse fertur*, the only laugh recorded in his dolorous life, *non opus est, pater, sortium jactatione*. He himself would most willingly choose God as his inheritance. And accordingly he enters the novices' school where he is invested by his biographer with the student's proper virtues: eager to hear, careful in repetition, prudent in judgment, solicitous to hold tenaciously what he has heard. In Glendalough he remains, novice, monk and abbot for the next twenty-two years, shaping himself in what its great school, the austere beauty of the mountains and lakes, and the needs of the people about them would teach him of the spiritual life, of Christian learning and the handling of men.

The Valley of Glendalough is the deep reservoir which fed St. Lorcan's actions. This man who spent the rest of his life in cities, passing between armed camps, arranging between contending kings and living among strangers the external life of negotiation had as his *point d'appui* a rock overhanging a dark mountain lake. In the sixth century a narrow cavern set in this rock and difficult of access drew St. Kevin to Glendalough with its promise of solitude and anchoretic severities. The anchorite's cell multiplied into the monastic hive. The valley became a university settlement, an ecclesiastical city, the seat of a diocese, made splendid with a cathedral, towers and churches which still constitute one of the remarkable ecclesiastical groups of Western Europe. In the twelfth century, when Lorcan went there, it still guarded an unimpaired tradition. The spirit of the cell still animated it and became his own. Lorcan's character was annealed in the ascetic training of the early Irish Church whose austerities would seem fabulous if they were not well authenticated. He stood in the direct line of descent from St. Kevin and the early anchorites. When, therefore, in his later years as Archbishop of Dublin he returned, as his habit was, to spend Lent in St. Kevin's Bed—the *spelunca de deserto*—and on the rocky shelf beneath it where still stands the ruins of Teampull na Sceilg, he was only adding the joys of lonely contemplation—*contemplativas delicias*—to austerities which had become part of his normal life.

The typical Irish monastery was a school of asceticism, of psalmody and of ecclesiastical science. But it was also, in a degree peculiar to early Ireland where the Abbot overshadowed the Bishop, the spiritual center of the countryside. The monastery was not the monk's refuge from a wicked world but his sally-port. The abbot stood in as close relationship as the chief to the population outside the monastic community and on his special plane had need of all the qualities of leadership. Coming of a ruling stock it is not surprising that Lorcan rose so quickly to the Abbotship to which *clero et populo id postulantibus* he was elected in 1153 when only twenty-five years of age. His tenure of office gave him the widest exercise in the art of ruling men. Within the household he had to reckon with the envy and malice provided by his early elevation; without the enclosure he had distress to alleviate in the mountainy lands, south, west and north, which gave precarious support to the population and he had to ensure peace and order along roads harassed by robbers. The ecclesiastical city was in his charge whose temporalities were richer than the Bishop's. His unbounded charity first becomes known during a famine which marked the beginning of his office. Into its relief he flung, not only the monastic resources of the monastery, but also his father's fortune, ministering to the poor, the Latin text notes, as a servant rather than as a prelate. He spent freely on Church building and from this period dates the beautiful priory of St. Saviour's at the eastern end of the valley. After four years of office his spiritual stature was so plainly evident that men sought to make him Bishop of Glendalough. He put the proposal aside not as the historian Lanigan maliciously suggests on the ground that holy men do not ambition bishoprics but pleading his non-canonical age. For ten years the administration of the monastery engaged his zeal and charity; he was in touch with the great reform synod of Kells in 1152 and one finds his name subscribed in 1161 to the Charter of the new Augustinian foundation at Ferns where years later the fugitive king Dermot, its founder, sought a monk's disguise when deserted by his kinsmen and friends. In the same year Gregory, the Archbishop of Dublin, died and Lorcan was elected in his place and was consecrated in 1162 in Christ Church in Dublin by Gelasius of Armagh, the Primate, in the presence of his suffragan Bishops.

The consecration was as significant in the history of the Irish Church as it was in his personal life. The predecessors of the new Archbishop, two of them schooled in Canterbury and St. Alban's, had in many cases received their consecration from Canterbury and professed obedience to that see. The vicissitudes of his immediate predecessor are evidence of the racial and ecclesiastical jealousies which his election allayed and the manner of his consecration is signal testimony to that new consol-

idation of the National Hierarchy which was a principal object of the
Irish Reform movement of the twelfth century.

Reform had been urgent for two reasons. The Norse had raided and
plundered the Abbeys for nearly two hundred years. Under their blows
the monastic system had given way over great portions of the country
and in spite of a growing concentration in certain centers, Armagh,
Derry, Kells, Clonmacnoise and Kildare, Christian morale had weakened. In the monasteries the Abbot or *comarba* who ruled as heir of
the saintly founder was commonly a layman. Ireland in the eleventh
century was as the Continent in the tenth. Rome inspired by Cluniac
ideals, as Dr. Kenney observes, had struggled successfully against the
absorption of the Church into the feudal system. In Ireland the reformers had to struggle against its absorption into the Irish system.
The vices of laicization were rampant. The temporalities of even the
primatial see of Armagh remained for generations in lay hands. There
was a collateral necessity to organize according to the hierarchic rule of
Christendom a Church which had forgotten diocesan organization and
episcopal control. The authority of bishop, archbishop, and primate
had to be defined and established upon a territorial basis. The Norse
wars being over, Irishmen resumed their close contact with Rome and
a Europe afire with the spirit of Gregorian reform, and to their eyes
these abuses and anachronisms with other canonical and liturgical backslidings became intolerable. In this matter, as Dr. Kenney states, inspiration, advice, example may have come from abroad, but the driving
force which effected the ecclesiastical revolution was from within the
Irish Church. Behind every reform movement there stands a saint. In
Ireland, as the preceding paper has shown, the saint was Malachy, having as precursors Cellach of Armagh and Gilbert of Limerick. Their
movement, carried on from synod to synod beginning with Rath Bre-
sail in 1111, achieved its main purpose in the Synod of Kells in 1152,
when among other decisions the sees of Dublin and Tuam were erected
to Archbishoprics and the number and limits of the present dioceses
were substantially fixed. Minor outstanding disciplinary reforms were
completed in subsequent synods held in 1162, 1167, and 1172, all of
which were attended by our Archbishop.

In this movement which had come to a head when Lorcan was still
in Glendalough, Dublin played only a subordinate if not indeed a passive part. But as a Norse town, standing apart like Norse Waterford

and Limerick, it presented the useful example of an already clearly defined diocese with a diocesan administration independent of monastery or comarb. Unlike, however, Gilbert of Limerick, who owed no allegiance to Canterbury, and Malchus of Waterford who quickly shifted his to Armagh, some of its Bishops had professed obedience to Lanfranc, Anselm and Ralph who were nothing loath to use the town as the bridge head of an assumed jurisdiction. With the gradual assimilation of Dublin to Ireland this assumption of authority could not fail to be questioned. Already in 1121 Cellach of Armagh had gone into possession of the see of Dublin "by the choice of the Foreigners and the Gael" and when Gregory was set up by a rival party and consecrated by Ralph of Canterbury, Gregory was unable immediately to occupy his see and had to return to England to be maintained there during the rest of Ralph's life.

This is, therefore, the significance of Lorcan's consecration by the Primate in Dublin. He was the first Irishman to be so consecrated and the last for many centuries. For it was his tragic destiny to have been the pledge of Norse-Irish union under the national monarchy and to witness the dissolution of both under a new invasion.

So, at any rate, Lorcan came from the inland valley of the two lakes to the metropolis with its crowded harbor. He whose frontiers were mountains was now penned within a walled town, exchanging the cloister for its chattering streets where he must have heard as much Norse, Norman-French and English spoken among its merchant folk as his own Irish. The integrity of his outer life is split. He moves henceforward perpetually between opposites, between Gael and Gall, Norse and Norman, King Ruaidri and King Henry. The other worldly man must put on the man of affairs, the monk-bishop become a politician, almost a soldier. He might lament like St. Bernard: "I am become the chimera of my century, neither cleric nor layman." We know the hot vehemence with which St. Bernard fused these contradictions and we are similarly still aware *post annorum multa curricula* of the saintly charm with which Lorcan drew the exigencies of his outer and inner life into harmony. In the few sentences of his biographer, confirmed by the less ornate surviving testimony of his bones, we perceive a man *elegantis staturae*, of tall stature and graceful bearing, carrying with seemly dignity the Bishop's pontificals. Beneath them a hair-shirt. He dispenses hospitality to rich and poor in his home beside his Cathedral where the present Synod house stands, a hospitality discreetly liberal, in his first biographer's phrase, among rich foods choosing for himself the plainest and coloring water with wine for courtesy and company's sake. Each day at his table he dines thirty to sixty of the poor that his other guests may be encouraged in well-doing. From the day he put on the white robe of the Augustinian Canon he took no meat, and on Fridays only bread and water. Three times daily he used the discipline; his nights were lonely vigils or spent in choir. Assiduous in attendance at the Divine Office, when at dawn the canons left the choir for their cells he remained in solitary prayer and when day came he passed out to the cemetery to chant the office of the dead. His life was what the old Irish homily calls the "white martyrdom" of abnegation and labor. The Bull of his canonization recites his constancy in prayer and his austere mortification. These were the secret springs of his energy and profuse charity. *Austeritas, benignitas.* This white-robed figure of whose speech hardly four sentences remain is seen always in the gracious gesture of giving and with the gravity of silence about him. Crowds depend upon him, recognizing in him a source of supernatural power and the records of his canonization attest his miracles. He lived through two famines and two sieges and saw the city of his adoption once sacked. He moves through them with the equilibrium of the saint and a saint's equal mind. But also with a saint's energy. He has hardly taken his seat in his Cathedral when his zeal turns to the reform of his clergy. His predecessors had been trained in a milder climate and under a more lax monastic rule. The service of the Cathedral had suffered. Looking abroad for a model he persuaded his secular canons to join him in community life as Augustinian regulars of the Arroasian rule and converted the Cathedral Church of the Holy Trinity into a Priory. His community became a school for bishops, Albin of Ferns, Marianus of Cork, Malachy of Louth who were subsequent witnesses to his sanctity.

In the Irish monasteries psalmody occupied a great space in the monk's life. Lorcan raised the Gregorian chant, still so little heard in Irish churches, to its proper place about the Altar and restored its appropriate splendor to the Divine Office. He commenced the rebuilding of his Cathedral and added to the number of the parish churches

which for a city of small size were already numerous—a deed of St.
Lorcan is witnessed by the priests of seven churches and four or five
others appear to have existed at this time. During a famine which afflicted the city the destitute flocked about his doors. He exerted himself
in the public relief not merely by prodigally multiplying his personal
charities but by organized assistance, quartering the city poor upon
the abbey lands of his Cathedral—Swords, Lusk and Finglas. When
these were filled and the famine still continued he sent others further
afield through Ireland recommending them to the popular charity and
chartering a vessel at no small cost to convey others to England. Then
came the scourge of war throwing city and country into confusion.
When he is in the very act of negotiating terms with the Normans the
city is seized by a sudden, treacherous irruption and the peacemaker
turns to save the wounded, to bury his dead, to guard the ecclesiastical
property from spoliation and to recover the looted Church vessels and
books. Henceforward he must double the parts of a Mercier and a Vincent de Paul. Resistance becomes a duty of patriotism. Fronting the
unjust aggression he becomes for a moment the center of the national
resistance, serving the irresolute Ard Ri with steadfast loyalty. No contemporary Irish record of the Archbishop's doings exists, but Giraldus,
a little pained perhaps to find a saint among his adversaries, says with
an *ut ferebatur* that the princes of Ireland were moved to action by the
patriotic zeal of the Archbishop who joined with Ruaidri in rallying
the country and its allies, sending missives abroad to Gottred of Man
and to the other Lords of the Isles. The confederacy which he formed
seemed for a moment like achieving its purpose and Strongbow, reduced to the sorest straits, used the Archbishop as the mediator of his
offer to do homage to Ruaidri in return for the lordship of Leinster.
The Ard Ri refused the terms, but taken unawares by a sortie of the
now desperate Normans saw his far-drawn forces scattered.

The rest of his political life is busied with embassies of peace. When
Henry II holds his state in Dublin to receive the submission of the
Irish princes, Lorcan journeys to Connacht on his behalf on a fruitless
errand to induce the Ard Ri "to go into the King's house". In 1175
the situation is reversed; Lorcan is Ruaidri's envoy to the King, negotiating the Treaty of Windsor, a mission requiring high qualities of
skill and statesmanship where the contracting parties represented the
feudal system opposed to Brehon law and Irish custom. The task was

not made easier by a mischance which came to him at this time. For, visiting the shrine of St. Thomas at Canterbury, a madman who had heard of the visitor's reputation for sanctity, thought that he would meritoriously make another martyr and felled the saint to the ground before the high Altar. The traces of this blow on the head were verified by the Cardinal Archbishop of Rouen in 1876.

Meanwhile synods had been held at Armagh, Cashel and Dublin which the Archbishop attended in his subordinate place. None of them shows any trace of his leading or statesmanship. The first was held in 1170 in the shadow of the invasion, Gelasius, almost a nonagenarian, presiding. It expressed the pious opinion that the national calamity was a divine judgment upon the sins of the people who bought as slaves the children whom their Anglo-Saxon parents sold to them contrary to natural law and to the Twenty-eighth Canon of Anselm's Council of London of 1102. The second, convened by Henry within twelve months under the Cistercian Bishop of Lismore, was Henry's quittance for Adrian's Bull. It gathered up some loose ends of the reforms initiated by Cellach a generation before, redressed certain surviving irregularities in discipline and made provision for a special treatment of the clergy. Its decrees were confirmed at a Dublin synod in 1177 with Cardinal Vivian as Legate. The final decree of the Cashel synod provides that "all divine matters should be conducted agreeably to the practice of the most holy Church and according to their observance in the English Church." Giraldus is our chief authority for these decrees, which he sets out verbatim. By unaccountably omitting from his text the words *ad instar sacrisanctae Ecclesiae* his English translator infuses a wholly unjustified Anglican flavor into the decree. This omission has misled later writers. Accepting it and representing as a synodal finding what is more probably merely the comment of Giraldus, a recent scholarly and sympathetic historian has been constrained to a mild criticism of St. Lorcan's share in that synod. Following the definition of this decree Giraldus' text proceeds: "It is right and just that, as by Divine Providence Ireland has received her Lord and King from England, she should also accept reform from the same source", with much else to the same effect. Upon which this writer passes the natural judgment that "it is strange that Archbishop Laurence, a truly Irish-hearted man, should have 'concurred' in this claim." I suggest, following Dr. Lanigan and the form in Wilkins' *Concilia*, that the language of the preceding

decrees makes it reasonable to detach these subsequent sentences from
the definition of the decree, and when one restores to the English
translation the omitted words of the original text which identify English observance with the recognized practice of Western Christendom
Lorcan's concurrence is not open to criticism. The fact that English
observance was at this time in accord with the practice of the universal
Church could not prejudice Lorcan's view of the matter.

Lorcan presided in his Cathedral at the obsequies in 1176 of Strongbow, whom a singular fate had united to his own family. The Cathedral in which the Earl was buried was then rising from the ground in
something of its present dimensions, and the Earl's name is associated,
second to the Archbishop's, in the building of the tower, the choir and
two chapels. His confirmatory grant to the Cathedral of churches and
termon lands is dated 1178, when he was probably watching the erec-
tion of the transepts. In the following year he left for Rome to attend
the Third General Lateran Council with five other Irish bishops. On
their passage through England Henry compelled them to take an oath
that they would seek nothing at the Council prejudicial to the king or
his kingdom. Some three hundred bishops were present at the Council
and from that great assembly Lorcan passed into the closest confidence
of the Holy See. He obtained from Alexander III a Bull confirming
the rights and privileges of the see of Dublin. Jurisdiction is conferred
over five suffragan sees and the Pope takes the Archbishop's church
in Dublin and all its possessions under St. Peter's protection and his
own, defining and confirming its possessions and ensuring it and the
property of his suffragans by strictest penalties against any interference
ecclesiastical or lay. Finally on his return home Alexander gives him
the supreme mark of his confidence in naming him Papal Legate.

In the brief space of life that was left to him Lorcan exercised his
new powers with exemplary decision. With the invaders new abuses
had crept among his clergy, abuses in the minor and even major orders, peculiarly hateful to the Archbishop, *castitatis et honestatis zelator.*
He is said to have refused his absolution to these offenders and to
have despatched no fewer than one hundred and forty to Rome. In
the steps he had taken in Rome to protect the rights of his see and
perhaps in the resolute purge of his clergy, which must have included
many newcomers, the King was offended. A new Thomas à Becket
touched his authority. And, therefore, when on a final peace mission

for Ruaidri Lorcan crossed the Irish Sea, bringing with him the king's son as hostage to Henry, he finds the Channel ports closed against his return by royal edict. Following the King of Normandy and landing near Treport at a cove which still bears his name the saint falls ill. He sees the Abbey towers of Eu and asks some shepherds what they might be. The Abbey belongs to the monks of St. Victor. *"Haec requies mea in saeculo in saeculi"*, replies the saint, and the dying man is received among the monks whose Abbey Church he will hallow with his bones. Two sentences are recorded of his dying hours. Asked by the Abbot to make his will: "God knows", says he, "I have not a penny under the sun." And again, but in his native tongue, thinking of his own people: *"Heu popule stulte et insipiens, quid inodo facias? Quis sanabit adversiones tuas? Quis medebitur tui?"* He knew himself the pastor and defender of his people, who would find themselves without such a defender for many years—for seven centuries.

A good and just man, Giraldus calls him; he died in exile—an exile and fugitive, the Abbot Hugues wrote to Innocent III, *pro libertate ecclesiae*—an exile as well, he might have written, of charity and patriotism. His life was written and rewritten at Eu from information eagerly gathered by the canons from the saint's disciples and other pilgrims from Ireland who journeyed to his shrine, from his nephew Thomas, Abbot of Glendalough, his intimates Albin, Bishop of Ferns, Marianus of Cork and Malachy of Louth, and from Jean Comyn, who succeeded him in the see of Dublin. In 1225, forty-five years after his death, he was canonized by Honorius III, and thereupon became patron of the Archdiocese of Dublin.

~

SAINT DOMINIC

[1170–1221]

Hilary Carpenter, O.P.

T IS THE PURPOSE of this essay to depict the character of St. Dominic in its historical setting so that the essential note of the apostolate originated by him and perpetuated in the Order he founded, may be the more accurately appreciated. No doubt it is largely because a great number of the Inquisitors later chosen by the Popes were Dominicans that the Founder of their Order has come to be regarded, even among Catholics, as a dark and sinister figure, the unlovable originator of the Spanish Inquisition. The mere historic fact that this latter Institution, besides not being Spanish in origin, was set up by Pope Gregory IX ten years after St. Dominic's death, is evidently not sufficient to dispel the cherished error, nor yet the equally historic fact that the tortures inseparably associated with it in the public mind were neither prescribed nor even permitted for decades after it had come into being. The public mind is seldom an historical mind; in the present instance it has been content to identify St. Dominic with a fellow countryman and a member of his Order, the grim Torquemada who was appointed to organize the Spanish Inquisition two centuries later. The two characters could scarcely have been more different.

The quality of a man's soul is almost invariably reflected in his outward appearance and manner. This was undoubtedly true of Dominic Guzman. Fortunately we have an eyewitness description of the Saint set down for us by one of his spiritual daughters, Sister Cecilia Cesarini: "The blessed Dominic was of moderate stature and of a slender build. His handsome face was fresh-complexioned, his hair and beard were yellow, flecked with grey, and his eyes beautiful. A kind of splendor radiated from his brow, inspiring all to respect and affection. He was ever smiling and joyous, unless he were moved to pity by his neighbor's suffering. He had long and beautiful hands. His voice was full, sweet and sonorous." The beauty, the light and the joyousness of his face were the outward counterparts of a soul possessed of the beauty, the clarity and the joyousness of divine truth and charity. These two, truth and charity, absorbed his whole being and few even among the saints have appreciated as he did, in mind and in heart, the ineluctable union of these two essential elements of the Christian life.

Contrary to the common estimation of his character, Dominic's nature was one of keen sensitivity and deep emotion. Those who lived closest to him bear witness both to his joyousness and to his tears; and it was this sympathetic generosity of soul, this power to rejoice and to suffer with others, that first won for him the devotion and love of those he would himself win for God and his truth. His absolute virginity of body and soul, signalized in the liturgy of his feast, was not the coldness of insensibility nor yet the false disdain of the Manichaeism he did so much to counter and destroy. His fasts, his vigils, his almost incredible and incessant acts of extreme mortification, far from hardening or denaturing his sensibilities, refined and purified them because of the great charity of his soul, so that he became the more attracted and attractive to others with none of the peril that so often threatens the relationships of human affection. He was afire with a passion for souls because he was aflame with the love of God; it was said of him that he spoke only to God or of God.

It is only when one appreciates the essential though entirely spiritualized humaneness of St. Dominic that one can appreciate the persuasive force of his intellectual powers which were even more remarkable in their appeal to others than these more obviously attractive characteristics. It may be observed, in passing, how strange a thing it is that those characteristics in man which pertain strictly speaking to his irrational side should be called humane, whereas those whereby he is made only a little less in nature than the angels should be commonly associated with a lack of humanity. It is tacitly assumed that a man can be softhearted only if he is softheaded. But with Dominic, at any rate, tenderness of heart was combined with crystal clarity of mind. He sought passionately for truth; from his early days books were for him a necessity of life, as his earliest biographer tells us; yet it is also told of him that, as a student, he sold his parchments, covered as they were with his own annotations, that he might give money to the starving poor. "I could not bear to prize dead skins", he said, "when living skins were starving and in need." Yet G. K. Chesterton could write, in his *Saint Francis of Assisi*, that "Dominic the Spaniard was, like nearly every Spaniard, a man with the mind of a soldier. His charity took the practical form of provision and preparation." This can hardly be true of the young student who sold the very sinews of war on an impulse to feed the poor, or of the mature Founder who dispersed his still small band of sons to the four corners of Europe within a few months of the establishment of his Order.

It must remain a mystery that the clear-sighted and profound vision of Chesterton should have failed to estimate the true greatness of St. Dominic, even though one can readily understand his almost connatural appreciation of St. Francis. He seems, in this instance, to have allowed himself to be content with the popular estimate rather than to have examined for himself the historical evidence. He records the meeting of the two saints at the Chapter of Straw Huts "because it was immediately before St. Francis set forth on his bloodless crusade that he is said to have met St. Dominic, who has been much criticized for lending himself to a more bloody one", though he admits further on that "St. Dominic devoted himself much more to persuading than to persecution." He saw that "about everything St. Francis did there was something that was in a good sense childish." What he failed to see was that about everything St. Dominic did there was something in every sense Christlike. Dominic loved the heretics and won them by love, even though he hated their heresy with all his soul. If he made war on their stiff-necked leaders it was never more than a war of words, and they were words of truth, not of passion.

The whole character and apostolate of Dominic is summed up in the single word that is the motto of his Order: *Truth.* Truth was for him not merely an attribute of the human mind—though that also seemed to him a thing of radical importance. It was also an attribute of the divine mind that could be reflected, must indeed be reflected, in the very being of man. Like all attributes of God, truth must be seen as subsistent in God, it must be seen as a Person in God. This divine truth is reflected in the being of man only when the Divine Person is reflected in the being of man. Dominic saw with overwhelming clarity that truth was desperately necessary to the mind of man because man, and especially the man of his own day, was desperately in need of God. If he laid such great store by the value of the intellect with which God had endowed him, it was only that he recognized in this vehicle of logical truth a powerful means to the attainment of the far more important ontological truth. He saw that only by knowing truth can a man become true. Truth, in its ultimate resolution, is a Divine Person, the Person of God who was made Man that man might be made a partaker in the divine nature. "*I am the truth*", said the Son of God. "*No man cometh to the Father but by me.*" A man can become true only by finding union with him who is Truth; but how can he seek unless he knows what he is seeking, unless he is first taught? And he only is competent to teach who himself knows divine truth and has been himself transformed by it. It was said of St. Dominic that he was *alter Christus*, another Christ. This was in a sense inevitable if he was to use his great gifts of nature and of grace for the special apostolate to which he was called, for which he was raised up, by God. No one realized more clearly than he the necessity of "doing the truth in charity" as the essential means of teaching the truth. When the moment came for the opening of his apostolate Dominic, like his Divine Prototype, "began to do and to teach".

The condition of the Church and of Christendom (if indeed the distinction is to be allowed) at the end of the twelfth century was one of exceptional need. Albigensianism, growing rife at that time in the south of France, evil as it was in itself, was a symptom of a still greater peril attendant upon a new sense of intellectual life and freedom. It is not without significance that the new champion of divine truth was born of Spain. It was among the Moors in Spain that the real menace to Christianity was to be found, for the Arabian misinterpretation of Aristotelian philosophy bid fair to establish in Christendom a spurious rationalism that would undermine Christian truth in a world emerging from the Dark Ages. But under the inspiration of Dominic this menace was to be turned into a saving grace by the fearless intellectual integrity of Albert the Great and Thomas Aquinas. For he was not merely to be a champion of the faith among the heretics of Languedoc; he was to live on in an apostolic movement inspired by his character, outlook and approach to truth. Dominic did not write the *Summa Theologica* or the *Summa Contra Gentiles*; but only a Dominican could have written them.

It is related by the early biographers of St. Dominic that his mother,

Blessed Jane of Aza, had a dream before the birth of her child: "She thought that she bore in her womb a dog and that it broke away from her, a burning torch in its mouth wherewith it set the world aflame." His godmother also told of a dream in which she saw the child's forehead lit by a radiant star which bathed the whole world in the splendor of its light. Whatever be the authenticity of these legends, they are unquestionably illustrative of the intellectual light and flaming charity that were to characterise the saint in his mission of truth. The circumstances of his birth encouraged the natural tendency of the child both to learning and to holiness; the nobility of his family would guarantee the one, while the sanctity of his mother would lay the foundations of the other. The strict discipline of his school and university years formed and strengthened him, shaping in him that sanity and equanimity of character to which all the witnesses at his Process of Canonization bore testimony, qualities which were, together with his unfailing sweetness and joyousness, the natural basis of his tremendous power of persuasion. But this discipline of learning was not confined to academic studies; even then his bed was the bare ground, his nights were often spent in prayer; for it was a discipline of learning inspired by the love of God.

"God's husbandry" was continued when Dominic went from the University to begin a priestly life as a Canon Regular at Osma under the Rule of St. Augustine, which was later to be the basic Rule of his own Order. Almost a decade was to be spent in learning the discipline of the cloister and the liturgy. "Straightway he began to appear among his brother canons as a bright ray of sunshine", wrote Blessed Jordan of Saxony who succeeded him in the government of the Order,

> in humbleness of heart the least, in holiness the first, shedding around the fragrance of quickening life like the sweet scent of pinewoods in the heat of a summer's day. . . . Day and night he frequented the church, ceaselessly devoted to prayer, scarcely venturing beyond the cloister walls. . . . But there was one especial petition which he often made to God, that a true love might be his to help effectively in the saving of men's souls, deeming himself then only a real member of Christ's Mystic Body when he could spend his whole being on gaining men, as his Lord Jesus had spent himself for them on the Cross.

When the preparation was finished and God's moment came to begin the apostolate, it was the apparent accident of his being chosen to accompany his Bishop, Diego, on a diplomatic mission that brought him face to face with the cancer of heresy that had taken malignant hold on the south of France and was eating into the vitals of Christendom. His first actual contact with it is significant. The host of the inn where they were to stay on their way north was himself a victim of this were-wolf resurrection of ancient Manichaeism, and Dominic lost no time in joining issue with the evil. That first night he spent in argument and persuasion, and the morning light found the innkeeper on his knees before his guest and before God. From this moment Dominic's sense of his vocation began to take shape, though he could take no active steps till another of those accidents of divine making showed him the way.

It is not to be thought that the Church was making no effort to combat the evil within her. The great and saintly Pope at that time, Innocent III, had entrusted to the Abbot of Cîteaux the organization of a preaching crusade against the Albigensian revival of Manichaeism, for preaching was then little known. On their return journey from the north Diego and Dominic passed by the great Abbey of Cîteaux (where the Bishop was so moved by the life of the monks that he himself took the Cistercian habit) and afterward made contact with the Abbot and his crusading monks at Montpellier. The efforts of the legate and his companions had proved fruitless; it was Bishop Diego who put his finger on the root cause of their failure. The leaders of the Albigenses, the "Perfect" as they were called, unlike the rank and file of their followers, were intensely ascetic in their mode of life. This parade of asceticism, all the more effective because not only was it not required of the rank and file but, on the contrary, justified every gross excess in them, was the first source of attraction to rich and poor, learned and unlearned alike. The papal emissaries, on the other hand, exhibited the outward trappings and mode of life normal to their ordinary state and present dignity. The primary appeal to these erring children of the Church was thus absent.

It can scarcely be doubted that this idea of a new approach to the problem originated with Dominic. At any rate he at once adopted wholeheartedly a way of life that appealed to all the instincts and discipline of his whole outlook. He made no secret of his vigils and his fasts and his increasing mortifications. It is Chesterton's view that Dominic "probably did not understand . . . the power of mere popularity produced by mere personality." This is far from true, even in the

precise sense Chesterton meant it. When the Subprior of Osma became Brother Dominic he threw into the scale of persuasion the whole
weight of his attractive personality. Not only was the cynical asceticism
of the Perfect outdone by the wholehearted asceticism of the follower
of Christ; to it was added the full force of those personal characteristics
that have already been emphasized. Moreover, once he had thus won
the respect and the affection of the people he was able to administer
to them the mental and spiritual enlightenment their souls needed. So
did this *alter Christus* begin "to do and to teach".

The heresy that Dominic first combatted was based upon the Gnos-
tic error as to the nature and relation of Matter and Spirit, itself a falsi-
fication of the early Greek philosophical theory of Contraries. Matter
was accredited to a Supreme Evil Principle as to its cause; Spirit to a
supreme Good Principle. In the Manichean resolution of Gnosticism
all being is divided into two great contrary classes, matter which is
wholly evil and spirit which is wholly good. It is thus in essential
conflict with Christian truth, for the Incarnation effected the supreme
union of spirit with matter when the Word was made Flesh. With the
Albigenses the basic error of the Manicheans was carried to its logical
conclusion by the leaders, largely because of the philosophical bent
which was at once the glory and the peril of the educated mind of
the Middle Ages. But while for the small group of the initiated this
logical conclusion led to extreme asceticism, real or assumed, for the
mass of their followers it led not only to the denial of the Incarnation
and of Christianity as a whole but to every conceivable excess of vice.
It represented a complete overthrow of Truth in respect of both God
and man. It could be countered only by the reassertion of that Truth
which is both God and Man. These heretics, some wittingly, some
unwittingly, had destroyed the keynote of their very humanity and so
lost God for whom that humanity was created.

While St. Dominic devoted himself to the combatting of this heresy
the conviction was steadily growing upon him that there was need
in the Church as a whole of an organized body of trained and saintly
preachers for the safeguarding and spread of divine truth. Except with
individuals his success was not widespread or immediate. In his disputations with the leaders the force of his arguments was recognized
again and again, and miracles were not wanting to confirm them. But
he realized that he could not pursue his apostolate alone. Already the

qualities of his character had drawn a small band of associates to his side. But he now felt the need of a definite sign from heaven; and one evening, as he prayed for it to Our Lady outside the gates of Fanjeaux, it was given to him. Out of the darkened sky came a globe of flame which hovered awhile and finally came to rest over the desolate church at Prouille. On three successive nights this vision was shown to him. He knew now that he must begin his special work in that spot and he knew how it must begin. He gathered together there a small company of women, most of them converts from heresy, and devised for them a rule of strict enclosure, penance and contemplation. This was his powerhouse of prayer. At the same time he housed nearby, to form a kind of "double monastery", his little band of men under an equally strict rule of poverty, study and liturgical prayer. The foundations of his Order were laid.

For eight years he continued his fight against heresy from this stronghold of Truth. They were the years of probation for the Order that was to be established finally only five years before his death. He and his little company of preachers, authorized by the legate Raoul in accordance with the desires of Innocent III and warmly encouraged by the Bishop, Foulques, preached throughout the diocese of Toulouse, Dominic himself singing aloud for joy the psalms and hymns of the liturgy as he strode along; and the burden of his preaching was what we have come to know as the Mysteries of the Rosary, Christ and him crucified. His deep devotion to the Mother of God, enshrined in his Order whose sons were to be called the Friars of Mary, opened up for him and for those to whom he preached a deeper and more intimate understanding of the Incarnation, of Divine Truth made Man. And to guarantee the accuracy of their preaching, he came with his companions to follow the lectures of the Englishman, Alexander Stavensby, afterward Professor at Bologna and finally Bishop of Coventry.

When, in due time, encouraged by Pope Innocent and the Roman Curia, he set himself to determine the rule and constitution of the Order to be presented for official approval, he called his companions to consultation with him on the matter, thereby establishing from the outset that democratic character which he imprinted indelibly on his Order. In the Bull of its institution, Pope Honorius III (who had by now succeeded to Innocent) addressed himself to Dominic: "Recognizing that the Brothers of your Order are to be the champions of the

faith and the true lights of the world, we confirm your Order and take
it under our own supervision." The dream of the mother was now
fulfilled; the personality of her son was enshrined in a living and permanent Order of Preachers; through these *Domini Canes*, these Dogs
of the Lord, Dominic would go forth with a flame in his mouth to set
alight the world.

The remaining five years of St. Dominic's life, till he died in 1221,
were occupied in establishing the Order throughout the length and
breadth of Europe and in his unwearying missionary journeys. By that
time the Friars Preachers were established in all the great centers of
learning in Christendom, including Oxford, and at the same time the
poor were everywhere having the Gospel preached to them. He could
now sing his final song, his *Nunc Dimittis*. As he lay dying in another's
bed (for he had none of his own) one asked him where he wished to
be buried. "Under the feet of my Brethren", he replied. As they were
about to start the Prayers for the Dying, he bade them wait a moment.
He had one last word for them. "I am going where I can serve you
better", he said. "Now begin."

SAINT FRANCIS OF ASSISI

[1182–1226]

C. C. Martindale, S.J.

O RECKELSSLY are the words "dark ages", "medieval" and so forth chucked about, that I venture to make one or two points clear. If anyone wants to use the—to my mind— clumsy misnomer: The Dark Ages, he should confine it to the period between, say, 750 and 950; the medieval period can be regarded as extending from 1050 to 1350, and that is a generous allowance. Saints Paul, Anthony and Augustine belonged neither to the dark, nor to the medieval periods; St. Edward was in a transitional period working up to the medieval world. Francis and Thomas are genuine medievals; and other tickets will have to be found for anyone to be mentioned after them. It is true that the "Dark Ages" can so be named largely because we have, till recently, studied them hardly at all: everybody is aware how completely many a man's estimate of the Middle Ages has had to be revised, since modern scholarship has concentrated on that period. The theory of unbroken human progress has long ago collapsed. In very many ways the thirteenth century was immeasurably ahead of either the sixteenth or the eighteenth; and the world-wide study devoted to the history of St. Francis, and the almost passionate affection in men of the most various creeds that his personality inspires, have contributed more than almost anything to place his supremely creative century in its right perspective.

Francis appears abruptly, aged about twenty, taken prisoner in a war between Umbrian Assisi and her rival town, Perugia. It was the stormy period of transition from the rule of the great lord in his castle, to that of the cities and their citizens, and such little wars were frequent. Francis was son of a very wealthy merchant; his father adored him, and indulged—nay gloried in—the lad's rocketing career. Francis, recklessly extravagant, yet lavish to beggars no less than in his dress; daring and

original to the point of the fantastic; small in frame but utterly untiring, almost ecstatically responsive to music and to color, yet with an
artist's swift reactions toward melancholy and dream; Italian through
and through, yet fascinated by French poetry and the chivalrous tales
related by the troubadours, Francis was acknowledged leader of the
young men of his city, was always chosen "master" of their "revels",
was acquainted with every form of license. And yet, unless I err, he was
saved from *committing* himself to what he mixed with by that glamorous
romantic veil that made him *need* to transpose even war, even love, even
dress, into a semi-mystical world of the imagination. After his capture
and imprisonment, during which he was so gay that his fellow captives thought him half-delirious, reaction came. Liberated, but weak,
he stood leaning on a stick staring at the cypresses and vineyards of
that gold-misted world and wondered that ever he had so much loved
them. . . . But the old spirit in part revived. He set out on another war,
against invading Germans. Then, having dreamed of a palace, full of
splendid armor, where a bride awaited him . . . he, half asleep, heard
himself asked: "Which is better—to serve the servant, or to serve the
Lord?" "Of course, to serve the Lord!" "Why, then, make a master
of the servant . . . ?" Half-dazed, he returned to Assisi; resumed his
mastership of revels, but would sit abruptly abstracted in the middle of
the feasts. He had suddenly noticed Poverty—the frightful poverty of
the Assisi underworld which stole out from its black squalor to gaze at
these golden lads. . . . His companions chaffed him, and asked him if
he was in love. . . . Yes, and with a princess more noble, more lovely,
than any that they knew. They guffawed; but it remained that he had
caught sight of Poverty and had begun to love her. To love her, even
while his very soul crept with horror at the idea of embracing her. . . .
He began to pray. He pilgrimaged to Rome and not only poured out
what money he had upon the destitute, but made a beggar of himself
for one day and returned to Assisi still sick at memory of the rags, the
filth, the stench, the humiliation. He felt he must conquer that—slowly.
Well, at least he would no more do his alms in secret, terrorized by the
idea of the mockery of his own "class"; he gave them publicly at his
own door. Not enough! not deep-biting enough, because still the act
as of one who stood above, done toward men who crouched beneath
him. He must *equalize* himself! He met a leper, and beating down his
loathing, kissed the hand into which he placed his gift. And the leper

lifted his face and gave, in his turn, to Francis the kiss of peace. . . .
The decisive step, unconsciously, had been taken. For awhile he stumbled around his new domain of Poverty. He saw a ruined chapel, San
Damiano. He had heard a voice: "Francis, restore my Church, which is
falling into ruins." Losing for a moment all perspective, he sold a lot of
his father's merchandise and carried the proceeds to the San Damiano
priest. The poor man was terrified, and refused it. Francis' father was
furious, seized him, beat him, imprisoned him, and in the long run
renounced his son, even as that son now renounced the whole of the
life to which he had been educated.

Since in a quarter of an hour's talk I have to leave out almost everything, let me insist on this. You will never understand Francis till you
realize that with all the love and loyalty of his heart he *married Poverty
for Christ's sake*. He regarded Poverty not only as no disgrace but as a
glory. She was the Princess Poverty. To pay court to Money, to devote
your life to Money, to engage yourself to Money, *that* was the illusion
in any case: to do so with your eyes open, *that* was the apostasy and the
degradation. And this, not merely because he saw in a philosophical
sort of way that the free man, the really rich man, was the man who
cared nothing for coins—even the pagans had seen that: the Stoic, the
Cynic, the Buddhist, have seen it very clearly. Nor did he become poor
just because in a philanthropic sort of way he was sorry for poor people
—poor people often resent that sort of commiseration most bitterly.

No. The point is that Francis saw the Truth that no man may be
assessed according to what he *has*, but according to what he *is*; and he
is, what God sees him to be; and God esteems him entirely according
to his Christlikeness; and Francis found himself becoming "poor" just
in proportion as he became like Christ. Christ, "being rich, for our
sakes made himself poor"; "even Christ pleased not himself." People
today are poorer than they were—but reluctantly, kicking against it. I
get letter after letter from America, from New Zealand, from Australia,
and now from South Africa, lamenting that so little work, and therefore money, is to be got. Men pray for the rebuilding of trade—the
chance to make a fortune. They want to build the social edifice over
again, BUT, out of the same materials, on the same architectural principles. Impossible. And thank God for it. Money-getting, money-having,
money spendable upon self—no life can thus be made. "Standard of
Life" is a term endlessly repeated nowadays. It used to be reckoned in

terms of motor-cars and cinemas, and "having a good time". Hopeless.
All that has to be turned upside down. "Standard of Life" is a spiritual
thing. The standard of an unjust millionaire's life is lower than that of
the honorable scullion on whose head he plants his gold-shod hoof.
Francis saw that; Christ taught that; and such is the verdict, in eternity,
of God.

If this is realized, I hardly care what else I omit. I cannot speak of
the gradual grouping of thousands upon thousands of men around St.
Francis; the formation of his Order, and of its outer ring, so to say, the
Third Order; nor of the exquisite idyll of St. Clare and the making
of the Second Order, composed of those "Poor Clares" of whom we
have so many in England, thank God, and whose history has always
been one of perfect fidelity to perfect poverty. Nor can I explain the
slow, prudent hesitating and finally most definite approbation obtained
from Rome for all of this; nor the Saint's expeditions outside Italy, even
to the Sultan's camps in Egypt. I shall not, on the one hand, describe
his bitter disappointments when he realized (as only his sweet simplicity could have failed to do) that the mass of his followers could not
possibly burn with his pure flame, nor love poverty and the cross as
he did; nor yet shall I trace the thousand streams of art, drama, song,
social and missionary and educational work that have flowed through
the world because of St. Francis. Cut out what was due to Francis in
the work of Dante, and Giotto; in philosophic and scientific areas, in
the work of Duns Scotus or Roger Bacon or St. Bonaventura; in the
realm of government, men like St. Louis of France; of charity, women
like Queen St. Elizabeth of Hungary, who, like Dante, were members
of his Third Order, and what an infinity will you lose! And what,
when we recall that in the sheer history of electricity itself, Galvani,
Volta, and Ampère were all members of that same Third Order! Why,
I must omit even that unique gem of literature, the Little Flowers of
St. Francis, and no more than mention his own Canticle of the Sun,
wherein he finds all nature—Brother Wind, the air and clouds and fair
and every sort of weather; Sister Water, so helpful and humble and
precious and pure; Brother Fire, gay, strong, lighting up the dark—
found all these to be, in *their* way, his brothers and sisters, no less than
those human men and women who in their far *better* way "for thy love,
Lord, forgive and are weak and are troubled and in peace endure—for
by thee, Lord, shall they be crowned." And before he died, he added:

"Praised be my Lord for our Sister, bodily death, from which no man may flee that liveth. . . . Praise ye and bless my Lord and give him thanks, and be subject to him with great humility!" But what it were a scandal and a shame for me to omit, were at least an allusion to that miracle which reproduced in his very flesh the external semblance of the death of Jesus Christ. In the year 1224, in the year and indeed the month and almost on the very day when the first Friars were landing here in England at Dover, Francis went up into the precipitous rocks of Mount Alvernia to pray in solitude. There it was that, during an ecstasy, he found the likeness of the wounds of Christ impressed upon his hands and feet and side. No one now doubts, or should doubt, of the historical character of this event. Concerning the mechanics of its physio-psychology, so to speak, experts still dispute, and by all means let them do so. Let instances be quoted of how a mother's love has caused to appear on her own body marks suited to the accident that she helplessly witnessed happening to her child. We are grateful for such proofs of what an overwhelming, penetrating, soaring and seraphic love can bring about. But what is to be said of the love lit up within the heart of a man such, that not only it unites his spirit even here on earth in unsurpassable intensity and purity with Christ, but overflows upon his very body—or rather, what do I mean by that "not only"? The true point is that not merely in the poor flesh of Francis were the marks of nails and lance anguishingly and accurately reproduced—a portent, without doubt—but that in his soul, so far as human soul can admit and support a love that is divine, the very love of Christ who lived and died for us, was reproduced. I have spoken, then, of Francis, and alas! have said hardly anything to convey to you what he was, but only, so to say, the two poles of his existence—the negative one, which means his rejection of all that human nature tends to make a god of; and his adherence with the very stuff of his soul to the GOD revealed in Jesus Christ, which is the positive definition of the life of Francis. He is not the elegant statuette that you perceive in artistic boudoirs; he is not the sweetly romantic preacher to the birds and the fish; he is not just the knight-errant of his Lord, wandering through the loveliness of Umbria; nor even, merely he who blessed Assisi from the hillside, as he approached it to die there, not seeing it, for tears and sickness had made his eyes go blind—and breaking bread into little pieces, for the last time, that he too might have, with his beloved, his final Supper, and dying on the ground just as the sun set and a myriad larks thrilled through the evening sky their happy hymn. Francis, having lived in this world and having so well understood us men, who must needs live within it, was himself not of it—no, he was not of it; and as for me, whose paganized youth he, more than any Saint, regenerated, I am glad, by the words of my lips, to have kissed, on my behalf and yours, the footsteps of his memory.

SAINT ANTHONY OF PADUA

[1195-1231]

Alice Curtayne

HE UNIVERSALITY AND PERSISTENCE of the cult of St. Anthony of Padua is such a tissue of paradox that it constitutes one of the great psychological riddles of hagiography. I do not pretend to solve the problem here but only to put the terms of it before you. The outline of his life sufficiently states the paradox.

He was born in 1195 probably near Lisbon and was given the name Ferdinand. He is said to have been a descendant of Godfrey de Bouillon, Duke of Lorraine, hero of the First Crusade and first King of Jerusalem. However that may be, Ferdinand's father was a knight at the court of Alfonso II, King of Portugal, where he held an office in connection with revenue. The boy was thus brought up on the fringes of royalty. He was sent to the Cathedral school, as his uncle was a canon of the Lisbon chapter and could keep an eye on the student. Ferdinand developed a religious vocation but showed an early independence of mind. One would have thought that his uncle's influence would have led him to the secular clergy, but instead, at the age of fifteen, he entered the Lisbon monastery of the Canons Regular of St. Augustine.

When he had completed two years here, he asked to be transferred to the house of the order at Coimbra, a day's journey to the north of Lisbon. He said he found the visits from relations in Lisbon too disturbing. He was accordingly sent to Coimbra and ordained there in due course. This monastery conducted a school famous for scriptural studies. Here Ferdinand studied with intense application for eight years and it was during this period he acquired the theological and biblical proficiency which was later to astonish the world.

One day, in the capacity of guestmaster, it devolved on him to attend to five Franciscan friars, who had applied at the monastery for hospitality. They were on their way to Morocco to found a mission there. While he attended to their needs in the refectory and dormitory, Ferdinand talked with the guests, whom he found very interesting. It was not his first acquaintance with the Franciscans. There was a little group of them in the neighborhood who frequently came to the Augustinian monastery for alms.

The five who went to Morocco became martyrs in a short while, having been butchered in circumstances of unusual ferocity. Their remains were brought back to Coimbra where they were given the honors of Church and State. The King and Queen attended the obsequies.

The affair made a deep impression on Ferdinand, who now found himself irresistibly attracted to the Franciscans. But it was not an easy matter for him to justify this new form of his vocation to his colleagues. The Canons Regular of St. Augustine were an old order, deservedly honored; the monastery at Coimbra had been founded by a saint. On the other hand, the Franciscan movement was still only in its infancy and was viewed with suspicion, if not open hostility, by the old established religious orders. Ferdinand had to go through a painful passage before he put aside the white habit and rochet of the Canons Regular in favor of the Franciscan habit and cord. He took a new name, Anthony.

The next time we have a clear view of him, he is in Italy, the home of the new movement. He probably attended the famous Chapter of Mats in Assisi in 1221. This was the last General Chapter of the Franciscans held during the founder's lifetime and more than three thousand friars were present. It was one of the most amazing meetings in Christian history. The country people of Umbria brought cart-loads of bread, wine, cheese and other edibles, as well as drinking utensils and plates, while the nobility of the district competed to serve the friars at their meals. At the conclusion of the Chapter, there was a reordering of all the Franciscan groups and the novice, Anthony, was sent to a small hospice for lay brothers at Monte Paolo, near Forli, in Emilia. Being an ordained priest, he was useful here to say Mass for the brethren. His other duties seem to have been chiefly menial. It would look as though, humanly speaking, he was extinguished.

It was quite by accident that his real ability came to light. Nine months after he had been sent to Monte Paolo, an ordination ceremony took place at Forli. It was usual to engage a special preacher for such an occasion. This time there was a serious hitch; the special preacher failed to appear at the appointed hour. There were a number of Dominicans at the ceremony and, one after the other, they were invited to oblige, but they all declined on the ground of not being prepared. The Father Provincial was in a really awkward predicament when his eye met Anthony's. He signalled him briefly to fill the gap. Here was someone anyhow who could not refuse because he was unprepared. He was bound to obey.

Anthony came slowly forward and gave as his theme, *Obedience*, a theme into which his life at Monte Paolo had certainly given him a deep insight. His hearers looked and listened with growing astonishment. After a second or two of hesitation, Anthony had perfectly recovered himself and was completely at his ease. It could be seen at once that he had all the requisites of a most successful preacher: poise, a good delivery, passionate conviction, personal weight, a profound knowledge of theology and scripture, a wonderful memory. There was almost a commotion when he ended that extempore sermon. There were very few good preachers among the Franciscans, yet the Church never had such need of preachers and the heretical sects could always provide them. Anthony was immediately appointed preacher to the province of Romagna and word to that effect was sent Francis, who returned a message to the Provincial that Anthony was to be appointed preacher to the whole of Italy.

Anthony from that hour belonged no more to the hospice of Monte Paolo. He became a nomad and traveled ceaselessly for the next ten years from the north of France to the south of Italy, devoting all his time, talents and energy to the sole work of preaching. He discovered within himself the power of enkindling the masses with his own fire. The people's response was immediate. The churches filled to hear him to the point that windows and doors would be packed with faces and all the spaces outside thronged too with people. He then began taking a platform out into the street the better to command his audiences. When city streets and squares could no longer accommodate the crowds, the platform had to be carried out of the towns to a meadow, or a bare hillside, and thither that spectacular mass of people—twenty, thirty, or forty thousand—would trudge to hear Anthony, walking for miles through the heat and dust of summer, or in the most inclement winter weather.

Anthony's fame as a saint has shifted focus. His posthumous glory has concentrated almost solely on his miracles. It is, then, surprising to find what a small part marvels played in his real life work. It is an error to read his story backward, or to imagine that the splendor surrounding his name since his canonization irradiated also the shabby figure of the preaching friar. He was not always stunning attention with miraculous control of the elements, of the animal kingdom, of disease. It is worth noting that when the miracles recorded for his canonization were sifted, out of the forty-six accepted, only one had occurred before his death. His fame in life was not due to the prodigies he worked. He earned that success in a very human way open to all.

One must not, however, go to the other extreme and deny him all contact with miracles. If he was not in the habit of making a spectacular display of prodigious power, marvels were certainly told of him. One curious factor must be noted about the miracles he worked in his life. It is for the really amazing events that the strongest evidence exists. For instance, we are compelled to accept the two stories of the sermon to the fishes and Bonvillo's mule, whether we happen to like them or not, for they have been certified by the critics of the sources of his life.

Neither these episodes nor his success as a preacher can be understood without reference to the forces against which Anthony engaged in combat. Three groups of heretics were then disturbing Christendom: the Catharists, the Albigenses and the Waldenses. They all worked from within the Church, calling themselves Catholic reformers, or apostolic, or primitive, Catholics, and they tried to set up a hierarchy within a hierarchy. The Waldenses were particularly subtle and dangerous. They supported the Church in every particular and received all the Catholic Sacraments, except Penance, which they sought from Waldensian preachers only. These groups of heretics were therefore not so much like a diseased limb that can be amputated fairly cleanly as an internal malady which has to be gradually eliminated from the blood. They all drew their theories from the Bible so that only a Biblical expert could refute them. This is where Anthony's eight years' preparation in Coimbra was such an advantage. He was so thoroughly grounded in the Scriptures that Pope Gregory IX, when he heard him preach, called him, "Living Ark of the Covenant".

Anthony's sermon to the fishes took place probably at Rimini and is related to his fight against the Waldenses. He had been preaching to an audience of these, all professedly Catholic. The first difficulty was to convince them they were not the cream of the Catholic flock. This audience had become so outraged at Anthony's outspokenness that they decamped in a body, leaving him talking to the air. After this, he went for a walk along by the Marecchia. The mere sight of the ocean brought to his mind in a flash every reference to fishes in the Old and New Testament, from Jonah and the Whale to the miraculous catch of fishes and so to the early Christian symbol of a fish scratched on a stone. He spoke his meditations aloud and presently the fishes of the sea rose in serried rings to the surface of the water to listen to him. They were seen by numbers of witnesses, people who had first gathered in surprise behind a friar who was apparently talking to the waves.

The story of Bonvillo's mule is also connected with his battle with heretics, Albigenses this time: It happened in Toulouse, a place so rotten with Albigensian ideas that Anthony, while there, carried his life in his hands. It was the only place in Europe where the heresy was fostered by civil power, for the government of this fief had favored it now for more than a generation. A man named Bonvillo argued publicly with Anthony against the Real Presence and ended up by demanding a sign. He said he would tie up his mule in the marketplace and leave it there without food for three days. At the end of that period, Anthony was to bring the Blessed Sacrament into the market and Bonvillo would bring oats at the same time: if the mule ignored the food and adored the Host, then Bonvillo would become a believer.

The populace agreed with Bonvillo in demanding this test and Anthony's protests were shouted down. The circumstances must have been both peculiar and formidable when the preacher was forced to assent. At any rate, Anthony seems to have made up his mind to stake a great deal on the power of prayer. At the end of three days, accompanied by lighted candles and swinging censer, he carried the Host into the marketplace, where the starving mule was pawing the ground in the midst of an immense crowd. Bonvillo at the same time thrust his oats under the animal's nose. But the mule turned from the food and kept his head on the ground in an unmistakable posture of adoration. He did not rise until Anthony had retired.

Both these stories are the theme for innumerable paintings and drawings. It is a human impulse to scoff at them, as imposing too great a strain upon credulity. Yet the evidence for them is such that it cannot be dismissed as worthless.

Anthony's sermons, then, were apologetic rather than devotional. This makes their appeal a greater wonder to the modern mind, which finds it difficult to understand the medieval preoccupation with apologetics. All the laity of that age who aspired to culture tried to make it include mastery of the content of the Faith. He did not actually preach from notes, but he relied almost wholly upon preliminary preparation with notes. This we know from one of the innumerable miracle stories: how once in France a novice stole his precious manuscript and Anthony was in acute distress over the loss. It is an illuminating incident. The prodigious crowds that were the talk of Europe assembling to hear him—the "Hammer of the Heretics" as he was called—and in the background he was wringing his hands because he could not find his notebook.

There was an element of surprise in his preaching which conveys to us today, across the centuries, some dim idea of what his personal magnetism must have been. He had tremendous moral courage. When it was necessary to attack an abuse, he did not know fear. It is said that famous preachers who came to listen to him shivered at his boldness. On one occasion he was invited to preach at a Synod at Bourges and the Archbishop, Simon de Sully, presided at the council. Anthony opened his sermon with *Tibi loquar cornute* ("You, there, with the mitre"), a public denunciation of the Archbishop who had invited him which almost paralyzed his hearers. A feature of his sermons was the virulence of his attacks on the secular clergy. He pitted himself also with extraordinary vehemence against the prevalent vices of his age, which were avarice, luxury and tyranny in government. His success as a preacher was due to this concentration on realities. He knew the needs of his day and met them. He eschewed abstractions.

His effect was such that, at the rumor of his coming, shops were shuttered up and the law courts closed. The people's demonstrative enthusiasm became such a physical danger to him, he had to be protected by a bodyguard of young men, who drew a cordon around the platform while he was preaching and held off the onrush of people afterward. Eye-witnesses have left on record vivid details: one said that the crowds cresting a distant hill on their way to one of these sermons looked like a dense flock of birds rising in flight; another said the lights flitting across the dark countryside the previous night reminded him of a strange concourse of spectres, for crowds used to gather around the platform the night before a sermon was announced, so as to make sure of a good place; yet another said that when Anthony paused in his speaking, the crowd would sigh in unison and the sound was like that of a great wind soughing.

The last Lent he preached in Padua was remembered for generations afterward because of the furor it caused in the city. The Paduans could find neither food nor accommodation enough for the crowds that invaded them. When Anthony was not actually preaching, or preparing notes for his next sermon, he was working like a Titan to cope with the enormous effect he was producing: endlessly hearing confessions, reconciling enemies, enforcing justice, arbitrating feuds, helping to close the affairs of usurers, even revising the social code and helping to frame the laws of the Commune. He was then at the highest point of his fame. Nothing whatever rivaled the interest of his sermons to those who had come within the sphere of his influence. The magnitude of the thing was perhaps the surest indication of its brevity. He was thirty-six. He had now been living this life for ten years without a break. He had latterly become afflicted by dropsy. His body was very swollen, his movements ungainly, his breathing difficult.

When Lent was over, he and two Franciscan companions got permission from a friend and patron, Count Tiso da Campo San Piero, to rest for a while in his country estate some distance outside the city. Among the trees in this retreat was a giant walnut with six thick branches growing upward from the crown. Here Anthony chose to make a cell for himself, binding the branches together with willows and roofing them with rushes. In this airy solitude, he tried to work during the summer heat. The Cardinal Bishop of Ostia had asked him for a copy of certain of his sermons and he was writing them out in obedience to this request. It was here that the intimation of death came to him on June 13, 1231. He told his companions to take him back to St. Mary's Padua, as he did not want to be a trouble to his host.

They placed the dying man on a peasant's cart, drawn by an ox, and thus began the miserable journey in the dust back to the city. Before they were half-way there, he was beyond speech, so they halted at the convent of the Poor Ladies at Arcella. Here they placed him sitting upright in a chair to enable him to breathe. He began to chant the Lauds hymn *O Gloriosa Domina* and, so chanting, he died.

The great Spanish artist, Murillo, found inspiration in the story of a vision with which Anthony was said to have been truly favored. He depicts the Child Jesus as resting on a sort of bank of sunset cloud and light, floating just within reach, while Anthony, who had been reading, leans suddenly forward, his dark, southern face transfigured with recognition. The sentiment of joy has been marvelously seized in the painting, so that it is impossible to look at it without communicating in that delight. This painting has been reproduced endlessly all over Christendom. It probably led to the statue with which we are so familiar—one might with justice write, drearily familiar—showing Anthony with an open book in his hands and the Infant Jesus resting on the book.

Here is the paradox. The well-known representations, though they commemorate a true occurrence, a fleeting moment of Anthony's life, yet show him as the exact opposite of what he really was. They suggest the cloistered contemplative, yet the world was Anthony's cloister and the two notes of his life's work were militant activity and ceaseless movement. He has become so monopolized by the Italians, and particularly by Padua, that it is generally forgotten he was a Portuguese. An aristocrat by birth, son of a knight at court, he has become the special property of the poor and the downtrodden. His devotees view him complacently as a character entirely simple, sweet and meek, but his biographers have difficulty in maintaining this consistent picture. To the student of his life and times, his character was intriguing and complex rather than simple; for instance he made three fresh starts in the religious life and there clung about him until he was at least twenty-six that faint suggestion of failure that attaches to anyone who makes several new beginnings. Sweetness of disposition was not his predominant characteristic: he had a tongue that could blister. He was bold rather than meek, as when he publicly slated an Archbishop who was among his audience. A man of profound learning, with no living rival as a Biblical expert, he has become the particular patron of the illiterate, the saint of trivial appeals, the finder of lost things. One of the most effective preachers the world has ever seen, recourse is had to him chiefly against the petty, almost the comical, ills of life.

His image is more ubiquitous than ever today in Catholic churches, bearing witness to that abiding appeal. More often than not it is an execrably bad colored plaster statue, so that—generally speaking—great art has not contributed to the extension of that cult. This saint of such a remote medieval period, the thirteenth century, still retains a secure hold on popular imagination, despite the multitude of saints that have been canonized and even the visions that have electrified the Christian world since his time, whereas hundreds of other saints have in the interval faded out of Christian memory.

～

SAINT THOMAS AQUINAS

[*1225(7?) –1274*]

C. C. Martindale, S.J.

 HERE IS A real pleasure in passing immediately[1] from St. Francis of Assisi, so simple, so gay, so all that is the opposite of "bookish", who has won the love of the world, to St. Thomas of Aquino, in Southern Italy, who with positively startling rapidity is regaining its homage, as having been perhaps the most commanding intelligence that Europe ever produced. I will first very briefly summarize his life. His ancestry was superb; through his father, Count of Aquino, and his mother, Countess of Teano, he was related to the Emperors Henry VI and Frederick II, and to the kings of France, Castile and Aragon. At five, he was sent to school with the Benedictines of Monte Cassino. Later, he went to the University of Naples—his intelligence had already revealed itself such that *not* to have left monastery for university would have seemed a crime. Here, far from yielding to that insidious climate and the corruptions that surrounded him, he resolved to become a Dominican friar, and his superiors sent him to Rome in view of yet further journeys to the great center of learning, Cologne, and the supreme focus of scientific study, Paris. But his parents indignant that the lad should renounce the pomps of his heredity for the black and white dress of the Dominicans, literally kidnapped and imprisoned him, and his brothers made the vilest attempts to destroy his chastity. Herein he conquered, and, managing to get books, filled his two years' imprisonment with intensive study. Finally, he reached Cologne and was put under Albertus Magnus a man of encyclopedic knowledge. At first Thomas listened so much and said so little that they called him the "Dumb Ox". But Albert said that his voice would one day fill the world; and indeed

---

[1] In the broadcasting series in which all the sketches contributed to this book by Father Martindale were first delivered.

216

Thomas was to eclipse his master, at least in accuracy of observation and force of argument, and, merciful endowment, terseness of statement. Ordained priest about 1250, and equipped with one University degree after another, he moved to and fro among the great intellectual centers of the period, especially in Italy and France, but in 1263 he was present at a Dominican general chapter in London, and his tall, burly, upright figure has been seen at Blackfriars by the Thames, and he may have actually fingered the ancient stones that not long ago were transported thence to their proper place today—the Dominican Priory at Haverstock Hill. It seems humanwise inexplicable how, during these years of continuous travel and teaching, yes, and of preaching and apostolic work, he can not only have produced his enormous literary output, but have *thought* the firm-woven texture of philosophy that his books contain, let alone have studied the authorities he uses and quotes, especially as during his last years he manifested an ever-increasing distaste for that sort of human knowledge and love for the understanding that comes through direct communication with God. And observe, that when he died, in 1274, in a Cistercian monastery, having endeavored to obey the Pope's mandate that he should go to the great Council of Lyons, he was not yet fifty!

Now, when I say that probably no one man has so influenced human thought as St. Thomas has, I may seem to you to be talking nonsense. Yet thinkers have thriven just in proportion as even unconsciously they obeyed his principles of thought, and have done flimsy work in proportion as they have scorned, or just not known of, the intellectual method that he brought to such perfection. But only within the last, say, forty years has his name, and has the whole character of his period begun to come back into their proper place in men's appreciation. For it was the fashion to suppose that no one had thought or said anything worth anything till the sixteenth, or, indeed, till the nineteenth century. That fantastic balloon has been pricked and the conceited air let out of it. Not only was the thirteenth century the time when practically all Europe's universities either came into being, or received their rapid development; not only was it the time of—on the one hand—the most intensive study of sheer *fact* (in Albertus Magnus, for example, and in his two pupils, Roger Bacon and Thomas Aquinas, you will find all that should have led up swiftly to an applied knowledge of high explosives, of lenses, and of internal combustion engines, and again, a perfect knowledge of the "sex" of plants and of such exquisitely subtle observations as the evaporation of sap through their cuticles)—but also of the boldest practical theorizing, connected for example, with the correction of the calendar based partly on the knowledge of the time taken by light to travel, and so forth. It was the period, again, of artistic development and of literary origins—it was then that the legend of King Arthur, the Romaunt de la Rose, the Golden Legend, the Nibelungenlied, and more still, took shape, which have influenced literature ever since; not to speak of the great developments in Law, in Guild-Life, in sheer exploration with consequent knowledge of geography, and it was then (as I hope to mention when speaking of St. Camillus de Lellis) that the very creation or development of hospitals still surviving occurred—St. Thomas', Bart's, etc.—and that a medical and surgical knowledge existed that later generations *forgot*.

And notice that the full education of the day was at the disposal of nearly everyone. Never has education been so "democratic" since then. An enormously higher percentage of the population then went to universities than goes now or can possibly hope to go. Not that this cost them nothing. Personally, I think that little tends so swiftly and directly to degrade intellectual ambition as free education. Anyhow, in St. Thomas' day when education really was esteemed, enormous sacrifices were made by students and their friends for the sake of learning. Scholarships, burses, collections of all sorts were made, to get the would-be student actually to the university, to supply him with his books, and very food; he, on his side, was willing half the time to go without most of life's necessities and all its luxuries, and to earn his very keep not only by manual work outside of school terms, so to say, as is nobly and inspiritingly done by so many young students in the United States today, but, by working within the Universities themselves during term, serving, for example, the professors and even their fellow students.

Therefore, had St. Thomas put his tremendous influence and intellectual energy at the disposal of his age alone, his work would have been wide, deep and lasting. But he made a new gift to that world, which has assisted human thought ever since and could assist it at the present moment far more even than it does, were it better used. The great Greek thinker Aristotle had reached our thirteenth century in small fragments only of his works, ill-translated, and mostly by way of Arab and Jewish authors, who had made current very distorted versions of Aristotle's

meaning, so much so, that the very name of that philosopher was sus-
pected and disliked. St. Thomas, practically singlehanded, turned the
whole of this situation once and for all upside down. He caused, with
the help of the Holy See, a complete and proper translation to be made;
he explained the whole system of Aristotle more perfectly than ever
yet it had been set forth; and he displayed the fact that, far from being
of necessity, or at all, hostile to the Christian Faith, the tremendous
treasures of antiquity could be brought into glad and free cooperation
with the teachings of Christ. This in itself is an enormous benefit, because it can preserve religion from the miasma of sentimentalism that
infects so much of it today. Do not imagine it is easy to think properly.
It is far harder than learning about airplanes, or hunting, or making
films. It is an *art*. And, it is very tiring. People seize every chance of
not thinking, and end by half arguing you ought not to think, anyway
in religion, but just to feel or to be what they dub "mystical".

Our popular press almost takes it for granted that nothing is to be
known for certain, by means of the intelligence, of God, of the soul, of
right and wrong; that in some vague way religion won't bear thinking
about too closely; that history, and scientific research are, no one quite
knows how, yet in their very nature hostile to religion. So the average man himself, hard-headed enough, accurate and precise, when, say,
business is in hand, permits himself an incredible looseness of talk when
spiritual things are concerned. Yet I suppose that nowhere in the world
—no, not in Aristotle himself—will you find such ruthless distinction
between speculation and proof, hypothesis and demonstration, such
relentless logic as in St. Thomas, such laborious accumulation of all
available fact, such shifting and reshifting and assessment of evidence,
such absolute freedom from the scientific or philosophic fashion of the
moment—for science has fads and fashions, slogans and cant-phrases
too. In deed, just now men of science (anxious to put science itself
at the disposal of the multitude) are showing (to my mind) a reckless-
ness of statement, indulging in an irresponsible guessing-in-public so
second-rate as to be worse (because due to a vulgar affection for publicity and sensationalism) than the days of Tyndall and Huxley, even,
witnessed, for these had a kind of crude, boyish harsh optimism about
them which absolves them from much that was precipitate and has had
to be abandoned. No; Aquinas read everything, and forgot nothing;
never mixed up the materials with which he was dealing, whether they

concerned sheer history, or human psychology (as when he treats of human passions, or of perfectly concrete matters like the effect of hot baths upon the mind . . .), or asceticism, or metaphysics, or revealed dogma and theology. Nowhere in his enormous work is the least dislocation to be found; nowhere a word used without its meaning having been previously made clear; nowhere a side-slip in an argument. We dare not say we have exhausted our understanding of any ancient philosopher whomsoever, till we see what his thoughts would have issued into by the time of, under the treatment of, St. Thomas; nor can we possibly do better, when reading any author later in date than St. Thomas, than to drive what he may write through the fine mesh of Thomas' own thought.

You are probably saying by now: "What on earth has this talk been about? Who cares twopence whether Thomas Aquinas was or wasn't a great thinker? And if he was, what has that got to do with being a saint?" But, well, St. Francis sufficed, all by himself, to prove that a man can turn right upside down the ordinary belief that Money is what man wants, and that his proper job in life is (as an American millionaire once said to me, with eyes wide open like a baby's with astonishment that I could suppose anything else) *making dollars*, whereas hardly a man knows the name of, and not one man remembers with esteem or affection, any of the rich men of Francis' day, while millions still love *him* with all their hearts. And Thomas Aquinas suffices (had he not had a single disciple instead of one generation after another of them) to upset the myth that Religion fears Thought, fears Science, is an affair of emotion, obscure tradition, of leaps in the dark, or even identical with mystical union with God—though this, when genuine, is a very sublime outcome of it. St. Thomas in his own person, in his books, in the thousands of books written about him, through the great Dominican Order to which he belonged, in the schools that still live, think, and develop by means of his impetus and method, disproves that myth. Religion does not fear Enquiry, but courts it; nay, is the first to apply it—I have never read any attacks on religion so drastic as those invented by Aquinas! But it was not just his intelligence that made St. Thomas a *Saint*. He thought singularly lightly of the intellectual side of his work. It is pathetic still to see his own manuscript of one of his greatest books, preserved in the Vatican Library, and to perceive how through paragraph after paragraph of abbreviated, almost shorthand script, his pen has drawn a line of yellowing ink, showing how dissatisfied he was with what we find so treasurable. His extreme humility, no doubt—like that, indeed, of any really great scholar—made him think but poorly of his work; any such man sees how tremendous is Truth, that the most of what man can know of it is but little. But deeper still, he had come to live in so habitual a communion with God, actually in the country whereof the most accurate theology is but the map, that, said he, "all I have written now seems to me but of little value." This man of many travels, of intimate understanding of his fellow men, was, through his love for Jesus Christ, in such close touch with God, that all life, let alone all knowledge, had become for him a means of a holiest Communion; and perhaps the best way of entering into contact with St. Thomas is through his Eucharistic hymns, fragments of two of which, O *Salutaris* and *Tantum Ergo*, are sung Sunday by Sunday by millions still today.

∼

SAINT MARGARET OF CORTONA

[1249–1297]

Alban Goodier, S.J.

 HEY WERE stirring times in Tuscany when Margaret was born. They were the days of Manfred and Conradin, of the Guelphs and Ghibellines in Italy, when passions of every kind ran high, and men lived at great extremes. They were times of great sinners, but also of great saints; Margaret lived to hear of the crowning and resignation of St. Celestine V, whose life and death are a vivid commentary on the spirits that raged throughout that generation. It was the age of St. Thomas in Paris, of Dante in Florence; of Cimabue and Giotto; of the great cathedrals and universities. In Tuscany itself, apart from the coming and going of soldiers, now of the Emperor, now of the Pope, keeping the countryside in a constant state of turmoil, and teaching the country-folk their ways, there were for ever rising little wars among the little cities themselves, which were exciting and disturbing enough. For instance, when Margaret was a child, the diocese in which she lived, Chiusi, owned a precious relic, the ring of the Blessed Virgin Mary. An Augustinian friar got possession of this relic, and carried it off to Perugia. This caused a war; Chiusi and Perugia fought for the treasure and Perugia won. Such was the spirit of her time, and of the people among whom she was brought up.

It was also a time of the great revival; when the new religious orders had begun to make their mark, and the old ones had renewed their strength. Franciscans and Dominicans had reached down to the people, and every town and village in the country had responded to their call to better things. St. Francis of Assisi had received the stigmata on Mount Alverno twenty years before, quite close to where Margaret was born; St. Clare died not far away, when Margaret was four years old. And there was the opposite extreme, the enthusiasts whose devotion degenerated into heresy. When Margaret was ten there arose in her own district the Flagellants, whose processions of men, women, and children, stripped to the waist and scourging themselves to blood, must have been a not uncommon sight to her and her young companions.

Margaret was born in Laviano, a little town in the diocese of Chiusi. Her parents were working people of the place; their child was very beautiful, and in their devotion, for she was the only one, they could scarcely help but spoil her. Thus from the first Margaret, as we would say, had much against her; she grew up very wilful and, like most spoilt children, very restless and dissatisfied. Very soon her father's cottage was too small for her; she needed companions; she found more life and excitement in the streets of the town. Next, in course of time the little town itself grew too small; there was a big world beyond about which she came to know, and Margaret longed to have a part in it. Moreover she soon learned that she could have a part in it if she chose. For men took notice of her, not only men of her own station and surroundings, whom she could bend to her will as she pleased; but great and wealthy men from outside, who would sometimes ride through the village, and notice her, and twit her for her beautiful face. They would come again; they were glad to make her acquaintance, and sought to win her favor. Margaret quickly learned that she had only to command, and there were many ready to obey.

While she was yet very young her mother died; an event which seemed to deprive her of the only influence that had hitherto held her in check. Margaret records that she was taught by her mother a prayer she never forgot: "O Lord Jesus, I beseech thee, grant salvation to all those for whom thou wouldst have me pray". To make matters worse her father married again. He was a man of moods, at one time weak and indulgent, at another violent to excess, and yet with much in him that was lovable, as we shall have reason to see. But with the stepmother there was open and continued conflict. She was shocked at Margaret's wilfulness and independence, and from her first coming to the house was determined to deal with them severely. Such treatment was fatal to Margaret. As a modern student has written of her:

> Margaret's surroundings were such as to force to the surface the weaknesses of her character. As is clear from her own confessions, she was by nature one of those women who thirst for affection; in whom to be loved is the imperative need of their lives. She needed to be loved that

her soul might be free, and in her home she found not what she wanted. Had she been of the weaker sort, either morally or physically, she would have accepted her lot, vegetated in spiritual barrenness, married eventually a husband of her father's choice, and lived an uneventful life with a measure of peace.

As it was she became only the more wilful and reckless. If there was not happiness for her, either at home or elsewhere, there was pleasure and, with a little yielding on her part, as much of it as she would. In no long time her reputation in the town was one not to be envied; before she was seventeen years of age she had given herself up to a life of indulgence, let the consequences be what they might.

Living such a life it soon became evident that Margaret could not stay in Laviano. The circumstances which took her away are not very clear; we choose those which seem the most satisfactory. A certain nobleman, living out beyond Montepulciano which in those days was far away, was in need of a servant in his castle. Margaret got the situation; there at least she was free from her stepmother and, within limits, could live as she pleased. But her master was young, and a sporting man, and no better than others of his kind. He could not fail to take notice of the handsome girl who went about his mansion, holding her head high as if she scorned the opinions of men, with an air of independence that seemed to belong to one above her station. He paid her attention; he made her nice presents; he would do her kindnesses even while she served him. And on her side, Margaret was skilled in her art; she was quick to discover that her master was as susceptible to her influence as were the other less distinguished men with whom she had done as she would in Laviano. Moreover this time she was herself attracted; she knew that this man loved her, and she returned it in her way. There were no other competitors in the field to distract her; there was no mother to warn her, no stepmother to abuse her. Soon Margaret found herself installed in the castle, not as her master's wife, for convention would never allow that, but as his mistress, which was more easily condoned. Some day, he had promised her, they would be married, but the day never came. A child was born, and with that Margaret settled down to the situation.

For some years she accepted her lot, though every day what she had done grew upon her more and more. Apart from the evil life she was living, her liberty loving nature soon found that instead of freedom she had secured only slavery. The restless early days in Laviano seemed, in her present perspective, less unhappy than she had thought; the poverty and restraint of her father's cottage seemed preferable to the wealth and chains of gold she now endured. In her lonely hours, and they were many, the memory of her mother came up before her, and she could not look her shadow in the face. And with that revived the consciousness of sin, which of late she had defied, and had crushed down by sheer reckless living, but which now loomed up before her like a haunting ghost. She saw it all, she hated it all, she hated herself, because of it, but there was no escape. It was all misery, but she must endure it; she had made her own bed, and must henceforth lie upon it. In her solitary moments she would wander into the gloom of the forest, and there would dream of the life that might have been, a life of virtue and of the love of God. At her castle gate she would be bountiful; if she could not be happy herself, at least she could do something to help others. But for the rest she was defiant. She went about her castle with the airs of an unbeaten queen. None should know, not even the man who owned her, the agony that gnawed at her heart. From time to time there would come across her path those who had pity for her. They would try to speak to her; they would warn her of the risk she was running; but Margaret, with her ever ready wit, would laugh at their warnings and tell them that some day she would be a saint.

So things went on for nine years, till Margaret was twenty-seven. On a sudden there came an awakening. It chanced that her lord had to go away on a distant journey; in a few days, when the time arrived for his return, he did not appear. Instead there turned up at the castle gate his favorite hound, which he had taken with him. As soon as it had been given admittance it ran straight to Margaret's room, and there began to whine about her, and to tug at her dress as if it would drag her out of the room. Margaret saw that something was amiss.

Anxious, not daring to express to herself her own suspicions, she rose and followed the hound wherever it might lead; it drew her away down to a forest a little distance from the castle walls. At a point where a heap of faggots had been piled, apparently by woodcutters, the hound stood still, whining more than ever, and poking beneath the faggots with its nose. Margaret, all trembling, set to work to pull the heaps away; in a hole beneath lay the corpse of her lord, evidently some days dead, for the maggots and worms had already begun their work upon it.

How he had come to his death was never known; after all, in those days of high passions, and family feuds, such murders were not uncommon. The careful way the body had been buried suggested foul play; that was all. But for Margaret the sight she saw was of something more than death. The old faith within her still lived, as we have already seen, and now insisted on asking questions. The body of the man she had loved and served was lying there before her, but what had become of his soul? If it had been condemned, and was now in hell, who was, in great part at least, responsible for its condemnation? Others might have murdered his body, but she had done infinitely worse. Moreover there was herself to consider. She had known how, in the days past, she had stirred the rivalry and mutual hatred of men on her account and had gloried in it; who knew but that this deed had been done by some rival because of her? Or again, her body might have been lying there where his now lay, her fatal beauty being eaten by worms, and in that case where would her soul then have been? Of that she could have no sort of doubt. Her whole life came up before her, crying out now against her as she had never before permitted it to cry. Margaret rushed from the spot, beside herself in this double misery, back to her room, turned in an instant to a torture chamber.

What should she do next? She was not long undecided. Though the castle might still be her home, she would not stay in it a moment longer. But where could she go? There was only one place of refuge that she knew, only one person in the world who was likely to have pity on her. Though her father's house had been disgraced in the eyes of all the village by what she had done, though the old man all these years had been bent beneath the shame she had brought upon him, still there was the memory of past kindness and love which he had always shown her. It was true sometimes he had been angry, especially when others had roused him against her and her ways; but always in the end, when she had gone to him, he had forgiven her and taken her back. She would arise and go to her father, and would ask him to forgive her once more; this time in her heart she knew she was in earnest—even if he failed her she would not turn back. Clothed as she was, holding her child in her arms, taking no heed of the spectacle she made, she left the castle, tramped over the ridge and down the valley to Laviano, came to her father's cottage, found him within alone and fell at his feet, confessing her guilt, imploring him with tears to give her shelter once again.

The old man easily recognized his daughter. The years of absence, the fine clothes she wore, the length of years which in some ways had only deepened the striking lines of her handsome face, could not take from his heart the picture of the child of whom once he had been so proud. To forgive was easy; it was easy to find reasons in abundance. Had he not indulged her in the early days, perhaps she would never have fallen. Had he made home a more satisfying place for a child of so yearning a nature, perhaps she would never have gone away. Had he been a more careful guardian, had he protected her from those who had lured her into evil ways long ago, she would never have wandered so far, she would never have brought this shame upon him and upon herself. She was repentant, she wished to make amends, she had proved it by this renunciation, she showed she loved and trusted him; he must give her a chance to recover. If he did not give it to her, who would?

So the old man argued with himself, and for a time his counsel prevailed. Margaret with her child was taken back; if she would live quietly at home the past might be lived down. But such was not according to Margaret's nature. She did not wish the past to be forgotten, it must be atoned. She had done great evil, she had given great scandal; she must prove to God and man that she had broken with the past, and that she meant to make amends. The spirit of fighting sin by public penance was in the air; the Dominican and Franciscan missionaries preached it, there were some in her neighborhood who were carrying it to a dangerous extreme. Margaret would let all the neighbors see that she did not shirk the shame that was her due. Every time she appeared in the church it was with a rope of penance round her waist; she would kneel at the church door that all might pass her by and despise her; since this did not win for her the scorn she desired, one day, when the people were gathered for Mass, she stood up before the whole congregation and made public confession of the wickedness of her life.

But this did not please her old father. He had hoped she would lie quiet and let the scandal die; instead she kept the memory of it always alive. He had expected that soon all would be forgotten; instead she made of herself a public show. In a very short time his mind toward her changed. Indulgence turned to resentment, resentment to bitterness, bitterness to something like hatred. Besides, there was another in the house to be reckoned with; the stepmother, who from her first coming there had never been a friend of Margaret. She had endured her return because, for the moment, the old man would not be contradicted; but she had bided her time. Now when he wavered she brought her guns to bear; to the old man in secret, to Margaret before her face, she did not hesitate to use every argument she knew. This hussy who had shamed them all in the sight of the whole village had dared to cross her spotless threshold, and that with a baggage of a child in her arms. How often when she was a girl had she been warned where her reckless life would lead her! When she had gone away, in spite of every appeal, she had been told clearly enough what would be her end. All these years she had continued, never once relenting, never giving them a sign of recognition, knowing very well the disgrace she had brought upon them, while she enjoyed herself in luxury and ease. Let her look to it; let her take the consequences. That house had been shamed enough; it should not be shamed any more, by keeping such a creature under its roof. One day, when things had reached a climax, without a word of pity Margaret and her child were driven out of the door. If she wished to do penance, let her go and join the fanatical Flagellants, who were making such a show of themselves not far away.

Margaret stood in the street, homeless, condemned by her own, an outcast. Those in the town looked on and did nothing; she was not one of the kind to whom it was either wise or safe to show pity, much less to take her into their own homes. And Margaret knew it; since her own father had rejected her she could appeal to no one else; she could only hide her head in shame, and find refuge in loneliness in the open lane. But what should she do next? For she had not only herself to care for; there was also the child in her arms. As she sat beneath a tree looking away from Laviano, her eyes wandered up the ridge on which stood Montepulciano. Over that ridge was the bright, gay world she had left, the world without a care, where she had been able to trample scandal underfoot and to live as a queen. There she had friends who loved her; rich friends who had condoned her situation, poor friends who had been beholden to her for the alms she had given them. Up in the castle there were still wealth and luxury waiting for her, and even peace of a kind, if only she would go back to them. Besides, from the castle what good she could do! She was now free; she could repent in silence and apart; with the wealth at her disposal she could help the poor yet more. Since she had determined to change her life, could she not best accomplish it up there, far away from the sight of men?

On the other hand, what was she doing here? She had tried to repent, and all her efforts had only come to this; she was a homeless outcast on the road, with all the world to glare at her as it passed her by. Among her own people, even if in the end she were forgiven and taken back, she could never be the same again. Then came a further thought. She knew herself well by this time. Did she wish that things should be the same again? In Laviano, among the old surroundings which she had long outgrown, among peasants and laborers whom she had long left behind, was it not likely that the old boredom would return, more burdensome now that she had known the delights of freedom? Would not the old temptations return, had they not returned already, had they not been with her all the time, and with all her good intentions was it not certain that she would never be able to resist? Then would her last state be worse than her first. How much better to be prudent, to take the opportunity as it was offered, perhaps to use for good the means and the gifts she had hitherto used only for evil! Thus, resting under a tree in her misery, a great longing came over Margaret, to have done with the penitence which had all gone wrong, to go back to the old life where all had gone well, and would henceforth go better, to solve her problems once and for all by the only way that seemed open to her. That lonely hour beneath the tree was the critical hour of her life.

Happily for her, and for many who have come after her, Margaret survived it: "I have put thee as a burning light", Our Lord said to her later, "to enlighten those who sit in the darkness.—I have set you as an example to sinners, that in you they may behold how my mercy awaits the sinner who is willing to repent; for as I have been merciful to you, so will I be merciful to them." She had made up her mind long ago and she would not go back now. She shook herself and rose to go; but where? The road down which she went led to Cortona; a voice within her seemed to tell her to go thither. She remembered that at Cortona was a monastery of Franciscans. It was famous all over the countryside; Brother Elias had built it, and had lived and died there; the friars, she knew, were everywhere described as the friends of sinners. She might go to them; perhaps they would have pity on her and find her shelter. But she was not sure. They would know her only too well, for she had long been the talk of the district, even as far as Cortona; was it not too much to expect that the Franciscan friars would so easily believe in so sudden and complete a conversion? Still she could only try; at the worst she could but again be turned into the street, and that would be more endurable from them than the treatment she had just received in Laviano.

Her fears were mistaken. Margaret knocked at the door of the monastery, and the friars did not turn her away. They took pity on her; they accepted her tale though, as was but to be expected, with caution. She made a general confession, with such a flood of tears that those who witnessed it were moved. It was decided that Margaret was, so far at least, sincere and harmless, and they found her a home. They put her in charge of two good matrons of the town, who spent their slender means in helping hard cases and who undertook to provide for her. Under their roof she began in earnest her life of penance. Margaret could not do things by halves; when she had chosen to sin she had defied the world in her sinning, now that she willed to do penance she was equally defiant of what men might think or say. She had reveled in rich clothing and jewels; henceforth, so far as her friends would permit her, she would clothe herself literally in rags. She had slept on luxurious couches; henceforth she would lie only on the hard ground. Her beauty, which had been her ruin, and the ruin of many others besides, and which even now, at twenty-seven, won for her many a glance of admiration as she passed down the street, she was determined to destroy. She cut her face, she injured it with bruises, till men would no longer care to look upon her. Nay, she would go abroad, and where she had sinned most she would make most amends. She would go to Montepulciano; there she would hire a woman to lead her like a beast with a rope round her neck, and cry: "Look at Margaret, the sinner." It needed a strong and wise confessor to keep her within bounds.

Nor was this done only to atone for the past. For years the old cravings were upon her; they had taken deep root and could not at once be rooted out; even to the end of her life she had reason to fear them. Sometimes she would ask herself how long she could continue the fight; sometimes it would be that there was no need, that she should live her life like ordinary mortals. Sometimes again, and this would often come from those about her, it would be suggested to her that all her efforts were only a proof of sheer pride. In many ways we are given to see that with all the sanctity and close union with God which she afterward attained, Margaret to the end was very human; she was the same Margaret, however chastened, that she had been at the beginning. "My father," she said to her confessor one day, "do not ask me to give in to this body of mine. I cannot afford it. Between me and my body there must needs be a struggle until death."

The rest of Margaret's life is a wonderful record of the way God deals with his penitents. There were her child and herself to be kept, and the fathers wisely bade her earn her own bread. She began by nursing; soon she confined her nursing to the poor, herself living on alms. She retired to a cottage of her own; here, like St. Francis before her, she made it her rule to give her labor to whoever sought it, and to receive in return whatever they chose to give. In return there grew in her a new understanding of that craving for love which had led her into danger. She saw that it never would be satisfied here on earth; she must have more than this world could give her or none at all. And here God was good to her. He gave her an intimate knowledge of himself; we might say he humored her by letting her realize his love, his care, his watchfulness over her. With all her fear of herself, which was never far away, she grew in confidence because she knew that now she was loved by One who would not fail her. This became the character of her sanctity, founded on that natural trait which was at once her strength and her weakness.

And it is on this account, more than on account of the mere fact that she was a penitent, that she deserves the title of the Second Magdalen. Of the first Magdalen we know this, that she was an intense human being, seeking her own fulfillment at extremes, now in sin, now in repentance regardless of what men might think, uniting love and sorrow so closely that she is forgiven, not for her sorrow so much as for her love. We know that ever afterward it was the same; the thought of her sin never kept her from her Lord, the knowledge of his love drew her ever closer to him, till, after Calvary, she is honored the first among those to whom he would show himself alone. And in that memorable scene we have the two traits which sum her up; he reveals himself by calling her by her name: "Mary", and yet, when she would cling about his feet, as she had done long before, he bids her not to touch him. In Margaret of Cortona the character, and the treatment, are parallel. She did not forget what she had been; but from the first the thought of this never for a moment kept her from Our Lord. She gave herself to penance, but the motive of her penance, as her revelations show, was love more than atonement. In her extremes of penance she had no regard for the opinions of men; she would brave any obstacle that she might draw the nearer to him. At first he humored her; he drew her by revealing to her his appreciation of her love; he even condescended so far as to call her "Child", when she had grown tired of being called "*Poverella*". But later, when the time for the greatest graces came, then he took her higher by seeming to draw more apart; it was the scene of *Noli me tangere* repeated.

This must suffice for an account of the wonderful graces and revelations that were poured out on Margaret during the last twenty-three years of her life. She came to Cortona as a penitent when she was twenty-seven. For three years the Franciscan fathers kept her on her trial, before they would admit her to the Third Order of St. Francis. She submitted to the condition; during that time she earned her bread, entirely in the service of others. Then she declined to earn it; while she labored in service no less, she would take in return only what was given to her in alms. Soon even this did not satisfy her; she was not content till the half of what was given her in charity was shared with others who seemed to her more needy. Then out of this there grew other things, for Margaret had a practical and organizing mind. She founded institutions of charity, she established an institution of ladies who would spend themselves in the service of the poor and suffering. She took a large part in the keeping of order in that turbulent countryside; even her warlike bishop was compelled to listen to her, and to surrender much of his plunder at her bidding. Like St. Catherine of Siena after her, Margaret is a wonderful instance, not only of the mystic combined with the soul of action, but more of the soul made one of action because it was a mystic, and by means of its mystical insight.

Margaret died in 1297, being just fifty years of age. Her confessor and first biographer tells us that one day, shortly before her death, she had a vision of St. Mary Magdalen, "most faithful of Christ's apostles, clothed in a robe as it were of silver, and crowned with a crown of precious gems, and surrounded by the holy angels." And while she was in this ecstasy Christ spoke to Margaret, saying: "My Eternal Father said of me to the Baptist: This is my beloved Son; so do I say to thee of Magdalen: This is my beloved daughter." On another occasion we are told that "she was taken in spirit to the feet of Christ, which she washed with her tears as did Magdalen of old; and as she wiped his feet she desired greatly to behold his face, and prayed to the Lord to grant her this favor." Thus to the end we see she was the same; and yet the difference!

They buried her in the church of St. Basil in Cortona. Around her body, and later at her tomb, her confessor tells us that so many miracles, physical and spiritual, were worked that he could fill a volume with the record of those which he personally knew alone. And today Cortona boasts of nothing more sacred or more treasured than that same body, which lies there still incorrupt, after more than six centuries, for everyone to see.

SAINT ELIZABETH OF PORTUGAL

[1271–1336]

Vincent McNabb, O.P.

AINT ELIZABETH was born in the year 1271, at Saragossa, Spain. She is known in Portugal under the Spanish form of her name, Isabel. The saint's father was Don Pedro, son and successor of Jayme the Conqueror, King of Aragon. Her mother was Constance, daughter of Manfred, the illegitimate son of the Emperor Frederic II.

If birth from such a stock assured a certain share in heroism, on neither side were the chances favorable to heroic holiness. On the one side, the grandchild of Manfred and the great-grandchild of Frederic II was not a saint by birth. On the other side, King Jayme was a Conqueror in other battlefields than those of heroic self-restraint. Indeed he almost rivaled Henry VIII in the variety of his matrimonial experiences. There is perhaps a faint forecast of the spiritual wisdom of his grandchild in one of the seven heads of advice Jayme gave to his son-in-law, King Alfonso of Castile. "If some only were to be kept in his grace, he could not keep the others, he should keep at least two parties—the Church and the people and towns of the country; for they are those God loves more even than the nobles and knights. For the knights revolt sooner against their lord than the others. If he could keep all of them with him, well and good. If not, he should keep these two parties, for with their help he could easily destroy the others."

At her baptism the child was called after St. Elizabeth of Hungary, the sister of her grandmother, Yolande.

The only remarkable fact which history has connected with the birth of the Saint is that she was born with a caul! Another fact, as much achievement as sign, is authentic history. Before the birth of Elizabeth, the King to rid himself of the murmurings against his loose living had banished his family from the court. But on the birth of St. Elizabeth, he longed to see his youngest grandchild, and for her sake he made peace with his son, Don Pedro.

The court of Don Jayme could hardly be called a model nursery for a saint; yet in view of her future trials it was a providential nursery for St. Elizabeth. Don Jayme, whose marriage with Eleanor had been declared null through consanguinity, tired of his next wife, Yolande, the sister of St. Elizabeth of Hungary, and in 1246 he tore out the tongue of the Dominican Bishop of Gerona who took her part. Teresa, who had supplanted Yolande in the King's affections, became wife and queen on Yolande's death. But before Teresa's own death the King's relations with a kinswoman and wife of a noble were the most striking features of St. Elizabeth's royal nursery.

In spite of the reproofs of Popes like Innocent IV, Clement IV and Gregory X, and saints like Raymond of Peñafort, the state of things at the court of Don Jayme continued to be so scandalous that on September 22, 1275, Pope Gregory X wrote to the King that if a change did not take place in eight days he had instructed the Archbishop of Tarragona to excommunicate him and lay Aragon under an interdict.

De Moucheron's idyll of the incestuous king won from his evil ways by his angel of a granddaughter is hardly compatible with the papal letters. Ten months after the last threat of Gregory X, the Conqueror was dead.

We are told that before his death (July 27, 1276) he had obeyed the Pope's command to send away Berengaria. Then he divided his kingdom between his sons, put on the habit of a Cistercian and died. Before his death, he used to say that "Elizabeth, his granddaughter and pupil (alumnam), would be the greatest and most illustrious woman to spring from the stock of Aragon."

Elizabeth was in her sixth year when the death of her grandfather, in whose care she was, restored her to her father, now King Pedro III. Her biographers gave her all the praise usually bestowed on the children of kings, and especially on such royal children as are afterward to be saints. It is said that her father received her as an angel of heaven. "On her charming face was painted a singular modesty joined to a gravity and sweetness most unusual. Already at her tender age she had the bearing and manner of a princess, she had wisdom and good sense, the love of prayer and of study. She was constantly seen saying her office, meditating out of holy books, going to the Sacraments, and showing the poor that deep compassion which she expressed in almsgiving proportionate to her allowance." Behind these accustomed generalities, which almost irritate the reader by what is left untold, we may find that truth which the future years were to develop. So marvelous are the authentic facts of the Saint as Queen of Portugal that the legends or platitudes told of her childhood are almost authenticated. Some of these things are made more certain by the fact that King Jayme the Conqueror, surely no mean judge of men and women, kept this "angel of God" by him till his death. If there are few legends in the life of this great Saint, it is not merely because her life was lived in the fierce light of a throne but that many of the authentic facts of her life are almost more marvelous than legend.

Elizabeth was scarcely twelve years old when her wedding became a move in the complicated game of European politics. This is but to say that the last person to be consulted about Elizabeth's future husband was Elizabeth herself. It makes her life seem very close to us when we read that Edward I of England sought her hand for his eldest son; while Charles of Anjou, King of Naples, sought to marry this great-grandchild of the Hohenstaufens to his heir Robert. Don Pedro was reluctant to part with his beloved daughter, being convinced that to her prayers he owed the happiness of his kingdom. But at last his reluctance gave way when Don Diniz, the young King of Portugal, asked for her hand.

The Portuguese King's motives for the marriage were tragic.

> Embroiled with his mother, whom he had at first associated with himself on the throne, at enmity with his brother, Don Alfonso, who laid claim to the crown, excommunicated by the Pope because of his resistance to the political pretensions [sic] of the bishops, King Diniz felt the need of resting on a loyal heart. But the affair was not simple. King Alfonso III, his father, had repudiated his wife, the Countess Matilda of Boulogne, had married Beatrice Guzma, illegitimate daughter of the King of Castile, had dethroned his brother, the legitimate king. Hence King Diniz found himself son of a usurper and of an illegitimate princess; himself illegitimate. At the petition of the States of Portugal, Pope Urban IV had validated the royal marriage after the death of the Countess Matilda; yet on the whole of the circumstances there rested not a few clouds.[1]

It is evident that Elizabeth was not a saint by circumstances.

---

[1] De Moucheron, pp. 18, 19.

The wedding by proxy took place in one of the halls of the royal palace at Barcelona. De Moucheron says that in accepting the hand of Diniz at the bidding of her father and mother she had "consummated her sacrifice and had renounced her secret vow of giving herself to God alone".[2] If the saint had already made a vow of virginity her freely accepted wedding shows her to have been taught that love is a sacrifice and perfect love a holocaust.

It might be questioned whether anything could be less romantic than such marriages as these. In poorer ranks of life a bridal dowry was usually given with the bride. But in these marriages of kings and queens a bride was usually given away with a dowry. Politicians, lawyers and military leaders were always consulted; the last person to be consulted was the bride. The last quality sought in bride or bridegroom was love. Two lives were thus entwined for better or worse till death parted them without the one quality which could make their union less than slavery. To such tyranny men and women must submit in order to be kings and queens. The common run of kings and queens escaped from the thraldom of wedlock without love by an open door of sin. Many of these unfortunate women became adulteresses. Some of heroic mold became saints. Of such heroism was St. Elizabeth.

Two months after Elizabeth left her father's home, the massacre of the Sicilian Vespers covered Don Pedro with suspicion. His only answer to these suspicions was to despatch an army which drove Charles of Anjou from Sicily into Italy. Pope Martin IV (Simon de Brion), who largely owed his position to Charles, showed his loyalty to his former patron and fellow countryman by excommunicating Don Pedro and declaring him deposed from his sovereignty of Aragon. St. Elizabeth was now the wife of one excommunicated king and the daughter of another.

She was only thirteen years old when her father died (November 2, 1285), absolved from his excommunication by the Archbishop of Tarragona. As her brother claimed the crown of Sicily and was actively supported in his claim by his mother, Pope Honorius IV had excommunicated them both (1286).

In 1289, she had the consolation of seeing a Concordat drawn up between King Diniz and Pope Nicholas IV. Her joy was complete when

[2] *Ibid.*, p. 22.

the Prior of the Dominicans and the Guardian of the Franciscans at Lisbon absolved the King from the Papal excommunication. At the same time the Pope removed the Papal interdict which for years had overshadowed Portugal. It is commonly felt that the success of these negotiations was largely due to the Queen.

St. Elizabeth was in her twentieth year (1290) when her first child was born. It was called Constance, after the Queen's mother.

The birth of St. Elizabeth's only son, Alfonso (February 8, 1291), her second and last child, was the occasion of her beginning those arbitrations which have made her the Patroness of Peace. A quarrel had sprung up between King Diniz and his brother, Alfonso. In order to ward off civil war, the Queen summoned an arbitration council of clerics and laics. Their terms of reconciliation were rejected by the King and his brother. Undaunted, the Queen persevered until in the end she had her way. It was a characteristic way: she made over to the niece of Don Alfonso a good portion of her own possessions.

The reign of King Diniz has been called the golden age of Portugal. By his wise laws and his endeavors to provide justice easily and speedily for his subjects, he became the Justinian of Portugal. His energy made Portugal an agricultural country of the first order. He reclaimed the sand-dunes along the coast by planting them with pine forests. So greatly did agriculture thrive that, although the population increased, there was always enough home-grown wheat for the people. He (1) reclaimed land, (2) became himself a land tiller, and (3) organized agricultural villages. The Queen built an institution at Coimbra, perhaps the first Agricultural College! It was for young orphan girls. They were trained in farming to enable them to marry the sons of farmers; and were provided at their wedding with farms on her immense estates. Don Diniz has been called the Laborer; St. Elizabeth the Patroness of Laborers.

The private life of this Portuguese Justinian was more akin to the spirit of the Koran than of the Gospel. It is said that when the Queen-wife first saw her place taken in the affection of the King by women of low morals she felt the sting of jealousy. But we have it on the authority of the oldest life of the Saint that she so conquered herself so as to keep "her peace of heart without stirring or anger either against the King or the women. Indeed she commanded that his children, who were many, should be cared for as the offspring of such a father, and should be given everything necessary."

One incident has become historic. St. Elizabeth, in her discerning charity toward the gently-bred poor, sent her alms by a young, discreet page. A courtier of the King, wishing to ruin the page and to advance his own fortune even by the Queen's dishonor, suggested to the avid ear of King Diniz the worst interpretation. The King, having secretly given orders to a lime burner to cast into the lime kiln the first person who brought a royal message, sent the Queen's page with the message. On his way to the lime kiln the page heard a churchbell ringing to Mass. He went into the church, remained for Mass and stayed some time afterward, absorbed in prayer. Meanwhile the King, who had heard no word from the lime burner, sent the calumniator himself as messenger. He arrived before the page, gave his message, and was thrown into the lime kiln! Soon afterward the page arrived, and brought back to the King the lime burner's inexplicable words, "Tell his Majesty that he has been punctually obeyed." We are told that the King saw the hand of God in this strange event. As a result, he made every effort in the future to conceal, if not to lessen, his amours.

It is interesting to know that St. Elizabeth, the Patroness of Peace, sometimes encouraged her husband to make war. In 1296 she was on the side of an armed intervention in the affair of the young King of Castile, Ferdinand IV. Her younger brother, Pedro, had already lost his life in Castile during the Wars of Succession.

But her love of peace soon prevailed. When Queen Maria, the Mother and Regent of the young King Ferdinand IV, invited her to a conference, she warmly accepted the invitation. In three days these two women succeeded in bringing more peace to their contemporaries by the Treaty of Alcanizes (1297) than men had accomplished by years of war. The young King of Castile married Constance, the daughter of St. Elizabeth. Alfonso, Elizabeth's son and future King of Portugal, married Beatrice, sister of King Ferdinand.

The Saint's home trials at this time were almost unbearable. King Diniz, in order to free his country during his Castilian war from all danger of war at home, was forced to make peace with his brother, Don Alfonso, with whom the chief danger lay. As Alfonso desired to see his children legitimized, he besought the Saint to intercede with her husband. Acting on principles of justice, not only did she refuse to beseech the King on behalf of his nephews, but she even drew up a formal protest against any attempt at legitimization. Yet the King's foreign policy so urgently needed peace at home that, on February 8, 1297, he drew up the solemn act of legitimization. It was accompanied by two other royal acts that baffle our modern imagination. He reserved the right of withdrawing the legitimization, on account of the Queen's protest. He made the Queen—or rather the Saint—guardian of his own illegitimate children. This document, making public the King's crimes, and the Queen's holiness, is dated Guarda, January 21, 1298. No chronicler has recorded the Queen's emotions on reading such a document; which doubtless were veiled behind a smiling acquiescence. But God's Saints are at once mysteries of Divine mercy and miracles of Divine power.

In 1302, the Saint's genius for peacemaking was stimulated by the threat of war between her brother, Jayme II, and her son-in-law, Ferdinand IV. The counsels of the Saint prevailed. The two kings of Castile and Aragon, having agreed to submit the matter in dispute to King Diniz, met for conference at Tarragona, a frontier town between the two kingdoms. At the suggestion of the Saint, the conference was opened on September 8 (1304), the feast of the Nativity of Our Blessed Lady. So successful was the arbitration of the King of Portugal that the Kings of Castile and Aragon not only healed their quarrels by accepting his judgment, but entered into an offensive and defensive alliance called the Treaty of Agreda.

As the next eight years of the Saint's life have left no record, some of her biographers have concluded that they must have been years of happiness. Their surmise has some show of likelihood from the fact that their silence comes to an end in the death of her son-in-law, King Ferdinand of Castile (November 7, 1312), and of her daughter, Queen Constance of Castile, some months later.

One of the only clues to the spiritual life of this Queen and Saint is given us at this time. We are told that from this date she multiplied her fervour, her austerities, her mortification, her fastings to the point of weakening her health. Lent and Advent were not enough for her. On three days of each week she scarcely took any food. She fasted from the Feast of St. John the Baptist till the Assumption and from the Nativity of Our Blessed Lady till Michaelmas. (These austerities are so contrary to flesh and blood as to scandalize the commonalty of men; yet they are so rare on the throne as to dispense the Saint's biographer from any explanation.)

Few of those who might be scandalized by the Saint's heroic fasting would be scandalized by her heroic almsgiving. In her person the Queen realized the words of St. Paul, "as poor, yet enriching many". For her, as for him, the world's riches, the commonwealth, springs not from the desire to concentrate wealth on ourselves, but to distribute it to others. For most men this is a dark saying. King Diniz was one of those average men, to whom a saint's ideal of personal poverty as a means of royal almsgiving was unintelligible. He grumbled at his wife's openhandedness, until a miracle silenced his reproaches. Perhaps covetousness is one of those royal vices that yield only to miracles. One winter's day, as the Queen bore in her lap a number of pieces of money for her beloved poor, she met the King. Usually such a meeting meant a royal largesse of reproach. But on this occasion there were no reproaches, for as the King drew near he saw in her lap only a handful of roses! Her biographer remarks naively that it might almost be looked upon as a family miracle, seeing that it is also recorded of her great-aunt, St. Elizabeth of Hungary.

Biographers of the Queen look upon the eight or nine unchronicled years after the Peace of Tarragona as the golden time of her life. From what we know of her husband's way of living there was little enough in her life except her own noble heart that could be called golden. All that history allows us to say with truth is that these so-called golden days were not so fraught with sorrow as the days that were to come. We venture to think that this woman's life was a great tragedy and that the unwilling motive of the tragedy was the woman herself. The devotion which her husband refused her was given by her son, Don Alfonso. When he came of age the King arranged that he should live with his wife, Doña Beatrice of Castile, in a palace of his own. This might have been looked upon as a fatherly kindness to his son, if the King had not kept in his own palace and near his person his bastard sons, especially Don Alfonso Sanchez of Albuquerque, whom he instructed in poetry.

The situation was too unbalanced to last. Don Alfonso determined to kill his half-brother, Don Alfonso Sanchez, and to usurp the throne (1317). Both designs failed. Only by the warning of his mother did Don Alfonso escape from the hands of his father. Some of the King's courtiers easily persuaded him that the Queen's presence at the Court was a danger to his policy. Yielding to their persuasions, the King banished his wife from Lisbon to the town of Alemquer.

King Diniz sought to strengthen his cause by appealing to Pope John XXII, at Avignon. So persuasive were his reasons that the Pope published a bull absolving Portugal from recognizing Don Alfonso as the heir to the throne. Elizabeth could not see her son deprived of his right without an effort toward justice. From Alemquer she appealed to the Pope. Her biographer adds quaintly that "*after this* she sought refuge in prayer and mortifications".

It is this exile at Alemquer that has drawn from the Saint's biographers their one attempt to record the spiritual life of the Saint. The attempt is too fragmentary to be satisfactory. She visited the sick, not merely to give them alms and womanly sympathy, but even to dress their wounds. Every day in her own palace she fed and waited on thirteen lepers. Once, victorious over her feelings, she kissed the loathsome sore on the limb of a poor woman. It was a miracle of charity which, we are not surprised to read, was followed by a miracle of power.

Once, carrying out the custom of the Portuguese sovereigns, she refused to drink wine ordered by the doctor. But as she lifted a cup of water to her lips, the water changed to wine. Again, while building the church of the Holy Spirit at Alemquer she found herself without money for the workmen's wages. In her straits she paid the workmen in roses; and lo! the former miracle of the money turned to roses was reversed and the roses given to the workmen were found to be pieces of money. These traditions are the simple folk's remembrance of a Saint and Queen who once brought charity and joy into their homes.

Sorrows were not wanting. Her husband was estranged from her. Her son was too busy about the success of his rebellion to remain with her. The Pope, to whom she had written with a child's trust, had not answered her letter. In that hour of supreme abandonment, her sisterly heart sought consolation from her brother, King Jayme of Aragon. In a letter to him, she cries out, "O my dear brother, what a life of bitterness I am leading! On whom but God can I lean?" It was years since the brother and sister had played together as children. But time had not dulled his affection toward one whose unselfish ways endeared her to her kindred. King Jayme sent to her in her trouble his brother, Don Sanchez. But Don Sanchez could effect nothing against the obstinacy of the Portuguese King and Infante.

There befell at this time what we, not she, would call a temptation. While still at Alemquer she received a visit from the principal men of Coimbra where she was deeply beloved. No doubt the atmosphere of a University town begot a sympathy with this peace-loving Queen who had even this year (1317) opened her convent of Poor Clares there with nuns from the fervent Convent of Zamora. The men of Coimbra explained to the Queen that she had but to give the word and the townsfolk would rise in her defense and lead her back to the Court. This proposal to rebel speaks eloquently of the charm wielded over these proud Portuguese by this Queen from Aragon! The Queen thanked them for their pains, but said that no doubt the King had some idea of utility or pleasure in keeping her at Alemquer, and that she would go back to the Court only in obedience to him. She added: "Let us commit our ways to Providence. Let us trust in God alone. He will know how to show our innocence and to take from the mind of my Lord the King the wrong impressions he has received of our conduct."

The men of Coimbra may have judged the Queen's refusal was dictated by a fear of their powerlessness. In this case, they may be behind the next attempt which came with a like aim; only to meet with a like fate. This time it was officers of the Court who came; making, not general offers of help, but showing their Queen squadrons of troops and beseeching her to allow them to escort her back in triumph to the Court. Her reply was a revelation of her whole attitude toward life and the honors of life. She said: "She would rather bear poverty and endure all the injuries inflicted on her than consent that such a war should be waged. She expressly forbade these generals to begin a war for these reasons."

But the victory so shunned by the Saint's humility was at length won by her humility. Of such paradoxes are the lives of Saints! The King, hearing of these two refusals, had sufficient intelligence or selfishness to realize that the Queen had better be at Court. She was therefore recalled from exile amidst the enthusiasm of the people to whom her self-sacrifice meant the stemming of a torrent of blood.

No sooner was the Queen at Lisbon than she began her beloved work of peace. Alone of all the Portuguese she was able to sheathe the sword of her son. She persuaded him to withdraw to Leiria and there to make his submission as son and subject to the King, his father. Her diplomacy obtained from the King a full pardon for all the insurgents.

A touch of artistry ennobled the King's gratitude. As a token of thanks to his Queen for having wrought a peace beyond the power of his armies he gave her the town of Torres Vedras. It was on her feast day, 1317.

The King's gift was nothing if not royal. He conferred on her all rights and revenues. Many documents still extant bear witness to the full powers granted by the grateful King and to the scrupulous care with which the Saint administered them. One of these, dated October 22, 1331, six years after the King's death, is of great interest to us who still keep poignant memories of the world's greatest war, with its accompaniment of Food Dictators and War Prices. The document bearing the signature of a Saint fixes the price of bread in the district of Leiria.

It was probably while the Queen was exiled at Alemquer that, together with her brother, King Jayme of Aragon, she arbitrated successfully between her brother Frederic and Robert of Sicily. She also had two joys, well calculated to lessen her sorrows. She received a letter of sympathy from the Pope; and she heard that her cousin Louis, Bishop of Toulouse, had been canonized as a Saint.

It was hardly to be expected that the Infante could see his illegitimate half-brother, Don Alfonso Sanchez, trusted by the King without a protest. Toward the beginning of 1320, the Infante made an attempt to procure the death of Don Alfonso Sanchez, whom the King sought to save. War broke out once more between the King and the Infante. The lawless bandits and criminals, who were a great part of the Infante's army, exercised their warcraft by sacking the Convent of Maomelas, and the royal tombs at Alcobaça. They killed the venerable Bishop of Evora (May 5), perhaps because he preached peace, or more likely because he had published, during the previous war, the Papal Bull releasing Portugal from its fealty to the Infante. Coimbra, so devoted to the Queen, soon fell into the hands of the Infante, who was at once besieged there by the King. In vain Pope John XXII exhorted them to peace, recognizing the Infante as heir and giving King Diniz a contribution for his fleet. On December 9 a bloody and undecided battle took place at Coimbra. Once more the Queen determined to mediate. With rare womanly skill, she sent the King to Leiria. Then, entering the city of Coimbra, she persuaded her son to go to Pombal, and there to be reconciled with his father.

The truce lasted about a year and a half. At the beginning of 1323 war broke out afresh. The Infante, now at the head of a formidable army, was able to strike at the heart of the country by hastening to besiege Lisbon. But the King was too skillful to shut himself up in his capital. He displayed considerable generalship by leaving Lisbon, in order to make a vigorous offensive against his son. The two armies came into touch on the battlefield of Alvalade. Then occurred an incident in the history of one whose life is full of incident. The two armies were already engaged. Arrows and stones darkened the air. The dead and dying lay thickly on the field of battle. Soon father and son would have been in deadly fight. But we must let the Saint's most recent biographer tell the story of what befell on the battlefield of Alvalade at that moment. "All at once, a mule at the gallop tore a way through the combatants and opened a path in the horrible confusion amidst the glittering swords. The mule bore a woman. It was the Queen! Braving the missiles that were raining around her, she seemed a heavenly vision; alone, for no one dared to follow her; with no other weapons than her weakness; her hands joined in supplication. The effect produced was irresistible, everyone stood still and ceased to fight. Meanwhile the King and his son, touched to tears by so great heroism and love, made a reconciliation once more on the field of blood. Then, at the bidding of the Queen, before the two armies, the Infante kissed the hand of his father; and the King, in pardon, gave his son his blessing. And in this great way was ended the parricidal struggle that had lasted five years."

The peace made that day between the King and his son by the holiness and heroism of the Queen Mother was to last until the King's death. Although the King lived little more than a year from the day when he gave his son his pardon and blessing on the battlefield of Alvalade, the after-history of his son when king would go to show that even in such a short period of peace between the two there was something so supernatural as to be worthy of the prayers of a Saint.

On May 30, 1323, John XXII empowered Gonsalvo, Archbishop of Lisbon, to absolve Diniz from the excommunications he had incurred through imprisoning clerics. It must have been a supreme joy to the Queen-Saint to kneel by his side as he received the Body of Christ— perhaps the first time since their wedding day!

Toward the end of 1324, the King fell ill at Santarem. The Queen never left his side, even though the King courteously urged her to prevent two deaths happening at the same time. On January 6, 1325, the King died, after sixty-four years of life, forty-six of reign and forty-three of wedlock.

Two days after the King's death (January 8, 1325) the Saint clothed herself in the habit of a Poor Clare. The declaration she made on this occasion is almost a curiosity of ecclesiastical literature. She declares that, by the King's death, she finds herself dead with him. She therefore fulfills a longstanding resolution to don the habit of a Poor Clare in which she hopes to be buried. She is at great pains to explain that this donning of the habit is only "by reason of sorrow, grief and humility and nowise by a religious vow, nor by profession, nor by obedience to any Order . . . We affirm that we have nowise made or formulated any vow, either simple or solemn, secret or expressed, nor any profession or obedience private or public." Moreover, she kept complete control over all her goods and possessions.

Eleven years of life remained to the Saint. They were spent in the shadow of Saint Clare at Coimbra where the spirit of the Poverello of Assisi flooded her soul. Twice she left her beloved convent-home to make pilgrimage to Compostella. Her first visit (1326) was made as Dowager Queen of Portugal. On the way, she touched the eyes of a child born blind and gave them sight. Her gifts to the shrine of St. James were so many and great that no one had seen the like before. One of her gifts was the jeweled gold crown of her coronation. In return, the Archbishop gave her a pilgrim's staff and shell. These she prized so much that she had them placed in her coffin after death. Everywhere the people of Spain received her as a Saint. On her return home she distributed her royal jewelry to her royal kinswomen. Much was melted down and made into chalices, crosses, reliquaries and other sacred vessels. Her royal robes became vestments for the Church's use.

Shortly after this, the Queen Dowager had to exert her powers of peacemaker between her son, the King, and Don Alfonso Sanchez. Perhaps it was in thanksgiving for this peace that the Saint made her second pilgrimage to Compostella. It was a striking contrast with her first, as she went on foot in strict incognito with only two maids. So well was her incognito kept that she seems to have been unrecognized either going or coming.

To this period must perhaps be assigned the miracle of the leper. She was spending Holy Week at her beloved orphanage of Santarem. On Good Friday she washed the feet of some poor people. One of these poor men, who was lame and a leper, was left behind in one of the corridors. A sentinel struck him heavily with a stick, inflicting a severe wound. St. Elizabeth, hearing of this, called the poor leper, and bound up his wound. Next day, both wound and leprosy had disappeared!

A famine that raged in the neighborhood of Lisbon in 1333 found the Saint's open-handed charity inexhaustible. It is needless to say that her official counselors counseled prudence and even foretold failure. But the Saint met their talk of prudence with her favorite evangel of charity, and withstood their dismal forebodings with a call to trust him who feeds the birds of the air.

The family quarrels between her son, Alfonso IV of Portugal, and Alfonso XI of Castile overshadow the last years of her life. Alfonso XI had given his hand in marriage to Doña Maria, daughter of Alfonso IV and granddaughter of St. Elizabeth; but he had given his heart to the beautiful Eleonora de Guzman. Already St. Elizabeth had accompanied her son, the King, to Badajos in Castile, where they extracted from Alfonso XI a promise to end the scandal of his present life. But his promise, if ever it had been sincere, was short-lived. Once again the private quarrels and vices of kings threatened to be the scourge of their peace-loving subjects. In the summer of 1336 war broke out, not so much between the Portuguese and the Castilians as between the Kings of Portugal and Castile. It was the last occasion on which the "Advocate of Peace" exercised her gracious function. Against the advice of all those who loved her, the Queen-Dowager left her home in the quiet convent home at Coimbra to give peace once more to two distracted countries. She was suffering from a tumor and an inflammation in the arm; perhaps from some form of blood-poisoning. But neither the fever-heats of her illness nor the intense midsummer heats of the plains of Alemtejo could check her zeal. She did not stay her haste until she met the two kings, her son and her son-in-law, in the little border town of Estremoz. It was the first Portuguese town she had entered after leaving Aragon as a child-bride and it was the first to hail her Queen. Hardly had she reached the town, in a dying state, than she summoned the two monarchs before her. One of her biographers has put into her mouth a fragment of a speech which may

well be given here. "What is your duty, kings sprung from a noble
stock, reared on such high principles, endowed with so much bravery?
Is it not to be reconciled and to live at one? Otherwise what will happen? Incurable ills for the State; the death of many innocent ones who
have nothing to gain by the quarrels of kings. Nor is this all. While
the lowly will be oppressed we shall see the proud exalted, and while
men honest and upright will be harrowed by fear and every sort of ill,
the others will rejoice because it is they who in every war profit by
the havoc to enrich themselves and are able in the general disorder to
further their audacity. Do not forget that when sovereigns are at war
they can no longer busy themselves with their administration; justice
is not distributed; no care is taken of the people; and this alone is your
sovereign charge, this the main point of your duty as kings."

It was her last effort for peace; and it was a failure. The next day,
Monday, the Saint's illness increased rapidly. On Thursday she made
her last confession. When the Bishop of Lamego, her chaplain, brought
the Body of Our Lord to her she summoned the last resources of her
indomitable will to rise from her bed. For the last time she bowed
down to the ground in adoration of Jesus Christ, who had bowed
down to earth for love of her. Later on in the day, when the Queen,
her daughter-in-law, was alone by her bed, the Saint looking at her
fixedly, said, "My child, bring a chair for this Lady." "Which Lady?"
replied Queen Beatrice, who could see nothing. "She who is drawing
near smiling, and in garments of white." Saying this, the dying Saint
raised herself as if in welcome. Her smiling lips were heard to utter:

> Maria Mater Gratiae,
> Mater Misericordiae,
> Tu nos ab hoste protege
> Et hora mortis suscipe.
>
> (Mary, Mother of Grace,
> Mother of Mercy,
> From the foe shield us,
> In the hour of death take us.)

These were her last words. It was Thursday, July 4, 1336.

She was buried in her beloved Convent Church of Santa Clara at
Coimbra, amidst her sisters of St. Francis of Assisi. Her memory became so precious to Portugal and her intercession was so miraculously

powerful with God, that after three centuries she was canonized by Pope Urban VIII (May 25, 1625).

It may be found after a further three centuries that in raising this Patroness of Peace to the altar, the Vicar of the Prince of Peace has given a model for all time to those who bear, or obey, rule.

SAINT JOAN

[1412 – 1431]

Ida Coudenhove

GREAT DEAL has been said and written about the "Maid of Orleans". She is more "interesting" than almost any other historical personage—interesting to the historian, to the psychologist, to the politician and to the poet. This personage, so public and yet so mysterious, more fantastic than the heroines of fairytales and sagas, and yet a part of reality; in whom all the brilliance of declining chivalry mingled with the gentle gleam of the eternal pastoral romance, and with the tantalizing and enigmatic phenomena of a new period of thought, this girl Joan draws the glances of men ever and again to herself.

Besides this, there is the interest in the "phenomenon of sainthood", which continues to increase and which is always still, unfortunately, associated with personages whose spiritual life was disguised under a most strange and marvelous material life—with Francis, Elizabeth, Catherine. . . . Nowhere are sainthood and adventure so inseparably woven together as in the extraordinary life of St. Joan. Her grim yet splendid fate, the glitter of her magic triumph and the horror of her tragic failure so obscure this fact from us that it is really difficult for us to discover what her real *religious* mission is.

But we are coming to understand more and more that the Maid of Orleans has a religious mission to us, to the whole of Christianity, and not only to her own nation—a religious mission and not a political or a romantic one. Looking at her, our attention is attracted by something new in the well-known visage of sainthood, which we have known and loved for so many other traits.

Can there be such a thing as a "new" characteristic trait in the face of the Christian? Many disillusionments have made us skeptical about it. The unprecedented is ever and again unmasked and found to be nothing but a compound of imitation and memory.

The "new" thing in Joan is not in the strictest sense of the word seen for the first time in her, but it is unusual, and shows itself in her in a striking way. Joan is the saint *who takes the world seriously*, who loves the world, who sacrifices herself for the world. That is her peculiar mission. That is the unprecedented thing in her religious personality, which, just at the present time, draws the Christian's attention to her.

To be sure Francis has long been called "The Saint who loves the Earth". The earth, yes, but not the *world*! He feared the world and fled from it, like any hermit of them all.

It is usual and natural, almost the normal thing with nearly all the saints we know, that they had, in a narrow, exclusive sense, a "religious" task to perform, and that they had to leave the world—*exire de saeculo*, so as to be free and remain free to perform that task. They had to be free for the work of praising God and of contemplation, free to perform works of love for the sick, the poor, prisoners, children; free to preach repentance and the Kingdom of God, to found an Order, a spiritual and religious school of Christian thought and life; free to reform the Church. When we open the life of a saint we expect an account of such works of piety, just as former generations required accounts of miracles and prophecies as the sole proof of sainthood. But Joan breaks through this rule.

She declared herself to be called of God—yes, and how? Solemnly, by voices and visions, like any prophet! But not by any means in order to heal the schism in the Church, the great, threefold schism, worse than the one in Catherine's days; not to show a new way of perfection, not to confute the numerous rebellious heresies of her restless age, not to give counsel, inspired by the Holy Spirit.

She was called, indeed, but to perform a purely earthly, worldly task, to free a people from a condition of unendurable political misery, to set a rightful king on the throne, to expel the enemy—"*bouter dehors les Anglais*". And she was to do all these things not at all on account of any possible or desired ecclesiastical consequences—not so that, in some way or other, a free, united French nation might conduce to reform —not so that the legitimate king might order the schism to end. No,

no, she wasn't thinking about anything of that kind. What she did had
no ulterior aim.

She doesn't leave the world because of her mission. Because of it
she goes into the world, right into the greatest press, into the most
splendid, most dangerous places, into the politico-military sphere, into
the court, into the camp, into war!

Can such a thing happen—can there be such a call from God—and
if this thing did happen in this one life, what does it signify?

There are two keywords to Joan's mission: "*La grande pitié de la
France*" and "*le bon plaisir de Dieu*".

"The great misery of France"—the endless wars, the foreign rule,
the ignominy of the interregnum, the lawlessness resulting therefrom,
because the king stood for the rights of the people amid the struggle of
contending Powers; the fall of the dynasty, whose last living scion did
not even know whether he could validly claim the crown, whether the
blood-royal ran in his veins; the disunion of the people, split up between
France, England and Burgundy, the arrogance of the conqueror, deeds
of violence, revenge, oppression, all over a plundered and despairing
land.

These were the things of which the great, armed angel, Messire Saint
Michel, told the listening shepherd child under the fairy tree. Was an
angelic mission—were crowned, heavenly virgins—needful for this?
Did not all Joan's childhood days resound with the news of horrors,
did not the messengers and the fugitives assemble in her father's, the
village justice's house? Since she was old enough to think, was not the
sight of exiles and fugitives, of wounded men, of every kind of victim
of the war, normal to her?

But she had to learn to understand how the matter stood. At this
point she received her call. She came to know that this distress had its
roots in sin. This misery was not just simply "willed by God". In it
stood revealed, in lightning flashes of terror, the offended will of God,
the transgressed law of the Most High.

The wages of *sin* are death, distress, "great misery".

For God has not only commanded that men should be baptized and
confirmed, that they should confess their sins and be present at the Holy
Sacrifice, that they should keep the festivals and honor the priest. He
has also made laws in accordance with which there should be righteousness, truth and peace among men. He has promised men that

his laws, so long as they are kept, will secure order, honor and peace. Men have mocked at his instruction, they have torn down the dykes which his wisdom made, and the floods of wickedness have flowed in, raging and ruthless, and are about to give a new, a frightful aspect to the earth.

Joan sees "evil" behind the misery of her people, and sees that God indeed desires peace between the nations, and order in every nation, but that men have desires different from God's, and, because of their greed and ambition, out of their wilfulness and arrogance, trample on his will as much as they can. The angel's call tells her nothing but that she, the "daughter of God", has to lead the fight for the Father's will against "evil" in this, its concrete form. And the will of the Father, the high will of God, is, in this case, decidedly and unmistakably to be read, even from the very sin and disorder which here and now oppose it and which are seen to be the great cause of the country's misery.

Shattered law must be restored, the rightful king must be crowned, the foreign invader must be chased back to the country which God had assigned to him, and must leave the French the land of their fathers —peace and justice must rule again, for so it should he.

She, Joan, is the chosen one, for she feels herself responsible, does this little girl in the Lorraine village, for the fate and the sins of the whole people. While nobody else does, while all the others put the blame on each other, she takes the blame on herself for this guilt and misery, goes to God with them, takes her stand before him, and asks for his command.

There are not only the individual fates of men, who may be saved or lost. There is also the fate of God's *will* in the world, God's will, which should rule the world, but may be defeated in it. There is a kind of piety, the possessor of which is actuated by a sense of concern for that Will, for its fate, more than by concern for his own fate or that of any man. This is not fainthearted fear in him. They know quite well, those loving, troubled ones of whom I write, that God "has men in derision" when they refuse his will. They know that he can strike them down with his iron scepter. But that is pain and tragedy to these pious folk, for they know that God wants his will to be fulfilled through men and not against them, and to be affirmed by their obedient freedom. Their sense of concern for God's will proceeds from an intensity of worship which casts them prostrate before God, who is the Lord, a worship which transmutes itself into a very passion of obedience and service, of passionate sacrifice for the honor of the Father. This their sense of concern proceeds, too, from a painful love for their fellowmen collectively, as nation or Church, from the love that suffers for the guilt of the community as for its own, takes it before God as its own, weeping, regretful, and ready for any penance. That is the way the prophets felt, the most moving books of the Old Testament are full of it. The Son of Man, who was at once the servant of Jehovah, and the "Lamb" to be sacrificed for his brethren, had it too.

But it takes on a new aspect in Joan, on account of the directness and simplicity of the means by which she would fain impress this worshipped, this painfully loved will of God upon reality. She would do it by means of violence and fighting, by means of heaven-storming boldness. This is doubly amazing, because we know about the simple piety of her childhood.

Where the earthly, the, worldly reality is so dense that one thinks no glimmer of divine light can make its way through, where the opposing powers rise up in all their violence, there lurks the special temptation *to despair of the victory of God's will* . . . the temptation to declare certain departments of human life and action—the political, the social, the economic—hopeless, impossible to reform, outcast, devilish, amoral —at any rate, inherently lost and desperate, beyond redemption. They can only be abandoned there on the left hand, a sinister hunting-ground for those who find their booty in them. One has to flee from them, to keep one's soul pure. The only way not to be dragged into the world is to renounce it. If one is dragged into it one will, as a part of it, be delivered over to its powers as their booty, and will have to refuse obedience to God, in order to exist . . . "and there is none living who has withdrawn his soul, still pure, from their service. . . ." The disorder of the world is incurable. The world can't be remodeled. To think it can is only to build castles in the air. One can only form and fortify enclaves in it, ruled by special regulations, within which enclaves it is possible to do the will of God. And then one goes on to say, with the logic of the fox who couldn't reach the grapes, that the world is doomed to destruction—that desperate world which isn't worth the trouble of shedding one's blood for in battle. It is better to confine oneself to the fulfillment of the other tasks which are concerned with the imperishable real, "purely religious" sphere.

Did Joan experience this temptation?

Charles Péguy, the poet, who died young (he fell in August, 1914), on whose spiritual legacy the best of France's believing youth live—who is fraternally akin to the Pucelle as Frenchman, peasant, soldier and Christian—has, in his *Mystère de la Charité de Jeanne d'Arc*, incomparably represented her fight with this temptation, and her victory over it by means of love. With more than a poet's clear-sightedness, he places both *before* the hour in which she was called. The whole volume is made up of a single dramatic conversation between the child Jeannette and Madame Gervaise, the hermit. It is well worth while giving a general idea of its contents.

Joan has fallen into an agony of grief: "the sadness of the Christian, which is the greatest sadness on earth"—into a sadness even unto death for the sins of the world, which stand revealed to her in the sins of her time, of her people—and as her own. For: "*Complice, complice, c'est pire qu'auteur.*" For she who daily hears about the abominations of war and the misery of France, and who takes refuge in pious wishes, in vows for the future, in helpless lamentation, in pharisaical horror at the wicked soldiers, in fruitless prayers, is she not an accomplice—like everyone else—like her father, mother, brothers, sisters and friends, like the village and the parish, like all whom she would fain love but must despise, for they are all as cowardly and guilty as she is? "*Complice, complice!*"

The pious woman, whom the child has called in in the anguish of her heart, that she may get the right answer to the questions from one consecrated to God, tries to comfort her. She speaks of eternal things, of the mansions in the Father's House, which the soldiers can't plunder; of the Lord's triumphant body, which no sacrilegious hand reaches, in spite of the crimes that are done on earth; of the variety of the earthly things that fall victim to the horrors of war. But Joan is not to be comforted thus. The supernal reality does not reconcile her to the terrible earthly reality which she sees around her. She wants to offer herself as a sacrifice to God, she would fain devote her childish body to the flames of hell, if this penance of hers could replace the sufferings of France. Madame Gervaise, frightened, blames her presumption. Not even to the Savior was it given to redeem *all*. His love broke, powerless, against Judas' sin:

> The Savior knew it well that all his blood
> could the beloved Judas not redeem.

It was the discernment of this which extracted from him his cry of abandonment on the Cross:

> Oh cry, at *which* the strength of Mary failed—
> and graciously the Father gave him death.

But Joan heard in the whole long story of the Passion and Death of the Lord only two things: he knew that he would not be able to save all, yet he undertook the task, and: the apostles forsook him and fled.

"We wouldn't have done that, we French, we Lorrainers, we peasants of our village", she cried. "No, not even the English would have done it. We here, in our village, are great sinners, we do all kinds of things, but we wouldn't have fled. . . ." Then she summons up her courage to say humbly: "With the help of God I shouldn't have fled." She hears no more the pious, frightened talk of the nun, admonishing her to be humble. She has attained to the perception of something unexampled. She gazes with longing aspiration down into the valley where the enemy is, and the strange book closes with the broken sentence:

> *Orleans, thou in the Loire vale* . . .

But we foresee that in her next hour of solitude the archangel will descend from Heaven, to take this child's dauntless heart at its word, to call upon it to do the will of his and her Lord, to undertake the Mission which she cannot fulfill to its completion, which she will yet fulfill until she perishes, for she "will not flee".

She quite understands that the vanity of the world is no reason for retreat from this hazard. Madame Gervaise, who, because of that vanity, has forsaken the world, may do so, but she, Joan, is still in the world. God has placed man in the midst of that vanity, and she is to be tested by it. The will of God will fulfill itself in it, hence it must be taken seriously, with the seriousness due to the will of God. In vain things, for them, for their sake, sin is committed, confusion is wrought, but in them may be found, too, faithfulness, obedience, steadfastness, confirmation, redemption.

Her mission is to try to subject this mighty vanity called "the world" to the will of the Highest. It is not an empty, an apparent test, it is not artificial, meant for a pure exercise in obedience, like the hermit's order to the monk to water the dry stick (and yet the stick began to grow green). It is laid upon her as a task really possible to fulfill, as a slight but real opportunity for her of serving her people and securing their liberty. She is charged to try, not to succeed.

Péguy, in another place, has made it clear in a very fine essay to what a great extent Joan was bidden "to carry out her supernatural mission with natural means". It was a supernaturally received mission, but the means for its fulfillment were most natural. They were troops, guns, money, strategy. No twelve legions of angels were promised her. St. Michael was only to advise her, not to fight for her. She is not invulnerable to cut or thrust, or immune from illness or mishap. Like the least of her soldiers, she depends only upon herself and upon the fortune of war, under God's hand. She knows it, too. She has been greatly wronged by being called a fanatic. She is sober, like every true saint; she is, moreover, sober like the real peasant woman she is. There is nothing of romanticism in her behavior. When excited people ask her for signs and wonders, prophecy or the healing of the sick, she laughingly replies: "Give me soldiers, and I will show you what kind of signs I am sent to show." And she failed not in courage, in prudence or in service. For a time, too, it seemed as if what she had undertaken might be successful, as, in earnest and joyful confidence, she had declared in the hail of the Dukes of Aquitaine, at Poitiers: "*les gens d'armes batailleront et Dieu donnera victoire.*"

She had, too, her hour of triumph, pure and lofty, after so many small but sorrowful cloudings (her first victory, and perhaps not only that, which revealed to her the frightful reality of battle, she wept over "with so many tears that thereafter she said that she had not known a person had so many tears to shed"). In her most blissful hour, in the holy hour of the coronation, in the lofty cathedral at Rheims, when she could kneel in homage before the crowned and anointed monarch who at last wore the crown of France which she had won for him, there breaks from her overflowing heart the words that so completely reveal her: "*Sire, ainsi s'est accompli le bon plaisir de Dieu.*"

At that time it seemed quite possible, and even imminent, in spite of all the "ifs" and "buts" of political and military luminaries, that after the coronation at Rheims she should march to Paris, take the capital and compel an honorable peace—and that then, as she ardently wished,

released from her mission, she should disappear into the quiet of her
native village. . . .

Why had it to be otherwise?

Perhaps it is an essential attribute of Joan as a religious personage
that she should perish. There was, perhaps, too, in the life of the Son
of God, in the spring of his Galilean fame, a time when it seemed as
if the people of Israel would accept his mission, when it seemed as if
he might, in another sense than that in which it finally came to pass,
lead his human brethren to the Father's feet.

Joan's fate reveals, in its humble and, as it were, hidden mirroring
of the Lord's life, what his fate reveals on so immense a scale: how
very deeply sunken the world is in wickedness. Her perishing revealed
what her victory would perchance have veiled: how great the world's
perdition is, how rotten is the whole framework of its vainglorious life,
how dangerous is the attack on the powers that manifest themselves in
it, how terribly alone is the Christian who dares to attack them, how
defenselessly abandoned is the pure, in spite of all ability and courage,
who scorns to meet the powers with their own weapons. But the honor
of the Lord whom he serves forbids him to use those weapons.

Thus it is essential to Joan's mission that she should have to do, in
the final conflict, with the spiritual tribunal. She has thus pressed forward into the most dangerous power-zone of the political, to the zone
where it is allied with devious and subservient ecclesiastical ambition.
She has pushed forward to the very front line of evil, where it wears the
mask of holiness and fights with the stolen and desecrated weapons of
religious authority and allurements, spiritual threats and punishments
("for a day will come when he that killeth you will think that he doeth
God service"). When it comes to this, only the undeserved death of
a righteous man can unmask the corruption.

No "*j'accuse*" of a zealous reformer, no flaming protest of revolt,
could so irresistibly drive wickedness in its power and glory from all
its defenses of phrase and pose, could force it so irresistibly to self-
betrayal, as this defenseless death of a child of God, as this blood crying out to Heaven.

By such a death the utter powerlessness of evil is at once revealed in
the midst of the eruption of its power, in the midst of the world which
is ever and again redeemed by the shedding of the most innocent blood
of the gentlest victims.

For here the fight which Joan had engaged in, the fight for the world between God and his adversary, is moved back from the exterior front, where she made her first attack, and concentrated on the narrow ridge of a decision that has to be made within her soul. She has to decide whether or not the power of lying and violence can force her heart to surrender, to deny the Holy Spirit who was her motive power, to deny her mission. And she conquers as she falls, preferring, with a free will, death to adjuration. She conquers, and her pyre, which could not consume her heart, was the symbol of the utter powerlessness of violence to conquer the soul.

She falls, of course, conscious of defeat, of shame, of forsakenness —else were her sacrifice not fully completed, and, with it, the victory which could only be really won at this price. The utter darkness of her destruction is the gravestone which only the angel of the resurrection rolls away—by human reckoning, many years later. In this, too, is mirrored, is shown in parable, the mystery of Good Friday.

Amid the intensity and the emotion of Joan's human, yet superhuman struggle to stamp the refractory, the lost world with God's will, as with a seal, questions concerning her personal salvation and personal holiness sink into insignificance. Or, rather, Joan sought both of these in unconditional obedience to her mission, so that "questions of method" don't, in her case, arise.

It is quite a remarkable thing that asceticism plays no part in the life of this medieval saint, or at least we know nothing of his doing so. Prayer, of course, takes a great part in her life. No Christian life, ordinary or extraordinary, would be conceivable without prayer. Joan prayed a great deal, as a shepherdess with her sheep and as a soldier in the field. She had the Holy Sacrifice celebrated daily in camp, daily she received the Body of the Lord. The withdrawal of the Sacrament was the worst and most malicious torture of her long martyrdom.

But the question of asceticism in the current sense of the Middle Ages, the question of a special way to perfection, a special means to attain it, the question of turning away from the world, of flight from the world, of bodily mortification, does not seem to arise in her life at all. She knows nothing of the great controversy about holy poverty which had occupied the minds of ecclesiastical circles for decades. She knows not religious fear of the things of the world, she loves magnificence and even luxury, fine weapons, clothes, horses, as naturally as she loved her village simplicity and the rigors of the camp. She does not shrink from accepting joyfully the silver armor and the splendid saddle and harness, she fixes exactly of what material her costly banner is to be made, of what color it should be, loving it "forty times more than her sword". During her examination she replies with simple pride to a question about her horse: "Which? For I had four!" She takes title and coat-of-arms, presents and privileges, for her and hers, with a quiet soul. Neither does she shrink from the people's excesses of enthusiasm and reverence, which were all about her as she rode, when she entered the provincial capital. She fears not at all the splendor of the court, the feasts and banquet. She hates only the roughness and noise of the drinking bout. Her demeanor was, as the esquire Perceval wrote home, "*d'une parfaite élégance*". She mastered the ceremonial of the court with untroubled grace. She liked knightly play with steed and lance, as well as any youth of her following.

Joan of Arc is a maiden—*the* maiden—*la Pucelle*. A task like hers cannot be fulfilled with a divided heart. But her maidenhood is in no wise painful, nun-like, hiding herself from men with veil and enclosure. She is Diana-like, as has been said of Catherine of Siena, who adopted a similar attitude, so unmistakable in its sheer unapproachability, in its consecrated inviolability, that man appeared no more in the guise of an enemy or a danger, but as a comrade, a friend and a brother. All witnesses are unanimous as to the cordiality, the ingenuousness, the graceful freedom of her "fraternal" attitude toward soldiers and knights. Her faithfulness to the king is unexceptionable, utter, passionate. The thought that any of these relations with men could signify a spiritual danger never appears even in the distance.

Joan leaves her father and mother to carry out the Divine command. She leaves them secretly, against their will. But it is not the fundamental renunciation of his family made by the monk. It is a painful measure, forced upon her by circumstances. She is always yearning for her parents; the childish, painful, sweet dream of returning to the arms of her forgiving parents, to her forsaken flock, to her spindle by the fireside, charms her in the midst of her camp life, before the walls of beleaguered towns, more than all her triumphs.

Her attitude toward her own "peculiarities" is important, if we would understand her attitude to the world, and she has been badly misunderstood by the poets and expositors of later days. The Maid of Orleans is neither an Amazon nor a man-woman, neither an adventuress nor a fanatic. She is not an "emancipated" woman, who rushes arbitrarily and "with amazing energy" over the bounds of her position and sex. She is but a brave, obedient child, lost for the sake of a great love— nay of two: the love of God and the love of her people. But she is constantly aware that in all her amazing adventure, she is "on leave"— separated for a while, for the space of her unexampled mission, from her "real", her own, her proper life, which she is to recommence when everything has been successfully surmounted. . . .

Perhaps what strikes us the most in that wonderful, helmeted being is the unstudied humility of her humanity, her simple contentment with the ordinary concerning which she admits: "it's what I'm used to"; her serene moderation in the face of the extraordinary things, un-precedented in her days, through which she lived, because she had to —from obedience, not from choice.

Thus, trait by trait, she takes form before us. We see her unvarying and unquestioned humanity, her stern passion for the fulfillment of God's will, her great compassion for the "great misery" of the peo-ple—that people which sees no way of escape, either by cessation of its misery or by flight from it. We see the boundless courage with which Joan comes forward and shoulders the burden, her obedience, her moderation, the capacity she showed in her heroic undertaking. We see the unarmed meekness with which she endures and stands fast —a meekness in which there is neither defiance nor yielding, and the pure courage with which she admits that the hazard has gone against her, but never doubts the righteousness of the way she has taken, and remains devoid of bitterness. We see her confidence, even in destruc-tion, that all is well.

And in and above all that, we see her Christian way of taking the world seriously, which she does even to the extent of acknowledging the necessity for her own death in the words: "*That is the way of the world.*" But she thinks it worth while to die through that world and for it, for in it the holy, the beloved will of God is making ready the way for its fulfillment.

Such is the Maid, as at last she emerges from behind the romantic mask of misunderstanding poesy, from behind the political prejudice of a merely national cult, from behind the exaggerated simplicity of the sly, Shavian psychology: a saint, a unique religious figure. And in spite

of the unrepeatable nature of her mission, do we not find in that figure,
the characteristic traits of the Christian of today, of the Christian of
tomorrow as we would have him be, for that work in the world which
is our heritage and our hope?

SAINT CATHERINE OF GENOA

[1447-1510]

R. H. J. Steuart, S.J.

N THE TWELFTH CENTURY there began a feud, destined to last for many generations and to undergo many confusing transformations, between the adherents of Hwelp (Or Welf) Duke of Saxony and those of the Hohenstaufen of Waiblingen, over their conflicting claims to the Imperial throne. It was more complicated than that, but that was the gist of it. Later in the same century the quarrel resolved into one for supremacy between the Papacy, in the person of Alexander III, and the Empire, represented by Frederick I, the redoubtable Barbarossa. This recasting of the issue in dispute, with the consequent shifting of the main scene of its activities to Italy, led to a softening of these two barbaric-seeming names into forms better suited to southern tongues, and "Hwelp" and "Waiblingen" became "Guelph" and "Ghibelline", the former being for the Pope and the latter for the Emperor. Later still both the original and the secondary causes of rivalry between the two parties became almost entirely submerged in new matters of difference, and though mutual hostility remained as bitter as ever, the names Guelph and Ghibelline soon had even less authentic reference to their origins than, for example, the modern political distinctions of Conservative and Liberal in this country, or of Republican and Democrat in America, have to theirs, and were simply convenient names for the largest and most active party factions among the many that distracted public life in the states of Italy during the Middle Ages.

To a noble Guelph family of Genoa, the Fieschi, which had numbered two Popes, Innocent IV and Hadrian V, among its members, there was born in the year 1447 a daughter, Catherine, known to us now as St. Catherine of Genoa. She was the youngest of three sons and two daughters. Her parents had the reputation of fervent Catholics and

263

appear to have brought their children up strictly in the practice of their religion. Reliable contemporary evidence encourages us to believe that the attribution of extraordinary spiritual qualities to the saints in their childhood with which hagiographers are so often lavish on *a priori* (one suspects) rather than on historical grounds, is at any rate justified in Catherine's case. It appears to be unquestioned that she had reached a high level of contemplative prayer by the time that she was twelve years old, and that in the midst of the luxury that surrounded her she contrived to lead a most austere and penitential life.

As one would expect, her thoughts turned early to the religious life, and at the age of thirteen she offered herself to the convent of Augustinian Canonesses in which her elder sister Limbania was already a novice. She was of course too young, and it is not surprising that the nuns would not receive her. Probably she intended to make a second attempt later on, but her family had other designs for her future. Her father had died this same year and her brother Giacomo now took his place as head of the house. About this time the rivalry between the Guelph and the Ghibelline factions in Genoa became acute and led to much civic disturbance. This was largely due to the fact that a new aristocracy of wealth had arisen in that state (as in other parts of Europe) and had ranged itself under one or the other standard with all the old bitterness even if with little of the old reasons for it. As formerly the Fieschi and the Grimaldi on the Guelph side had led their party against the Ghibelline Spinolas and Dorias, so now the Fregosi took up the argument with the former against the Adorni on the latter, and Genovese order and prosperity threatened to break down altogether under their senseless bickerings. It was Louis XI of France, over-lord of the Republic, who saved the situation. He handed over suzerainty to Francis Sforza Duke of Milan, a person who as an Italian was more acceptable in that position than a foreigner could be, so that when the Duke sent his forces to establish his authority under the Ghibelline Doria it was a Guelph Fieschi who threw open the city gates for their entry, and there ensued thereupon a general reconciliation which for a considerable time at least brought peace to the distracted State. It was in order to cement this new unity that Giacomo determined to marry his sister to Giuliano Adorna, son of one of the chiefs of that powerful house. Catherine was not consulted at all until after the date and place of the ceremony had been already fixed: but she had been brought up in the tradition of unquestioning obedience to family authority, and there was no appeal. So on February 13, 1463, she being then sixteen years old, the marriage, for which she felt the utmost repugnance, was celebrated. Ghibelline and Guelph were now man and wife—a triumph of politics in her brother's eyes, a thing little less than disastrous in hers.

It would be difficult to imagine a more ill-assorted pair. Allowing for a margin of exaggeration on the part of Catherine's biographers, it appears that Giuliano Adorna was indeed in character and habits almost the antithesis of his young wife. The best that can be said in his excuse is that he was a man of his time and traditions. He was quick-tempered and aggressive, a gambler, lax in his morals, passionately devoted to every sort of show and luxury, serious about nothing but the pursuit of pleasure and diversion. The retired and penitential tastes of Catherine were utterly unintelligible and most disagreeable to him, and he let pass no opportunity of ridiculing and annoying her. Her reaction was to retire still more into herself and to redouble her austerities, and she became so weak and emaciated in consequence that her family were seriously alarmed. Interiorly, too, all was darkness: prayer, penance, good works, all seemed meaningless and worthless: God appeared to have abandoned her for ever, and faith was one ceaseless desperate effort under which she seemed from instant to instant to be on the point of breaking down altogether. She tells us that this terrible state of unrelieved desolation lasted for full five years. What we should expect to hear next would be that thereafter, having been tried and proved to the limit of her endurance, there had then flooded into her soul such light and warmth and strength as could only be purchased at that price. It is, in our degree, by a similar reflection that through our own bleak intervals we keep our hope, however painfully, still alive. But the saints live on a heroic plan: with those whom God finds responsive to his call he has no reserves, no half-measures, one might almost say no pity. He sifts and searches and dredges their soul, goes near to losing them their mind, to breaking their heart. That "conversio" which in all the adult saints is the essential preliminary to transforming love must be all-embracing, it must reach down to the ultimate depths of their volition, out to the furthest boundary of their possible experience. It must be *lived*, and lived *out*, not merely understood and accepted, however willingly—*if thou wilt be perfect . . . all whatsoever thou hast!*

One understands then, after the first surprise of hearing that it happened, how Catherine passed from her searing purgatory of desolation not up and on to a settled level of peace and security, but rather downward and backward to beyond where she had so nobly begun so long ago. For the importunity of her family and friends, lending its weight to the strain already put upon her resistance, prevailed at length, and partly to free herself from their perpetual reproaches, partly to ease her own intolerable distress, partly (it may be) from some interior questioning as to the complete purity of her motives in the possibly too introverted life which she had been living, she began to emerge from her solitude to take part in the social activities normal to her position, in a word, to reenter the world which she had so resolutely and so long forsworn. Immediately she became the object of regard and attention on all sides. She was courted and sought after, drawn into every kind of gaiety and amusement, committed to all the thousand and one futilities that constitute the main occupation of what is called Society. It is certain, however, that there never was any question of grave sin.

It is almost with awe that we learn that this, too, lasted for five years. It needed all that time for her to learn from that grim teacher, the experience of loss and failure and all-but despair, how God is all, how he has made us for himself alone, how our hearts must for ever wander restless until they find their way to him. She had to taste, too, the unavailing anguish of those who know that they have thrown a pearl of great price away—mystically to dip into the very blackness of the Pit. No less a defeat than this was, could have won her the victory in the end. For hardly had she taken the first step which, do what she might, *must* be followed by others in the same direction than she realized what she had done, and was doing, and might yet do. Her soul was filled with an agony of remorse that poisoned everything: night and day in her heart she accused herself of apostasy, and frantic with longing to find her way back she yet could see no light and no hope wherever she turned.

Five years: and then, on the feast of St. Benedict, going on an impulse to her sister's convent she sent for the chaplain of the nuns and asked him to hear her confession. It demanded an immense effort to do this because she had no idea of how she was ever to extricate herself from her entanglements: but she determined fiercely that come what might she would open her mind without reserve to the priest and would blindly follow his guidance at no matter what cost. Hardly had she knelt down with this resolution formed than, as she relates, there seemed to strike upon her mind and heart and soul a ray, of fire rather than light, conveying such an overmastering love of God and such a conviction of his transcendent goodness and her own sinfulness that everything else was wiped out of her consciousness and on the instant all doubt and fear left her for ever. She fell at once into an ecstasy, repeating over and over again the words, *Non piu mondo! Non piu peccato!*; "No more world! No more sin!"

She found it impossible to make her confession even when she had returned to her senses, but as soon as she could move hurried back to her home where she collected and immediately disposed of all her fashionable clothes and ornaments, afterward shutting herself up alone in her room for several days. When she emerged from her retirement she made a general confession of her whole life, and then without a moment's delay entered upon a course of prayer and penance which she maintained unmitigated by any circumstances whatever for the remaining thirty-seven years of her life. A year later there came to her an interior certitude of the forgiveness of all her sins and the acceptance by God of her atonement for them in full. From that moment to the day of her death she thought no more of them. Her conversion seems to have been as complete as it was instantaneous. She was never again subject to any fluctuations of faith or fervour, she never for an instant lost sight of the presence of God, and she was never again tempted through any of her senses.

There must have been much real good in her husband in spite of his disorderly behavior, for we learn that he accepted the new state of things without demur and willingly agreed that thenceforth they should live together as brother and sister, and though for some time to come there did not appear any great change in his mode of life, yet within a few years we hear of his complete reformation and that as a member of the Third Order of St. Francis he joined with Catherine in the heroic works of mercy among the poor and in the hospitals of the city to which she devoted herself until her death in 1510 at the age of sixty-three, he having predeceased her by thirteen years.

But, as so often happens with the saints,—and indeed with other categories of remarkable persons—the real value of the life of St. Catherine of Genoa, her chiefest title to our gratitude, is to be found in what

superficially at least might seem to have been almost a side-issue of it.
For it is as the interpreter and apostle (really "sent" one feels) of the
doctrine of Purgatory that she made her most permanent contribution
to the spiritual life of the Church, and what we know of her own inner
experience helps us to realize how fitted she was for that task. That
experience had taught her as no other master could that in the germ
of love for himself which God has implanted in our nature resides all
the potentiality of our perfection and our happiness: that if this be not
cultivated nothing will grow in its place: that the wickedness of sin
is wholly in this, that it is the negation of love. "Who are you?" she
once asked of the evil spirit during an exorcism: "I am one", was the
answer, "in whom there is no love."

She had learned by dreadful and dismaying experiment that the love
of God alone—not any other means or any other aims however noble
in themselves—is able both to stimulate and to satisfy the yearning of
the human heart, and that the worth of any act that a man can perform is no greater than the love of God of which it is the token. And
she knew by the same experiment that our love of God is one thing
with his love of us—his self-expression, as it were, in his own regard,
through and as ourselves—so that not to love him is in fact to deny
him, for it is to reject him who *is* love. The words that two centuries
before Margery Kempe of Lynn, in faraway England, had heard in her
prayer, she would have understood and rejoiced to hear: "Not all your
prayers and penances and good works mean so much to me as that you
should believe that I love you."

But the first necessity of love is for union, and union in its closest
sense is in the harmony of wills: by every sin (which is essentially an
act of discord) this harmony is interrupted and impaired and something
more disastrous to the sinner and more dishonoring to God than any
mere temporal evil has been done and must be undone and made good
either here or hereafter. The guilt of the sin is forgiven by repentance,
but a shadow, a weakness, something of a wrong orientation, remains
in the will that offended, and right love between the soul and God is to
that degree inhibited. How difficult the circumstances of our present
life make the process of recovery all must be aware, and indeed the
Church seems in practice to assume the necessity of an after-life atonement for the generality of the saved. Here we see even the plainest
truths but darkly, and the mere lapse of time may act as a kind of men-

tal or moral anesthetic: it is not until the day when that which is perfect is come and we know even as we are known, that we shall fully
understand what our hearts were created to give and what they have
in fact given or withheld. In the first indivisible instant of the soul's
separation from the body all the guilt of venial sin is remitted by that
supreme act of submission by which it surrenders itself. There is now
no other possible object of the will but God, nothing has any power
to draw it away, were it in the very slightest degree, from him, for
himself. The whole total of energy in the liberated soul is converted
uniquely Godward: its entire being presses undeviatingly, unequivocally, solely and wholly to that Absolute Being in whom alone it has
its own being: at last its constitutive instinct for blessedness in God
only has broken free from the trammels of all other attraction. But
though from outside itself there comes now to the soul no hindrance
to its full and immediate possession of God, within itself it perceives
that through no fault but its own there is still something that holds it
agonizingly back. This is the aftermath of sin, the sediment left by the
weaknesses, the bad dispositions, the wrong choices and tastes, which
the soul has taken into itself in the repetition of sinful acts committed
throughout its mortal life. There remains no guilt, no aversion from
God, attached to it: the freedom of the soul is now such that no influence but good has power to touch it: it cleaves wholly indeed to God,
but the *instrument* of its adhesion through its own fault, through the
effect of the accumulation of ill uses to which it has been put in life
—has, as it were, become "unhandy". One might fancy a craftsman
unable to give full expression to his perfect ideal because, though his
own vision and skill are unimpaired, through his misuse of them his
tools will not serve him as they should.

And as in life it seems to be the ineluctable law that we must pull
down and build again what we have built wrong, and this with greater
pain and labor than it would have cost us in the first place to build
aright, so (the Saint seems to teach) we have in Purgatory to struggle
through to God by somehow retracing toward him the steps that in life
we took away from him: in some mystic way to relive our temporal
past, not in detail but in respect of that essential quality in it which
gave it a final character displeasing to God, the ill-use namely of our
free will. That is the bare statement of what we call the "punishment"
of Purgatory: but she goes on to show how terrible the process is, and

why. The torment of Purgatory, indeed, she declares to be less than that of Hell only in that the latter is without hope and is constituted in hate and aversion from God, whereas the former proceeds from love and drives the soul nearer to him. Yet again, in another sense this very difference is a chief cause of the intensity of the purgatorial sufferings. For the soul, now exclusively turned to God, is aware that only through its own fault is its knowledge (which is possession) and with that its love, of him still imperfect: and as with impetuous energy it bends and thrusts itself toward him, so do the knowledge and the love increase in clarity and vehemence and so in consequence does the anguish of the still untranscended separation grow. Extremes meet: increasing joy multiplies the suffering, and the greater suffering leads to greater joy, so that it seems true to say that the pain of Purgatory is more intense the nearer the soul is to its deliverance. The process of approach to final union with God is through a transformation of all self-regard into that perfect charity which has no will but his, so that for the souls in Purgatory the reality of their suffering is not the pain that it causes themselves but the realization of the cause and meaning of that pain, their opposition to (or dis-harmony with) his will which to them, says the Saint, is so catastrophic a thing as to obliterate in their conscious-ness the very recollection, as such, whether in the gross or in detail, of their sins that brought it about, well though they know their own responsibility for it. Yet with it all—and it would be wicked folly to treat its agonies lightly—the souls in Purgatory enjoy a happiness far surpassing our imagination. St. Catherine, indeed, does not hesitate to say that she can think of no greater joy than theirs except it be that of the Blessed in heaven. For with them all happiness is resolved into this one thing, that God's will be perfectly done: and in their sufferings they see this being accomplished, and more and more perfectly, as the relics of their sins that hindered it are by his love burnt away from them. But it would be a mistake to limit the teaching of the Saint to the purgation to come after death. Her doctrine of Purgatory was also her doctrine of life. Here, as there, she teaches, it is true that all our happiness stands upon the oneness of our will with God's: and here, too, for all the obscurity of our apprehension, we can by supernatural faith learn to judge the worth of all things by that unique standard. Sin, then, should be of all imaginable misfortunes the gravest, and repentance and for-giveness will not be the last of it. There will be needed reparation in kind, deliberate reversal of the evil choice, positive goodwill in small things as in greater—to lay, as it were, even in advance, the stress of our emphasis on the one overruling aim of all in self-defense against the frailty of our unstable fancy.

It is from such a consideration of Purgatory, too, that we are helped to an understanding of how pain may be, and ought to be, the means both of self-expression and self-escape. For we are never so true to ourselves as when we are true to God, by committing ourselves, that is, wholly to him. And the more completely we do this the greater is our pain that there is yet more to do, for by so much the more clearly do we come to understand how that if we are to have him, he must have all.

~

SAINT JOHN FISHER

[*1459–1535*]

David Mathew

INCE THE CHURCH has been promised persecution, the lines of the regional episcopates should in the ideal order lead to martyrdom. It is in this manner that the centuries of effort and the humdrum of laborious confessors receive their seal. Thus the spirituality of Catholic generations, long undisturbed, had gone to the molding of the mind and temper of John, Bishop of Rochester, who died in 1535 for Christian truth; in defense of the doctrine of Christ's foundation of an indefectible and visible Church.

Coming at the close of the medieval period and summing up in himself the theological inheritance of the Catholic Ages, it is difficult to reconstruct the picture of this man, the accidents of whose life seem so remote. Some impression of Bishop Fisher can be gained by a study of those Holbein drawings from which his tired, farseeing eyes gaze wearily on the great reign and its overblown splendor. Through his habits and his mode of life, tenacious and slow, the effects of temperament may be discerned; while each facet of his thought reflects the heavy and massed influence of tradition. Yet each reaction to the increasingly complex world by which he was surrounded only serves to emphasize his deep simplicity. The moment of his last arrest, which formed the prelude to his martyrdom, seems the converging point for all these forces. At this stage, too, a view can be gained from the State Papers of the domestic interior at Rochester, the minute detail of his poverty, the broken peace.

By the spring of 1534 Henry VIII's divorce case was over, the religious schism quite effective, the breach with Rome almost complete, and the bishop could gain but little consolation from the Easter festival. On the following sixteenth of April his arrest, as the defender of the ancient discipline, seemed the mere final step, long since forseen, in what was to the bishop's thought this tragic progress. The movement of men's minds appeared to him inscrutable, that rejection and questioning of the verities with which, since childhood, he had been familiar. For just thirty years he had ruled his see, riding on visitation through the Kentish country, with a period of preaching or confirming to vary the rhythm of his constant prayer. And now he was to leave the scene of his austere labors. Behind him lay the skeleton of works which an ardent faith had forced upon him, a declaration of Christ's presence in the Sacrament, a defense of chastity. The elaborate notes of sermons, the carefully piled examples of erudition in which the formalism of his training stood revealed, belonged to that period of his life which was quite finished. With the order for his arrest the sum of these active labors of mortification and study was complete. Henceforward he had merely to follow his own conscience and accept God's Mercy. The skepticism of the new age, the king with his carnality and self-communings, the sacrilege of heresy bore down on one whose life of prayer had led him far from worldly interests. Religion, in the sense of the practice of the Sacramental life and the absorption of the Testaments which the Church had guarded, alone seemed clear. It was the reality from which the world was moving. Serene amid this indifference, the bishop prayed with the forms that he had used in his distant boyhood as he had knelt by his father's grave beneath the rood in the minster at Beverley. He would always raise his heart to God in the same allegiance. The words of the Easter Sequence *Victimae paschali laudes* came with the memory of the voices of the clerks and the singing men of his cathedral. Here was the old medieval simplicity and the questioning to which his mind responded: "Tell us, Mary," so the words of the Sequence continued, "what thou hast seen in the way". Men spoke of the noisy Germans, disputers of a tavern theology, Magister Luther and Oecolampadius. The bishop retained the ancient questioning, *Dic nobis Maria, quid vidisti in via?*

This same Faith and the tranquility bred of an earlier and more peaceful time were alike implicit in every movement of the chaplains and the servants in that great ill-built house, the palace of Rochester. This had been the scene of his austerities and his quiet ruling. The bare untapestried walls of the sleeping chamber, with the green and white embroidered silk behind the altar in the corner and the rough blue sarcenet curtains by the window had that familiarity which can only come from a cell loved and well kept. Beside one wall there stood the bishop's bed with its counterpane of red linen sewn on the underside with canvas, which covered the hard straw matting of his night's discomfort. Each detail of the room bore witness to a struggle for detachment from the things of sense and a determined following of the ancient ways. During thirty years the bishop had looked out upon the view from these same windows, the flooding and uncovering of the tide banks, the gulls, the empty shore.

About him the worn equipment of the house and its empty spaces suggested that love of the poverty of the Gospel, which he followed without the constraint of vow; this desire which has so often marked those detached souls for whom the raised loneliness of the episcopate has something of the height of Calvary. The study place and the dining chamber both bore his austere impress, the table and the long forms and the bishop's chair with its black velvet. All here brought to the mind the withdrawn existence of one for whom the spiritual values would alone seem real. The grave and careful reading of a clerk moving through the Gregorian homilies would mark a fitting background to the scene, while the bishop sat alone in his dark moth-eaten tippet, his wide jaws moving slowly as he munched the bread in his thin pottage.

Upon the bare table stood a skull to keep him company, beyond the mazer bowl and the little silver cellars. Such silver ware, small in quantity and in value, yet indicating that formality which his episcopal ranking still demanded, had come, as had so many of his possessions, from his patroness the Lady Margaret, the old king's mother. Personal acquisition did not square with his conception of the pastoral rôle.

Beneath him in the town the travellers from the Cinque Ports jostled, and in the Medway lay the Gravesend wherries. With the casual strangers he had little contact, but the innkeepers and the other townsmen and the close gathered households of that Kentish country were of his flock. He could not fail to remember that God would hold him as steward for their Faith and his own. And the emphasis on this fact stands out more clear, since his great age at length forbade him his cherished pastoral contact with the poor. Now as he stood, supporting himself with a stick on account of his weakness, it was clear that he would be called upon for his final duty to seal his testimony to the truth of Christ. Erect, with the hair shirt constantly grating on him, his emaciated figure only added to the impression of unexpected height. In his face the blue veins showed more strongly now that his seventies were far advanced. The spare white-haired figure, with those eyes which mark his detachment from the world so clearly, suggests the last months of some early bishop, weakened in body, but strong willed to die. Bishop Fisher's thoughts upon this matter, his great sense of the duties of the pastoral office and of the feeding of the sheep, are presented in the sermon which he preached upon the books of Martin Luther. "And Peter", the bishop had declared, "was made by Christ, to whom he commysed in his absence the cure of the Christen people sayenge: *pasce oves meas, pasce, pasce.*" One word sums up the Bishop of Rochester in life and death—*pasce, pasce*.

The meaning of his arrest, the steps by which the king had separated from the Holy See, the casting off from the unity of Christian Faith were seen without illusion, events sharply defined and evil. It was not with the court that his own sympathies had ever lain, nor his career depended. The piety and old-fashioned scholarship, the careful fine calligraphy, the controlled appreciation of good letters, would all seem to have marked out Dr. Fisher for a life of learning and quiet pastoral care; the stole, the doctor's cap; hardly the mitre. The crucial accident which had uprooted him from his Cambridge life appeared before him, that choice as confessor to King Henry VII's mother, the Lady Margaret. How remote it now must seem, the cameo-like form of the Lady Margaret, the high coif and the folded linen beneath the chin, the mild wide eyes, the figure, prim and diminutive. He could see her still with her hands folded before her Book of Hours, while her quiet speech fell on matters of the spirit, as she told of the dream of Saint Nicholas before her marriage; a miniature from an older time. Hers was a figure staid and a little aloof, as she arranged her household and her bounties in the purposed and now withered chastity of her third espousals. It was upon these bounties that there had hinged the bishop's chief administrative labors, the founding of St. John's and Christ's Colleges at Cambridge and the Lady Margaret chairs of Divinity. But twenty-five years had passed since the Lady Margaret had died, and customs changed quickly. That reading of Hylton and the ghostly counsel, the filagree of her devotion, to Our Lady's Nativity for instance, the whole devout way of living had now vanished down the wind. Yet such a spirit had never been at ease in the court atmosphere, and in the new, rather tasteless, glitter the king's gentlemen could develop freely, subject to the requirements of good breeding, a hearty and respectful avarice. The new strange world in which the bishop moved appeared in the light of his detachment with frosted clearness.

As to the king, it was not hard to judge him, the crude theological antitheses, the full-fleshed yet equivocal laughter, the mind clogged a little by the body, that Yorkist inheritance, large-boned and raw. To place Queen Catherine of Aragon would seem less easy. Her outward aspect, likewise, was so familiar, the long brown hair, once beautiful, now dulled, the wide and pleasant features, placid and dignified. She was devout in her own Spanish fashion, to Walsingham and the Franciscans; she used with persistent care the Latin Office. Yet it was difficult for the bishop, a Yorkshireman, direct and very humble, to fathom her reserved mind and its mainsprings, the heavily conscious royalty of the new Spanish kingdom, the barred, yet tremulous, Castilian pride. He was not her confessor and was only consulted upon occasion. On the other hand he had formed a sharp impression of Mistress Boleyn. He knew her home at Hever, with its new terraces, and he had been the ordinary of that unsound knight, Sir Thomas Boleyn, the leman's father. Yet the personalities of this struggle seemed far away, like that garishness which had come in with Wolsey.

Even the bishops of the court party moved in circles, which his own orbit never touched, while day by day their contact with the king enmeshed them in those toils of the royal policy from which his own detached life kept him free. "Now be many chalices of gold", the Bishop of Rochester had written, "but almost no golden priests". Difficult as it is to indicate his own remoteness, some impression is conveyed by his biographer. "Truly", this Marian admirer wrote of Fisher, "of all the bishops that we have knowne or heard of in our daies, it may best be said, that this bishopp hath well lived and well and truly lurked: for who at any time hath seen him ydle walk or wander." Through the strange phrases the special quality of his life comes clear.

As he moved on toward prison the new court life was present to him, that magnificence, high colored, rather vulgar, which the late Cardinal Wolsey loved. Even now there remained a suggestion of that unseemly power in Master Cromwell, the King's new secretary, with his little eyes and quick, too pleasant speech. It was an unsavory remembrance that

Master Cromwell had survived from the late cardinal's gaudy wreck. The bishop had no prejudice against new men, for he was one himself, a mercer's son from Beverley; but he could feel the loss of true religion. The politicians shared the courtiers' indifference, and there arose the image of the noisy, crafty Brandon, with slashed sleeves and ostrich feather and the groups in apple green and russet satin at the king's ponderous archery. Whatever the self-tortured king might do, the courtiers had calmed a facile conscience and the appetites led them and the bishop knew to his sorrow the riches of the Church. All finesse was abhorrent to his firm straightforward mind, and few signs of the new age seemed so repellent as this gambling upon religious truth. The courtiers possessed a prudent anticipation of prosperity as they maneuvered to obtain the weather gauge. The bishop could see them as they flocked around the uneasy Boleyn, the concubine with her dark eyes and her forced French ways and her virulent laughter. There was something of gambling fever in the life of these parasites, as they moved through the king's new palace of Placentia by the river. Placentia—the very name conveyed a flushed, false pleasure and the impermanence of that house of cards, the royal favor: Bishop Fisher passed on slowly to the calm peace of the Tower.

The bishop stood for the old ways and the heart of England. It was clear that he must now defend his flock, as they dug and plowed and chaffered, faithful and simple. The literary and scholarly friendships of the past had worn thin in this testing time. Erasmus was now remote and his action doubtful. As the bishop remembered that great scholar, whom he had first befriended in Cambridge long ago, their conversations seemed so far away, faint like the smile which lit his guest's lined face, when his courteous fancy turned on learned matters. The detail of the visits seemed most distant; the heavy cloak and rich black fur from out of Germany showing dark against the poor wall hangings, as the scholar played with an ivory sand caster or other toy in his quiet talking. No man could be more pleasant to those whom he admired than Erasmus. The young painter from Basel whom he had sent— Hans Holbein, a mere name upon the memory—had spoken of him. But in this stress a certain triviality marked such scenes. The bishop was absorbed in his single duty to protect, as an *alter Christus*, the flock of Christ.

Behind him lay his own small diocese, and the experience of the

German wars had shown the insecurity of religious practice, once the unity of Christian Faith was broken. He knew that he could count on Sir Thomas More's clear conscience, but the strength of the new monarchy, the pervading influence of the Tudor power and the well-executed maneuvers of the court had left them now in isolation. The vitiated atmosphere of the court, from which all his life he had kept free, would hinder most great men from that prayer for fortitude which martyrdom exacted. The king's counselors were subtle, as had been proved in the case of the nun of St. Sepulchre's at Canterbury and her treasonable sayings, in which the bishop had so nearly been involved; but all that was required in these last stages was to go forward in the light of Faith.

In the churches, hospitals and chapels the Holy Sacrifice of the Mass was offered and the shriving and receiving of the Sacrament renewed the life of Grace for the Christian people. The religious houses stood as firmly rooted in the countryside as the oak in which Saint Simon Stock found refuge; while the changing pattern of each shrine stood clear. An atmosphere of high spiritual doctrine marked Dartford, the bishop's sister's convent, Dominican, a school for manners and good letters, with its strict well-born community, whose diluted conservatism still showed through their courteous phrases. The calefactory at Greenwich brought back another scene: the form of Master Forest, keen and busy, and the tough, austere Franciscans; while at Aylesford in its quiet elms the shadow of Saint Simon lay upon the Carmelites in their simplicity. At Boxley, just beyond his borders, there stood the abbey of the Rood of Grace. Here was the ordered religion of the Christian centuries, now threatened. The light of the spring days fell upon these houses with the first apple blossom in their orchards in the calm weather. The bishop could not forget for an instant that God had raised him up as their protector. In this lull before the storm there was no movement. The disturbances of the court found no reflection in the religious peace which lay unbroken on the See of Rochester. The freshening breeze from off the Channel slowly turned the sails of windmills.

The closely woven skein of town and country had led the bishop to that understanding of the rural life implicit in the outlook of that time. He had written long ago of the winter season and of "the trees whan they wydred and thyr leues shaken from them and all the moystour shronke in to the rote and no luste of grenenes nor of lyfe appereth outwardly." When he put the worldly things behind him he had a sense of all that he was leaving, as he rode away and his old eyes slowly drained the Kentish fields.

In another region, also, the freshness and the limitations of the medieval knowledge defined his thought, while the restrained quality of his imagination kept the whole, as in a miniature, within due limits. The very restrictions of his knowledge had brought the Holy Land closer to him than to the later ages. "The Blessyd Martha", he had declared in one of his more carefully wrought out sermons, "was a woman of noble blode to whom by inheritance belonged the castel of Bethany". The Ancients, too, had come within his ken, and he was still sufficiently medieval in his concepts to realize spontaneously and humbly how closely he approached the sum of knowledge. "Where is now", the bishop had declaimed with his naive rhetoric, "the immemorable company and puyssance of Xerxes and Cesar, where is now the grete victoryes of Alexander and Pompey, where is now the grete rychesse of Cresus and Crassus." "The grete rychesse of Cresus and Crassus." How remarkably the phrase suggests the Elizabethans and their tall forests, but what unsympathetic hands have strewn these acorns?

The intermingling of these strands of thought, the curveting simplicity of the bishop's pastoral rhetoric, is seen in his sermon on Martin Luther. "Such a clowde", he wrote of the early heretics, "was Arrius which stered so greate a tempest that many years after it vexyd the chirche of Christ. And after hym came many other lyke clowdes as Macedonius, Nestorius, Eutices, Donatus, Iouinianus, Pellagius, Joannes Wicleff with other moo. . . . And nowe suche another clowde is raysed a lofte oone Martyn luther a frere, the whiche has stered a myghty storm and tempeste in the chirche and hath shadowed the clere lyght of many scryptures of God." his following of the evangelical counsels is here reflected; that prayer and meditation which had armed him, the devotion to the scriptures of God. Thirty years of a tranquil episcopate and the slow maturing of religious experience, absorbed since childhood, had gradually prepared the bishop for his time of trial. An incessant search for God had left his spirit free and untrammeled, while from the moment when he yielded himself to his last captivity this freedom of the soul breaks through each word and movement.

It was on the Thursday after *Dominica in Albis*, in that Eastertide of

1534, that he was brought down to the Tower. Through this week in the liturgical calm of the Paschal Season the Proper of the Mass had remained unchanging. "And there are three that give testimony on earth," the meaning would come to him as his failing eyes peered toward the Missal with the Lady Margaret's portcullis on the cover, "the spirit and the water and the blood". How strongly the Epistle would sound forth as a demand and a warning. *Et tres sunt qui testimonium dant in terra: spiritus et aqua et sanguis.* It was a not unfitting prelude to the leadership of the white robed army, *te martyrum candidatus.* As the gates of the Tower of London closed behind him the bishop had marked out his future. The imprisonment lasted for a year, and finally, on June 22, 1535, the Bishop of Rochester was put to death for his refusal to accept the Royal Supremacy and for his statement that "the king our sovereign lord is not supreme head in earth of the church of England". In the previous month he had received the title of Cardinal Priest of the Church of Saint Vitalis, so that Peter's approval sealed his action. He died that the English provinces might still remain within the unity of Catholic Faith.

It is well to consider now the final actions of this determined life, which bind together each divergent trait. Among the principal accounts of the actual martyrdom are the Rastell fragments, the work of an eyewitness, and the various manuscripts of the English Life, the earliest of which can be traced to the reign of Queen Mary. As a pendant to a description of his outlook these papers make each salient feature clear. The details of his last hours show again the workings of a life's simplicity.

"The xxii day of June next following," so runs the Rastell fragment, "abowt fyve a cloke in the morning, the Levetenant of the Towre came to this holy mann in his bedde asleep and wakyd hyme and shewed hym . . . that the kinges pleasure was that he shuld suffer in that fornonne."

" 'Well,' quoth the bishop, 'if this be your erant hyther, it is no newes unto me; I haue looked dayly for it. I pray you what is it a cloke?' "

" 'It is,' quoth the Levetenant, 'abowt Fyve.' "

" 'What time,' quoth the bishop, 'must be myne howre to goo owt hence?' "

" 'About tenne of the cloke,' sayed the Levetenant."

" 'Well, than,' quoth the bishop, 'I praye you, lett me slepe an howre or twyne. For I may say to you, I slept not much this nyght, not for feare of death, I tell you, but by reason of my great sickness and wekeness.'"

"With which aunswere the Levetenant departed from hyme till about nine a cloke. At which tyme he came againe to the bishops chambre, and found him upward, putting on his clothes; and shewed him that he was come for hyme."

"'Well,' quoth the bishop, 'I will make as convenyent hast as my weeke and syckely aged body will gyve me leve. And, I pray you, reache me there my Furred typpett to put abowt my necke.'"

"'Oh, my Lord,' quoth the Levetenant to hyme, 'what nede you be nowe so carrefull of your health? Your tyme is very shorte, lytle more than half an howre.'"

"'I think none otherwise,' quoth the bishop; 'but, I pray you, yett gyve me leave to put on my Furred typpett, to kepe me warme for the whyle until the verie tyme of execution; for I tell you truth, though I haue, I thank our Lord, a very good stomacke and willing mynd to dye at this present, and I trust in his goodnesse and mercy he will styl contynewe it and encrease it, yet will I not hinder my health in the meane tyme not a minute of an howre, but will preserue it in the meane season with all suche discrete wayes and meanes as almighty God of his gracious goodnes hath prouyded for me.'"

"Then was he caryed downe oute of his chamber betwene twaine in a chayre and so to the Towre gate."

The next passage appears in the early English Life, attributed to Richard Hall, and therefore has only such authority as that work will carry. "But as he was mounting up the staires", so runs this extract, "the sowtheast sonne shyned verie bright in his face; whereupon he said to himself these wordes, liftinge up his handes, *Accedite ad eum et illuminamini et facies vestrae non confundentur.*" How significant are these words, "Come ye to him and be enlightened." But for the last words on the scaffold we have an eyewitness' authority: "Than spake he . . . in effecte as follows," the Rastell fragment continues, "Christian people, I am come hyther to die for the fayth of Christes catholyke church."

A carol, very familiar to the religious thought of Bishop Fisher's time, reflects in dawn clear phrases the England and the cause for which he

died. In the first reference to Our Lady the intimate religion of the
little shrines and churches lies revealed.

> For in this rose contained was
> Heaven and earth in little space,
> *Res miranda.*

The miracle of the Incarnation is suggested, the nearness of Bethlehem,
the lowing cattle, God's Presence in tranquility in the fields. And then
the last couplet brings to mind the spirit of the bishop's martyrdom.

> Leave we all this worldly mirth,
> And follow we this joyful birth
> *Transeamus.*

~

SAINT THOMAS MORE

[1477-1535]

G. K. Chesterton

F ANYONE had looked for the name of Thomas More in the century or so after his death he would probably have found first the isolated mention of a sort of legend: that he was the Man Who Died Laughing. He is mentioned in this manner in more than one of those quaint collections of freaks and monsters and old-world anecdotes such as were common in the whole period from Aubrey to Isaac Disraeli. The story is something of a simplification and an exaggeration; but it is not one which the admirers of Thomas More will in any sense desire to deny. There is no doubt that he died jesting; and that he would have been the first to see the fun of having his death commemorated in a jest-book. In other words, he was not only a humanist, but a humorist; a humorist both in the contemporary and the modern sense. Anyhow, most modern people know what they mean by a humorist; whereas, the more modern they are, the more they dispute about what is meant by being a humanist. And sometimes, I grieve to say, a humanist seems to mean a man who is not very human and not at all humorous.

If, on the other hand, anyone confine his curiosity about Thomas More to an enquiry about the popular notions surrounding the name in quite modern times, he would probably find that More has mostly been remembered as the author of *Utopia*; in some sense as the author of all the Utopias; even all the six or seven separate Utopias of Mr. H. G. Wells; a rather serious responsibility for Thomas More, if looked upon in that earnest light. And here again the impression is not false; and need not even be disproportionate, if it is stated in its proper proportion. Thomas More was most emphatically a man of the Renaissance; a man whose mind went outward as well as inward; and thought of the ends of the earth as well as of the end of the world.

He was quite as much of a reformer and rational pioneer as Erasmus
or Colet; though certainly more devout than the former, and probably
more tactful than the latter. The two men were his friends; and the two
friendships make up a great part of his life. Moreover, it is true that his
life reaches its first natural turn or turning-point with the publication
of *Utopia*; and that if we take that date with the subsequent date of
his resignation of the Chancellorship, we shall have the two pivotal
points of his general movement; before the last and finest passage of
all. Everyone knows that he was the son of a judge of Henry VII, Sir
John More, and became the page of Archbishop Morton, who proph-
esied great things of him even in his childhood; that he became a typical Hellenist, learned especially in the New Learning; that his natural
gaiety and good manners made him popular with everybody, and not
least with Henry VIII, who sought his companionship, asked his advice
and at length persuaded him to a reluctant acceptance of the dangerous
dignity of Lord Chancellor. It is also well known that More was well
aware of the danger of such dignities. Somebody congratulated him,
after an interview in which Bluff King Hal had been slapping him on
the back with uproarious amiability, and More answered grimly, "If
my head would win him a castle in France, it should not fail to go." It
was indeed destined to go, to be used in the storming of a larger and
more ancient castle, which was also a cathedral. But, as I have said,
the modern instinct is so far right that if we wish for a moment that
marks the morning of his career, with its widest liberty and liberality
and even relative irresponsibility, we could not take a better one than
that of the publication of *Utopia*, during one of his holidays abroad in
1516. It is undoubtedly full of all the ideas of his time, and many ideas
of his own; artistically and imaginatively it responds to a real appetite
for experiment and a gigantic gesture making for elbow room; which
were of the best promise at that time. We see something of the same
thing later, in the Utopian speech made by one of Shakespeare's characters, on landing on the magic island of *The Tempest*. But when this
is said, there is something else to be said, which for some reason or
other very seldom is said, about the significance of *Utopia* in the life of
Thomas More. It must be taken in conjunction with that other stray
legend of the laughing man; and the knowledge that More was not the
sort of humanist who sternly refuses to be a humorist.

Unfortunately many modern humanists, who know that he even

jested in his death, cannot bring themselves to believe that he ever jested in his youth. The fact is that *Utopia* is one mass of the sort of questions which are asked by jesting youth, as by jesting Pilate, even if neither of them waits for an answer. Why should we have all this complicated botheration about private property; how about having property in common, like the monks? Why not assassinate the one foreign statesman who is certainly planning a world-war, instead of massacring millions of harmless people who never wanted any war? Are animals immortal; or why aren't they? Wouldn't it really be a jolly good thing for the country if all lawyers were kicked out of it? Would not divorce be a very comfortable solution of a lot of uncomfortable problems, if only it could be allowed? Might not Nudism be at least a temporary measure; as connected, for instance, with what is now called Companionate Marriage? Is it really impossible to have a simpler society, with all the Gordian knots of life cut with this sort of private pocket-knife of common sense? Those are the sort of random rationalistic questions which filled his head, and his period, and his first fantastic book; and if Mr. Bernard Shaw had put them into the mouth of a highly Nonconformist negress, many might now suppose that they were quite novel. But if it be asked how or why a Catholic, let alone a great and holy Catholic, even entertained such ideas, the answer is that a thinking Catholic always does entertain them—if only to reject them. Thomas More did primarily entertain them and did finally reject them. A Catholic is not a man who never thinks of such things. A Catholic is a man who really knows why he does not think they are true. But when people begin to think they are true, to think that far worse things are true, to force the worst things of all upon the world, the situation is entirely different; and cannot be related in any way to the jokes which a young Renaissance humorist put into a book like *Utopia*. This is the point of the supposed difference between More the author of *Utopia* and More the Chancellor of England. The difference is that England exists, unlike *Utopia*; and this somewhat eminent Englishman wanted England to continue to exist; and especially the England that he loved.

For this is the main moral charge against Thomas More; indeed, the only moral charge against Thomas More. The ordinary English authorities, in the Victorian tradition, pay a tribute to his virtues and talents, his charity and charming personality, but say that the great "stain" on his character is the fact that he did when chancellor the work that would have been done as a matter of course by any other chancellor; and that this work included the suppression of heretics. They are forced to admit that he only did what all the other people would have done; what all the heretics themselves would have done. He could not possibly have been a chancellor without doing the work of a chancellor, and he had long refused to be a chancellor, and was then much blamed for throwing up his chancellorship. But, though it is clear that More only did rather reluctantly what all his friends and foes would have done resolutely and ruthlessly, there is more in the matter than that; and there is a sense in which he really was resolute and might well force himself to be ruthless. It was connected, not with any change in Thomas More, but with a change in the whole world around him.

In the early days in which he wrote the *Utopia* the new world was really expanding into wider horizons. As it expanded geographically to the discovery of America, so it expanded psychologically to the discovery of Utopia. It may be that even in that liberty there were the beginnings of the peril. But the liberty was liberty; it had not yet hardened into heresy. For a heresy is only a fossil liberty. The young Renaissance romancer was in a double sense free of his Utopia; he was free to enter it, but also free to leave it; he was free in it, and also free from it. He was not to be tied for life to the idle fantasies and hypotheses which he had thrown out in the daydreams of his youth, to be the laws of fairyland. In all that the new movement was an expansion; but there came a definite time when the new movement ceased to be an expansion, and the wise could see that it was already becoming a contraction. The Renaissance was an expansion; but the Reformation was a contraction. Even by the time of More, men as clear-sighted and sensitive as More could see that the coming of a new tyranny out of the North had altered all the conditions of liberty; and especially of the old liberties and levities of the South. It was no longer a question of the dubious broadening of the old broad philosophy; it was a question of a new and narrow religion. The author of *Utopia* had had his fancies; but the Chancellor of England realized that other fancies, far less humane than his fancies, were quite likely to become facts. The new men, the new reformers, were not men like his old cronies Colet or Erasmus, and they were meaning business. Nobody accused them of being jesters, and some of them never laughed in their lives, let alone in their death. And they were heartily and horribly in earnest. They really meant to drive out all the priests, as the author of *Utopia* had never really meant to drive out all the lawyers.

The Calvinist was fanatical about the fixed predestined necessity of good men going to hell, as even Mr. Hythlodaye had never been fanatical about horses going to heaven. A new sect really began by going about naked, on ordinary occasions, whereas nobody supposes that More wanted people to do so, even on the very extraordinary occasions his romance describes. In other words, *Utopia* was written by a particular man, in a particular mood, at a particular moment, when he was lighthearted and full of levity because he believed that civilization was growing more civilized. At the later period he definitely believed that civilization was in danger of going to the dogs; to all the mad dogs of religious melancholia and barbarian self-conceit. It measures the depth of his understanding of the real moral danger, that he seems to have been especially indignant about the denial of free will. Everybody then alive thought that poisonous doctrines ought to be materially suppressed like poisonous drugs. He had no more doubt about these poisonous doctrines than about poisonous drugs. He felt as a man would feel struggling with the growing power of gangsters and gunmen in Chicago. That is the only change there was, and it was not a change in Thomas More or even in Thomas More's opinions. It was the change from liberty to martial law.

The change, such as it was, was masked for some time by a fact often forgotten: his essential agreement with the king. What then was the essential point of his disagreement with the king? The answer is the study of the two characters; and especially of More's character. For the king, let it be remembered was, or seemed to be, quite as much of an orthodox Catholic as More, and much more of a persecutor or crusader than More. Henry Tudor was rigid in every detail of Catholicism; perhaps too rigid to be a Catholic; to the very end he thought himself rather more Catholic than the Pope. In his hatred of the heresies he was quite as decided as More and much more merciless. What was the matter with him was that he was the sort of rigid Churchman who always does, consciously or unconsciously, want to be head of the Church. There are High Church laymen, there are even Catholic laymen, in whom their respective priests will mournfully recognize the type. "Everything in the parish church must be absolutely Catholic or Anglo-Catholic; but as to what that is—why, I will decide."

Now Thomas More was a layman of exactly the opposite type. He was, indeed, in his interior life, intensely sacramental and even ascetic; and his real religion was of the sort that the saint possesses and the saint never parades. But, by the standard of a certain fussiness about ecclesiastical affairs, which sometimes marks the clerical layman, he might almost be called a lazy layman. He was the sort of Catholic who specially incurs contempt by "leaving everything to the priest". But, above all, there was at the back of his mind a sort of grand humility and philosophic abnegation, which can never be understood by the clericalist who merely wishes to boss things. The issue between Henry Tudor and the friend whom he rather reluctantly murdered is really this; Henry was a strict Catholic, wishing to keep everything straight, but insisting that the man to keep them straight must be himself; while More was really a more liberal Catholic, admitting that things sometimes needed to be sharply put straight; admitting (above all) that he himself might need to be put straight; but insisting that the man who put things straight should *not* be himself, but another. Henry always wanted to be judge in his own cause; against his wives; against his friends; against the Head of his Church. But the link which really connects More with that Roman supremacy for which he died is this fact: that he would always have been large-minded enough to want a judge who was not merely himself.

Mr. Belloc has pointed out, in a brilliant and penetrating essay, that More died for the Papacy because it was a part of the truth; not because it was his favorite part, or to him and his friends a particularly sympathetic or popular part. And this, of course, is profoundly true; the need for the Papacy is far more obvious now than it was then. Nevertheless, there is this true relation between the martyr and the doctrine for which he died; that he died, not only defending the Pope, but defying the sort of man who wants to be Pope. There is no true Pope who wants to be Pope. More was the sort of man who would write a hundred wild satires or romances like *Utopia*, by way of a joke; but he was also the sort of man who would wish that a better man might judge whether the joke had gone too far. Therefore when Henry and his hangers-on began at last to press him upon the supreme question of Henry's rightful supremacy, he knew that the claim was wrong in spirit and motive; and after an interlude of odd silence and reflection, suddenly rose up and defied it. He did not at all want to die; he was the kind of man to enjoy life to the last; but he did die, and having thus released his soul, he died laughing.

SAINT JOHN OF GOD

[*1495 – 1550*]

Alban Goodier, S.J.

EW PEOPLE in this world who have made any name for themselves in any sphere began life under such adverse conditions as did St. John of God. He was born in Montemayor-el-Novo, in Portugal, in 1495. His parents were respectable, but not of the richest class; they looked upon their only son as the chief treasure they possessed. But they were not to possess him long. One day, when John was eight years of age, he disappeared. Whether he had been deliberately kidnapped, or whether he had been seduced from his home by some enticing stranger, is not clear; at all events a short time after he found himself an outcast, a homeless waif, in the streets of Oropesa, in the kingdom of Castile, on the opposite coast of the Spanish peninsula from the place where he was born. There, in a foreign land, he had no one to care for him, nothing on which to live; he had to be content with whatever means of subsistence he could find, and he settled down as a shepherd-boy on the neighboring countryside.

He remained in this solitary life till he was twenty-two years of age; during all that time there seems to be nothing to record about him. Then came a change. It was an age of wars and conquests; and even country villagers, especially in Spain, when the day's work was over, could talk of little else but the new countries being discovered, the great battles being fought, the wonderful deeds being done, by the heroes of the time, from the Emperor-king, Charles V, known among themselves as Charles I, to the common soldier. Men would come home from the wars, and would fire them with marvelous tales, which lost nothing in the telling; voyagers would return from their wanderings across the seas, and would describe the strange people they had met, and the strange sights they had seen, in America or in the Indies. Occasionally one would come back with his pockets apparently full of gold,

and would build his own house and settle down at home, independent
for the rest of his life; and many a country-bred youth would tell himself that the same could be his if only he would go and do likewise.
Then would follow some recruiting officer, who would dangle before
these young men's eyes the glittering bait of service in the Emperor's
armies; and many would lay aside their plows, or leave their sheep on
the hillside, to go after the drum of the sergeant and enlist as soldiers.

In the course of time John the shepherd caught the fever like others. When he was about twenty-two years of age he joined a company
of footsoldiers, and in that company fought for the Emperor, Charles
V, first against the French in Fontarabia, later in Hungary against the
Turks. For some eighteen years John was a trooper employed in various parts of Europe. But while helping to win battles, he lost almost
everything else. On the hillsides of Castile he had preserved some practice of religion; now he lost what little of faith and devotion he once
possessed. He laid aside his morals; he was ashamed to be thought better than the comrades-in-arms about him; in the course of years John
became as hardened in body and soul as anybody else.

Still, not quite everything was gone. Sometimes, when he lay alone
on his bed of straw at night, memories of his childhood would come
back to him. Though he had been taken from his home at the age
of eight, he never forgot the pictures of his early days. The cottage
in which he had lived as a child with a contented father and mother
would rise up out of the mist; or again the hillsides with the sheep,
where he had wandered many a day, all alone, but light-hearted and
utterly free. These recollections he would contrast with the life he was
living; with the noise and confusion of it all, the wealth that occasionally came from loot, but as quickly disappeared, the revelry and drink
and sin, above all the cruelty. Here indeed was a trait which he never
lost. However wild his life, John had always a weak spot in his heart
for the poor and suffering; however reckless his behavior, no beggar
ever came to John but got relief, if he was able to give it. The trait is
not uncommon in men of his kind, as anyone will know who has had
to deal with them.

One or two events contributed to deepen these reflections. Once
when he was out on a looting expedition he fell from his horse, was
severely injured, and narrowly escaped being taken by the enemy. As
he lay on the ground expecting death, instinctively the prayers of his

childhood came to his lips. He appealed to Mary to save him, and somehow he was rescued. On another occasion he was set to guard an enormous heap of booty. When he was relieved it was found that much
of the treasure had been rifled. Naturally the suspicion fell on John;
even if he had not been partner in the theft, at least he had failed in
his duty. He was condemned to be shot; and that would have been his
doom had not some more tolerant officer intervened to win his pardon. Experiences such as these strengthened his disgust for the army;
he determined to be rid of it as soon as he could, and to return to the
peace he had known.

John was over forty years of age before his day of freedom came.
After the campaign in Hungary his regiment was at last disbanded, and
the men were landed on the coast of Galicia. Immediately he set about
making something of himself; and since in those times it was usual for
penitents to begin by being pilgrims, John made a pilgrimage on foot
to St. James of Compostella. At the shrine, as became a true pilgrim, he
put himself right before God; he made his confession, and determined
that in some way the rest of his life should be spent in atonement.
With the joy of forgiveness came thoughts of his early childhood, and
with them a great longing to know what had become of his family. He
accordingly went into Portugal, to the town where he was born; he
found there an uncle, to whom he contrived to make himself known.
From him he learned that his mother had died long years ago, partly
of a broken heart because of the loss of her son; after her death his
father had entered a Franciscan monastery, and there had ended his
days. As may well be imagined, this discovery made a deep impression
on John, especially at this moment. He looked upon himself, not only
as a reprobate trooper, but as having been in some way the cause of
his mother's and his father's death, and therefore unfit to live in their
country any longer.

John accordingly left Portugal, and returned once more into Spain.
But to what could he turn for a means of livelihood? An ex-soldier,
at the best of times, was always an object of suspicion among self-
respecting citizens. Such a man had been accustomed to a lawless life;
he was not overscrupulous about the things that belonged to others;
usually he knew no trade, and was too old and unwilling to learn one;
his behavior and language were no good example to the young men
and women about him; altogether, prudent fathers and careful mothers

had no wish to have him as a member of their establishments. When, then, John sought employment, he only fared like others of his kind. He had nothing to recommend him; his age was a further obstacle; he was miserably poor; in the end he counted himself fortunate to find a situation as a shepherd once more, in the service of a wealthy and benevolent lady who lived near Seville.

Thus at the age of forty-two, John began again where he had left off twenty years before. But now he was a very different man. In his hours of solitude on the hills with his sheep he set himself at least to try to pray; during his prayer it came upon him more than ever what a wasted life he had lived. Indeed, it had been more than wasted; he was appalled at the amount of harm he had done to others. There were only two conclusions to be drawn. On the one hand, if he received his rights from men, he would certainly deserve from them nothing but contempt; on the other hand, he who had done so much harm, who stood responsible for the lives of so many, perhaps his mother included, could never be content to remain in comparative ease among his sheep. In some way he must give what remained of his life in atonement for the lives of those he had ruined; he must do some good to balance the harm.

What should he do? He would take the first thing that came his way. There was much talk at the time of the sufferings of Christian slaves among the Moors of Africa. He would go over to them; if he could get money he would spend it all in their ransom; if he could not, then perhaps he could substitute himself for one of them. With this plan in his mind, John gave up his shepherd's life and made his way to Gibraltar. Here he came across a Portuguese who for some reason had been exiled from his country, and was about to settle with his family across the strait at Ceuta. He was utterly destitute; this decided John to go with him, and at least to begin by serving him. They came to Ceuta; there John found work on the fortifications which were being built, handing over his earnings to his destitute fellow countryman.

But this did not last long. In a very short time a priest who worked in the settlement discovered him. When he learned something more of his new parishioner and his past, he spared no pains to persuade John to return to Spain; Africa was no place for men like him. He pointed out to him the risk he ran by living in his present surroundings. In part they were too like those of his old days; his companions were not dissimilar, soon the old temptations would return and he would fall. There was the added danger of association with Muslims. Already some of his kind had joined their sect, lured by their moral code, which suited their fancy better than their own; if John was not careful he would follow them, and his last case would be worse than his first.

John listened to the warning of the priest and returned to Spain. He had failed in his first attempt, but he was in no way discouraged. He had made up his mind to spend his life in the two things we have seen, securing for himself the kind of justice he deserved, and somehow doing good to others; how these things were brought about mattered very little. Soon he invented for himself a trade which served his purpose very well. We next hear of him going from village to village, with a wheelbarrow or a hawker's basket, selling pious pictures and medals and objects of devotion to anyone who would buy; when he found a customer he did not part with his wares till he had given him, over and above, an exhortation to use his purchase well and be good. In this manner he came to Granada. While on this journey, tradition tells us that he found a small child on the roadside, ill-clad and barefooted, who asked John to carry him part of his way. Without more ado John lifted the child on his shoulders, and trudged along with his double burden. But the weight was heavy, and John was none too strong; when he reached a drinking fountain on the road John proposed to the child that they should stop and rest. The child came down from his shoulders but was suddenly transformed. "John of God", he said, "Granada shall be your cross", and immediately disappeared.

Arriving at Granada, John continued the trade he had chosen for himself, but on a larger scale; if he could not preach, or help souls by any powers of his own, at least he could do good by such means as this. He rented a shop at a street corner near the city gate, and there continued to sell his pictures and pious objects. He was also a constant visitor at the neighboring church. Now it chanced that a preacher at that church was Blessed John of Avila, the friend of St. Teresa, of St. Francis Borgia, and of others well known for their sanctity. One day (it was the feast of St. Sebastian, a great day in Spain) John of Avila was preaching; he had taken for his subject the glory of being made a fool for the sake of Jesus Christ. John of God was among his hearers; during the sermon it struck him that here was an obvious and simple solution of his first problem, that of making people treat him as his past life deserved. If he could do nothing else at least he could do this; if he could be nothing else at least he could be a fool. No sooner was the sermon over than he set to work. As the congregation poured out into the street, John went before, crying out for mercy, tearing his hair, beating himself on face and body, rolling in the mud, sitting on the pavement at the feet of the passers-by. So he moved from street to street, amid the ridicule of the neighbors, and to the intense amusement of the children who followed him in crowds. The more they laughed the more John persisted in his folly; he played his part to perfection. Soon the neighbors were convinced that the keeper of the shop at the corner of the street was of unsound mind. He had always been queer, so they said, now they saw that he had fits of insanity, and they began to be sorry for him.

But John was far from being content with their pity; he must be treated as a madman or all his efforts would be in vain. Accordingly on another day, when service was about to begin in the church, John rushed in, threw himself on the ground, and began again to cry out for mercy, louder than ever before. Of course there was a commotion; it was now quite clear that he was mad, and had become a public nuisance. Some pious members of the congregation took hold of him, and carried him off forthwith to the nearest lunatic asylum. At last John had got his wish; he was really taken for a fool, and was to be treated accordingly; to assure himself that this treatment should continue, in his prison he began to play the lunatic more than ever. Now in those days the chief cure for lunacy was the whip. John, therefore, as a particularly troublesome patient, was taken out every day and scourged; but the more his keepers scourged him, the more did John persist in his folly.

At length one day what was going on reached the ears of Blessed John of Avila. Now Blessed John, probably through the confessional, had come to know the shopkeeper a little; and though he easily allowed that he might be what men would call eccentric, he was certainly not mad nor in any sense a lunatic. Hence he was not slow to guess his penitent's maneuver, and determined to put an end to it. He went to the hospital, and asked to see John alone. Then he gave him a sound scolding. He pointed out to John that he was untruthful; he was pretending to be mad, whereas he was quite sane. He was unjust; he was living on the alms intended for lunatics, while he was quite able to look after himself. He was wanting in charity; for he was giving endless trouble to everyone about him, though he had resolved to spend himself in their service. All this made John see his folly in a new light. He became immediately sane, and Blessed John of Avila was soon able to secure him his release; possibly some may have thought that he had worked a miracle.

John came away from his prison, and again betook himself to his little shop. But by this time, as the lunatic episode proves, it had grown too small for his zeal and his energies; he could not wait all day for good people to come to him, he must find something else to do. First he went on a pilgrimage to Our Lady of Guadalupe, and apparently came back with his mind made up; at last it would seem, after all these years, he had discovered his true vocation. He came back to Granada, rented another house, and immediately began to gather in it all the refuse inhabitants of the town. It did not seem to matter who they were; homeless tramps and vagabonds, cripples begging at church doors, the poor in the streets wherever he might find them, prisoners let out of jail, all seemed the same to John; he invited them all to his house so long as there was a board on which they might lie. Often enough, when he found on the road beggars too deformed to be able to crawl to his lodging, he hoisted them upon his back and carried them there himself; John with such a load became a familiar sight in the streets of Granada.

Within the house John did all the work himself. He had at first no servants, no nurses; his experience in the wars now stood him in good stead, for there his natural charity had taught him something about wounds and bandages. So he set to work with the little he knew. He could wash his patients and dress their sores; he could kiss their feet and let them feel that somebody cared; he could put them to bed and give them a sense of home; he could sit by their side and be merry with them, and then could induce them to go to confession and pray; it was all very rough and ready, but it suited his household. Under such management it was wonderful how this gathering of the refuse of Granada soon became a model of quiet and content. At first the neighbors resented his conduct; in no long time they were glad to let John go his own way. For the maintenance of his establishment he went out to beg. He had been a hawker and had learned how to use his voice in the streets; moreover, with his keen sense of humor, he had discovered ways to induce men and women to buy his wares. He made use of the same methods now. He went about the town, rattling a tin can in his hand, shouting as loud as charity could make him, and the burden of his cry showed that his humor had not deserted him. "Do yourselves a good turn, Ladies and Gentlemen, do yourselves a good turn", was the form of appeal he adopted; and its novelty made his hearers laugh, but it also induced them to open their purses. Money began to come in by this single channel; very soon those who gave John alms followed him to see what he did with it. Their eyes were opened; they were astonished to discover what a single man could do unaided, and a man without any qualifications whatsoever. He was neither nurse nor doctor, neither priest nor religious, his education was virtually none, he had no one to help him except his own patients, who occasionally caught the fever of his charity. Very soon there grew up about his house a group of more wealthy men and women who took a pride in calling themselves his benefactors.

Thus in an incredibly short time John found himself a kind of public character in Granada. He rose to the situation. On the one side he accepted any means that was likely to help him in the service of stricken humanity, on the other side his net was extended so as to include every type of outcast. He was not content with gathering up the beggars off the streets; he went and searched them out in the hovels in which they lived. Even houses of ill fame were the object of his raids; indeed, it is clear that they soon became a matter for his special concern. He went in among them, scolded and exhorted and sympathized with those who lived in them, as often as not was only laughed at for his pains, but in return brought away many a penitent and set her up in an honest way of life.

Meanwhile the work he was doing attracted the notice of the ecclesiastical authorities. There were those who were suspicious, who had little faith in such freakish ways; there were others who could not but see the astonishing fruit of John's work. He was called to meet the bishop, who also at the time held the post of Mayor of Granada. The bishop asked him his name; John replied that once upon a time a child he had helped in a country lane had called him John of God.

"Then John of God shall be your name always", the bishop answered, and this was how he came to have the title. Then the bishop asked him about his dress. For John, even in this august company, presented a sad appearance; he was wearing a suit of clothes he had taken from a beggar in exchange for his own. The bishop bade him wear a habit; by this dress it would be clear to all that he acted with the bishop's approval. The next step was a hospital proper which the citizens of Granada gave him; and by a hospital we must understand a kind of workhouse, though even a workhouse, as we now interpret it, would be much too good a name. Henceforward John had to give himself to administration; he had a staff of volunteers who worked under his direction, many of them men whom he had rescued from misfortune, who were ready to make amends in the way he showed them.

But John could never have been a saint had he merely prospered; prosperity alone never makes a saint. Besides a few friends, he had many enemies; the kind of work he did almost inevitably provoked opposition. First were the outsiders, who looked on from a distance. They denounced this excessive consideration for the outcast; such treatment as John gave them could only encourage vagabonds and idlers in their evil ways. There were others who put him on his trial for the misuse and squandering of the moneys entrusted to him; practically he was accused of embezzlement. Often enough, it must be confessed, there seemed to be justice on their side; for John did not keep accounts, and money slipped through his fingers as quickly as it came. For instance, once when he went to Valladolid to beg from the court established there, he came away with a large sum of money, but arrived at Granada without any. He had given it all away on the road, chiefly in Valladolid itself; and when his friends at home blamed him for having come back empty-handed he would only say:

"God is in Valladolid as well as in Granada, and we can give to him there as well as here."

Again there were many, young and old, who never forgot that he had once been an inmate of a lunatic asylum, and treated him accordingly. Once a boy met him, carrying a bucket of dirty water. He poured the contents over John the lunatic; whereupon all in the street burst into laughter. But John burst into laughter with them; which made some think him only a greater fool, while others thought him a saint. Another time John's cloak accidentally brushed against a Spanish gentleman, and fell to the ground at his feet. The gentleman was indignant, and dealt John a staggering blow. John recovered himself, picked up his cloak, and then stood before his assailant for another.

But these were only the outside trials which signified nothing to

John and troubled him very little; what affected him more were the
persecutions coming from inside the hospital. There were the many
quarrels among the patients themselves, almost inevitable when we
consider who they were; and John, in his efforts to be peacemaker,
came in for blame from many sides. They would denounce him for
injustice, or extravagance, or something else; there were times when it
seemed that all his labors had come to nothing. Most troublesome of all
were the women whom he had rescued from a life of sin. He had been
more than once warned that to do more for these poor creatures than
to take them from their evil surroundings was dangerous. They were
treacherous by nature, they were ungrateful, they were notoriously
unstable, their very repentance, in most cases, was only a pretense; if
he did more for them they would only turn upon him. John was well
aware that this was only too true; nevertheless, he went on as before.
He found them a home, as we have already seen he procured the means
to give many of them a new start in life; still it was only to receive in
return, for the most part, what his friends had told him would come.
In the home he had provided for them these poor, restless creatures
were difficult to control. They were never satisfied; no matter what he
gave them they always asked for more. They looked upon themselves
as something superior to the beggar man about them who had made
himself their slave. Abuse was all he deserved, and he received it from
them in overflowing. When he could not find for them all they demanded, when he attempted to suggest to them better thoughts than
those they had always in their minds, then they would turn on him
with ridicule, call him a hypocrite and a bigot, hint to him that he
knew too much about their lives to be himself wholly innocent.

And John, with his usual good humor, would take their abuse in
good part. It was characteristic of him throughout his life that he never
took offense; he knew himself too well for that. He would join in the
laughter against himself; he would tell these women that what they said
against him must be true. Once when one of them was particularly
abusive, raking up his early life against him, he gave her two silver
coins that she might go into the street and proclaim to all the world
what she had charged him with in private. On another occasion, when
a visitor chanced to overhear the abuse that was being poured upon
him and wished to interfere, John begged him to leave his accusers
alone. "I beg you of your charity", he said, "to let them have their

say. They know me better than you, and they know that I am a bad lot, worse than they."

John of God was a saint in a category all his own. He lived his own life without anyone to help him, he grew in sanctity after his own manner, he did his work almost entirely singlehanded. The order which he founded, the Brothers Hospitallers of St. John of God, grew almost without his knowing it; it was the fruit of his example and inspiration, its first members were men whose lives had been akin to his own, and whom he had won to do as he did in atonement. And the divine consolations he received were characteristic of himself. We have mentioned the Child that was so heavy a burden in his early days, when he first made his way to Granada. Once, in later years, as he prayed before a crucifix, he seemed to see before him his Lord, Jesus Christ, Our Lady, and St. John. Our Lady stepped forward from the group with a crown, not of gold, not of roses, but of thorns in her hand, and pressed it hard upon his head. "John," she said, "it is by thorns and sufferings that you must win the crown my Son has waiting for you in heaven." John felt the thorns piercing his very brain; still he could only reply: "From your hand, Lady, thorns and sufferings are welcome; they are my flowers and my roses."

Another time he found a beggar in the street, deserted and apparently dying. As usual he took him upon his shoulders, and carried him to his hospital. There he laid him on a bed, and began to wash his feet. But the feet had gaping wounds in them; John looked up in surprise, and found the beggar had been transfigured. He seemed to be all shining, and the brightness seemed to envelop John himself. When he was again alone, and was walking through the hospital, so brilliant a light shone about him that the sick in the ward took alarm, thinking he was on fire; and John had much difficulty in assuring them that all was well.

So John went through the last fifteen years of his life, keeping his two resolutions, to atone for the harm he had done to others in his early days by doing only good to them now, and by ignoring his own very existence. He gave when he had nothing for himself; when he was ill, which was often, he took no notice of his illness that he might serve others who were worse. But there came a time when he could hold out no longer. One day, when he was out on an errand of charity, he chanced to pass along the riverside, and saw a man in the river drowning. Without more ado he went into the water and saved him, but he came home that evening shivering and in a high fever. He struggled on to his ordinary work, but at intervals he was obliged to lie down in his own hospital, alongside of those he called his children. These children took alarm; to do such a thing was unlike their father; they would get out of their beds and crowd around his couch, so that John was in danger of being suffocated. A benefactress came to the rescue. On one of her visits to the hospital she discovered what was going on, and wished to have John taken to some other home where he might be better tended. But John demurred; not until she had been supported by the express order of the bishop would he consent to be removed.

In this way he came to die; when the end seemed certain the bishop himself gave him the last sacraments. Then he was asked whether he had anything on his mind. Yes, he had. His answer was characteristic of the man, the model of practical charity.

"There are three things that make me uneasy", he said. "The first is that I have received so many graces from God, and have not recognized them, and have repaid them with so little of my own. The second is that after I am dead, I fear lest the poor women I have rescued, and the poor sinners I have reclaimed, may be treated badly. The third is that those who have trusted me with money, and whom I have not fully repaid, may suffer loss on my account."

He was reassured on these points and his mind was set at rest. Then, even more characteristically, he requested those round his bed to leave him alone for a few minutes; he had lived his life alone, he would die alone. When they were gone he rose from his bed and knelt before a crucifix. The nurses entered shortly after and found him still kneeling there, his face resting on the feet of the Savior, but he was quite dead. His body remained kneeling till it was taken up to be laid out for burial. It was March 8, 1550, a little after midnight. At the time of his death John was fifty-five years of age.

～

SAINT IGNATIUS LOYOLA

[*1491–1556*]

R. H. J. Steuart, S.J.

HE STORY OF St. Ignatius Loyola is too well known to need retelling here. The figure of the ex-soldier whose chosen career appeared to have been cruelly arrested by a malignant chance, and who turned with astounding readiness from a manner of life for which every circumstance of birth and tradition had seemed exclusively to fit him to one to which nothing in his previous experience had had any relevance whatever, is familiar to everyone. It has impressed itself deeply upon the history, both ecclesiastical and secular, of the post-Renaissance world, and it has in its time attracted on the one hand more admiration and on the other more animosity than has perhaps that of any other single individual within the last four hundred years. For St. Ignatius has a serious claim to a very large share in that renovation within the Church of which the miscalled Reformation without had, under God's overruling providence, been at least the indirect occasion, and that fact alone has earned for him the permanent hostility of a large section of opinion all over the civilized world. He was besides a pioneer in a great many of the movements which were to put an end, almost within his own lifetime, to the deadly apathy and decadence, spiritual, moral and cultural, which were rotting the vitals of Christendom. Further, he was the author of a quite new conception of the religious life which has had its influence upon nearly every Institute or Congregation founded since his day, and of a highly systematized type of spirituality which has made a hardly less wide and lasting impression upon the general practice of the Catholic Faith.

On all these counts, severally and collectively, he has been, and still is, lavishly praised and violently abused. It is the fate of dynamic men such as he to rouse both extremes of opinion just because they themselves cannot help being extreme: they may be loved or they may be hated, they cannot be ignored.

The more one learns about the state of Europe at the time of the Reformation the more one is appalled at the desperate straits to which, over a large part of the Western World, Catholic life had been reduced, and the more one marvels at its rehabilitation and at the quality of the men to whose courage and energy that was due. In many parts, especially of the northern countries, schools had ceased to exist and universities had sunk to incredible depths of ineptitude: the teaching of the Sacred Sciences had degenerated into a round of dreary futilities, and secular learning had practically come to a halt: there were everywhere priests who could not translate a line of their breviaries nor even pronounce the words of Absolution, and who never opened their mouths in a pulpit or took any care whatever of the instruction of their people: there were Bishops, too, whose sole interests were worldly and political, and there were religious of both sexes whose stagnant lives, when they were not positively scandalous, were at any rate of no profit either to their neighbors or to themselves. And this is only skimming the surface of the matter. Rabelais, who was a contemporary of Ignatius, could have verified with chapter and verse all the topics of his caustic satire.

One understands how on all counts this age became one of revolt, for whether men admit it or not, when their religion fails them so does everything else and they *must* strike out for something new to live upon, and it was dreadfully true that at that time many felt that in fact religion had failed. It is only when we remember the assurance of Christ that the gates of hell will never prevail against his Church nor he desert her while the world lasts, that we cease to wonder how she can have survived even as a remnant.

We need not dwell here upon the course of Ignatius' vocational development, for whatever specific object he may at the outset have had in his mind when he began to collect followers about him, his ideal very soon fell into focus as service—to be calculated without limit or reserve—of the threatened Faith. They would go to Rome and there place themselves wholly at the disposition of the Vicar of Christ to be used just as he might direct. They would call themselves "of the Company of Jesus", using the word in the military sense of a compact fighting force under one direct command. That form of the title is still in use in some languages but in Latin it became "Societas", and the name "Jesuit" ("Jesuita") for its members was really an accident, being at first applied as a nickname in derision of their supposed arrogance to themselves of a specially favored intimacy with Our Lord. It is interesting to find the word used by the Carthusian Ludolph of Saxony more than two hundred years earlier, where he says that as here we are through the grace of Christ in Baptism named *Christiani* so in the life of glory we shall through Jesus our Savior be called *Jesuitae*!

Again, it is beside our purpose to recall the many vicissitudes of the new-born Institute before at last it acquired the full canonical status of a religious Order, or to remark upon the attraction that it seemed from the first to exercise upon so many of the best minds of the day so that Ignatius saw rapidly grouping themselves under him a body of men of the finest quality and capacity both spiritual and intellectual. With them he founded schools for the Humanities and for Higher Studies wherever these were lacking and were needed—and that was nearly everywhere: he resuscitated the languishing Faculties in many Universities, particularly in northern and central Europe: trained a new and competent clergy to minister to provinces which heresy had ravaged unchecked by their late pastors: sent devoted missionaries to every quarter of the known world: and found men of high ability and zeal and courage to employ upon any and every charge which could further the greater glory of God. It has been said that the immense work in all these fields which was done by his Society at that time has justly entitled it to be regarded as the savior of Catholic culture in the greater part of Europe.

To this service he subordinated every other consideration, and in the means that he employed for this one end he looked uniquely to their fitness for the purpose and cared nothing at all for the subsidiary and unessential forms. So in the Order that he founded there is no choir, no habit, no assuming of religious names, no insignia of prelacy, no apparatus of domestic ceremony: all Superiors except the General are appointed, not elected: the noviceship lasts for two years, with a third year of repetition for the priests after ordination: and no ecclesiastical dignities may be admitted save and except under the direct command of the Sovereign Pontiff. To many of those who had been reared in another tradition he appeared as a dangerous innovator, and these made no secret either of their opinion or of their hostility to

him. Ignatius did not quarrel with them. Without any inclination to
criticize the ideals or methods that approved themselves to others, he
yet felt quite assured that for the kind and quality of work that he had
in mind this stark disciplining of the means to the end was a necessity,
and he offered immovable resistance to all the influences that tried to
divert him from his plan.

All his activities were distinguished by daring, determination, and
method, by a kind of ruthless logic, and by an idealism which never
ceased to be practical. He was always a Knight, but always a man of
affairs too: he had at once the vision of an artist and the caution of a
statesman: he feared nothing except to be untrue to the best that he
could see, and with all his powers of sympathy he was unable to find
any excuse for what was small or second-rate or disloyal. So well did he
hold the balance between the extremes of rigidity on the one hand and
of over-suppleness on the other, that he has been roundly charged with
both. But his rigidity (which was then, indeed, absolute) was only for
principle, and he was adaptable only in the same interest. He himself
relates how at the beginning of his conversion he determined to show
his independence of all worldly conventions by keeping his hair and
nails untrimmed and refusing to address people by their proper titles,
thinking that thus he would acquire greater liberty and authority for
his spiritual ministrations. But when he found that the precise contrary
was the result he surrendered his resolution without demur.

But a saint is not a saint for what he does except in so far as that
is the veridic outcome of what he is. If he *is* a saint the two will
be commensurate, but not necessarily so to human vision, for the in-
cidence of circumstance and opportunity upon which the former so
largely depends is for God's providence alone to determine. The saints
themselves knew this well, and that the most that anyone can do is no
greater than the most that he means to do, and the nearer they drew
to God the more they saw how little more than nothing that is. One
remembers how after his great ecstasy on the feast of St. Nicholas, two
years before his death, all that he had written seemed to St. Thomas
Aquinas "like so much straw" so that he never took up his pen again
and the *Summa*, that greatest of all monuments of human thought, remains unfinished.

The life of St. Ignatius, then, for all its magnificent achievement,
has as its main significance for us the revelation that it affords us of

what he was; and in his case, perhaps more than in that of most of the saints, that revelation is very clear and unmistakable. For the course of his life ran patently along the lines of thoroughness, undefeatable idealism, and an almost *physical* grasp of the sovereignty of God's will as absolutely paramount in the least of matters as in the greatest, and all was tempered (like a fine steel instrument) with that sound sense of realities which is the principle of endurance and (contrary to what is often assumed) the basis of genuine sanctity. And it is probably not too much to say that no other saint provides such facilities for studying at first hand what one may call the "mechanism" of his holiness. Taking it in its broadest sense, it was an attitude of mind which would prefer any conceivable alternative to the sacrifice of truth and right and would never be content but with what is best and noblest, be their price what it might. Men of that type may be met with in many settings, not necessarily all Christian or even all religious, but they only come to their full expression there, for only there can the human heart really find its true self. In his "Spiritual Exercises", the textbook of his School of Holiness, St. Ignatius traces the development under grace of such a soul and with a sure hand lays out its course, for he himself had lived it as he wrote it. Not that Iñigo de Loyola was yet St. Ignatius when he came at last out of his solitude of Manresa, for there was still very much that he had both to learn and to unlearn. But he was ready now to do both: the ideal was irrevocably established, the resolution grounded, and for its implementing—ignorant though he might yet be of how that would shape itself—he was prepared. In proof that this is no exaggeration is the fact that he never had occasion throughout the remainder of his sixty-four years of life to make any substantial alteration in what he had written.

One might say, in very brief and summary fashion, that the method of the Spiritual Exercises is, by means of an ordered scheme of meditation upon the vital and fundamental truths concerning God and man and their mutual relations—the latter specially focused in the life of Christ—helped by various ancillary rules and instructions, to bring a man to a clear apprehension of the issues at stake, place before him the highest ideals of their treatment and fulfillment, furnish him with sound motives for choosing nobly according to the light and grace that he receives, and urge him to make his "Election" (as it is therein called) not, obviously, for or against the service of God, but in regard

of the state in which he realizes, thus enlightened, that he will serve
him *best*. By then he should be able to act upon certain conviction
and he should be responsive to the finest ideals that have presented
themselves to him: he should be safeguarded, too, from all danger of
error, presumption, or delusion.

But the "treatment", if one may call it so, does not end with a rea-
soned election. Unless the service of God be apprehended for what (if
it be sincere) it really is, a work, namely, of love—and of love, first, in
return for love—it will be in peril from the instability and inconstancy
that attach to all imperfectly motived resolutions: so the "exercitant"
is invited to turn to the consideration, with all the earnestness at his
command, of the Passion of Our Lord in which his limitless love for
men, translated into the medium of their own expression, is so con-
summately exhibited. And this is clinched by an exercise in which
through the argument of God's goodness to men, proceeding from
his own essential goodness, are presented irresistible motives for their
wholehearted love of him in return and their generous surrender to
his will.

But apart from its intrinsic merits of logical cogency and psychological soundness the outstanding worth of the book resides in no
small degree in the eminent commonsense which is therein allied with
lofty idealism. The author sets himself to arouse the noblest and most
chivalrous instincts of the human heart, but he keeps control of them:
reason alone is not a sufficient spring of lasting action, for after all the
mind is only a part of the man: but on the other hand emotion or
affection, though they have greater stimulating power, rest upon a less
permanent basis and have need of the services of reason as an armament
against their own mutability. Hence in his presentment of the carefully
selected subjects that he proposes for consideration he endeavors always to engage simultaneously the attention of the two faculties, thus
ensuring as far as may be a unified appeal to the whole man.

That St. Ignatius intended his Exercises to be an exhaustive treatise
either upon the whole of the spiritual life or upon the science of prayer
in particular, no one would claim. Primarily the book had one aim,
to effect the spiritual conversion of whoever would submit to its discipline, and as an almost certain consequence to indicate to him the
special will of God in his regard; and clearly a system which successfully does this will also successfully influence and guide the subsequent

conduct of him who has profited by it and be for him a permanent reference and support. The manner of prayer (or rather, the chief manner, for the author employs several) employed to this end is what is universally called "discursive meditation" obviously, because the main purpose of the Exercises is to inform the soul through the reasoning powers of the mind—but the actual prayer-value, so to call it, of meditation is not the thought that it provokes but the movement of the will that follows upon the thought. The actual *meditation*, therefore, is the means, not the end, and that St. Ignatius was fully aware of this is indicated by the words of the Fourth Addition to the First Week: "In that point in which I find what I desire there will I rest without being anxious to proceed to another until I have satisfied myself."

Further, it is abundantly and unequivocally evidenced both by his letters to St. Francis Borgia and others, and by his own observed practice, that the Saint was a mystic and a contemplative of the highest order: yet in the Exercises there is no definite reference to that degree of prayer. The word "contemplative" is indeed employed in certain connections, but as Father Joseph Rickaby, S.J., says,

> St. Ignatius uses the word Contemplation in quite another sense than St. John of the Cross and other mystical writers. Ignatian contemplation is not a form of the Higher Prayer: it is what an artist would call a Study of a scene in Our Lord's life. We may call such contemplation a *mind painting*.

Suarez explains the apparent omission as follows:

> In this degree of contemplation or unitive life one must distinguish the beginning, which is all that concerns the progress of its growth, from the end, which is union with God by a certain simple intuition of the truth. In the first stage one must follow the ordinary methods of prayer and meditation, directed to the end that one has in view: for the second, no definite form or method can be laid down since it is a very simple act and is exercised rather in receiving than in seeking, though human cooperation is not altogether excluded. It is for this reason that our Father Ignatius, while adequately setting forth all that pertains to the initial stage of this final degree of contemplation both as to matter and form, was content to direct those who would understand along the right path, for what comes after belongs to the province rather of the Holy Spirit than of man. He has therefore said but little about the actual union with God and the simple act of contemplation.

He has said but little (if indeed anything) about it in so many words but a great deal by implication, for the whole apparatus of the Exercises is directed toward the closest union with God through a searching preparation of the soul for the Divine visitation whatever form that may take, and it goes as far toward accomplishing that object, one feels, as human instrument could without trenching on what Suarez here calls the *magisterium Spiritus Sancti*.

The prayer contained in the "Contemplation for obtaining Divine Love" which crowns the structure of the Exercises—"Take, O Lord, and receive, all my liberty, my memory, my understanding, and all my will"—might have been written, word for word, by St. John of the Cross so aptly and authentically does it sum up the aspiration of the soul brought at last to the realization of God as the one all-sufficing object of its desire—"Give me thy love and thy grace, and this is enough for me." That there cannot be much lacking to the Spiritual Exercises as a veritable School of Holiness, and that they cannot be charged with falling far short of what is amply sufficient for the highest possible spiritual development of a Christian soul, seems to be at least insinuated by the fact that of those who joined the Society in the lifetime of its founder and were trained by him upon their model, four besides himself have been canonized: and it has been calculated that from his day down to the present there has never been a time when there was not a Jesuit saint in the world.

Ignatius is one of the few saints who have, so to say, deliberately *explained* themselves. The main and obvious theme of his doctrine, clearly exposed both in the Exercises and in his own life, is the conquest of self; a plain statement of the fact that the service of God, in whatever shape it engage us, signifies no other thing than the submission of our will to his. And the first step to this must be truth in that most unpalatable form of all, truth about oneself, so that there may be an equation between our real selves as we learn them to be and the ideal of the Christ-life that the will of God may be done in us now as it is in heaven.

Nothing is to be too high or too difficult, but on everything there is to be the curb of reality, acting like a bridle on a horse not as a check but as a control.

His device was the Greater Glory of God: meaning that in this life the task would never be over.

SAINT FRANCIS XAVIER

[*1506–1552*]

Alban Goodier, S.J.

ROBABLY THERE IS no saint whose name occurs in the Church's calendar, perhaps there is no hero in history, who has more enthusiastic admirers than St. Francis Xavier. Certainly it would be hard to find more highly colored panegyrics than those which have been written of him, from his own brethren in France and Spain to our own poet Dryden. The boundless range of his horizon, his life of utter devotedness, the splendid fruit of his labors, all appeal to every man who looks for greatness, and compel him to pay homage. The most materialistic and the most utilitarian, whatever they may think of saints as such, are forced to acknowledge that here, at least, was a man, even while he was a saint. That one should surrender all that Xavier surrendered for the sake of his fellow men, that he should seem to have known no limits to his giving, or to the people to whom he gave, but perhaps, above all, that he should have succeeded in doing the work he did, all this appeals to the man of action and results, who reckons work done by the price that is paid for it and by the fruit that is reaped. Hence it is that panegyrists, both inside and outside the Church, dwell most of all on this aspect of the saint as that which appeals to every man.

At the same time, one cannot help asking oneself whether as a matter of fact this side of his life is the one which is really most to be admired. One cannot help asking whether St. Francis Xavier himself, were he now in heaven allowed to select, would choose this glorious picture of himself as the one which redounded most to his credit, or as the one he would most bring before men's notice in proof of the manhood that was in him. To anyone who reads between the lines of the story of his life the fact of the other side is only too evident. In his own day, and among his own people, he was by no means the great success

we, looking back, can see him to have been. On the contrary, we are
not without proofs, both internal and external, that to many at least
of his contemporaries he was thought a failure. While here and there
he had a few staunch friends, and while his capacity for friendship is
manifest in every letter that he wrote, still there is, throughout his life,
a certain isolation and loneliness which cannot be mistaken. At times
he seems almost to cry out against it; when, for instance, he writes to
all his brethren in Europe, saying he would gladly write to each one if
he could; when in his moments of distress he addresses a single faithful
follower in India; when he leaves all alone and hides himself away to
seek the one Friend who, he knows, will never fail him.

Still more evidence have we of his own deep conviction that he
was himself of little worth. By nature highly strung and sanguine, he
suffered from strong reactions; endowed with talents and gifts beyond
the ordinary, he was weighed down with the littleness of men around
him, blocking his way at every turn; a man of broad horizons and
boundless ambitions, he seemed for ever tempted to depression and
despair, and to surrender every task he undertook. The real greatness
of the man must surely lie in this, that he did what he did in spite of
every discouragement, from without and from within, and that he died
with his eyes stretched forward to a yet further horizon, counting all
he had so far done as nothing, probably counting it a failure.

From the day when he decided to throw in his lot with St. Ignatius
he was a disappointment to those who had hitherto known him. His
family was disappointed with him. It was noble, but now was not rich;
it had lost its all because of its staunch support of the French claim
against the Spanish for the lordship of Navarre: in the campaign which
led up to the fall of Pampeluna, his own brothers had fought on the
side of the French victors. Now, since the reverse, it had done what
it could to give this youngest son a fresh start in life; since he could
not serve under a Spanish conqueror, he should be offered a career of
learning, a career in the Church. Yet here he was, at the mere instigation of an eccentric beggar-student, and a Spaniard besides, whose past
was more than suspicious, sacrificing all his prospects, and starting on
some wild-goose chase to convert the Holy Land! It must be confessed
that many a more Christian family than even that of Xavier would
have been justified in its disappointment on a less apparent ground
than this.

Again, the University was disappointed with him. It had given him every advantage; it had appointed him to a professorship; it had marked him out for a career which only needed his own energy to lift him up to the highest rank of the new élite of Europe. Yet all the return he made was, in a moment of enthusiasm, to throw it all up at the suggestion of one who had already come to be looked upon with reserve. Surely there was ground for the resentment of the authorities against the intrusion of Iñigo Loyola; and their judgment that Francis Xavier was, after all, fickle and lightheaded, a dreamer of dreams and unreliable, was not without a basis of good evidence.

Then to his companions, the first members of the Society of Jesus, his life seemed so arranged, his character so singular, as constantly to lead to disappointment. In the enthusiasm of his conversion, he wished to go to the Carthusians, and it needed all the influence of Ignatius to prevent him. On their first tramp to Rome, he had carried his penance to an excess which any man of judgment might easily have avoided, and only a miracle prevented him from becoming a burden to them all. Arrived in Italy, he was sent to Bologna. There he made his mark; he was a born preacher and apostle; evidently he was the man to reform that and other cities; and he was called away from the midst of it all to sit at a desk, seemingly useless and unknown as a mere private secretary. Nevertheless, here again he succeeded. His brethren saw the wisdom of having such a man at the elbow of their Father General. One so gifted, so far-seeing, so sympathetic, so devoted, would be of untold service in framing the new Constitutions and in directing the fast-growing Order; yet, on a sudden, they found that, at a single day's notice, he had gone away to Portugal, thence to be lost to civilization altogether.

In Portugal again he found his place. There he had to wait for more than six months until the fleet for the Indies was equipped. The time was spent in the apostolate, the spirit of Bologna revived; prisoners in jail were evangelized, especially the victims of the Inquisition, and even accompanied to the stake. But his chief labor was among the nobles, those whose lives and example counted for so much that was evil, whose conversion would mean so much for the world they ruled. And with these he succeeded. Such a preacher had never been known at Court before; so great a reform had never before been brought about. It would clearly be a mistake that such a good work should be cut

short; king, and people, and clergy clamored that Xavier should be left
in Portugal, and another sent to the Indies in his place. It was not for
the first time that the report went round concerning him that here was
a good man being utterly thrown away.

So many changes in five brief years, and Xavier was already thirty-
five. He set sail for India on his birthday, 1541, full of the tales which
he heard of the countries awaiting him, white for the harvest, of kings
and people who were only too eager to receive the saving religion of
the beloved Portuguese. When he arrived he found things very different, though probably he was not surprised. Goa, a city of luxury
and slaves, where Europeans vied with Asiatics in every worst vice
and excess—this was the base from which he had to work. A people
hating a religion which came to them with fire and sword, some in-
veigled with promises of reward, others compelled to intermarry with
Portuguese soldiers and camp-followers—if indeed it may safely be
called intermarriage—such were the races "craving" for the water of
baptism. A priesthood of the laxest morals, a convent in which every
nun had her serf attendant—such was the material with which he had
to work. Churches there were in abundance, standing almost side by
side. Sunday, when women and some men were borne to church, and
slaves carried their prayer books by their side, was a day to be seen
in Goa. For the rest, religion was chiefly of account as a means to
conquest and wealth.

Into such a welter of religion and luxury and tyranny Xavier was
thrown, and the first result was only to be expected. He was for ever
at war with the Portuguese officials; and that not so much, or not only,
because he interfered with their authority, or because he thwarted their
cupidity, or because he brought home to them unpleasant truths which
they had hoped to have left behind them in Europe, but also because he
never seemed to be satisfied with what was given him. He had come to
India under the protection of the Portuguese flag; the faith should go
with the flag, so they thought, even the best among them, and a people
won to the faith was a people won to Portugal. But this restless man
was not content with this. Not even the vast expanse of the Portuguese
possessions sufficed for him, nor all the money they bestowed on him
to succor his starving neophytes. He would go where he chose; he
would demand protection and help for work that would bring them
no return; though officially sent out by the king of Portugal, he would

serve the crown just so far as it pleased him and no more. It cannot be denied that the complaints that went home to Portugal, and even to the General, St. Ignatius, in Rome, were not wholly without foundation, and to one who did not know better must have seemed very convincing indeed.

But while this was the conclusion of some men, not utterly unreasonable as men count reason, a still greater disappointment was felt by the man himself. By nature Francis Xavier was one who lived with high ideals, and who seemed destined to find his only—happiness in working for a definite goal. Yet one after another the goal he set before himself was snatched from his grasp. There is evidence to show that as a child he would gladly have followed his brothers in the service of his country; his family could not afford it, and he must make his own way in the world. At the University, beyond a doubt, he reveled in the thought of all that lay before him; the hope must surely have lingered in his mind that his master would bid him win his place as a scholar for the greater glory of God. Instead, he was told to give it all up, and tramp to Rome and take ship for Syria. He did as he was told, and was rewarded by a craving for the life of contemplation. He even doubted, so someone tells us, whether that were not his vocation; instead he was not even allowed the journey to the holy places, but was thrown into the cities of Italy to preach and give instructions.

Again he did as he was told, and again a new ambition lay before him. He could preach, and he knew it; he could teach because he knew what he knew; he would give himself heart and soul to this work, for God, and for man's salvation. He had scarcely begun and caught on, when he was ordered to put it all aside and retire into the hidden life of a private secretary. Still, even here there was something to live for. On the one hand there was the great task of building up a great religious order; on the other was the constant companionship of the one friend of his bosom. Here he could live, and do great work, and be happy; and on a sudden he was told to be ready in a day to depart for Portugal and the Indies, to go out of everything for which he had lived, to go out of life as he knew it altogether.

Here a fact should be remembered which adds to the pathos of the situation. There is no record whatever that Francis Xavier had ever set his heart on the foreign missions, or had ever felt for them any particular vocation. With other saints and great missionaries it was different.

St. Peter Claver trained himself for the slaves from the beginning of his so-called conversion. Blessed Charles Spinola looked forward from the first to work among the heathen. The North American missionaries and the missionaries in China were all practically volunteers. With St. Francis Xavier there is no record that it was so. He was simply told to go and he went; all his University ambitions, all his contemplative longings, all his schemes for the good of his Order, were annihilated once and for ever. Humanly speaking, the parting was death; it had not the spring of a young missionary going out to the goal of his desires; and perhaps there were other reasons besides sanctity for the singular silence of the man at the moment of parting, usually so demonstrative, so simple in the expression of his emotions.

When he began his work in India, the same disappointment and failure seemed to dog his steps. Of the few companions he took out with him, not more than one seems to have persevered. The first and daring mission among the natives, where the faith found good soil, was all but swept off the face of the earth by an inroad of heathen invaders. His extraordinary powers as Papal Nuncio, and plenipotentiary of the king of Portugal, were practically never used except against those who thwarted him. It was his failure in the king's dominions that drove him farther afield, to the extreme East, and thence to Japan. More than once he had to complain, so far as he dared, of the poor material that was sent out to help him, poor alike in intellect and in spirit; and one finds him almost beside himself, as he cries out to the men of genius who are wasting their lives, so he calls it, winning themselves renown in the Universities of Europe. As the years wore on, and everything he did seemed to fail, he declared his longing to leave the Indies alone, and to go to Abyssinia, to Arabia, to Madagascar, anywhere so that he might do some little good before he died, for all he had done so far had apparently been brought to nothing. Exhausted in body and soul, he buried himself for weeks at a time in the garden of the College at Goa.

What was this College at Goa? Let us take its story as a key to the inner life of the Apostle of the Indies.

Of all the works Xavier set on foot none was more dear to him than the College of St. Paul. Since he could not hope to have from Europe missionaries of either the number or quality he needed, he determined to make missionaries of his own in India; and that these might be trained uncontaminated, as far as possible, by the life, heathen or Christian, around them, he would bring them up apart, under his own supervision. In other words, the College, which he took over and reconstructed as his own, was to be a nursing home for native priests and catechists, from whatever part of the East they might come. That these might grow up with a spirit of their own, independent of all European contact or subjection, none but pure Asiatics were to be accepted. That such an institution might prosper, it was obvious from the first that it would need a Rector on whom he could rely. In all his service, Xavier had only two such men. One he had been compelled to send south to the Fishery Coast, to control the work he had there set on foot. The other was not a Portuguese; he came from the Netherlands and, knowing the Portuguese, Xavier on that account feared to appoint him.

Accordingly he had written to Europe, asking that a worthy Rector might be sent. Rodriguez, the Provincial, responded, and there arrived in Goa, while Xavier was away in the South, a young Jesuit father, Antonio Gomez, with his letters of appointment as Rector in his pocket. He was duly installed, and at once, both in the College and in the city, things began to stir. Gomez was a devoted disciple of the University of Coimbra. He had made his name there, he knew no other; for him the University, with its life and methods, were the acme of perfection, on whose model all other colleges must be built. He was, besides, an excellent preacher, far more impressive, if one may judge from reports, than Xavier himself. His manners were beyond criticism; he was sought after by the highest people in Goa, from the viceroy and bishop downward, as a guest in their homes, as a confessor for the fastidious Goan ladies. He had, moreover, the confidence of his Provincial, Simon Rodriguez, in Europe; the decree for his appointment had been given him without any consultation of Xavier. He was a man of unbounded self-confidence and assurance; besides, having come out some six years later than Francis, he could claim both greater experience in the management of schools, and even a better knowledge of the spirit and working of the Society of Jesus itself.

When, then, he was installed as Rector of the College of St. Paul's, Antonio at once set about his reforms. He began with the brethren, his own religious community. Regulations were drawn up and enforced, concerning eating and drinking, sleeping and recreation, spiritual duties and work, strictly according to the practice of Paris and Coimbra. The conditions of the East were ignored; that the spirit of the Society should be relaxed because of mere climate was unthinkable. He ruled with a rod of iron, as became his notion of a strong superior; should any subject prove recalcitrant, he announced that he had authority to send insubordinates to Portugal, if necessary in chains.

Next, he turned his attention to the students. These undisciplined and mixed young men, coming as they did from various parts of India and the further East, were ordered to conform to the ways and customs of Coimbra. The result was inevitable; in a very short time they began to climb over the college walls and run away. But this troubled the Rector very little. He had other and better designs in view. The College of St. Paul must be raised to the status of a university; only as such would it be worthy of the Society of Jesus. To this end it was essential that European students should be admitted, the sons of the officials and magnates of Goa and of all the Portuguese dominions. Education was all important for such as these, and the labors of the Society would be most profitably spent on their training. Out of these, moreover, far more becoming vocations might be looked for; as for the candidates whom Fr. Francis had in mind, for them the apostolic schools would suffice, scattered in various places, preferably away from the metropolis of Goa.

Francis on his return saw what was being done; he remonstrated, but to no purpose. Gomez had been sent to teach the Society in the East, Xavier himself included, the ways of the Society in Portugal, not to be taught the ways of a lax and undisciplined community. What was to be done? The crisis had come in the few months Francis had been in Goa between his return from the East Indies and his departure for Japan. All had been arranged for the voyage; if he lost this opportunity he might not find another for a year. To leave all authority in the hands of this man would be fatal; yet on his other expeditions he had always done this with the former Rector. He must give Gomez another appointment. He must send him out of Goa, to Ormuz, to Din, to Bassein, to one of the Portuguese settlements where his learning and talents would have full scope, and where he would have less opportunity for mischief. In his stead he must run the risk of appointing the one trusty subject he had at hand, the Hollander, Fr. Gaspar Baertz.

So Francis determined, but circumstances were too much for him. Fr. Gaspar saw only too well the difficulties before him, and pleaded to be excused; a Dutch superior would be pleasing neither to the members of the Society nor to the Portuguese authorities. Fr. Antonio on the other hand was aggrieved; he questioned the right of Fr. Francis to override the decision of their common Provincial in Portugal. To strengthen his cause he called in the aid of his friends, the viceroy, the bishop, and others; these expressed surprise that so excellent a man, so exceptional a preacher, so great an influence for good should be removed from the city. In the end, much against his will, but left with little other choice, Xavier was compelled to yield. The Portuguese, Antonio, was allowed to stay, the Hollander, Gaspar, was sent to Ormuz. As a compromise, however, the authority of Antonio was strictly confined to the College; the care of the missions and missionaries was confided to an other.

Thus Xavier started on his voyage to Japan with a heavy heart, for he knew very well that he left behind him the seeds of serious trouble. Still, he must go. This state of things was nothing new. Whatever he had undertaken had usually come to grief; his plans had been regularly brought to naught by just those from whom he had naturally a right to expect most assistance. In two months he reached Malacca; a month later he was on his way to Japan. But not without a last sad note which betrays the anxiety he carried with him. Before he left Malacca he wrote to the Provincial of Portugal:

> As you know well, the office of superior is very dangerous for one who is not perfect. I ask you therefore to send, as rector and superior of the brethren in India, one to whom this office will do no spiritual injury. Antonio Gomez does not possess the necessary qualifications.

It was long before his request was heeded. For two years and more Xavier was away in Japan; when he returned to Goa, Gomez was still at his post. In those two years he had done serious harm; and in the meanwhile, while Francis was wearing himself out exploring Japan, he was telling his own tale to superiors in Europe. But not without the knowledge of Francis; in spite of his preoccupation far away, he found time to write to Fr. Antonio, warning him, and begging him to do his simple duty. Thus we find him saying:

> I entreat you, for the love of our Lord, so to behave that all the members of the Society may love you. Write to me and tell me of your spiritual life. If you will do that, you will lift a great burden from my heart.

It was all of no avail. Gomez received the letters of Francis, but chose
to go his own way. He claimed to have better training than Francis;
he knew better how the Indian mission should be worked. He had the
ear of his Provincial in Portugal; Francis had not. He had the College
under his complete control expressly by the Provincial's order; Francis
had other things to do. Therefore it was only just that he should be
given a free hand; he, and not Francis, had the right to lay down the
policy of the mission. Scarcely had Francis sailed away from Goa than
the native students were dismissed in numbers; in their places were received Portuguese youths, many of whom could scarcely read or write.
Of these many were hurried through to ordination; this was adduced
as a proof of the wisdom and success of his policy, and Gomez then
wished to close the College to native students altogether.

Such was the news which reached Francis after a year or more of
his time in Japan. There was trouble everywhere among the brethren
in India; unless he returned it would increase. He had no alternative
but to return. In November, 1551, he set sail from Japan, and reached
Malacca in forty days. Here he received an abiding consolation, humanly speaking the greatest he had ever had during all his time in the
East, and one that buoyed him up to face the still greater trouble to
come. It was a letter from Ignatius, the first that had reached him for
four years. Its contents had much between the lines, which even we
may easily read. We know that during this time Ignatius had had no
little trouble with Simon Rodriguez, the Provincial of Portugal; in fact
with all the Portuguese Province altogether; it was to the Province of
Portugal that his famous Letter on Obedience was written about this
time. The trouble was not unlike that between Francis and Antonio;
it was chiefly a question of jurisdiction and authority. Since Simon
was what he was, and since the spirit of Coimbra was the spirit of
Antonio, Ignatius saw the difficulties of his son Francis in the very
complaints that were made against him. There was only one thing to
do. He could not send him help, but he could set him free. With his
usual vigor of action, he constituted India and the East a Province of its
own, independent of the Province of Portugal, and appointed Xavier
its first Provincial. The letter which conveys this message concludes
with words whose full meaning only Francis and Ignatius could have
understood; but they are characteristic, both of the saint who wrote
them and of the saint to whom they were written:

I shall never forget you,
Entirely your own,
Ignatius.

That sentence was enough. It told again of that *interna charitatis et amoris lex* which always ruled the heart of Ignatius, and which he placed above all constitutions for the government of his Society. It made up for many disappointments. Before this Francis had asked for men of better calibre than those he had received, and had been told he could not have them. They were wanted elsewhere. He had described the fields he had explored, white for the harvest, and had appealed for men to whom he could trust them; he received a scanty handful, and of these many he had to send home again, or dismiss from the Society altogether. And we are now, be it remembered, within a year of his death.

Francis sailed from Malacca to Cochin, and here further trouble awaited him. During all his time in India he seems to have had only two men on whom he could entirely rely, Antonio Criminale, an Italian from Parma, and Gaspar Baertz. Arrived at Cochin, he was welcomed with the news that the former had perished, murdered by Muslim raiders; and with his death again had been undone much of Xavier's work on the Fishery Coast. Gaspar was away in Arabia. Meanwhile the news from Goa was heartbreaking. Antonio, the man who should have been his right hand, and in whom he had been compelled to place all his confidence, had gone from bad to worse. From being Rector of the College he had constituted himself Vice-Provincial. He had ignored and crushed the gentle Fr. Paul, whom Francis had appointed to control the Society in his absence, claiming that his credentials from Rodriguez superseded all restrictions from Xavier. In that capacity he had given trouble everywhere. All the native students had at last been dismissed from the College. Down along the Fishery Coast he had thrown everything into confusion. Customs which Francis had wisely conceded Antonio had prohibited. What was not done in Portugal could never be allowed among Indian natives. In his scheme for extending colleges he had usurped the properties of others; churches assigned for the use of the Society he had claimed for his own. In Goa itself the Jesuit fathers were almost in open revolt. They no longer knew whom they were to obey.

To add to the confusion, just before the arrival of Francis in Goa,

another father had come out from Portugal, sent as superior by Rodriguez, the Provincial. But when he presented his credentials it was
noticed that they did not bear the signature of Ignatius; evidently Rodriguez had appointed him on his own authority alone. Moreover, he
was a new man, utterly unacquainted with the conditions in the East;
and the fathers had had bitter enough experience with Antonio to risk
another reformer from Portugal. He must await the arrival of Father
Francis before he could be allowed to supersede even the dreaded existing superior.

Xavier arrived in Goa in February, 1552. He was there only two
months before he set off again on his final voyage to China. But in
those two months much had to be done. Now that he was Provincial
with power to act independently he could remove Fr. Antonio from
office; at the same time he feared to repeat his last experience with the
newcomer from Portugal. In spite of many remonstrances, Antonio
was sent to Diu, far up the coast; Francis would listen to no entreaty,
not even that of the Viceroy himself. Still he would not install in his
place the newly-appointed Fr. Melchior Nuñez. The story is that when
they met Fr. Francis asked him: "What qualities do you possess to fit
you to be a Rector?" Fr. Melchior replied: "Six years of theology and
three of philosophy." "Would that you had six years of experience",
was Xavier's answer, and he sent him away to Bassein to gain it. In
his stead, in spite of the reasons which before had made him hesitate,
he appointed Fr. Gaspar. In his hands he left everything; secretly he
added this, that in the next year, when the ship set sail for Portugal,
Antonio was to be dismissed and sent home with it.

On Maundy Thursday of that same year Francis set sail again, never
to return. At first all seemed to go well. He was received with honor in
Malacca, where he gave a friend, a certain Pereira, a letter, appointing
him ambassador, to go along with him to the "King" of China. Then
began more trouble. The Governor of Malacca refused to let Pereira
go; he turned also on Francis, and many of his court followed suit.
Francis sailed away with another wound in his heart, accompanied by
two servants, the one a Chinese, the other an Indian. "Never in all
my life have I endured persecution like this, not even from pagans or
Muslims", was his summary of his last sojourn on Portuguese soil; and
in a farewell letter to Fr. Gaspar he wrote:

Master Gaspar, you cannot imagine how I have been persecuted here in Malacca.

But even that was not all. He left Malacca in July; in November he lay a dying man on the hillside of Sancian. The ship that had brought him had slipped away home without giving him a word of warning; there remained in the harbor a single Portuguese sloop, waiting for good weather. Xavier lay beneath a temporary shelter, open on every side, the cold north wind beating mercilessly upon him. His companions and nurses were his two boys, one a Chinese, the other an Indian; during all his illness not a single European from the vessel in the harbor went near him. So he died, deserted in death as for the most part he had been in life; within sight of a goal which again he was doomed not to reach, repeating again and again in mingled sadness and resignation: "Jesus, Son of David, have mercy on me." Meanwhile in Goa a letter from Ignatius was awaiting him, bidding him come home to Europe. He had failed in his childish ambitions, failed as a University professor, failed as a monk or a hermit, failed as an Italian preacher, failed as a Court orator, and after all that he was to reap a harvest which he was never to know. No, St. Francis Xavier, the Apostle of the East, was not wholly a success; had he been that he would have failed to resemble his Master, the Failure of Calvary. And in that very failure, more than in all his triumphs, is the real greatness of the saint to be found. For through it all he never once flinched or surrendered. He appealed to be brought home, but he did not linger for the recall. He appealed for better support, but he went on using what he had at his disposal. He saw in all his failures proof of his own incompetence; but he strove with might and main to give without reserve the little he had to give. Xavier was great, not so much because of what he did as because of what he failed to do.

This, then, is the other side of the life of one of the most successful of the chosen servants of God. There is a greater greatness than the greatness of success; and that is the greatness of failure. For that is the greatness of being, without the encouragement of doing; the greatness of sacrifice, of which others less great may reap the fruits.

What became of his beloved College of St. Paul? A visitor to Goa will find there a deserted town, with nothing standing but its churches. Palm trees grow in the marketplace, where once the grim rites of the

Inquisition were performed. If he asks where stood, and what is now left of, the College of St. Paul, he will be told that the spot is out of the way and its ruins are not worth a visit. But if he insists, he will be taken a mile or so from the center of the town toward the sea, along a road flanked by palms, and there he will find standing on his left a single wall, pierced by an arched doorway, and will almost wonder how it still stands, all alone and unsupported. It is the façade of the old church of the College; the foundations of the rest are hidden beneath a tangle of bush. If he goes a little farther, and climbs the wall that skirts the road, he will find himself in a similar waste of undergrowth. Let him work his way up through this, and he will discover, still standing among the trees, the little chapel in the garden where Xavier used to hide for a month at a time from his labors, and, on the left, the well where he cooled his heart when it threatened to burst in an ecstasy of love.

The buildings of the College have gone, but the College itself still lives. Some years after the saint's death the place where the College stood became hopelessly malarial, and students and staff had to leave it. They went inland, to a more open country; and now at Rachol the great seminary of Goa preserves the tradition unbroken. It is not without significance that of all the works established by St. Francis Xavier, this, which was dearest to his heart, and cost him more than all the rest, is the only one that has survived. His spirit still broods over Southern India; there more than anywhere else may the Catholic faith be seen in all its vigor. Still, even here it would be hard to say what single area bears certain proofs of his labor. Much has been entirely swept away, by persecution and invasion; what may have survived has been merged in the work of the missionaries who have come after. Only at Rachol, the tree which he certainly planted, and watered with his heart's blood, still lives and bears the fruit for which he expressly planted it.

~

SAINT TERESA AND

[*1515-1582*]

SAINT JOHN OF THE CROSS

[*1542-1591*]

Father Bruno de J.M., O.D.C.

VERY MAN who reflects knows that he cannot remain within his own limitations: he must find a way to over-pass them: and this because of the frailness of a nature composed of spirit and matter. It is a plain fact of experience that if we do not go on, we fall back. The soul must command the body, and must itself be commanded by him who created it and maintains it in being. It is essential that the soul remain in contact with the Being in whom "we live and move and have our being", the Being more intimately present to the soul than the soul is to the body.

Concentrating their gaze upon their own depths, leaving behind the world of sensations and images which cannot express the very essence of pure spirit, facing Nothingness, the Void, the Night, the Mystics come close to the inmost point of their being: and there meet him who is. In him and the life flowing from him, they live intensely, know the joy of Existence Itself—Existence himself—open themselves wholly, love. Knowing, because Christ has revealed it, the marvelous life of the Three divine Persons, they participate in that perfect Community, wherein each gives his whole substance to the others and receives theirs wholly. They know the plenitude of bliss in total self-giving. The things that give us joy here below, St. Teresa of Avila assures us, are lies and no more, if they turn the soul, no matter how slightly, from the life within itself.

To reach so high a state, the Mystics had to be nailed to their cross and reach out beyond self, to bear the agony and through it come to liberation: but they chose aright, and theirs is the better part. They are extraordinarily free, and extraordinarily fruitful: for they make steadily for their goal, without deviation: and their goal is God who is supreme Goodness. The rest of us turn endlessly about the objects to which our passions tether us. We should and could advance into the world within: instead, for the most of our time, we live a barren life, unworthy of man, a life which—if we are fortunate—may show us the face of our own despair. Because they accept Creation and Redemption as primary facts, the Christian Mystics are splendid models of humanity. "Their accumulated vitality pours out in an incredible energy, daring, power of conception and achievement", says Bergson. He holds that neither in ancient Greece nor in India was there a mysticism in such plenitude: the soul of the Christian mystic was not absorbed in itself but opened wide to a universal love. The burning charity which characterises and completes the mysticism of Ramakrishna and Vivekananda is due, Bergson says in *Les Deux Sources*, to a Christian influence from the West. Our great mystics are men and women of genius, and as we come to know them we are astounded at the gifts God has lavished on them, not only in the order of grace but of nature too. There is vast human richness in the creative activity of the reformers of Carmel, in Teresa's prose style, in John's lyrical gift. These heroic humanists dominate sixteenth-century Spain. Teresa was born in 1515 and lived till 1582. John was born in 1542 and died in 1591. "I know not how I am so loved", said she: and he—"Where there is no love, it is for you to bring love." They abounded with life. They loved and were loved. They are worth knowing.

Come with me over the threshold of one of these Carmels: one is like another, time and place make no difference. You enter the vestibule, never closed during the day, and announce yourself—*Ave Maria Purissima*. In the parlour they receive you warmly, as a brother—this in spite of the grilles, whose spikes may be as long as seven or eight inches: that is their length at Segovia and Alcala. You may even be asked to sing: and if you mind that, you are no son of Teresa. At the convent of St. Joseph, in Avila, I was shown Teresa's flute and *basque* drum with its little bells. I had made no mistake when I went looking for traces of the saints. I found Saint Teresa in every one of her convents: at Valladolid there was the manuscript of *The Way of Perfection*; at Salamanca, the small holy water flask that she wanted tied on to her belt at the start of a journey; at Seville, her cloak (Father Silverio wanted to put it on me), and the portrait painted by Juan de la Miseria, and the manuscript of *The Interior Castle*.

But Avila is best. In that medieval walled town Teresa was born. Her father, Alonso Sanchez de Cepeda, was a veritable patriarch—he left twelve children to mourn him. Her mother, Beatrice de Ahumada, was gentle, self-effacing, quiet-spoken: she dressed like an old lady and read romances of chivalry behind her husband's back. Like him she was devout; she died at thirty-three, her death making as little stir as her life. I can give no better portrait of Teresa than her confessor and biographer, the Jesuit Ribera, has left us:

> Mother Teresa was reasonably tall, lovely in her girlhood and still beautiful in age. She was plump, her skin white, her face full and her cheeks rosy. Her complexion was pink and white: when she fell into prayer, her color rose and she was extremely beautiful. Her whole expression was of purity and peace. Her hair was black and curly, her forehead wide, level, shapely; her eyebrows were chestnut, long and thick, more straight than arched. Her eyes were black, rather prominent. They were not large but very well placed, bright and expressive; when she smiled, they sparkled with joy and gaiety: when she looked grave, they were very grave indeed. Her nose was small, with a slight rise half-way, full at the tip and slightly down-pointed; the nostrils round and small. Her mouth was not big, not small; the upper lip thin and straight, the lower strong, rather heavy, a rich red. Her teeth were quite beautiful, her chin shapely, her ears neither large nor small, a squarish shortish neck, strong and very pretty hands. On the left side of her face were three small moles that added to her attractiveness. In general her appearance was agreeable, and she moved gracefully. She was so kind and friendly that she pleased practically all who saw her.

Teresa herself, writing to Salcedo, adds the perfect footnote to this minutely detailed catalogue. "You say you would give six ducats to see me? It strikes me as too much. For that I ought to grow bigger to visit you. In fact you are worth more than I, for what value has a poor little bit of a nun?"

With some such picture in one's mind, there is no great difficulty in seeing Teresa alive and real in her first convent—the Incarnation at Avila. Let us visit her there. One day she had gathered a few friends in her cell. They were expressing their horror at the ravages heresy was making in France. Suddenly Teresa felt a call to establish a more contemplative life in her order. So far Carmelite convents for women had no Constitutions strictly so-called. For the most part they used the Constitutions followed in the men's monasteries: these usually had some passing references to the nuns. The first-known ordinances are those given by Blessed John Soreth to the Beguines of Guelder, who were part of the Order. The idea came to her to draw up something closer to the primitive idea of Carmel. From canons to magistrates, all Avila was soon turned upside down. With four nuns from the Convent of the Incarnation, Doña Teresa de Ahumada, with no capital and no income, founded the little convent of San José. Sheer madness, obviously. This was in 1562.

There are meetings, pregnant with the richest possibilities, that God has prepared from all eternity. A man can be an excellent religious, spiritual, mortified, and yet not be capable of heroism. But tasks arise that call for heroism: and the Reform of Carmel was one of them. What heroic man would Providence raise up to aid Teresa? On August 16, 1567, the Master General sent from Barcelona to his beloved daughter Teresa a patent giving her permission to found two convents of "contemplative Carmelites". Teresa wanted a counselor. The Carmelite Fathers spoke highly of John of St. Mathias. A companion of this man John told Teresa admirable things of his way of Life—as that he practiced the primitive Rule, was a model of penance and recollection. One day, with the permission of the Prior of St. Anne, John of St. Mathias (who was to be John of the Cross) came to see Teresa, at the house of Blaise of Medina. After praying in the great gilded room that had been made into a chapel, he saw the *Santa Madre*. It was the first time. These two geniuses of sanctity knew each other instantly for what they were.

John was the first to speak. He was a small man, a Castilian, with black brooding eyes, a brown face that could grow brilliant in ecstasy. He was born on the high tableland of old Castile, between Avila and Salamanca, in Fontiveras, a village lying at the foot of its church. He was of noble blood. Gonzalo de Yepes, his father, was grandson of Francisco Garcia de Yepes, man-at-arms to John II. In spite of his ancestry, Gonzalo had listened only to his heart when he chose for wife a poor girl, Catalina Alvarez. After thirteen years of trouble and happiness together, they had their third child, John—"my John" as the mother called him, rocking him in her arms: "John of the Cross", as the angels called him, seeing what he was to be. He knew poverty and toil as a child.

Gonzalo died soon after and Catalina had to face life with her three sons as best she might. At eleven, John was sent to study at the College of the Children of Doctrine at Medina del Campo, where he had come with his mother. He was "very good and sensible". Later he entered the service of Alonso Alvarez of Toledo, administrator of the smallpox hospital. He had already begged money for poor children, now he begged for the contagiously sick poor. His work for the hospital left him no more than "a brief moment in the morning and again in the evening" for study. Even at night, he was always being sent for. At such times they would find him studying, his mother tells us, in the wood pile: we know from other sources that he went there to do penance. He studied and prayed. Wisdom, gift of the Holy Spirit, did more for his education than the lessons of the Jesuit Fathers. The spectacle of the world, the splendor and baseness of man—he saw much of man and the world at the great fairs of Medina del Campo—cut whatever attachment to the world still held his heart. He left the hospital—very secretly, his brother Francisco adds—and went off to join the Order "founded for the service and honor of Mary".

From Medina, John was sent to Salamanca. There for three years he followed courses at the great University as well as the teaching given by his own Order at the College of St. Andrew. Early in September, 1567, he left the town with its forty parishes, its thirty convents, its great houses with their armorial bearings. Salamanca faded away behind him. He crossed the red plain of Leon with its circlet of hills. He had thrown away the promise of a career in the University. He had of his own choice abandoned the gold ring and the cap of a Doctor of Theology. What the force was that drove him further and higher he told Teresa at their meeting in Medina. He had just celebrated his first Mass and found in his heart only the desire "for greater perfection and for the solitary life", the desire "to leave the world and be submerged in God": he had made up his mind to become a Carthusian.

When Teresa came to speak, she unfolded her project: not a dream, you understand, but a project, authorized in due form by the Master General of the Carmelites. And John agreed to set about a reform of the men like that which Teresa had begun for the women—but on condition "that he would not have to wait long". In these words we see Saint John of the Cross whole and entire. He was a mystic, a man in love, a man of decision. He did not waver or shuffle, he took the shortest road, straight up the hill. Teresa was a woman of action: "Works, not words." She, like John, had a longing for the solitary life. She cried out: "What a torment for a poor soul that has attained this degree of union, to have to begin to deal with men again, to be condemned to see the miserable farce of life acted out before its eyes." But if you love, you must give your strength and your genius. That is what Christ demanded of Teresa and of John for the renewal of the Carmelite order.

In the autumn of 1568, after a year in the school of Theology at Salamanca, John of St. Mathias, now John of the Cross, began, in a hut at Duruelo, on the bleak Castilian plateau, the work of reform conceived by Teresa. The "Carmelite thing" had been born anew in her heart, already mystically on fire from the Seraph's dart. During the summer she had instructed her "son" at Valladolid. He was then only twenty-six. She was fifty-three.

In a total union of minds, St. Teresa and St. John were to succeed in a most daring enterprise—an organic union of the solitary life of the Hermits of Mount Carmel and the apostolic mission of the Mendicant Orders, of which the Carmelites had been one since their arrival in Europe in the thirteenth century. Both of them knew that outward action must flow from a state of the soul. Saint John set about transposing Mount Carmel itself into the psychological order and making it the figure of our own ascent. Carmel was a lifegiving symbol: its ascent a thing to be accomplished within the soul: and only the soul stripped of all that is not love is ready for Love.

The Dominican Ibañez sent Teresa "two sheets of paper laden with arguments and theological principles" to dissuade her from founding convents without money. But, Teresa said to herself, "The greatest honor of the poor lies in being really poor." As we have seen, San José was founded without any resources: and Teresa went on practicing the theological virtue of hope. "Teresa and three ducats, that's nothing: but

God, Teresa and three ducats, that's everything." She realized that the convent at Rio de Olmos could not survive. What matter. She simply gave away whatever was worth keeping to a regular convent. "It is not proper for a house of thirteen poor little nuns to make a great noise when it collapses. The true poor make no noise. . . . For thirteen poor women, any corner will do. If you have an enclosed place with a few shelters where you can be alone and pray, splendid. . . . Poverty must be everywhere, in our dwelling, in our clothes, in our words, above all in our thoughts."

You will remember how John installed solitude and poverty in a hut at Duruelo, which was a hamlet of twenty cottages. In the distance, the dark Sierra de Gredos: the valley spread out like two great wings. It was an open, fertile place. The life of the Reform was to grow out of the life of Elijah the prophet, father and head of the Carmelites, from the life of the hermits of Palestine and Egypt. With his companion, Padre Antonio, John found the cottage a "place of delight". Following Teresa's plan, he built small hermitages at the two corners of the choir looking toward the chapel. They were so low that your head more or less touched the roof. Actually you could only either sit or lie down in them. Here the old trunk of Carmel was to bud forth anew. "What they have joyously harvested with the sickle of contemplation in solitude, they must thresh on the floor of preaching and sow broadcast."

For Teresa action too proceeds from this interior harvesting. You can see why the Nuncio, Sega, called her "a restless vagabond woman". All founders, all reformers, have been, as their master was, "a scandal to the Jews, folly to the Greeks". But God's work makes its own way through man's malice and blindness. Teresa and John united their gifts, completed each other miraculously. In spite of the difference in age and temperament, John exercised a strong influence over the Spiritual Mother of interior souls. From the *Life* and *The Way of Perfection*, both written by Teresa in 1561, to the *Thoughts on the Canticle of Canticles*, written in 1574, and *The Interior Castle*, there is not only a progress due to the experience of a soul that has attained full awareness of self, but also an increasing doctrinal firmness which surely owed something to John. "I look here and there for light," says Teresa, "and I find all I need in my little Seneca". She stood before him, as in prayer; in his absence, she declared: "No one realizes the riches and treasures God has placed in that holy Soul; they are very great." "Father John of the

Cross is truly my soul's father; he is one of those who have brought me most good by their words. You can, I assure you, have the same confidence in him as in me. He unites the greatest experience with most profound knowledge.''

Conscious of the lights she was receiving, Teresa knew that she must transmit them. At Salamanca, after a few too short days, Teresa was back once more in her poor cell. In the distance the tinkling of bells died away, and the last students were homeward bound at last, rapier or guitar under their cloaks. All was at peace. By the light of a small lamp, Teresa was busy at her writing. With a quill pen she covered the large, almost square, sheets of paper she used with her big masculine script at an incredible speed. The doctrine that she set out was so accurate that when John of the Cross came to write in his turn, he did not linger over the stages anterior to the mystic espousals—''raptures, ecstasies, subtle flights of the spirit, because'', as he said, ''Blessed Teresa of Jesus, our mother, has left admirable writings upon these things''—writings that he hoped soon to see given to the press.

To the list of Teresa's writings that we have just given, we should add the history of her *Foundations*. As for the works of St. John of the Cross, they are all subsequent to the purifying trial that he underwent in 1577 at Toledo.

For all its refined art—Jewish, Moorish, Christian—and the warmth of its coloring and the blazing sky over it, Toledo stands up bleak and bare as a symbol. Barrès said aright: ''It is a cry in the desert.'' To Toledo John, dressed in the habit of the Mitigated, in the company of one of the harshest of monks, was to come bearing his cross. It would be long and wearisome to set out here the dispute between the Mitigated and the Discalced. Sufficient if we grasp that there is no worse suffering than the suffering dealt us by our own, and that God often allows men this ultimate crucifixion to bring their work more surely to completion. St. John was to suffer horribly. The Chapter General of Piacenza ordered the Discalced Carmelites to withdraw within three days into one of the regular monasteries ''even if it were necessary to use the secular arm to make them.'' Father Maldonado, right-hand man of Tostado, the Vicar General, executed the decree to the letter. For him, there was no question of John's being a reformer. He had examined him thoroughly at the Convent of the Incarnation at Avila. Why, if he was a saint, did he not abandon novelties which scandalized the Order in which he had made his profession? Surely that would be more humble, more charitable, and so more perfect. But a saint judges by divine norms, and he is not afraid to cause pain if souls are called to spiritual growth upon the cross that he sets before them. Father Maldonado, making no impression by his arguments, fell back upon the decrees of Piacenza and applied them with Spanish rigor. On the night of December 3, 1577, he laid hold of John to take him to Toledo.

The rumor got about and Teresa wrote to Philip II to complain of Maldonado. From his palace at Madrid as from the Escorial, Philip kept the matter of the Reform under prudent, unemotional surveillance.

The Carmelite convent at Toledo was the prison chosen for John of the Cross. This particular convent no longer exists. It was to the east of the town, looking down upon the bridge of Alcantara. Here it was that John of the Cross had his torment, immured in the tiniest space, made into a "nothing" that Love might have its way with him. Air and light came into his dungeon only from a window high up. He had to stand on a stool to read his Office. At the beginning of this imprisonment every evening, later on on Fridays, he was brought to the refectory to take his bread and water on the floor. It was the fast of ignominy, prescribed for the incorrigible. Then he stripped to the waist, and the friars circled round him lashing him as they passed. "He remained motionless as a stone." He had no intention of turning back, even if it cost him his life to go forward. Why, they kept hammering at him, this foolishness of a reform of Carmel and a new way of life? And who was to lead it? "A little friar like him?" At the sight of such savagery and such patience, the young novices told one another "He is a saint." And they wept.

To add to these sufferings, the demon tormented John. His soul seemed shriveled and devitalized as by a leprosy spreading and devouring it—extinguishing the ideal, lowering the level of being. These sufferings are those described by St. Teresa in the "Sixth Mansion" of the *Interior Castle*: mockery, insults, sarcasms, physical crosses, anguish of soul, inclination to welcome the suggestions of the demon. Teresa's psychological analysis foreshadows the admirable synthesis of the *Dark Night*, John's masterwork. In his prison John had an overwhelming sense that no one could now know his true face: and still he bore the weight God laid upon him, dragging on in the darkness, crushed, all but annihilated. It is by Death that we come to Life: and it is of Life that we die. Distress in the spirit, time of divine dereliction: "My God, my God, why hast thou forsaken me?"

> Where then hast thou hidden,
> Beloved, leaving me in agony?

It was the ultimate denudation, the ultimate in humility: in such a love there is no illusion. But in such a love there is liberation. The liberation that love brought John was total. In his prison he sang. In his verses the literary critic admires the magnificence of the poetry: for the spiritual man they are filled with a profound, almost inexhaustible symbolism—and this is true of the *Spiritual Canticle* as of the *Dark Night*:

> In this blissful night
> Secretly, no man seeing me,
> I seeing nothing,
> With no other light or guide
> But that which burned in my heart.
> And it led me
> Surer than the light of noonday.

Strengthened by so searching an experience, St. John—after an escape miraculously aided by the Blessed Virgin—was able, when he got to Andalusia, to trace for his disciples the plan of the mount of Perfection. I see him in the midst "of trees laden with delicious fruits". facing the splendid range of hills beyond the Guadalquivir. He is sitting on the red earth and working. The solitude of Calvario is not silent. You can hear the grave murmur of the fir trees, the plash of the fountain, the Arab song of a peasant some way off. "With his eyes like two lights and his cheeks like flame", he was drawing up a spiritual itinerary, the road map of "kingly souls".

Just run through St. John's works in their logical order: in the *Ascent of Carmel*, he teaches the soul how it must bear itself in relation to God all along the spiritual way; the *Dark Night* analyses as it had never before been analyzed the purgative work of God in the sensible part and the spiritual part of the soul; the *Spiritual Canticle* treats of the espousals and the spiritual marriage of the soul with God; the *Living Flame of Love* sketches the supreme transformation of the soul in God. Of the *Letters*, we possess only a few, mainly of spiritual direction, some of them of great value.

I shall make use of the works of both saints to draw out a sort of practical synthesis of their doctrine.

John of the Cross and Teresa of Jesus were working upon a spirituality eremitical in origin, very simple, very old. Granted that the two saints were psychologists of genius, living in the sixteenth century, speaking from their own experience; but they were the heirs of a mystical tradition that came out of the East. It was in the soil of Carmel that they sought for and found the pearl of contemplation. Evidences of this tradition, lovingly outlined by Father Jerome of the Mother of God, have just been assembled under the title *Les Plus Vieux Textes*, in the series *Vigne du Carmel*, edited by Father François de Ste. Marie. Nothing more substantial in this field has appeared since *Les Saints Déserts des Carmes Déchaussés* of the late Father Benedict Zimmerman. Such a collection of texts appeals not only to the sons and daughters of Elijah; in this subhuman age, when men are seeking refuge in Hinduism, it will quite certainly interest many spiritual souls in search of a way of deliverance. Without contact with God, no good thing is accomplished here below. The contemplative is the sage, the man the City must hold in honor. His zeal is to Love what the flame is to the brazier. The spirit of the contemplative prophet, "like to fire", which mystics within the Church and without have claimed as their own, becomes all the more actual as we see the signs multiplying of Apocalypse. Not without trembling do we at Carmel celebrate every July the feast and solemn octave of our father Elijah, precursor of Christ, victim of Antichrist who is to come at the end of the world. Gigantic and sublime, Elijah proclaimed that Jahveh before whom he stood was the living God.

"It is said in our original Rule that we must pray without ceasing", St. Teresa reminds us. And John of the Cross says, "Let not your spirit take its food save in God." Jesus has ordered us to be ever at prayer: and he adds that we must pray in secret, almost without the sound of words.

Prayer is a contact of love in the obscurity of faith with him who, present to all that he sustains in existence, reveals himself mysteriously to his friends. Raised by baptism to the supernatural order, we know not only that God exists and what his attributes are as we can grasp them by reason, but what he is in himself. That is to say we know the mystery of the most holy Trinity; and we live thereby if we make use of the proximate means of divine union, the three theological virtues of Faith, Hope and Charity, given to us by sanctifying grace. These alone being essentially supernatural, enable us effectively to participate in the Triune intimacy of God. As they have their home in the highest faculties of the soul—intellect, memory and will—it is obvious that the imagination and the senses can aid our prayer only for the moment. St. John of the Cross tells us that little time need be given to the imaginative representation of truth, a great deal more to the intellect's examination of the mystery represented, the goal of meditation being to rest lovingly in God and listen to him. "Each time that the soul by meditation obtains this loving knowledge, it produces an act; and repeated acts, whatever they be, at last engender a habit" (*Ascent of Carmel*, Book 2, Chapter 14). This indeed is the prayer of *active* recollection of which the *Way of Perfection* treats. Teresa requires that we close our lids, abandon creatures, enclose ourselves wholly in the small heaven of the soul: we are not bound to fix our thought upon him, nor enter into much inner discourse or high and learned considerations: simply we must within ourselves, in the depth of the heart, turn the soul's gaze upon Jesus. "If we continue thus for some days, and make serious efforts, we shall see the profit that will flow to us. As soon as the soul sets itself to pray, it will see the senses returning in upon it like bees coming back to their hive and entering to make honey." "This way of praying aids the spirit to attain recollection much more speedily than any other", Teresa tells us. All the same, if it is to develop all its power and dominate our life, we must work at it for six months or even a year.

To "tranquilize the soul", to enable "the spirit to develop the habit of acting only interiorly", to aid intelligently, as the saint demands, toward the concentration necessary for the flowering of this interior life, experience shows that it is best to place the body at ease, the head erect, muscles relaxed, and breath coming easily—all of which is the exact opposite of the practice which Teresa condemns in the "Fourth Mansions", namely the effort to hold one's breath in order to produce passive recollection. What she is insisting on is that, the divine operations being "wholly pleasant and tranquil, whatever is laborious brings more hindrance than help." She cannot "bring herself to use human methods and things which his Majesty seems to have reserved for himself." Let us look again at the preparation for active recollection. If one does what we have just set out, there soon ensues a tranquilization, or rather an opening out of the being thus brought to rest. All one need do is "control his gaze that he may look upon Our Lord within him", and murmur the sacred words of the Our Father, or indeed any words of love; and after a while, the closed eyes being unable to open —"effort would be necessary to hold them open" absorption in God grows deeper.

"I give you all these recommendations"—so a twelfth-century Carmelite reports Our Lord as saying—"in order that from a pure heart, an honest conscience and a sincere faith, there should pour forth without obstacle so fervent and powerful a charity, uniting your heart to me totally and unresistingly and so peacefully that it feels absolutely nothing contrary to my love, no obstacle, but reposes wholly at peace in my love" (*L'Institution des Premiers Moines*).

"All created things, our sisters, which charm our eyes and our ears in solitude, rest us and strengthen us", writes one of the last hermits of Mount Carmel at the end of the thirteenth century, "They silently hymn their beauty and excite our soul to praise the wonderful Creator" (*La Flèche ardente*). Thus we see John of the Cross "diligently searching out secret places, favorable to contemplation. At the evening prayer, he went out to the garden and had the friars do the same among the trees and in the great solitude that was to be found in this convent at Granada. And there he remained with great devotion and quietude."

Surely this very ancient fashion of going to God is very simple. To-day, when we are impatient of constraint, when we have a taste for the soberer things and a thirst for the Absolute, it presents itself to us as an ideal and a very practical ideal. I have insisted of set purpose on what our masters of speculative mystical theology have chosen to call "a quiet contemplation". "By this way more rapidly than by any other," Teresa tells, "God will instruct the soul and will grant it the prayer of quiet."

Nor must we separate asceticism from mysticism. The one is made for the other. And a day may come, indeed should come, when the action, till now latent, of the Gifts of the Holy Spirit received in Baptism will take charge of the spiritual activity just described. It is to the supreme Gift, Wisdom, an experimental knowledge, that the soul owes its entry into a genuinely mystical passivity. Contemplation, as we have seen, was already supernatural as to its object during active recollection: now it becomes supernatural as to its mode. God plunges the soul into the state of loving contemplation without any preliminary effort on our part. The fearful should take courage. The image of the Blessed Humanity may disappear, the sacred words of the Our Father grow still, but St. John of the Cross sets out three very important signs by which the soul may come to know that it can and should let itself be borne along into this passivity.

1. Meditation becomes impossible. The imagination lies inert. There is only aridity in what had brought delight.

2. Neither the senses nor the imagination can fix themselves voluntarily on any object within or without. There may still be involuntary distractions.

3. Finally, and especially, the soul rejoices to find itself alone with God in a general attention of love, but indistinctly and with no hold by the intellect upon any particular thing.

It is absolutely essential that these three signs should be found together in a soul if it is legitimately to abandon itself to this passivity in which is neither form nor image. The first sign is not sufficient without the second, for it might easily be that the inability to form images and meditate arises from distraction and lack of concentration. And the third sign is also of absolute necessity, for the inability to occupy the spirit either upon God or creatures might proceed "from melancholy or from some evil humor in brain or heart causing a slackening in the senses", which might cause one to think nothing and will nothing and find pleasure in this total relaxation, without desire for anything besides. The soul should both habituate itself to quietude and grow in a general loving listening to God, the cause of peace and joy.

Soon there comes a purifying aridity. In relation to this passive purification of sense, John returns at the beginning of the *Dark Night* to the three signs given above from the *Ascent of Carmel*. In addition to the impossibility of meditation, the inability to fix itself either on creatures or on the things of God, the saint here demands, in place of joy at finding oneself alone with God, a sorrowful memory of this same God: but he adds that this aridity is not always given to us for the passive purification of sense; it may be the accompaniment of sin, imperfection, want of energy, tepidity, or even a bodily indisposition.

By now we are at the stage of the prayer of quiet. In this prayer, only the will is engaged. After the Fourth Mansions described by St. Teresa, we enter the Fifth, namely, thought, memory and imagination, and we have the prayer of union. Finally, the ecstasy of the Sixth Dwellings suspends the external senses.

Those souls are rare which have had the privilege of the authentic experience of the mystical states described in the Sixth and Seventh Dwellings of the *Interior Castle*. There are a fair number who have known the passive night of sense, quiet, and even the prayer of union; but not many who have experienced the passive night of the soul which follows ecstasy. This "strong cleansing", a kind of anticipation of purgatory is, St. John tells us, the privilege of very few. But it is this, according to him, which enables men here below to attain the transforming union, spiritual espousals and marriage. The saint himself reached these high summits of the mystical life in his prison at Toledo. At the urging of his disciples he wrote down the splendid poems which are the hymn of his liberated soul. This was mainly at Granada, around 1584.

By then Teresa had been dead two years. Her death was very simple and quiet and beautiful: "It is time for us to see each other, my beloved Lord", she was heard to murmur as she received the viaticum. Then Extreme Unction was administered and she lay on her side, a crucifix in her hand. She fell into ecstasy, conversing with a mysterious interlocutor. At moments her face was luminous, as before some marvelous sight. Then she groaned two or three times, and uttered her last sigh. Her beauty grew no less with death. Her face was radiant. Her body remained supple as in life. Fr. Gracian told us that years later it was found incorrupt and a sweet fragrance came from it, her flesh being as young and soft as a child's.

Thus John of the Cross remained sole depository of the new Carmel. Escaped from Toledo, as we have seen, he bore it with him to the foot of the Sierra Morena in the Andalusian desert. He came down by slow stages toward the lower ground, a moving grey and white speck in the blood-red expanse of rocks. After crossing the Guadalimar, he came into Beas de Segura. In the heart of the town he knocked at the door of the Convent of St. Joseph, whose prioress was Anne of Jesus, the future foundress of the Carmelite Order in France. In this convent at Beas he cultivated certain souls of truly exquisite spirituality. Later,

having left the Calvario, he would come back from Baeza and even
from Granada to Beas for a month and more, to be near those he loved
with special love: "Till I come, do like the ewe lamb: chew over what
I have taught you." And his teachings were certainly substantial. In the
notes of Magdalen of the Holy Spirit, for instance, we find a famous
passage of the first book of the Ascent:

> Always seek for preference
>   not the easiest but the hardest;
>   not the most charming but the most boring;
>   not what pleases but what repels;
>   not what consoles but rather what afflicts;
>   not what saves us trouble but what gives us trouble;
>   not the most but the least;
>   not the highest and most precious but the lowest and most despised;
>   not the desire of something but the non-desire; do not seek what is
>   better in things but what is worse, and for Jesus Christ put yourself
>   in denudation, emptiness, and renunciation of all that exists in this
>   world.

The advice he gives here should not cause us to see him as the dry-
eyed ascetic spoken of by Huysmans. John of the Cross was a man of
tenderness, driven to react against its excesses. The detachment that
his soul demanded brought no diminution of friendship, but the very
reverse. Friendship is itself only if virtue preserves it from a self-seeking
sensuality and from animal passions. When the Reform was properly
under way John brought his mother, his brother Francis and his sister-
in-law to Duruelo and gave them charge of the kitchen and the laundry.
St. Teresa emphasizes that it is an error to think that those who have
set their foot upon the way of renunciation neither love nor can love
anyone but God. "They love, and they love more than others, with
a more genuine love and more passion and their love is much more
profitable. In fact it is love."

On the feast of the Blessed Trinity, 1579, John of the Cross founded
the College of Our Lady of Mount Carmel at Baeza. Just three years
later, in March, 1582, the friars of the Carmel at Granada elected him
prior. There he built with his own hands an aqueduct and a cloister, the
most beautiful of Carmelite cloisters. But nature was the cloister he
preferred. He would go to the bank of the Genil or the Darro, bringing
the friars with him that they might wander among the pistachio trees,
the pomegranates and the camellias.

Every day after the three hours' sleep with which he indulged his "little beast", John of the Cross arose. He went to the corner of a staircase from which he could see a great expanse of sky and countryside. At his feet he saw the wilderness close by wherein, as we have said, he had his friars pray their evening prayer. At dawn the snowy peaks of the Sierra Nevada shone brilliant to the left. Behind the hill of Los Martires the mass of the Alhambra showed red and orange; higher, the Generalife stood up white, the summer residence of the Sultans, hung with texts of the Koran, ringed round with myrtles. Granada, paradise of the senses, Granada still Muslim, still an arena for the passions and all devilry, contained within itself a whole generation growing up Spanish and Christian on the surface but no more than that. The Moors of Granada had put up with Baptism as preferable to banishment.

It is interesting to note that at the very time when John of the Cross was finishing the *Ascent of Carmel* and the *Dark Night* at Granada, the celebrated Mooress of Ubeda was still teaching there the mystical doctrine of Islam. Her influence remained very much alive throughout that region. She was an amazing woman, now ninety-three; "she had no equal in the world of the learned for instructive ideas, and was known to all nations. Learned men came to compliment her on the great feastdays. Great was her power of divination." A century before her birth, a century and a half before John's, there died at Fez Ibn Abbâd Allah, born at Ronda, not far from Malagar. You will find in the *Études Carmélitaines* a fascinating article by Don Miguel Asin Palacios, entitled "Un précurseur hispano musulman de saint Jean de la Croix", treating of this man whom Massignon calls the true master of primitive Islamic mysticism. One is struck with "the profoundly Christian attitude of abandonment to the charismatic gifts adopted by the Spanish Muslim Sufis of the school Shâdhîlî, particularly by Ibn Abbâd of Ronda", writes Asin Palacios. "In the night of anguish, God reveals himself to the soul much better than in the luminous light of expansion . . . the soul therefore must not despair if it does not feel the consolation of the presence of God in prayer . . . this consolation is for the Shadhilis, as for St. John of the Cross, a sort of spiritual gluttony. . . . Obviously we must seek the common origin of the two attitudes in the doctrine of St. Paul as professed and lived by the Fathers of the Desert and by the Christian monachism of the East." Which seems to imply, concerning the "dark night"—which Dionysius, Ruys-broeck, Tauler and Catherine of Genoa have merely adumbrated—that St. John of the Cross, after having experienced it and hymned it in his Toledo prison, received confirmation of it from Mount Carmel itself by the way of Islam and the Fathers of the Desert. St. Anthony the Hermit gave it as his view that the ascetic should compare his whole life daily with that lived by the great Elijah. And, according to Louis Massignon, the eighteenth Sura of the Koran became "the fundamental support of all Islamic mystical vocations, causing them to invoke as spiritual director the holy Intercessor Elijah."

The "dark night" is an essential phase of that Carmelite mystical experience which issues into the sunrise joy of God. It seems proba-ble that Elijah knew it, when he fled into the desert and begged God for death—"Lord, I am not better than my fathers." It seems to me that this purification was essential before he could attain Horeb and perceive God in the soft and gentle wind. In the *Institution des Premiers Moines*, the Lord speaks thus to the least-privileged son of the great prophet: "Because you could not clearly see my face and because with the hindrance of your corruptible body you will not be able to remain long in the glorious contemplation of sweetness experienced, you will pray, if you wish to persevere in perfection, and you will say, groaning: 'God. O my God, I seek you at the dawn of day, my soul is athirst for you. My very flesh is parched for you. In this desert place, dry and impenetrable, thus it is that I present myself to you in the sanctuary to contemplate your power and your glory.' But lest your desire to see me and your hunger to taste of the sweetness of my glory dry you up in groaning and sadness of heart beyond remedy, for your consolation I have ordered ravens to bring you nourishment."

"The beauty of Carmel will be given", says St. Gregory of Nyssa, "to the soul which shall resemble a desert place: it is a gift of the spirit."

It was at Granada that John wrote the *Spiritual Canticle* and the *Living Flame of Love*, his two great works to the glory of the Trinity. Whatever tendencies certain Islamic mysticisms may have aroused to-ward naturalism and diabolism, St. John answered them magistrally, destroying all our delusions in advance. We are very far here from the paradise which the Koran promises to pious men. "There will be streams there whose water will be incorruptible." One remembers the ice-cold waters from the Sierra in the marble basins of the Moorish palace. And truly an abyss of cold pleasures separates the Alhambra, with its colonnades and stucco ornamentation, from the humble and recollected cloister of Los Martires. And it is not only in his treatises that Father John lays the rigorously exact foundation of an authentic mysticism. About him he uncovers the tricks of the demon, morbid errors, false attitudes. "Servants of God must not obey their superior in anything that would trouble contemplation", claimed the Illuminists. But John of the Cross, though he defends fiercely the liberty of souls to obey the impulse of God, has no trace in him of Luther's kind of independence. In the prologues to the *Spiritual Canticle* and the *Living Flame of Love*, he declares not only that he bases his teaching upon Holy Scripture, but that he submits to the judgment of more enlightened men, and above all "to the judgment of our Mother, the Holy Catholic Roman Church, under whose guidance none can go astray." He submitted in all humility to his superiors, even to his own disgrace. By his fidelity to the supernatural and by the force of his genius, St. John of the Cross occupies a peak of wisdom between the Illuminism of the pseudo-mystics and the earthboundness of the anti-mystics of his own time and all times.

In his last aphorism, John of the Cross writes: "Leave all those other things that remain to you and turn to a single thing which draws all with it, namely, holy solitude accompanied by prayer . . . and there, persevere in the forgetfulness of all things. . . ." To forget is to look beyond. "In the evening of this life", he says, "you will be examined upon Love". Love accepts all humiliations and all cruelties as acts of justice, and memory forgets the names of those who do them. Thus St. John of the Cross forgot the injustices done to him by his superior, Nicolas Doria and his lieutenants, and died at peace.

The moment was at hand. Fever had hold of him. Obedience took him from the bundle of heath and reeds he slept on. He went by preference to Ubeda, and not Baeza, where he would have found a prior who wanted him and loved him. He mounted the small mule that a friend got for him. There was a boy to lead it.

We shall not follow him to the very end of his life upon this earth. But remember one single fact—that, seeing him in such an abyss of grief and knowing his great love for music, they had guitar players brought to his bedside. But John wished to suffer, with no relief whatever, "the beneficent gifts" God sent him.

John of the Cross, proclaimed a Doctor of the Universal Church by Pius XI on August 24, 1926, is more alive, more actually operative than ever. International congresses of religious psychology have been devoted to him in France. Theologians, poets and philosophers come to him. From the point of view of nature as of grace he towers high. This star of the dark night seems to fascinate and illuminate our age even more than the sun of Teresa. I have just seen the psychological portrait which, without knowing either his life or his doctrine, Madame Suzanne Brésard, of the Institut Carrel, has drawn of the saint from examining his handwriting. It is a striking confirmation of all that we knew and all that we guessed. Gustave Thibon has greatly admired this analysis; what strikes him in St. John's handwriting is the objectivity, the clarity. Here is a saint who knew trials and even despair but had no inner conflicts, or possibility of conflict. With St. Teresa there was the possibility, though she surmounted it. Her lyric gift, her imagination, are of the heroic and not the sentimental type. More built for human contacts than St. John, she could make a better display—but it was a display of what was there.

In exalting the living religion of Teresa of Avila, the heroic humanism of John of the Cross, we made no mistake. Like El Greco and Victoria, they express for us not only the high soul of Spain, but the human soul in its totality, unmutilated, lovingly at grips with the essential reality of the divine. But it is with the authority of personal experience that they communicate to us that inexpressible element which the great painter and the great musician can do no more than stammer.

~

SAINT CAMILLUS OF LELLIS

[*1550–1614*]

Alban Goodier, S.J.

AMILLUS DE LELLIS had a good but timid mother: his father seems to have been the very opposite. Both were of respectable, some say of noble, families; and the surname confirms it. But the father, himself the son of a fighting man, had become such a ne'er-do-well that he had long since dragged the family name in the mud. He was a soldier all his life, or rather he was an adventurer; he served in the armies of various monarchs, hiring himself out to whoever would pay him in the manner common at that time, and was actually in the imperial army which sacked Rome in 1527. He appears to have been chiefly conspicuous for having all a soldier's vices of the period; he was a careless spendthrift and a persistent gambler. The chief consolation he gave to his wife was that he was seldom at home.

When Camillus came into the world, he brought only anxiety to his mother. He was the only child that survived his infancy; even before his birth she had a dream which she could only interpret as portending misfortune. Her husband gave her no help, and she had the burden of bringing up her boy as best she could, with a sorry example before him. As for Camillus, from the first he showed only signs of taking after his father. As a child he was lank and ungainly, unusually tall for his years, in appearance anything but attractive, lazy by nature and hating to be taught. He had a violent temper and an obstinate self-will, which were not improved by the fact that his mother feared him, and for peace sake allowed him his own way so far as she was able. He was only twelve years of age when she died; what with her reckless husband, and what with her wayward son, who had learned thus early to pay no heed to her, life was too much for her, and she was taken away.

For a time after her death Camillus was placed under the care of relatives, who took little interest in him; his character was not such as to win sympathy, and he was allowed to drift very much as he chose. He was sent to school, but he detested it. When he ought to have been learning he did little but dream of his father's adventures, and longed for the day when he would be grown-up enough to run away and join him; when he was out of school he found low companions for play-mates, and very early became addicted to gambling. One only thing could be said for him. In spite of his waywardness he learned from his mother a deep respect for religion. He believed in prayer, though he seldom prayed; in the sacraments, though he seldom received them; in later years we shall see how this pulled him through many a crisis, and in the end was his saving.

At length the day of liberation came. Being so tall, and having early learned to swagger as a full-grown man, he could easily pass as being much older than he was; when he was barely seventeen he shut up his books, joined his father in a foreign camp, and enlisted as a soldier. There he allowed himself to live as he would; before he was nine-teen he had learned everything a wicked youth could learn, and made free use of his knowledge. Under his father's tuition, in particular, he became an expert gambler; from that time onward the two together, father and son, were the center of gambling wherever they went. In fact they made gambling a profession.

There was plenty of fighting in those days, and soldiers of fortune had little difficulty in finding occupation; when their funds had run out, and idling had become a burden, Camillus and his father had only to offer their services to any general who was in need of men, and because of their previous experience they were easily accepted. Thus it was that they found themselves in all sorts of camps, sometimes fighting with friends, sometimes with enemies; an authority seems to say that at one time they were found even on the side of the Turks. Fighting to them was fighting, the cause was no affair of theirs. So long as they were paid their hire, and enjoyed the wild life they desired, the rest mattered little to them.

But this kind of existence could not go on for ever. Even among the rough soldiers of their time Camillus and his father were too great a disturbance in the camp, and once at least were turned out. Their gambling, aggravated by their own violent temper, led to quarrels; gambling and quarreling produced only insubordination. They took to the road, wandering from hamlet to hamlet, earning what they could by their cards. One day, as they were traveling together on foot with a view to joining the army in Venice which was being raised to fight the Turks, both of them fell ill on the road. But the father was the worse of the two; and Camillus had perforce to put up with his own sickness as best he could while he found a place where his father could be cared for. Alas! it was too late. His father's illness was too far advanced, his worn-out body had no resistance left. Camillus' only consolation was —for in spite of the life he was leading it was to him a strange and abiding consolation—that on his deathbed the old man broke down in sorrow for his past, received the last sacraments with true fervour, and died an evidently penitent man. Thus for the first time the faith he had inherited from his mother served Camillus in good stead.

Left alone in the world, and with this last scene stamped indelibly upon his memory, Camillus began to reflect. He was reduced by his gambling habit to utter destitution of both body and soul; death might overtake him at any time, as it had overtaken his father, and there might be no one to help him in his need. He would mend his ways; he would escape from all further temptation by hiding himself in a monastery, if a monastery could be induced to accept him; there and then he took a vow to become a Franciscan. He remembered that he had a Franciscan uncle somewhere in Aquila; he would begin with him. As soon as he was well enough he tramped off, came to his uncle's door, told him his tale, and asked that he might be admitted into the Order. His uncle received him kindly and listened to his story, but was not easily convinced. Vocations did not come so easily as that: Camillus would need further trial that his constancy might be proved. Besides, at the moment he was in no fit state to enter on religious life. Not only was he worn in body, but he had a running wound above his ankle, which had started long ago with a mere nothing, but had obstinately refused to be healed. The Franciscans were kind, but they could not think of receiving Camillus as a postulant, and he was once more sent adrift.

And he did drift; first to old boon companions, with whom he took up again his gambling habits; then, since the running sore in his leg became a nuisance to others, he began to wander alone from place to place, scarcely knowing how he lived. It was indeed a long and trying probation for one who was to become the apostle of the derelict and dying. At length he found his way to Rome; and here the thought occurred to him that if he could gain admission to some hospital the wound in his leg might be tended and cured. He applied at the hospital of S. Giacomo; as he had no money with which to pay for a bed, he offered himself as a servant in the place, asking in return that his running sore might be treated. It is well to remember that at this time, since the Franciscans had rejected him, his chief ambition was to be cured that he might once more return to the life of a soldier.

On the conditions he proposed he was received and given a trial. At first all seemed to go well. Camillus was in earnest, and meant to do his best; away from his old surroundings the better side of Camillus appeared. He went about his work with a will, sweeping corridors, cleaning bandages, performing all the most menial duties of the place, for he was fit for nothing else. The doctors on their part did theirs, attending his wound, and giving him hope of a permanent cure; under this *régime* one might have trusted that a change had come in his life at last. But unfortunately for him, in spite of the work allotted to him, he had many idle hours on his hands; and there were never wanting other idle servants about him with whom he was able to spend them. In spite of all his good intentions his old passion for gambling returned and he could not resist. He secured a pack of cards, and to while away the time he taught his games to his companions. But soon the authorities began to notice that something was going wrong in the servants' quarters. The men were less ready at their work; they were dissatisfied among themselves; quarreling became more common, for with the return of the gambling habit Camillus' ill-temper returned in its wake. A search was made of his room; the tell-tale cards were found hidden in Camillus' bed. Without more ado he was pushed into the street, his leg still unhealed, and without a coin in his pocket.

So for a second time Camillus' efforts to mend his ways came to nothing. He became despondent; his evil habits had the better of him and he seemed unable to control them; he would go back to soldiering again and take his chance. Hence the next we hear of him is once more in the armies of Venice; he fought in those ranks against the Turks, while he was still only nineteen years of age. He continued there for two years, fighting by land and sea. Still even here his evil genius pursued him. He distinguished himself, it is said, on the battlefield, but in camp once more got himself into trouble. On one occasion, at Zara, a gambling quarrel led to a challenge; a duel was arranged between himself and another soldier, and only the interference of the sergeant of his company prevented it. In the end good enough soldier as he was, his seniors seem to have grown tired of him and he was dismissed.

But dismissal did not cool Camillus' fighting spirit. Since Venice would not have him any longer, he went and joined the army of Spain. Later on, in 1574, he is found in a company of adventurers, under one Fabio; its chief attraction for Camillus was that every man in it was addicted to gambling. In this company he fought in North Africa and elsewhere; at last, on their way to Naples from Palermo, their galleys were so tossed about by a storm that they were given up for lost, and they finally landed with nothing but the clothes on their backs and their weapons of war. The company had to be disbanded, and once again Camillus was a homeless tramp. He went straight to the gambling dens which he knew well. There he staked all he had—his sword, his gun, his powder flasks, his soldier's coat, and he lost them all; he was thankful that at least he had his shirt on his back, for even that, on a former occasion in that same place, he had staked and lost, and had been forced to part with in public.

He now sank lower than ever; what was worse, he found a companion in his misery. The two formed a sort of partnership. Gambling from town to town became their trade, with begging to make up when they had lost everything. Worst of all, Camillus in a kind of hopeless despair seemed to have no will left; he went wherever and did whatever his evil comrade directed him to go and to do. They had a vague idea that they would travel about and see the world; if fighting came their way, they would join up again as they had done before; this was Camillus' condition in 1574, when he was twenty-four years of age. Just then, if one had searched all the dens of Italy, it might have been difficult to find a more hopeless case than that of Camillus de Lellis.

And yet just then the change came. The two tramps had come to Manfredonia. One morning they were begging, with others of their kind, standing on the steps outside a church. It chanced that among the passers-by was a man of wealth, well knownfor his charitable works. He noticed the tall, soldier-like youth among the beggars. He spoke to him, expressed his surprise that one such as he should be begging his bread among cripples and other helpless creatures, and told him that he ought to work. Camillus made the usual excuses; he said that he was a disbanded soldier and that now no one would employ him. The rich man took him at his word. At the time he was building a monastery outside the town; he gave Camillus no money, but sent him with a note of instruction that he should be given employment on the building.

Camillus accepted the offer, and made up his mind to try; but first he must take leave of his old companion and dissolve their partnership. His comrade, when he heard his announcement, could not but burst into laughter at this sudden conversion. He mocked at Camillus, so quickly turned pious; he showed him the liberty he was throwing away. He sneered at the idea that Camillus would ever persevere; he warned him that the old craving would come back again and he would give way. He would gamble with the other workmen, many of whom would not need to be taught; he would quarrel as he had done before; he would again be dismissed, and would be left more destitute than ever. Besides, the work offered him was only a trap. Under such management he would be watched everywhere; he would be always under restraint; he might as well go to prison. How much better would it be for them both to get out of Manfredonia and look for work elsewhere! Then they could do as much or as little as they liked, and when they were tired of it could go out once more on the road.

At first Camillus listened to his tempter and yielded. It was true he could not trust himself; it was also true that he could not easily surrender the free life he had been living. He turned aside, and went down the street with his companion, following him blindly as he had done before. They left Manfredonia and made for the next town, more than twelve miles away. But on the road there came to Camillus a great grace. He had felt the goodwill of the man who had offered him work; thought of the Franciscan monastery brought back to him memories of his early efforts to amend, five or six years before; it seemed to him that here was an opportunity which should not be missed, and which might never occur again. With a mighty effort, the greatest he ever made in all his life, he shook himself free. To the surprise of his companion he suddenly turned round, and began to run back to Manfredonia as fast as his legs would carry him. Next morning he found himself enrolled among the laborers on the monastery building.

Still it was no easy task. As might have been expected from one with a past like that of Camillus, he found hard work anything but a trifle. He hated the drudgery; moreover there came upon him the consciousness that he was born for something better. There followed dreams of the life he had lived. With all its squalor and misery at least it had been free; however low he had sunk he had not starved; and there had come occasions when he had had a good time. Then his old companion discovered his whereabouts, and would come around the place. He would taunt Camillus with his slave's life, would contrast his own freedom as he went to and fro at his pleasure, would provoke in him the temptation to gamble which Camillus could scarcely resist. And last there was the wound in his leg. The more he labored the worse it troubled him; the particular task that was assigned to him only tended to aggravate the pain.

Nevertheless Camillus labored on. The skilled work of the builder was beyond him, but there were other employments to keep him always occupied. He drove the donkeys that carried the stones for the building in panniers on their backs; he took the messages into the town; he brought the other laborers their food and drink. Curious neighbors could not but observe this tall youth in rags with that about him which showed that he had seen better days, but he took no heed. The only remaining sign of his former life was the soldier's belt he still wore; the children in the street were quick to notice this and made fun of the trooper turned donkey-driver. Camillus was stung by these trifles; he could endure many things, but could not endure to be ridiculed. Still he held on; whatever happened he must keep to his post; that was almost all his ambition for the present, and his many past failures had taught him where he must be on his guard if he would succeed. If he would check his gambling propensity he must keep to himself and away from danger; if he would conquer his habit of idle dreaming he must be always occupied; if he would subdue his temper he must submit to whatever was put upon him; if he would suppress the multitudinous temptations that surged within him, he must make himself work and work. He could look back afterward and recognize that those months spent as a driver of donkeys were the turning point of his life.

It was a humble beginning, solitary, drab, without sensation of any kind; it had not even the dramatic climax of a sudden great conversion like that of Augustine and others. Nevertheless, it was the beginning of a saint. Camillus worked on, and soon two things followed. He began to have more confidence in himself, and he began to win the good opinion of others; with the first came an aspiration to rise to better things, with the latter the means to attain them. We are explicitly told that when first he undertook the work at the building his only ambition was to get through the winter, and to earn a few crowns with which to start life again in the spring; after all, even that was something when we consider what he had been immediately before. But he had no intention, and even feared, to go further. When some Capuchins, for whom the monastery was being built, offered him some of their cloth to replace his rags he refused it; he was afraid lest to accept it might lead to other things, perhaps to his becoming a friar. But before the winter was over all this had changed. One day, as he was driving his donkeys back from the town, he received the reward of his perseverance. He seemed to see himself, and all the life he had hitherto lived, in an entirely new light. The memory of the vow he had made long ago came back to him, and he began to ask himself whether his present occupation was not an opportunity given to him to fulfill it. The thought sank deeper; he remembered how once he had hoped that this might be an escape from his miserable life. He spoke of it to one of the friars, and he was encouraged. Encouragement revived desire and soon he was at the superior's feet, asking that he might be received.

In this way Camillus gained admission into a Franciscan monastery. But his stay did not last long. No sooner had he begun his novitiate than the wound above his ankle began to grow worse. He was told that he must go; with this impediment upon him he could not be received; but for his consolation he was given the assurance that so soon as ever his running sore was healed he would be taken back. Armed with this promise Camillus set to work in earnest; he would begin again where he had begun before and failed, but he would not fail again. He would go to Rome, to the hospital of S. Giacomo, where he had received so much benefit before both for body and for soul, but from which he had been so ignominiously, and so deservedly expelled. He would ask to be given another chance, to be taken in on the same terms as formerly. For almost a year he had kept away from gambling; he had learned to work as he had never worked in all his life; the Franciscan fathers would give him a good character; he himself would let the authorities see that they might trust him; perhaps they would let him try again.

Camillus came to Rome, and all seemed to go well; it was in 1575,

a holy year. He was given another trial at S. Giacomo, and this time
there were no complaints. Camillus had heard of St. Philip Neri, of
his wonderful power in supporting sinners; he made himself known
to him, and St. Philip took him in charge. Under his wise guidance
Camillus kept steady; he worked at the hospital for four years as a
menial servant, after which it appeared that the wound in his leg was
healed. Then once more he wished to return to the Capuchins. St.
Philip tried to dissuade him, but he would not listen. He had made a
vow; the Capuchins had promised that when his leg was healed they
would have him back and he would go. But scarcely had he entered
than the trouble began again; the wound broke out afresh and he was
told to depart, this time with the emphatic injunction that he must not
hope to try any more. Thus for the third occasion Camillus' ambition
to become a friar was frustrated. He tried again the next year, with
the Observantines of Ara Coeli, and was again refused only then did
he give up all hope altogether.

"God bless you, Camillus," was St. Philip Neri's welcome when he
returned, "did I not tell you?"

Camillus was thirty years of age when he made his Franciscan experiment. For the last five years he had served faithfully at S. Giacomo; therefore, when he had failed at the monastery he was gladly
taken back. More than that, he was appointed superintendent of the
servants, and that in those days included the nurses, who were all men.
Now it was that the real Camillus began to appear. Whether it was his
Franciscan experience which had given him new ideals, or whether it
was St. Philip who was training him to better things, from this moment Camillus became a new man. He had already learned the value of
unceasing work as a cure to his many temptations; now he discovered
that the more he gave himself to helping others the happier man he
became. He began to love the patients in the hospital, not merely to
serve them; and the more he loved them the more he was troubled by
the treatment they received, even in so comparatively well-regulated
a hospital as S. Giacomo. One evening, as he stood in the middle of
a ward, the thought occurred to him that good nursing depended on
love; that the more it was independent of mere wages the better it
would be; that if he could gather men about him who would nurse
for love, and would leave the wages to look after themselves, then he
might hope to raise nursing to the standard he desired.

With this object in his mind Camillus carefully selected five men from among his fellow servants in the hospital. He told them of his ideal, and of the way he hoped to attain it; the men rose to his suggestion, and agreed to throw in their lot with Camillus, pooling all their earnings, and living as much as possible together. But soon it was found this did not work; living in a public hospital, part of a general staff, they could not keep separate from the rest. If they wished to carry out their intention to the full they must have a home of their own.

Meanwhile another thought had come to Camillus. He had noticed that not only the servants often failed in their duty to the sick, but the priests failed as well; if he would have his company of nurses equal to his ambition, then it must include priests also. He would become one himself; illiterate as he was he set to work. First he found a chaplain of the hospital who undertook to teach him Latin during his leisure hours; later, since by this means he made slow progress he entered himself as a student at the Roman College, taught by the Jesuit fathers; and, at the age of thirty-two this lank figure of over six feet was henceforth to be seen among the little boys learning the elements of grammar. Naturally the boys were amused; they nicknamed Camillus the "Late Arrival", and would offer him their services to help him in his lessons. But Camillus persevered, and in 1584, when he was thirty-four years of age, he had the consolation of being ordained.

Now at last it may be said that the life of Camillus really began. He took a house by the Tiber, in the lowest and most pestilential part of the city, and there set about the service of the sick wherever he might find them. One incident here is worthy of mention; it is said to be the only occasion when St. Philip Neri made a mistake in the diagnosis of anyone entrusted to his spiritual care. So long as Camillus was safe at his work in the hospital of S. Giacomo, St. Philip was happy about him; when he heard that he had left the place, and had taken up his abode in the lowest quarters of the town, he was not a little distressed. Knowing Camillus' past, and his propensity for gambling, he was much afraid that his new surroundings would only revive the old temptation. Moreover, he was convinced that this new departure was only another mark of that restless and obstinate nature which had already made his penitent seek in vain for admission among the Franciscans. He spoke sharply to Camillus; he advised him, for his own security, not to give up the work he was doing at S. Giacomo; if he disobeyed, Philip would be compelled to give him up. But Camillus held firm to his project; he knew he had found his true vocation and he would not yield, even though he loved St. Philip as more than a father; and from that moment, for a period at least, Philip Neri and Camillus de Lellis parted company. It is one more instance of the difference that can come even between the most charitable, and the most understanding of saints.

It is not our object to speak of the wonderful Order, the Brothers of a Happy Death, which grew out of these humble beginnings; it is more to our purpose to watch how the mind of Camillus himself seemed steadily to expand, and how to each new light he responded without any reserve. At first he had the idea of founding an institution of hospital nurses; soon he realized that the sick outside hospitals were in far more need of good nursing than those within, and at once he made them the object of his special care. Next, in a time of pestilence, he saw how the stricken were, almost of necessity, neglected and allowed to die as they might; he bound himself and his followers by vow to visit pestilential areas whenever there was need, and in fulfillment of that vow numbers of his disciples gave their lives. Following on this was his care of those actually dying. When the end was certain, many, especially among the poor, were left to their fate and nothing more was done for them; Camillus made the comfort and help of the dying so much his special object of charity that from that work alone his order ultimately took its name.

So did his charity expand, and the memory of his own early days spurred him on, some would say, even to extravagance. No case was too abandoned for him to help; none too wicked for Camillus to put it away. Once, in 1590, in a time of famine and distress in the city, when, besides, the winter was exceptionally severe, Camillus was distributing clothes to the poor in his courtyard. Two of the recipients, as soon as they had the clothes in their hands, immediately gambled them away or sold them, and then ran off lest Camillus might discover what they had done. But Camillus was too quick for them; his old days told him why they had run away, and he sympathized. He followed after them and caught them up; then he brought them back and clothed them again as if nothing had happened. Naturally his friends remonstrated. They thought Camillus had not noticed what the rascals had done, and told him, bidding him leave them to their fate. But Camillus did not change.

"What, my brothers," he replied, "do you see nothing but the rags of these poor creatures? And do you see nothing beneath the rags but the poor creatures themselves? St. Gregory gave to a man in rags, but the man was Jesus Christ himself."

This story is only one of many. Of all the great apostles of charity perhaps there is none of whom so many stories are told of extreme generosity to the poorest of the poor. And we in modern times have reason to preserve the memory of Camillus, for we owe him two great debts. In the first place he may be said to be the founder of the modern nursing spirit; in the second place, without any doubt, we are indebted to him for the institution of the Red Cross. When the Order which he founded was formally approved by the Pope, that its members might be distinguished from other regulars, Camillus asked that they might be permitted to wear a red cross on their cassock and mantle. By an apostolic brief, dated June 26, 1586, the permission was granted; and three days later, on the Feast of Saints Peter and Paul, Camillus with a few of his followers came to St. Peter's, each wearing the red cross, and there dedicated themselves and their work to God for all time.

But the charity of Camillus was not confined only to the sick and dying; it spread out to every phase of wretched humanity, no matter where he found it. As he grew older he seemed to recall with greater vividness the miseries of his early days; often enough, when his companions or others ventured to protest against what seemed to them excess, he would only answer that he himself had once been in the same or greater need, and would go on as before. When he traveled, he invariably filled his purse with small coins, to be given to beggars on the way; sometimes, for the same purpose, he would have bags of bread tied to his saddle. He would imitate literally the Samaritan in the Gospel; if he found a sufferer on the road, he would take him to the nearest inn, have him cared for, and leave behind money for his maintenance while he stayed. Indeed, this constant habit of paying for the needs of others whom he met anywhere, and who seemed in any way poorer than himself, was often a source of no small embarrassment to those who traveled with him. Camillus never seemed to care; he was always giving; when his stock ran out he would keep an account of the needs of others and would send them shoes, and clothes, and the like as soon as he was able. Not even the poverty of his own house would stop him; once when a father-prefect had forbidden the distribution of bread at the gate, because there was not enough for the community, Camillus bade him revoke his order.

"Did you sow and reap this bread?" he asked him. "I tell you, that if you will not do good to the poor, God will not do good to you; in the hour of your death it shall be measured out to you with the same measure with which you have measured out to such as these."

And again, when his disciples were afraid of his seemingly reckless giving, he said to them:

"Trust in God, O cowards, and cast your bread into the river of life; soon you shall find it in the ocean of eternity."

Or when at last they suggested that it was enough to help those who came to them, he said:

"If no poor could be found in the world, men ought to go in search of them, and dig them up from underground to do them good, and to be merciful to them."

Indeed, if one may distinguish the charity of Camillus from that of any hero of his class it was specially this: he was for ever "digging out the poor from underground to do them good". No one knew the slums or the ghetto of Rome better than Camillus; and all whom he found there, Christians or Jews or Turks, were all the same to him. He frequented the prisons; he would shave and wash the wretched convicts, and bade his companions do the same; he had special care of those condemned to death. Even the undiscovered poor did not escape him; he would inquire from neighbors whether they knew of widows or children in straitened circumstances, and when he found them, those widows and children would find parcels of money and clothes coming to them from they knew not where.

Lastly we must mention his care of the very animals. He once found a newborn lamb lying in a ditch, apparently forgotten by the shepherds. He got off his horse, picked up the lamb and carried it in his cloak to the nearest sheepfold, where he gave it to those who would look after it. Another time he came across a dog with a broken leg. He cared for it and fed it regularly; when he had to leave the place he asked others to continue to look after it.

"I, too, have had a bad leg," he said; "and I know the misery of not being able to walk. This is a creature of God, and a faithful creature, too. If I am as faithful to my master as a dog is to his, I shall do very well."

As we read incidents and sayings like these we seem to see the secret of the sanctity of Camillus; a depth of human sympathy, and virility, and love of life itself, which was at once the cause of his early wanderings and of his later heroism. In all greatness there is a certain disregard of consequences, be it in good or in evil; we say that the greatest mountains cast the deepest shadows. So was it with Camillus. In his early years this disregard led him to choose the life he did; later it would almost seem that it left him without any power to choose for himself at all. But one day, on a sudden, he seemed to awake. He saw something he had not seen before; he felt within himself a power to be and do which was not his own. Up to that time he had often tried and failed; from that moment he failed no more. He made many mistakes; for years he was compelled to grope about; feeling his way, not knowing where he would end, perhaps not altogether caring. Still, during those years of groping it is clear that his willpower was being strengthened every day. It is not a little significant that whereas at the age of twenty-three he had not the will to resist a fellow tramp, when he was thirty he could hold his own conviction against even a St. Philip Neri.

Once this willpower had been gained the rest of the growth of Camillus is comparatively easy to explain. He was a soldier by profession, for whom life had no surprises, to whom no degree of degradation came as a shock; he had gone through the worst and he knew. But he also knew that however low a man may fall he remains still a man; when he himself had been at his lowest he had never quite lost the memory of better things, nor the vague desire that he might be other than he was. From his own experience he was sure that the most wretched of men was more to be pitied than to be condemned; and if to be pitied, then to be helped if that was possible. With this knowledge, burnt into his soul during ten bitter years, and with the will now developed to act, the hero latent in Camillus began to appear. Nothing could stop him; not the anxious warning of a saint, not the discouragement of religious superiors, not the appeals of seculars who bade him be content with the good he was doing, not his own want of education, which seemed to exclude all possibility of the priesthood, not his naturally passionate nature, signs of which are manifest in him to the end. Like other saints, he began with nothing; as with them, the bread he gave multiplied within his hands; even more than has been the case with most saints, the stream he has set flowing has not been confined within the limits of a religious Order, but has overflowed its banks, and has materially affected the whole of our civilization.

Such has been the working of the grace of God in and through Camillus de Lellis, the trooper, the tramp. He founded his Congregation, and it was approved, in 1586, when he was thirty-six years of age. It was raised to the rank of an Order in 1591, and Camillus was appointed its first General. He held that office till 1607, when he persuaded his brethren, and the ecclesiastical authorities, to allow him to resign. He lived for seven years more, a humble subject in the Order which he himself had founded; and, as is not uncommon in the lives of saints, if we may judge from certain signs, they were not the happiest years of his life. In 1613 it became evident to himself and to his brethren that he could not live much longer, and at his own request he was taken to Rome, that he might die in the Holy City. But his preparation for death was characteristic of his life; so long as he could drag himself about he could not be kept from visiting the hospitals. When he could no longer go out, he still continued to visit the sick in his own house; and when that became impossible, then he set himself to writing many letters, to the many in the world who had helped him with their alms, and to his own brethren, that they might continue the good work. For himself, he did not forget what he had been.

"I beseech you on my knees to pray for me," he said to the General of the Carmelites, who visited him on his deathbed, "for I have been a great sinner, a gambler, and a man of bad life".

As his mind began to wander it always went in the direction of God's mercy; he seemed never to tire of thanking him for all he had done, through the merits of the Precious Blood of Christ. At length the end came. He stretched out his arms in the form of a cross, pronounced again his thanksgiving for the Blood of Christ, and died. It was in the evening of July 14, 1614.

SAINT FRANCIS DE SALES

[1567–1662]

R. H. J. Steuart, S.J.

HE LIFE of St. Francis de Sales, 1567–1662, still within the afterglow (or the penumbra) of the Renaissance, covered a very remarkable period in the Church's history. Luther had been dead twenty-one years and the Counter-Reformation had gathered great strength in the interval, to which St. Francis himself later contributed in no small measure by his amazingly successful missionary excursions into the Savoyan province of Le Chablais. The Council of Trent, which embodied the true principles of reform within the Church, had held its final session four years before he was born, and these principles had been, and were still being practically exhibited and illustrated by the astonishing galaxy of saints that adorned this new era of her history. The lifetime of St. Francis de Sales was contemporaneous with, or at least overlapped at one end or the other, that of nearly a score of the most illustrious figures in the annals of sanctity. St. Pius V, the Dominican Pope, from whose white habit the now established dress of the Supreme Pontiff derives, reigned over the Church for the first five years of the saint's life. St. Charles Borromeo, St. Philip Neri, St. Teresa, St. John of the Cross, St. Francis Borgia, were still living during his early youth, as also were the three boy saints, Stanislaus, Aloysius, and (a little later) John Berchmans. Other contemporaries were St. Vincent de Paul, the three Saints Peter (aptly symbolic name for the day!) Canisius, Claver, and Fourier, St. Jane Frances de Chantal, St. John Francis Regis, and St. Mary Magdalen de Pazzi.

Contemporaries, interesting from a rather different point of view, were Queen Elizabeth of England, and that hardly less enigmatic personage Henri IV of France. St. Francis was a child of four when the Turks were overthrown at Lepanto, and he had just come of age when the Invincible Armada sailed out to defeat and destruction.

His day was like a throwback to the Apostolic Age, a second visible coming of the Holy Spirit. There can be little doubt that this epoch marked a veritably new date in the practice, as distinguished from the doctrine, of the Church—importing something of a condescension to a sanctified humanism, a "vulgarization" (the word is not intended to carry the slightest reproach) for the benefit of the ordinary average Catholic, of a thing hitherto considered as more or less esoteric and altogether exceptional. Of this Gospel St. Francis was the Apostle. Preeminently he showed the way to a readjustment of worldly circumstances with spiritual demands. His doctrine amounted to a synthesis of the sometimes apparently contradictory postulates of the life of perfection, showing that these are reconcilable, and should be reconciled, in any state of life, however far it might seem superficially to diverge from the accepted canons of the science. He said of himself that he was not "a man of extremes": no, but he envisaged nothing less than the best, though it might seem to the casual student of his writings and direction that he was sometimes content with the second-best. No error concerning him could be more fundamental than this. All his aim was to extract the best obtainable (obviously not always the best imaginable) from his penitents. He may, as a shrewd analyst of saintly psychology has hinted, have now and then put just a little too much honey on the lip of the cup that he presented to them: but he was one of those miraculous geniuses who see centuries ahead of their own time, and experience has—proved that the guidance of St. Francis de Sales, devised for the vacillating and bewildered souls of his day, is quite peculiarly adapted to the needs of souls certainly not less bewildered and very much more vacillating, who in our own day have to grapple with problems so different from theirs.

He has been called the chief of the "modern" saints. This means, one supposes, that his type of sanctity was one with which the modern mind, no longer torn between the early violent recoil from pagan mentality and the late partial relapse into that mentality brought about by the Renaissance, finds itself in sympathy, for the outstanding characteristic of his school of holiness was *balance*, in which are involved breadth and moderation and tranquillity. His was the sort of sanctity that attracts admiration but does not frighten, and that seems (surprisingly) to *fit in* with the average human life instead of clashing with it. The average man can see himself in that galley instead of having to regard it as a station demanding a special physical and spiritual constitution,

almost a special order of being. He has been accustomed to think of
the saints as persons so peculiarly privileged, so aided and protected, so
unlike himself in every particular, that by no stretch of his imagination
can he fancy them as objects for his practical imitation. In addition, he
has come to think that a saint who is not a religious, or at least a priest,
is something anomalous. The net result of prepossessions such as these
has been to remove sanctity to an almost inaccessible region, far over
the horizon of the average Christian, and to establish the belief that it
must be a hard, bleak, dreary path that leads to it, for is it not true that
the saint must never take pleasure in anything for its own sake: that
he must find no rest in any creature, nor seek it: that he must disown
all credit for the good that he does, nor even admit to himself that he
has done any good: that the world must be his bitter and unrelenting
enemy wherein he may find no joy nor satisfaction: that the so-called
natural affections must be sterilized into complete impersonality, his
native faculties denied the opportunity of exercise, his body treated as
a thing inherently bad and corruptive?

Persons who think like this do not pause to ask themselves whether,
indeed, such a philosophy of life could stand the test of practice for a
week. One supposes, justifiably perhaps, that the question of practice
does not trouble them. But even as a matter of pure speculation one
wonders how they can square such a theory with the unquestionable
fact that Christ has laid the achievement of holiness upon us as an
obligation: for it is a Commandment, according to him, that we should
love God with the whole of ourselves—mind, heart, soul and strength
—and holiness, to put it in a phrase, *is* no other thing than the love of
God. If they are right, then God has so ordered our life that the one
thing that we are here to do with it is also the very hardest of all the
things that we could do with it—so hard, indeed, that the overwhelming majority of us simply cannot do it.

No doubt it is true that things have been said about the saints, and
perhaps even by the saints, which lend a very colorable authority to
such views. It is indeed the sin of one school of hagiographers that
they have been so constantly at pains to make the lives of the saints
seem as extraordinary and as unusual and difficult as they could—*ipsi
viderint!* It is one thing to live a heroic life and quite another order of
things to be able to give an account of its principles. If they were not
human they were not saints, and if they were human they were liable

to inequality in the power of expression as other human beings are, and were as truly the subjects of differentiation by character, sex, nationality, upbringing, age, social condition, intellectual power and other like circumstances as anyone else. Canonization affords us a guarantee of their doctrinal and moral orthodoxy, but not at all of their analytical or expository ability. We should not pay an equal attention to the ascetical teaching of St. Thomas Aquinas and of Brother Giles. The Curé d'Ars had certain rigorist, not to say Jansenist-like, principles of direction which few would approve today. St. Bernard, on his deathbed, asked pardon of his body for his overharsh treatment of it.

The life and teaching of St. Francis de Sales came as a ray of new light upon the problem. He used to say that the saints are indeed the salt of the earth, but that for that very reason they must be *in* the earth —their life must be capable of being lived among the surroundings and accidents in which the lives of ordinary men are lived—or what profits their savor? For goodness, he insisted, does not do violence to our nature: it does not restrict but expands it: grace, falling upon it, illumines it and brings out its beauty as the light of the sun brings out the beauty of a stained glass window. And this illumination is an all around effect: no more than do the rays of the sun in the example which he gives, does it select some details and leave others unlit.

It is true that in ordinary material (or at least non-spiritual) affairs we can usually attain to excellence in any one direction only at the cost of sacrificing other possibilities of achievement; but it is characteristic of the life of the soul that its perfection has a use for, demands the exercise of, *all* its powers. The only narrowness that he would admit is such as is inseparable from the qualities of firmness, of determination not to compromise, of exclusiveness of aim, which do sometimes involve the refusal or neglect of opportunity: for the use of some of the "creatures" which God has given us for our sanctification is that we should *not* use them—certain common instincts, for instance, otherwise legitimate, which may be lawful and helpful for one and harmful for another, or right and good under one set of circumstances but bad under another.

He would not, however, have anyone think that holiness is a cheap thing: quite otherwise, he once said that sanctity was the greatest of all miracles. But one feels that he had then in his mind the promise of Our Lord that to those who have faith—the *real* things, such as he demanded so rigorously of his Apostles, were it only as small as a mustard seed, a pinpoint—greater miracles of grace than those symbolic material ones which had so astonished them, would be commonplaces: the most mountainous obstacles would be removed and cast into the sea. But he strenuously combated, as a pernicious falsehood, the common persuasion that sanctity is so difficult a thing as to be practically out of the reach of the ordinary Christian, and he insisted that there are no circumstances of human life which need be inimical to its attainment.

For this he was, even in his lifetime, abused and derided. Mr. Worldlyman likes to think that Christian Perfection is an anomalous thing: he would be very uncomfortable if he believed otherwise. The Jansenists were of that cast of thought, and it pleased them to make the way, not of the transgressor alone but of the aspirant no less, a hard one. So that when, thirty-nine years after his death, the Bishop of Geneva was beatified pious people were seriously scandalized; and still more so when, after four more years, he became St. Francis de Sales. He had made it all too easy, they said: almost as if they grudged anyone becoming a saint. He had made holiness—the Love of God mind you!—*too* easy. A contemporary author thought that he had said something very biting when he called the path to holiness, as traced by the Saint, "a pleasant road". And all that St. Francis had said (or done) was to show that it is not strange to love God: that God has not made it frantically difficult to do so: that he has not given us one kind of nature and then made demands upon us which could only be met if we had a totally different one. He had only said that God has made us for himself so that we shall be for ever restless until we rest in him, and that we can rest in him now, if we will, and yet be ourselves.

His method of direction was gentle, as was Christ's: but nevertheless, like him, he made uncompromising demands upon those who submitted to it. We are to learn of Christ meekness, kindliness, and humility of heart: but we are unfit to be his disciples if we do not hate our life, carry our cross, forsake all. Gentleness in this matter is by no means the same thing as softness or weakness: it allows for sensuality and frivolity but it does not condone them, it aims to win rather than to terrify people out of them. If St. Francis de Sales permitted to some of his penitents interests and amusements which another in his place might have condemned as positively incompatible with a devout life, it was not because he imagined that these things were going to sanctify them nor because he thought them the best things for them to do, but because he knew very well that few persons are ready for a sudden "conversion of manners" if that is to be permanent, and that if their desire of perfection, however small at the moment, was genuine, these things would very soon become distasteful and be abandoned without any further urging from him. For above all he required genuineness and sincerity, and where he saw that these were lacking he limited any further dealing with such a soul (if he could not disembarrass himself of the charge altogether) to preserving it at least from total loss. But where he discerned the marks of a true vocation to perfection, he became an exacting guide. He taught incessant watchfulness over one's faults and evil tendencies, even the smallest, and unremitting effort to practice the Christian virtues in a high degree. But though he would never minimize or economize in this matter, neither did he favor violence over it. Violence too often defeats itself since it bears in itself the seeds of impermanence: and he forever preached tranquility, patience with self, cheerfulness, even in the midst of the most resolute struggle. All was to be subordinated to *fidelity*. But fidelity is nothing if it costs nothing, and it would cost nothing if it did not imply the likelihood of many revulsions of feeling, many failures and backslidings, many doubts and fears and defeats. Holiness, he insisted again and again, is a matter of the will: and it is consummated not necessarily in achievement but essentially in perseverance. And it is a matter of love, not of fear. It comes, normally, little by little as real love comes, invading the soul not (except in certain very special cases) as by some sudden and tremendous illumination but gradually, peacefully, though irresistibly, as daylight steals into the sky at dawn.

Holiness, in his conception of it, should be an all-around quality without abruptness or eccentricity: it should not involve the suppression in us of anything that is not in itself bad, for the likeness to God which is its essence must be incomplete in the proportion that it does not extend to the whole of us. So we must be truthful to ourselves, about ourselves, and we shall lose as much by not seeing the good that really is in us as by fancying that we see good that is not there at all. It is as right and due that we should thank God for the virtue that his grace has established in us as that we should ask his forgiveness for our sinfulness that hinders his grace. It is no derogation from the truth of this statement to recognize that, in point of fact, the nearer we draw to God the less will we think of either, for this indicates no more than that there is growing within us the realization that all our goodness is his and that our very wretchedness makes us the fitter objects of his mercy and power.

St. Francis de Sales did not confuse the Counsels with the Precepts: he was mindful of Our Lord's words to the young Ruler, "If thou *wilt* be perfect". But he let it be known that his manner of direction would be of little service to one who having faced the issue should voluntarily choose the lower level.

SAINT VINCENT DE PAUL

[*1580-1660*]

C. C. Martindale, S.J.

T THE BACK of all modern philanthropy—work for children, the sick, prisoners—stands St. Vincent de Paul. He was living while Shakespeare lived: Milton outlived him. I could narrate the miserable history of France contemporary with him, but I need not. It was a land in which armies were sweeping to and fro, with their train of fire, murder, rape. A land where rapacious nobles intrigued against the king, and one another. A land where St. Francis de Sales and St. Jeanne de Chantal lived, and tried to do, but unsuccessfully, what Vincent succeeded in.

His parents were small farmers, in southwest France. They kept no servant. Their son started as a shepherd. Intelligent, but visibly no use as a farmer, Vincent was put to school, his parents pinching to send him there. He became a "private tutor" and a snob on the strength of it. He was ashamed of his shabby father, who limped. He studied in Spain, then for seven years at Toulouse; he was ordained and hoped for a bishopric from his patrons. Then, returning home by sea, he was captured by Turkish pirates and taken to Tunis.

Here, having (like other slaves) been paraded round the town, thumped in the ribs, examined as to teeth, made to run and wrestle, he was sold first to a fisherman and then to an aged alchemist, man of Science in those days. This man, sent for by the Sultan, and dying of home-sickness on the way, bequeathed Vincent to a nephew, who resold him to an apostate Christian from Nice. One of this man's three wives was touched by Vincent's piety, and in the long run they all escaped to France. Here a Cardinal Vice-Legate, Montorio, took a fancy to Vincent—partly because of the queer arts he had learned in Africa; he was a ventriloquist and could make a skull "talk"—and finally took him to Rome and in 1609 sent him home on a diplomatic mission to Henry IV of France, who was trying to unite all Europe against Austria and Spain. What this mission was Vincent never revealed; and such was the change in him, that he sought no personal remuneration or recognition from it.

He lived, at first, in extreme poverty in Paris; he was appointed almoner by the ex-queen Margaret de Valois; he met and lived with M. de Bérulle, the Oratorian; he was made parish-priest of the destitute parish called Clichy. He therefore learned by experience what royalty, what Paris, what the fields, what life in community, were; and abruptly, he was sent to be tutor to the "young devils" (as their aunt described them), sons of the overwhelming nobleman, Philippe Emmanuel de Gondi, Comte de Joigny, General of the Galleys.

In that palace, Vincent lived as austerely as a monk. He ended by dominating, if not the children, at least their parents. He persuaded—a true miracle—the Lord to renounce a duel; the Lady, to visit the sick. Appalled at becoming a "personage", Vincent literally fled to a very modest parish: here, during the plague, he made some astonishing conversions among nobles, and perceived that—such was their generosity—charity needed some organization. He wrote a simple Rule; and this, 1617, is the true origin of the Sisters of Charity and of much besides. A Community of Priests was foreseen, who should work in villages, seek no preferment, and live from a common purse. But the Gondis insisted that Vincent should come back and live with them. However, almost at once, Mme. de Gondi died; and the Count became—can you credit it?—himself an Oratorian. Vincent was free to begin his life's work; but he was fifty years old!

I have to leave to one side an extraordinary episode. Gondi had been General of Galleys, which were manned by criminals chained to their thwarts and stripped to the waist in order to be flogged. Such vessels, in warfare, caught fire, blew up, or were sunk. They were a hell. Vincent, who had become intimate with the filth, reek and wickedness of Paris prisons, equipped a hospital whither the most infectious diseases might be carried, was appointed chaplain-general to the galleys in 1619. Did he learn his business from within, by himself becoming for a while a galley slave? It is not certain; but I think he did. I now mention a few of the other things he did, disregarding mere dates. He was sure that the formation of priests was essential. I think that the country clergy of France had simply despaired. The peasantry were "black animals" who lived by grubbing on roots, while armies swept to and fro, and a few great lords lived in crass luxury. The dumb misery of the countryside at the one end; pulpit "oratory" and tyranny at the other. Vincent created his Lazarists, priests so called because at first they lived in a monastery dedicated to St. Lazarus. Then he remembered towns. He felt he had deserted the thousands of miserable paupers within the walls of cities. Then he remembered his own enslavement in Tunis— at least forty thousand Christian slaves existed in Northern Africa— some of them, little English boys, carried off by pirates. Not till 1830 did Algerian pirates cease from off the seas, nor the African sun and African vice cease to tempt Europeans to crime and to apostasy. Then his priests began to go northward—to Ireland: Cashel and Limerick. To Scotland, and the Hebrides. Then to Poland; then to the "White Man's Grave", Madagascar. Egypt, Brazil, China beckoned to him.

But in the Catholic Church there is no such thing as priest versus laity. He resolved to animate the laity too with the will to serve for Christ's sake. Women, who had wished to dedicate their lives to God, had been forced, by tradition and popular opinion, to do so within closed convents. Vincent brought them out of their enclosure, and created both those Sisters of Charity (whose wide white caps are bound to be familiar to all of you who know the world at all), and those "Ladies of Charity" who, without becoming Sisters, devote their lives so far as possible to the service of the needy.

Vincent found that by 1650 there were forty thousand completely destitute persons in Paris out of a population of five hundred thousand. Four out of every fifty persons were completely destitute. He began with the children, whom their frantic parents cast out into institutions of which it is not too much to say that they became the homes of dreadful cruelty, if not wholesale massacre. He, in his land, was the first to look after little children. And he knew each baby by its name. In those days, when to venture alone outside the house was ruin to reputation, he told his nuns that they must know no convent but the sickroom, no cloister but the street. And—would you believe it?—Court-ladies, who, appalled by the insincerity, the sham, of fashionable life, would else have buried themselves in cells, no less than the heavier-witted women of the rich but inelegant classes, flocked to his call. I have no room to speak of his work for the insane: his house at St. Lazare (of which you may know the name because of a big Paris station that still bears it) was filled with those who were only not mentally but morally defective.

Nor have I room to speak of his connection with the secular, political, and royal history of France. He hated those duties: still, when Louis XIII required to die in Vincent's arms, the Saint was there. Enough to say that even during the ghastly siege of Paris, in the very Court there existed his group of devoted women, working for the relief of those whom the Court considered rebels. Ladies lavished their jewels upon his work; tradesmen poured out their wares gratis upon him. But by now he was very old, and very tired. Sleepiness invaded him—he said that the brother was ahead of the sister—sleep had anticipated death. His legs swelled; he sat all day in an armchair at his enormous correspondence. Then they grew ulcerated; he was nailed to his bed, and could raise himself only by a cord from a hook in the ceiling. All his old friends and associates were dying; he knew that he, too, would very soon follow them; but never did the smile fade from his clean cut lips, nor his mind (as his letters prove) waver. They whispered sentences from the Scriptures to him: he loved to answer "Paratum!" ("Ready"). (I have asked myself whether Thackeray, when he wrote Colonel Newcome's "Adsum", "Here, sir!" had been reading of St. Vincent.) Finally he said: "I believe", and then, "I trust", and at four in the morning of September 27, 1660, seated in his armchair, he died, perfectly serene, at the precise hour at which for so many years, he had risen to pray.

Vincent began, if you remember, with the qualities of a peasant rather ashamed of his estate and determined to better himself. Not *perfectly* scrupulous about money; looking forward to rank—even ecclesiastical; showing unmistakable signs of what he himself called his "dried up, caustic temper", and victim of "black and boiling moods". I think it was his experience of slavery that supplied his drastic lessoning—that turned him into a man utterly detached from money, undazzled by even royal rank; and won somehow for him by a kind of universal instinct the title of "le bon M. Vincent"—untranslatable word, not merely "good", but implying a lovableness in the goodness—no condescension in the kindness—almost, our *dear* St. Vincent. But in that kindness was no softness: his innumerable letters are shrewd, vivacious, affectionate, but most uncompromising: from those who proposed to join him and to work with him, he demanded *all*. Alas! it is so easy to serve Christ by fits and starts, when in the mood, in some ways only, with reserves.

Once more, the secret of the Saints is, that they judge life and work upon the scale of Christ. Christ *never* deserts; gives himself no holidays; keeps nothing back at all. Hence, maybe, Vincent's courage. His portraits show him with almost clumsy features, yet with eyes as wistful as they are humorous, and you would probably not guess from them his ardor, indeed, his audacities. Yet this man, willing to wait so very very long for the time *really* to work, was wanting to sanctify *all* priests; serve all hospitals and prisons; save all little children—and so, by uncloistering his nuns, he has indeed come to stand at the back of those millions of devoted women who all over the world and ever since have been doing their part of the work that was and is so needed; and it is hardly too much to say that this is the man who is inspirer of all such women's work in our modern world; and it was his name that was so spontaneously and immediately chosen by Ozanam, whom I hope to mention on May 1, when he, in his turn, inaugurated those Conferences which set laymen everywhere at the service of the disinherited by life; and for me it is really like going home when, from time to time, I visit that great Vincentian house that stands on the steep slopes and beneath the smoky skies of Sheffield.

SAINT PETER CLAVER

[1581–1654]

C. C. Martindale, S.J.

HEN SPEAKING of St. Francis Xavier, I was so fascinated by the man as to say but little of his work, or rather, of the people he worked for. Peter Claver also was a missionary; but this time I shall want to say almost more about the mission than the man.

Never believe that the Saints are somehow born so, born the finished product, or at any rate doomed inevitably to become what they do become. How wavering and unsure were the beginnings of this man! Son of impoverished gentlefolk, he was sent for education to the Jesuit college at Barcelona. Like many an impressionable lad, he began to feel attracted to the sort of life his masters were leading: but he vacillated; whether to ask to join the Jesuits or not, he could not decide. Finally he did join them; and again hesitated—was he, after all, meant for something more aloof from external work? more of a monastery? He, like Xavier, met the right man at the right time—not, in this case, an overwhelming spiritual genius like Ignatius, but an old laybrother Alonzo Rodriguez, porter in the College of Majorca whither Peter was sent for his philosophical studies. This old ex-business-man, whose wife and children all had died, had himself lost not one atom of his old power of shrewdly estimating character, nor any of his Spanish flame. He kept talking to the young student, whom his very studies intimidated, of the heroic life as spent in the far missions of the West Indies, and Peter Claver asked to be sent there. His request was granted, but he was told he had better be ordained before he went there. Frightened at the whole idea of the dedicated life, frightened—after embracing it—by the thought of vowing himself to it, disheartened by his very training once he had taken it up, he now shuddered at the irrevocability of ordination. He left Seville, in 1610, not yet a priest.

Even in America—his career was fluctuant, he ceased to want to be a priest and asked to become a laybrother; but here, too, he met the necessary man—Fr. de Sandoval, an amazing character whose work lay entirely among the slave population there. Somehow companionship with Sandoval worked the miracle; Claver was ordained; and almost abruptly his heroic career, destined to last into his old age, began.

These "negroes" were slaves. The history of slavery as such has not always been so very terrible. That of the slave trade always has. Or rather, it became so, the moment competition entered into it. England cannot be exempted from blame for these horrors. The moment cheap imported labor became desirable countries vied with one another to obtain the most lucrative contracts: the bodies of men became sources of revenue to would-be monopolists who bought cheap and sold dear. As from 1713, England was the chief holder. The time came when Newport in America was called "another Liverpool". Bristol was no better: not till 1826 did the British colony of Jamaica permit free right to marry to those slaves of whom their masters spoke as "black cattle", asking whether an orangutang were not a sufficiently good mate for a black woman.

In Claver's time, Portugal had the contracts. Slaves, victims at the outset of bloodshed and rape, were packed in bundles of six, necks and ankles chained together, wedged (wrote Sandoval) under decks where neither sun nor moon could penetrate, in a stench into which no white officer could put his head for fear of fainting. Maize and water was their food, once in twenty-four hours. About a third died on board; out of one cargo of five hundred, one hundred and twenty died in a night. A *duty* on such natives as died after landing was sheer incitement to kill off those who arrived living but *likely* to die. Yet so colossal were the profits, that even so it was worth keeping up the trade. Arrive they did, starving, covered with sores, more than half crazed eating dirt to hasten their end, so frantically homesick were they; and turned out into a yard filled with such a reek that even the heroic Sandoval went into an icy sweat when a slave ship was announced, remembering what he had been through last time. Among this it was that Claver labored unceasingly for *thirty-eight* years.

When a ship was signaled, he went to the port, with medicines, disinfectants, lemons and brandy; he took always interpreters, needed indeed for men terrorized by having been told that their blood was to be used for dyeing the ship's sails, their fat for caulking its sides. He took them to their yards; washed them; dressed their wounds; made beds for them; downright mothered the maddened mob.

Now some colonial officer, listening, may exclaim: "Ah! Another sentimentalizing Missionary!" Forgive me, but—nonsense! Catholics are realists; so were Spaniards then; so was Claver. He exactly assessed the passionate love they felt for him: accurately he estimated their dense-ness, their glee; their prancings, their debauched or furious relapses; their ecstasies, their orgies. He could quell by sheer personality a whole mob running amok. To him men looked, not to scourge or gun, to put order into riot. And when, like him, you have again and again to rush to the air to be sick because of the stink, there is no room left for sentimentalism, especially if you know you must go back, and go on going back.

His work was not haphazard. With the physical healing went spir-itual instruction always. And with what happened at Cartagena, his headquarters, went an endless following-up; untiring correspondence; regular tours of visits from village to village into which men had been sold, went an influence such that he could check, by a mere message, the flight of an entire population from a volcano—let them wait, he said, till he should arrive next day. Next day he came; led the negroes still quivering with panic, round the still-active crater, and painted a cross upon its lip. No one was injured. The hesitating youth had be-come the indomitable man, and walked serene along the very razor edge of peril.

At home, he concentrated upon two hospitals: St. Sebastian's, a gen-eral one; St. Lazarus, his favorite, restricted to lepers. True he ne-glected no human item—lint, bandages, ointments, stuff for mosquito curtains; saw to the lancing of sick men—nay, arranged concerts and so forth for them; but they—wise men—knew that this was but the almost negligible fringe of his mere *work*—as nothing compared with his *Self* or what stood as symbol of his Self—his mantle, just like those cloths and kerchiefs carried from the very body of St. Peter, in the Acts. That mantle served as robe for the leprous; veil for lupus-gnawed faces; pillow for the dying. "Infectious?" Why, the very contact healed. The very edge of his cassock was ever in rags, so did they tear shreds from it: his very signatures were cut from certificates, the very hair that the barber had clipped from his head, the towels stained with the blood that doctors had drawn from him when he himself was sick, for all this people fought, so sure were they that he was what he was—a man filled full of GOD.

And with hospitals, went prisons. Constantly he was called to assist at executions. He wiped the criminal's wet forehead; he held him while the rope was being fitted to his neck. Once, if not oftener, it broke. Human Justice was inexorable. Claver held the shrieking man to his heart while a second rope was fitted. It, too, broke. A third rope made the poor victim die. But in a book left behind him in his cell, after a visit from Claver, the man had scrawled these words: "This book still belongs to the happiest man in the world." No wonder that the tale—be it historical, or, better than materially historical, a symbol—was broadcast, that a servant threw the water Claver had used for a baptism into a pan where some dead stalks were lying. Next day they had grown green and had reflowered into life.

By 1650, Claver was old and broken. Year of torrential rains, and steaming heat. From Havana, plague reached Cartagena. The Jesuits flung themselves into this new service. Claver caught it; recovered; but found himself almost helpless. *Strapped to his horse*, he still insisted on visiting harbor, hospital, leperhouse. Often he fainted as he went: at last he was shut up within a sickroom of his own. And (to our feeling) a tragic thing happened. Claver was left, in his last months, practically alone. Tragically, yet not inexplicably: the Jesuit community, doing double and triple duty (its ordinary job, and its work among the plague-stricken, and work among a population struck almost as fatally with panic), returned home so exhausted that it could but fall into fitful sleep. But "tragically", not at all to Claver. This man (for, after all, temperaments do not change) all his life, had really wanted solitude, thought, prayer, but had been told by God that he must serve, must do the maximum of exterior work. He loathed it and loved it; was terrified of it but *did* it with a super-heroism. This man, then, at the end, was *put* into a solitude. Assisted only by one slave (who could not guess what a white man might need, and this white man would never condescend to ask, let alone complain) Claver lay there all day in the shattering heat, the flies, amid the hateful scraps of food. In front of him hung the picture of Alonzo Rodriguez, the Majorcan laybrother of—how many years ago? Claver's life had been a unity. He had willed to serve, for Christ's sake; and for Christ's sake he had wholly served. When ships came to Cartagena, the cannon thundered; tapestries were flung from balconies; reviews glittered; officials galloped by. Had he ever noticed them? Not he. In an interior solitude, but never loneliness, had his life been spent—Christ, Souls, his Self. Solitude—not non-human-ness. I tell you, he sickened of, he almost fainted from, the horror of his task, but he *did* it.

In the mid-summer of 1654, the old man said that he was dying. In an hour, the city knew it. Fr. Diego de Farina was appointed Claver's "successor". Claver dragged himself to his room and kissed his feet. On Saturday, September 5, he was told that the City had decreed that the old Jesuit college, his room included, must be demolished to make place for better buildings. He said it did not matter (and even till Monday he refused to receive the Last Sacraments). On the Monday, the hammers of the workmen could be heard. He remained serene. But, that night, they gave him the Last Sacraments of the Church and he became unconscious. Again, in a moment, the town knew of it. Even solitude was done with.

A throng besieged the college doors—officials, grandees, laymen, priests. The Jesuits barred the gates. They were burst in. One cry was heard: "We wish to see the Saint!" The passionate crowd would have stripped everything, so mad were they for relics. A friend could protect, alone, Claver's little picture of Alonzo, which in his unconsciousness he clung to. Then children filled the streets, refusing to move, calling for St. Peter Claver. Then came the negroes in a new army, breaking through even the children, and so into Claver's cell. Only after midnight, with unthinkable difficulty, was the house cleared, save for but a few. And between one and two o'clock of Tuesday, September 8, Feast of our Lady's Birth, St. Peter Claver died.

Do you want a hero? Do you want a man co-crucified with Christ? You have him. Peter Claver.

SAINT JOSEPH OF CUPERTINO

[*1603–1663*]

Alban Goodier, S.J.

F EVER A TINY CHILD began life with nothing in his favor it was Joseph of Cupertino; he had only one hopeful and saving quality—that he knew it. Other boys of his own age were clever, he was easily the dullest of them all. Others were winning and attractive, nobody ever wanted him. While they had pleasant things said to them, and nice things given to them, Joseph always wrote himself down an ass, and never looked for any special treatment. He went to school with the rest of the children in the village, but he did not succeed in anything. He was absent-minded, he was awkward, he was nervous; a sudden noise, such as the ringing of a church bell, would make him drop his school books on the floor. He would sit with his companions after school hours, and try to talk like them, but every time his conversation would break down; he could not tell a story to the end, no matter how he tried. His very sentences would stop in the middle because he could not find the right words. Altogether, even for those who pitied him, and wished to be kind to him, Joseph was something of a trial.

Ill fortune seemed to have set its seal on Joseph before he was born. His father, a carpenter by trade, was a good enough man in his way, but he was a poor hand at dealing with money; what little he earned seemed to slip at once through his fingers. At the very moment when his son came into the world his house was in the hands of bailiffs, and his effects were being sold up. Joseph was born in a shed at the back of the house, where his mother had hid herself out of very shame. With such a beginning Joseph had very poor prospects. As a child, utterly underfed and sickly, he was a very miserable specimen of humanity. He seemed to catch every disease that came his way; many a time he was at death's door, and, to tell the truth, if he had died it would have been

375

a great relief to those responsible for him. Even his mother wearied of him. She, too, was good in her way, but she was hard by nature, and circumstances had made her harder; Joseph was ever in fault, and for every offense she punished him without mercy, according to her notions of a mother's duty. When he was little more than seven years old he developed a running ulcer which would not heal; and his mother was the more embittered against him, for now she supposed that even if the boy grew up he would probably be always to the family nothing but a burden.

Nobody wanted Joseph; even his mother did not want him; Joseph learned this lesson very early and accepted it. He did not seem to want himself, he did not know what he wanted; at times he seemed scarcely to know what he was doing. So abstracted was he that he would forget his meals; and when his attention was called to the fact his only reply would be: "I forgot." Since he could make nothing of books, he was apprenticed to a shoemaker. It was of little use; Joseph was too much distracted, too much absorbed in other things not practical for a workaday people; and he never learned to make or mend a shoe. But he went on trying and his master tolerated him, merely to give the boy something to do.

At length, one day, in the midst of this aimless life, when Joseph was already seventeen years of age, there came into his village a begging friar. At once a new idea came into Joseph's mind. He could not be anything in the world, because he seemed incapable of learning anything; strangely enough this thought had never troubled him much. But surely he could at least be a friar, and go about begging his bread. Brains were not needed for such a life as that; and as for the life itself, it appealed to him with a strange fascination, as having an ideal of its own. Besides he had two uncles in the Order; that gave him hope and encouragement.

He was easily given leave to go away from his home and try; but to find entrance into a monastery was by no means so easy. He had done no studies worth the name, and therefore could not be received; many other reasons were easily forthcoming. He applied at one convent; and the door was closed to him at once; at another, and was told it was quite hopeless; at length he found a community which agreed to take him on trial as a laybrother. But it was of no avail; with the best of intentions to he kind to him, the brethren found him a test of their patience. Not only was he very dull and difficult to teach, but his fits of piety and abstraction, which had been with him from the beginning, made him quite unbearable. He had a way of suddenly standing still in the midst of some occupation, and forgetting everything. He would go down on his knees in the most unlikely places, utterly oblivious of everything around him. He might be washing dishes in the scullery, he might be carrying food into the refectory; one of these fits of abstraction would come on, and down everything would crash in pieces on the floor. In the hope of curing him, bits of the broken plates were fastened to his habit, and he carried them about, as a penance, as a humiliation, as a reminder not to do the same again, but he did not mend. He could not even be trusted with serving out the bread, for the reason that he forgot the difference between brown bread and white.

It was no use. Materially or spiritually Joseph's stay in the monastery could serve no good purpose; his habit was taken from him and he was told to go. That day, as he afterward declared, was the hardest day in all his life; it looked as if everything in heaven and earth had conspired to shut him out; and he never forgot it. He used to say that when they deprived him of the habit it was as if they had torn off his skin. But that was not the end of his troubles. When he had recovered from his stupor on the road outside he found he had lost some of his lay clothes. He was without a hat; he had no boots or stockings, his coat was moth-eaten and worn. Such a sorry sight did he appear, that as he passed a stable down the lane some dogs rushed out on him, and tore what remained of his rags to still worse tatters.

Having escaped from the dogs, poor Joseph trudged along, wondering what next would happen. He passed some shepherds tending sheep. They took him for a dangerous character. When questioned he could give no account of himself and they were about to give him a beating; fortunately one of them had a little pity, and persuaded them to let him go free. But it was only to pass from one trouble into another. Scarcely had he gone a little further down the road when a nobleman on horseback met him. The latter could see in Joseph nothing but a suspicious tramp who had no business in those parts, and thought to hand him over to the police; only when, after examining him, he had come to the conclusion that he was too stupid to be harmful did he let him go.

At last, torn and battered and hungry, Joseph came to a village where one of his uncles lived. He was a prosperous tradesman there, with a thriving little shop of his own; and Joseph hoped he would find with him some kind of comfort, perhaps another start in life. But he was sadly disappointed. Nephews of Joseph's type, even at their best, are not always welcome to prosperous uncles, much less when they turn up unexpectedly, with scarcely a rag on their backs. Joseph's uncle was no better and no worse than others. He looked at the poor lad who stood before him, soiling his clean shop floor with his dirty, bare feet, disgracing himself and his house with his rags, and he was just a little ashamed to own him as a nephew. Evidently, he said to himself, the boy had inherited his father's improvident ways, and would come to nothing good. He was already well on the road to ruin; to help him would only make him worse. Besides, Joseph's father already owed him money; how, then, could he be expected to do anything for the son?

So instead of offering him assistance, Joseph's uncle turned upon him; blamed him for his sorry plight, which, he said, he must have brought upon himself; railed at him because of his father's debts, which such a son could only increase; finally pushed him into the street, without a coin to help him on his way. There was nothing to be done; he must move on; nobody wanted Joseph.

At last he reached his native town, and made for his mother's cottage. His father was still in difficulties; during Joseph's absence things had gone no better than before. He came to the door in fear and trembling, remembering well how both his father and his mother had long since tired of his presence. Still he would venture; it was the only place left where he might hope for a shelter and he must try. He opened the door and looked in; inside he found his mother, busy about her little hovel. Weary and footsore, hungry and miserable, no longer able to stand, he fell on the floor at his mother's feet; he could not speak a word, though his glistening eyes as he looked up at her were eloquent.

But they failed to soften his mother. She had gone through hard times enough and was unprepared for more. What? Had he come back to burden them, now when things were worse than ever? And further disgraced besides, for had he not been expelled from a monastery? How the neighbors would talk, and scorn the mother for having such a son; an unfrocked friar, a ne'er-do-weel, a common tramp, and that at an age when other youths were earning an honest livelihood! She could restrain herself no longer. As he lay at her feet she rounded on him.

"You have been expelled from a house of religious", she cried. "You have brought shame upon us all. You are good for nothing. We have nothing for you here. Go away; go to prison, go to sea, go anywhere; if you stay here there is nothing for you but to starve."

But she was not content with only words. She had a brother who was a Franciscan, holding some sort of office. In high dudgeon she went off to him, and gave him a piece of her mind about the way his Order had dismissed her son, and put him again on her hands. She appealed to him to have him taken back, in any capacity they liked; so long as she was rid of him, they could do with him what they chose. But as for readmission, the good Franciscans were immovable. Joseph had been examined before, and had been declared unsuitable; he had been tried, and had been found wanting; the most they could do was to give him the habit of the Third Order, and employ him somewhere as a servant. He was appointed to the stable; there he could do little harm. Joseph was made the keeper of the monastery mule.

And then the change came. Joseph set about his task; since it was now clear that he could never be a Franciscan, at least he could be their servant. He said not a word in complaint; what had he to complain of? He told himself that all this was only what he might have expected; being what he was, he might consider himself fortunate to find any job at all entrusted to him. He asked for no relief; he took the clothes and the food they chose to give him; he slept on a plank in the stable, it was good enough for him. What was more, in spite of his dullness, perhaps because of it, Joseph had by nature a merry heart. However great his troubles, the moment a gleam of sunshine shone upon him he would be merry and laugh. The troubles were only his desert and were to be expected; when brighter times came he enjoyed them as one who had received a consolation wholly unlooked for, and wholly undeserved.

Gradually this became noticed. Friars would go down to the stable for one reason or another, and always Joseph was there to welcome them, apparently as happy as a lord. It was seen how little he thought of himself, how glad he was to serve; since he could not be a begging friar, sometimes in his free moments he went out and begged for them on his own account. His lightheartedness was contagious; his kindly tongue made men trust him; it was noticed how he was welcomed among the poorest of the poor, who saw better than others the man behind all his oddities. He might make a Franciscan after all. The matter was discussed in the community chapter; his case was sent up to a provincial council for favorable consideration; it was decided, not without some qualms, to give him yet another trial.

In this way Joseph was once more admitted to the Order, but what was to be done with him then? His superiors set him to his studies, in the hope that he might learn enough to be ordained, but the effort seemed hopeless. With all his good intentions he learned to read with the greatest difficulty, and, says his biographer, his writing was worse. He could never expound a Sunday Gospel in a way to satisfy his professors; one only text seemed to take hold of him, and on that he could always be eloquent; speaking from knowledge which was not found in books. It was a text of St. Luke (11:27): *Beatus venter qui te portavit.* Nevertheless he succeeded in being ordained, and the story of his success is one of those mysteries of grace, repeated in the lives of other saints, down to that of the Curé d'Ars in the last century, by which Christ himself lets us see that for his priesthood he chooses "whom he will himself", no matter what regulations man may make.

It came about in this way. Minor Orders in those days were easily conferred, and even the subdiaconate; but for the diaconate and the priesthood a special examination had to be passed, in presence of the bishop himself. As a matter of form, but with no hope of success, Joseph was sent up to meet his fate. The bishop opened the New Testament at haphazard; his eye fell upon the text *Beatus venter qui te portavit*, and he asked Joseph to discourse upon it. To the surprise of everyone present Joseph began, and it seemed as if he would never end; he might have been a Master in Theology lost in a favorite theme. There could be no question about his being given the diaconate. A year later came the priesthood, and Joseph had again his ordeal to undergo. He was examined with a number of others. One by one the first candidates were tested, and their answers were far above the average. At length the bishop, more than satisfied with what he had heard, cut the examination short, and passed the rest unquestioned. Joseph was among the fortunate candidates who were asked nothing, and was ordained along with the rest. He was twenty-five years of age.

There were many, by this time, besides the very poor, who had come to realize the wonderful simplicity and selflessness of Joseph, hidden beneath his dullness and odd ways; a few had discovered the secret of his abstractedness, when he would lose himself in the labyrinth of God. Nevertheless, he remained a trial, especially to the practically minded; to the end of his life he had to endure from them many a scolding. Often enough he would go out begging for the brethren, and would come home with his sack full, but without a sandal, or his girdle, or his rosary, or sometimes parts of his habit. His friends among the poor had taken them for keepsakes, and Joseph had been utterly unaware that they had gone. He was told that the convent could not afford to give him new clothes every day. "Oh! Father," was his answer, "then don't let me go out any more; never let me go out any more. Leave me alone in my cell to vegetate; it is all I can do."

For indeed, as we have seen, Joseph had no delusions about himself; and his ordination did not make him think differently. He had been sorely knocked about in life, but he always understood that he deserved it. The poor in the villages, when he went among them to beg, showed him peculiar respect and friendship; but he always took this to mean that they looked on him as one of themselves, indeed rather less than they were, and they were kind to him out of pity. True he was a priest, but everybody knew how he had received the priesthood. He could assume no airs on that account. On the contrary, knowing what he was, he could only act accordingly. In spite of his priestly office, Joseph could only live the life he had lived before. He would slip down to the kitchen and wash up the dishes; he would sweep the corridors and dormitories; he would look out for the dirtiest work that others shirked, and would do it; when building was going on in the convent he would carry up the stones and mortar; if anyone protested, declaring that such work did not become a priest, he would only reply:

"What else can Brother Ass do?"

And when he got Brother Ass alone in his cell, he would beat him to make him work harder.

But now began that wonderful experience the like of which is scarcely to be paralleled in the life of any other saint. It was first in his prayer. Joseph's absent-mindedness, from his childhood upward, had not been only a natural weakness; it was due, in great part, to a wonderful gift of seeing God and the supernatural in everything about him, and he would become lost in the wonder of it all. Now when he was a friar, and a priest, besides, the vision grew stronger; it seemed easier for him to see God indwelling in his creation than the material creation in which he dwelt. The realization became to him so vivid, so engrossing, that he would spend whole days lost in its fascination, and only an order from his superiors could bring him back to earth. It would come suddenly upon him anywhere; as it were from out of space the eyes of God would look at him, or on the face of nature the hand of God would be seen at work, disposing all things. Joseph would stand still, exactly as the vision caught him, fixed as a statue, insensible as a stone, and nothing could move him. The brethren would use pins and burning embers to recall him to his senses, but nothing could he feel. When he did revive and saw what had happened, he would call these visitations fits of giddiness and ask them not to burn him again. Once a prelate, who had come to see him on some business, noticed that his hands were covered with sores. Joseph could not hide them, nor could he hide the truth, but he had an explanation ready.

"See, Father, what the brethren have to do to me when the fits of giddiness come on. They have to burn my hands, they have to cut my fingers, that is what they have to do."

And Joseph laughed, as he so often laughed; but we suspect that it was laughter keeping back tears.

Then there came another visitation. In the midst of these ecstasies Joseph would rise from the ground, and move about in the air. In the church especially this would come upon him; he would fly toward the altar or over it, or to a shrine on a special festival. In the refectory, during a meal, he would suddenly rise from the ground with a dish of food in his hands, much to the alarm of the brethren at table. When he was out in the country begging, suddenly he would fly into a tree. Once when some workmen were laboring to plant a huge stone cross in its socket, Joseph rose above them, took up the cross and placed it in the socket for them. A little thing would suffice to bring about these levitations; a word of praise of the Creator and his creature, of the beauty of the sky or of the trees on the roadside, and away Joseph would go.

Along with this went a power over nature, over the birds and beasts of the field, surpassing even that of his Father, St. Francis of Assisi; and Joseph used his power playfully, as St. Francis used it. There was a convent of nuns not far from the monastery, where Joseph sometimes called for alms. One day, when they had been good to him, he told them with a laugh that in return for their kindness he would send them a bird to help them in their singing. The next time they went to office, in flew a sparrow by the window. All the time they sang he sang too; when the office was over he flew away again. And so it happened every day; morning and evening the sparrow was there, as regular as any nun. But one day a sister, passing him by, gave him a push with her hand; the sparrow flew out at once and did not return any more. When next Joseph came to the convent, the sisters told him that the sparrow was gone, but they did not tell him the reason.

"He is gone, and quite right," said Joseph; "he did not come to you to be insulted."

However, he promised he would make amends to the sparrow; and in due time he appeared again, and joined in the office as before.

But that does not end the story of the sparrow. He would become so familiar that the nuns could play with him; one of them tied a tiny bell to his foot. All went well till Maundy Thursday; on that day he did not appear, nor during the rest of Holy Week. When Joseph called on Holy Saturday to receive his Easter offering, they told him the sparrow had gone.

"No wonder", answered Joseph, "I gave him to you to join in your music; you should not have made him a bell-ringer. Bells are not rung during these days of Holy Week. But I will see that he returns."

And he did. The sparrow returned, and did not leave again so long as Joseph remained in the neighborhood.

Let us take another story from the many that are found in the life of this servant whom God loved. Joseph had a special interest in the shepherds of the neighborhood; with people of that class he was always most at home. It was his custom to meet them every Saturday in a little chapel at a corner of the monastery grounds, and there recite with them the Litany of Our Lady and other prayers. His congregation was usually a large one, swelled by people from the village. One Saturday Joseph went to the chapel as usual, and found not a soul there. It was harvest time; shepherds and villagers were out in the meadows and had forgotten to tell him that that day they could not come. Joseph, knowing nothing of the reason, talked to himself about the fickleness of men in the service of God. As he spoke he looked down the valley in the distance. The sheep were in the fields, but there were no shepherds; only a few children to tend them. Joseph raised his voice.

"Sheep of God", he cried, "come to me. Come and honor the Mother of God, who is also your Mother."

Immediately the sheep all around looked up. They left their pasture, leaped over hedges and ditches, formed themselves into orderly companies, and gathered round Joseph at the chapel door. When all were assembled, Joseph knelt down and began:

"Kyrie eleison."

"Baa," answered the sheep.

"Christe eleison."

"Baa."

"Sancta Maria."

"Baa."

And so it went on till the litany was finished. Then Joseph stood and blessed his congregation; and the sheep went back to their pastures as if nothing unusual had happened.

Such were some of the stories the brethren had to tell one another of Joseph and his ways. There were many more, especially of miracles he wrought among the poor. He would touch blind eyes and they would see; he would lift up a sick child and it would be cured; he would write out the benediction of St. Francis and it would be passed round a village and work wonders. But there were some among the brethren, as there are always and everywhere, who did not believe in these things. They were incredible, they were impossible, they could not have occurred as the evidence declared. Besides, Joseph was not the kind of person to whom such things would happen; he had too many faults to be a saint, he lacked all kinds of virtues, he was generally a trouble in the community. Therefore he was an imposter, a maker of mischief, who "stirred up the people, beginning from Galilee even to that place." He was reported to the Vicar General; the Vicar General believed what was said, and Joseph was called to stand his trial before the Inquisitors of Naples. The Inquisitors examined him; after close testing they were unable to convict him of anything. Still they would not dismiss him; his case was at least doubtful, and they sent him for further examination to the General of the Order in Rome. The General received him, at first, with little favor. Generals of religious orders have enough to do, and more than enough to give them trouble, without being tried by such subjects as Joseph. Moreover, Joseph never could say anything for himself; if superiors were hard on him he was tongue-tied and could only submit. But this very submission, in this case, was his saving. Father General saw his humility; he began to doubt whether all was true that was said against him. In the end he himself took him to see the Holy Father; and in the Pope's presence as, perhaps, might have been expected, Joseph was humiliated by having another of his "fits of giddiness".

But for all that, though nothing positive could be proved against him, during the rest of his life Joseph was submitted to a new kind of trial. It was the beginning of his Passion, and it lasted to the end. The explanation is not quite clear. It may have been that the tribunal of the Inquisition doubted whether it was safe to allow him, with his strange power, and his strange character, to wander about at will. It was not certain whence these powers came; devotees might make of them more than they ought; yet others might take scandal at Joseph's peculiar ways; many were the arguments adduced to make it clear that he must be piously but firmly kept in safe custody. The Inquisition of Perugia received a peremptory order to take him at once from his own monastery and to hand him over to the Father Guardian of a Capuchin convent, hidden away among the hills, there to be kept in the strictest seclusion. For a moment, when he heard the sentence, Joseph shivered. "Have I to go to prison?" he asked, as if he had been condemned. But in an instant he recovered. He knelt down and kissed the Inquisitor's feet; then got into the carriage, smiling as usual as if nothing had happened.

Arrived at the convent, Joseph was treated with the strictest rigor. Under pain of excommunication he was forbidden to speak to anyone, except the religious around him. He was not permitted to write letters or receive them; he might not leave the convent enclosure; all intercourse with the outside world was cut off. Why all this was done Joseph did not know, and he never asked; but he wondered above all why he had been taken from his own Conventuals and delivered over to the Capuchins.

Nevertheless, in spite of all this care, he could not be hidden. In course of time it became known where he had been spirited away; and pilgrims who had learned to revere him came to the place for the privilege of hearing his Mass. He was transferred to another hiding place, where again the same regulations were enforced. Here the same thing occurred, and once more he was taken away. For the last ten years of his life he seems to have lived virtually in prison, always being kept away from the crowds who persisted in seeking the man they proclaimed to be a saint.

Meanwhile within his places of imprisonment the same wonderful experiences continued. He would be shut up in his cell and he would see things going on elsewhere. He would kneel down to pray before a statue in the garden, and the friars would see him rise in the air, still in a kneeling position. They would come to speak to him, and would be surprised that he read their thoughts before they spoke; sometimes he would read there more than they wished him to know. One morning he came down to the church to say Mass, and announced to the brethren about him that the Pope had died during the night. Another time he made the same announcement; the occasions were the deaths of Urban VIII and Innocent X.

In 1657, six years before his death, Joseph was given back to his own Conventuals, and by them was transferred to another place of seclusion, from which he never emerged. The regulations were the same, the surveillance, if anything, was stricter than ever. He was assigned a tiny cell apart from the community, and a little chapel in which he might say his Mass apart from others. Indeed, scarcely anything else could be done. For years before he was secluded it had been impossible to admit him to office with the rest of the community; his ecstasies had become so frequent, and so continuous, as to throw all into disorder. For the same reason he had been made to take his meals apart. Now, in his last home, he was left to himself; and he lived, this dull man whom no one could teach, and no one wanted, almost continually wrapt up in the vision of that which no man can express in words.

But the time at last came for his release. When, in 1657, Joseph had been taken to his last place of confinement, he had said he would never leave it. He added one thing more for a sign. He told his companions that the first day on which he failed to receive communion would be the day on which he would die. And so it came about. On August 10, 1663, he was seized with an intermittent fever. So long as it was only intermittent he continued to rise every morning to say Mass. The last day was the feast of the Assumption; on that day, says the Act of his canonization, he had ecstasies and experiences surpassing anything he had ever had before. Then he was compelled to take to his bed; but still he persisted in hearing Mass when he could, and never missed communion. He became worse, and extreme unction was administered. When he had received it, he had one request to make; it was that his body should be buried in some out-of-the-way corner, and that it should be forgotten where it was laid. He fell into his agony. There came constantly to his lips the words of St. Paul: *Cupio dissolvi et esse cum Christo*. Someone at the bedside spoke to him of the love of God; he cried out: "Say that again, say that again!" He pronounced the Holy Name of Jesus. He added: "Praised be God! Blessed be God! May the holy will of God be done!" The old laughter seemed to come back to his face; those around could scarcely resist the contagion. And so he died. It was September 18, 1663. He was just sixty years of age.

SAINT BENEDICT JOSEPH LABRE

[1748–1783]

Alban Goodier, S.J.

HERE IS no condition of life which the grace of God has not sanctified; this is the first reflection that must rise in the mind of anyone who studies the history of Benedict Joseph Labre. He died a beggar in Rome in 1783. Within a year of his death his reputation for sanctity had spread, it would seem, throughout Europe. The man and his reputed miracles were being discussed in London papers before the end of 1784. During that year the first authentic life of him appeared, from the pen of his confessor; it was written, as the author expressly states in the preface, because so many tales were being told about him. In 1785 an abridged translation was published in London; surely a remarkable witness, when we consider the place and the times—it was only five years after the Gordon riots—to the interest his name had aroused. We wonder in our own day at the rapidity with which the name of St. Thérèse of Lisieux has spread over the Christian world; though St. Benedict's actual canonization has taken a longer time, nevertheless his cultus spread more quickly, and in spite of the revolutionary troubles of those days, and the difficulties of communication. Rousseau and Voltaire had died five years before; ten years later came the execution of Louis XVI, and the massacres of the French Revolution were at their height. In studying the life of Benedict Joseph Labre these dates cannot be without their significance.

Benedict from the beginning of his days was nothing if not original. His originality consisted mainly in this, that he saw more in life than others saw, and what he saw made him long to sit apart from it; it gave him a disgust, even to sickness, for with which ordinary men seem to be contented. Other men wanted money, and the things that money could buy; Benedict never had any use for either. Other men willingly became the slaves of fashion and convention; Benedict reacted against it all, preferring at any cost to be free. He preferred to live his life untrammeled, to tramp about the world where he would—what was it made for but to trample on?—to go up and down, a pure soul of nature, without any artificial garnish, just being what God made him, and taking every day what God gave him, in the end giving back to God that same being, perfect, unhampered, untainted.

But it was not all at once that Benedict discovered his vocation; on the contrary, before he reached it he had a long way to go, making many attempts and meeting with many failures. He was born not far from Boulogne, the eldest of a family of fifteen children, and hence belonged to a household whose members had perforce to look very much after themselves. From the first, if you had met him, you would have said he was different from others of his class. The portrait drawn of him by his two chief biographers seems to set before us one of those quiet, meditative youths, not easy to fathom, unable to express themselves, easily misunderstood, who seem to stand aside from life, looking on instead of taking their part in it; one of those with whom you would wish to be friends yet cannot become intimate; cheerful always (the biographers are emphatic about this), yet with a touch of melancholy; whom women notice, yet do not venture too near; a puzzle to most who meet them, yet instinctively revered; by some voted "deep" and not trusted, while others, almost without reflecting on it, know that they can trust them with their very inmost souls.

Benedict had good parents, living in a comfortable state of life; their great ambition was that from their many children one at least should become a priest. Benedict, being the quiet boy he was, soon became the one on whom their hopes settled; and they spared no pains to have him educated to that end. He chanced to have an uncle, a parish priest, living some distance from his family home; this uncle gladly received him, and undertook his early education for the priesthood. Here for a time Benedict settled down, learning Latin and studying Scripture. He was happy enough, though his originality of mind dragged against him. His Latin was a bore, and he did not make much of it, but the Scriptures he loved. On the other hand, the poor in the lanes had a strange attraction for him; they were pure nature, without much of the convention that he so disliked; and he was often with them, and regularly emptied his pockets among them. Besides, he had a way of wandering off to the queerest places, mixing with the queerest people, ending up with long meditations in his uncle's church before the Blessed Sacrament.

But in spite of these long meditations, Benedict's uncle was by no means sure that with a character such as his, and with his wandering propensity, he would end as a priest. Meanwhile the thought came to Benedict himself that he would be a Trappist; the originality of their life, with its ideals the exact contrary to those of ordinary convention, seemed to him exactly like his own. He applied to his uncle; his uncle put him off by referring him to his parents; his parents would have none of it, and told him he must wait till he grew older. At the time of this first attempt Benedict was about sixteen years of age.

He remained some two years longer with his priest-uncle, who continued to have his doubts about him. While he was still trying to make up his mind, when Benedict was about eighteen, an epidemic fell upon the city, and uncle and nephew busied themselves in the service of the sick. The division of labor was striking; while the uncle, as became a priest, took care of the souls and bodies of the people, Benedict went to and fro caring for the cattle. He cleaned their stalls and fed them; the chronicler tells the story as if, in spite of the epidemic, which had no fears for him, Benedict were by no means loathe to exchange this life of a farm laborer for that of a student under his uncle's roof.

But a still greater change was pending. Among the last victims of the epidemic was the uncle himself, and his death left Benedict without a home. But this did not seem to trouble him; Benedict was one of those who seldom show trouble about anything. He had already developed that peculiar craving to do without whatever he could; and now that Providence had deprived him of a home he began to think that he might do without that as well. But what was he to do? How was he to live? At first he had thought that his natural aloofness from the ordinary ways of men meant that he should be a monk. His family had put him off, but why should he not try again? He was older now, arrived at an age when young men ordinarily decide their vocations; this time, he said to himself, he would not be so easily prevented.

Benedict returned to his family with his mind made up. He loved his parents—we have later abundant evidence of that; natures like his have usually unfathomed depths of love within them which they cannot show. He would not go without their consent. He asked, and again they refused; his mother first, and then all the rest of the household with her. But he held on in his resolution, till at length in despair they surrendered, and Benedict set off with a glad heart in the direction of La Trappe.

He arrived there only to be disappointed. The abbey at which he applied had suffered much of late from the admission of candidates whose constitutions were unfitted for the rigor of the life; in consequence the monks had passed a resolution to admit no more unless they were absolutely sound in body. Benedict did not come up to their requirements. He was under age; he was too delicate; he had no special recommendations. They would make no exception, especially so soon after the rule had been made. Benedict was sent away, and returned to his family, and all they said to him was: "We told you so."

Still he would not surrender. For a time he went to live with another parish priest, a distant relative, that he might continue his studies, and above all perfect himself in Latin. But the craving to go away would not leave him. If the Trappists would not have him, perhaps the Carthusians would. At least he could try. Once more he told his parents of his wish, and again, more than ever, they opposed him. They showed him how his first failure was a proof that he would fail again; how he was throwing away a certain future for a shadow; how those best able to judge were all against him; how with his exceptional education he might do so much good elsewhere. Still he would have his way, and one day, when he had won a consent from his parents that at least he might try, he went off to ask for admission among the Carthusians of Montreuil. But here again he met with the same response. The monks were very kind, as Carthusians always are; they showed him every mark of affection, but they told him as well that he had no vocation for them. He was still too young to take up such a life; he had not done so much as a year of philosophy; he knew nothing of plain chant; without these he could not be admitted among them.

Benedict went off, but this time he did not return straight home. If one Carthusian monastery would not have him, perhaps another would. There was one at Longuenesse; he was told that there they were in need of subjects, and postulants were more easily admitted. He tramped off to Longuenesse and applied; to his joy the monks agreed to give him a trial. But the trial did not last long. Benedict did his best to reconcile himself to the life, but it was all in vain. Strange to say, the very confinement, the one thing he had longed for, wore him down. The solitude, instead of giving him the peace he sought, seemed only to fill him with darkness and despair. The monks grew uneasy; they feared for the brain of this odd young man; they told him he had no vocation and he was dismissed.

Benedict came home again, but his resolution was in no way shaken. His mother, naturally more than ever convinced that she was right, left no stone unturned to win him from his foolish fancy. Friends and neighbors joined in; they blamed him for his obstinacy, they accused him of refusing to recognize the obvious will of God, they called him unsociable, uncharitable, selfish, unwilling to shoulder the burden of life like other young men of his class. Still, in spite of all they said, Benedict held on. He could not defend himself; nevertheless he knew that he was right, and that he was following a star which would lead him to his goal at last. Since the Carthusians had said that he could not be received among them because he knew no philosophy or plain chant, that a year's course in these was essential, he found someone willing to teach him; and much as he disliked the study, he persevered for the year as he had been told. Then he applied once more at Montreuil. The conditions had been fulfilled; he was now older and his health had been better; he had proved his constancy by this test imposed upon him; though many of the monks shook their heads, still they could see that this persistent youth would never be content till he had been given another trial, and they received him.

But the result was again the same. He struggled bravely on with the life, but he began to shrink to a shadow. The rule enjoined quiet in his cell, and he could not keep still. After six weeks of trial the monks had to tell him that he was not designed for them, and asked him to go. He went, but this time not home; he made up his mind never to go home any more. He would try the Trappists again or some other confined Order; perhaps he would have to go from monastery to monastery till at last he found peace, but he would persevere. At any rate he would no longer trouble, or be a burden to, his parents or his family. On the road, after he had been dismissed from Montreuil, he wrote a letter to his parents; it is proof enough that with all his strange ways he had a very wide place in his heart for those he dearly loved.

My dear Father and Mother,

This is to tell you that the Carthusians have judged me not a proper person for their state of life, and I quitted their house on the second day of October.—I now intend to go to La Trappe, the place which I have so long and so earnestly desired. I beg your pardon for all my acts of disobedience, and for all the uneasiness which I have at any time caused you.—By the grace of God I shall henceforth put you to no further expense, nor shall I give you any more trouble.—I assure you that you are now rid of me. I have indeed cost you much; but be assured that, by the grace of God, I will make the best use of, and reap benefits from, all that you have done for me.—Give me your blessing, and I will never again be a cause of trouble to you.—I very much hope to be received at La Trappe; but if I should fail there, I am told that at the Abbey of Sept Fonts they are less severe, and will receive candidates like me. But I think I shall be received at La Trappe.

With hopes such as these he came to La Trappe and again was disappointed; the good monks declined even to reconsider his case. But he went on to Sept Fonts, as he had said he would in his letter, and there was accepted; for the third time he settled down to test his vocation as a monk. The trial lasted only eight months. He seems to have been happier here than anywhere before, yet in another sense he was far from happy. This youth with a passion for giving up everything, found that even in a Trappist monastery he could not give up enough. He craved to be yet more poor than a Trappist, he craved to be yet more starving; and what with his longing to give away more, and his efforts to be the poorest of the poor, he began to shrink to a mere skeleton, as he had done before at Montreuil. Added to this he fell ill, and was disabled for two months. Once more the community grew anxious; it was only too clear that he would never do for them. As soon as he was well enough to take the road he was told that he must go, that the strict life of the Trappist was too much for him; and with a "God's will be done" on his lips, and some letters of recommendation in his pocket, Benedict again passed out of the monastery door, into a world that hurt him.

Nevertheless, in those few months he had begun at last to discover his true vocation. Though the longing for the monastic life did not entirely leave him, still he was beginning to see that there was now little hope of his being able to embrace it in the ordinary way. He was unlike other men; he must take the consequences and he would. He could not be a monk like others; then he would be one after his own manner. He could not live in the confinement of a monastery; then the whole world should be his cloister. There he would live, a lonely life with God, the loneliest of lonely men, the outcast of outcasts, the most pitied of all pitiful creatures, "a worm and no man, the reproach of men, and the outcast of the people". He would be a tramp, God's own poor man, depending on whatever men gave him from day to day, a pilgrim to heaven for the remainder of his life. He was twenty-five years of age.

He set off on his journey, with Rome as his first objective, a long cloak covering him, tied with a rope round the waist, a cross on his breast, a large pair of beads round his neck; his feet were partly covered with substitutes for shoes, carefully prepared, one might have thought, to let in water and stones. In this dress he braved every kind of weather, rain and snow, heat and the bitterest cold; he faced and endured it all without ever wincing or asking for a change. Over his shoulder he carried an old sack in which were all his belongings; chief among these were a Bible and Prayer Book. He ate whatever men gave him; if they gave him nothing he looked to see what he could find on the roadside. He refused to take thought for the morrow; if at any time he had more than sufficed for the day, he invariably gave it to another. Moreover, as a result of his poverty, Benedict soon ceased to be clean; the smell of Benedict was not always pleasant; even his confessor, who wrote his life, tells us very frankly that when Benedict came to confession he had to protect himself from vermin. Men of taste, even those who later came to look on him as a saint, could scarcely refrain from drawing aside when he came near them; and when they did, then was Benedict's heart full of joy. He had found what he wanted, his garden enclosed, his cloister that shut him off in the middle of the world; and the more he was spurned and ignored, the more did he lift up his eyes to God in thanksgiving.

With this light dawning on his soul, soon to grow into full noon, Benedict set out on his travels. He had gone through a long noviceship, living as it were between two worlds, one of which he would not have, while the other had repeatedly closed its doors to him; now at last his life proper had begun. We can discover his final decision in a letter he wrote to his parents from Piedmont, when he had now left France, and was half-way on his journey to Rome. It is a letter full of soul and warmth; it teems with sympathy and interest for others; there is not a word which implies bitterness or disappointment; the man who wrote it was a happy man, in no way disgruntled; evidently his only fear is that he may give pain to those he loved.

My dear Father and Mother,

You have heard that I have left the Abbey of Sept Fonts, and no doubt you are uneasy and desirous to know what route I have taken, and what kind of life I intend to adopt.—I must therefore acquaint you that I left Sept Fonts in July; I had a fever soon after I left, which lasted four days, and I am now on my way to Rome.—I have not traveled very fast since I left, on account of the excessive hot weather which there always is in the month of August in Piedmont, where I now am, and where, on account of a little complaint, I have been detained for three weeks in a hospital where I was kindly treated. In other respects I have been very well. There are in Italy many monasteries where the religious live very regular and austere lives; I design to enter into one of them, and I hope that God will prosper my design.—Do not make yourselves uneasy on my account. I will not fail to write to you from time to time. And I shall be glad to hear of you, and of my brothers and sisters; but this is not possible at present, because I am not yet settled in any fixed place; I will not fail to pray for you every day. I beg that you will pardon me for all the uneasiness that I have given you; and that you will give me your blessing, that God may favor my design.—I am very happy in having undertaken my present journey. I beg you will give my compliments to my grandmother, my grandfather, my aunts, my brother James and all my brothers and sisters, and my uncle Francis. I am going into a country which is a good one for travellers. I am obliged to pay the postage of this to France.

Again I ask your blessing, and your pardon for all the uneasiness I have given you, and I subscribe myself,

Your most affectionate son,
BENEDICT JOSEPH LABRE
Roziers in Piedmont, Aug. 31, 1770

This was the last letter he appears to have written to his family. He had promised to write again; if he wrote the letter has perished. Indeed, from this moment they seem to have lost sight of him altogether; the next they heard of him was fourteen years later, when his name was being blazoned all over Europe as that of a saint whose death had stirred all Rome. And he never heard from them. He had told them he could give them no address, because he had no fixed abode; from this time forward he never had one, except during the last years in Rome, and that for the most part was in a place where the post could scarcely have found him, as we shall see.

Except to give an idea of the nature and extent of his wanderings during the next six or seven years, it is needless to recall all the pilgrimages he made. They led him over mountains and through forests, into large cities and country villages; he slept under the open sky, or in whatever sheltered corner he could find, accepting in alms what sufficed for the day and no more, clothed with what men chose to give him, or rather with what they could induce him to accept; alone with God everywhere and wanting no one else. During this first journey he called on his way at Loreto and Assisi. Arrived in Rome, footsore and ill, he was admitted for three days into the French hospital; then for eight or nine months he lingered in the city, visiting all the holy places, known to no one, sleeping no one knows where. In September of the next year we find him again at Loreto; during the remaining months of that year, and though the winter, he seems to have visited all the sacred shrines in the kingdom of Naples. He was still there in February, 1772, after which he returned to Rome. In June he was again at Loreto; thence he set out on his tour to all the famous shrines of Europe. In 1773 he was tramping through Tuscany; in 1774, after another visit to Rome, he was in Burgundy; during the winter of that year he went to Einsiedeln in Switzerland, choosing the coldest season of the year for this visit to the mountain shrine. 1775, being a Jubilee year, he again spent in Rome; in 1776 he was making pilgrimages to the chief places of devotion in Germany. At the end of that year he settled down definitely in Rome, going away henceforth only on special pilgrimages, most of all to his favorite Loreto, which he did not fail to visit every year.

Naturally enough stories are recalled of the behavior of this peculiar man on his journeys. He seems never to have had in his possession more than ten sous, or fivepence, at a time; when charitable people offered him more than sufficed for the day he invariably refused it. At Loreto, where he came to be known perhaps more than anywhere else, at first he lodged in a barn at some distance from the town; when compassionate friends found a room for him closer to the shrine, he refused it because he found it contained a bed. In Rome, as we have already hinted, his home for years was a hole he had discovered among the ruins of the Coliseum; from this retreat he made daily excursions to the various churches of the city. Except when he was ill he seldom begged; he was content with whatever the passers-by might give him of their own accord. Once a man, seeing him in his poverty, gave him a penny; Benedict thanked him, but finding it more than he needed, passed it on to another poor man close by. The donor, mistaking this for an act of contempt, supposing that Benedict had expected more, took his stick and gave him a beating. Benedict took the beating without a word. We have this on the evidence of the man himself, recorded in the inquiry after Benedict's death; it must be one instance of many of its kind.

But for the rest Benedict's life was one of continued prayer; he was a Trappist in a monastery of his own making. So far as he was able he kept perpetual silence; those who knew him afterward related that he seemed to go whole months together without allowing his voice to be heard. He lived in retirement and solitude; he would accept no friend or companion; he would have only God; a few who had come to notice him, and who helped him when he would allow them, were invariably treated as patrons and benefactors, but no more. When a convent of nuns, at which occasionally he applied, had observed him, and began to show him more interest and respect, Benedict discovered their esteem and never went near them again. All his possessions were a few books of devotion and a wooden bowl; the latter had split, and he had kept it together with a piece of wire. He fasted and abstained continually, sometimes perforce, sometimes by chance; by constantly kneeling on the hard ground, or the stone floors of the churches, he developed sores on both knees. He deliberately tried to be despised and shunned, and when men could not refrain from showing contempt in their manner, then would Benedict's face light up with real joy. Let his confessor, who wrote his life a year after his death, describe his first meeting with him:

> In the month of June, 1782, just after I had celebrated Mass in the church of St. Ignatius belonging to the Roman College, I noticed a man close beside me whose appearance at first sight was decidedly unpleasant and forbidding. His legs were only partially covered, his clothes were tied

round his waist with an old cord. His hair was uncombed, he was ill-clad, and wrapped about in an old and ragged coat. In his outward appearance he seemed to be the most miserable beggar I had ever seen. Such was the spectacle of Benedict the first time I beheld him.

For what remains of Benedict's story we cannot do better than follow the guidance of this director. After the priest had finished his thanksgiving, on the occasion just mentioned, Benedict approached him and asked him to appoint a time when he would hear his general confession. The time and place were arranged. During the confession the priest was surprised, not only at the care with which it was made, but also at the knowledge his penitent showed of intricate points of theology. He concluded that, beggar though he was then, he had evidently seen better days; indeed, he felt sure that he had once been a clerical student. He therefore interrupted the confession to ask whether he had ever studied divinity. "I, Father?" said Benedict. "No, I never studied divinity. I am only a poor ignorant beggar."

The confessor at once recognized that he was dealing with something unusual. He resolved to do for him all he could, and for the future to keep him carefully in mind.

As it has so often been in God's dealings with hidden saints whom he has willed that men should come at last to know, that apparently chance meeting was the means by which the memory of Benedict was saved. It took place in June, 1782; in April of the following year Benedict died. During those ten months the priest to whom he addressed himself had ample opportunity to watch him. As the weeks passed by he grew in wonder at the sanctity that lay beneath rags; and yet he tells us that, not a little fastidiously clean as he seems to have been himself, it never so much as occurred to him to bid Benedict mend his ways. To hear his confession cost him an effort, yet he never thought twice about making that effort; only at times, for the sake of others, the appointed place was out of the way.

He saw him last on the Friday before Holy Week, 1783, when Benedict came to make his confession as usual. He remarks that though always before Benedict had fixed the day when he would come again, this time he made no appointment. The next the priest heard of him was that he was dead, exactly a week later. But he was not surprised. For some months before, when once he had come to know Benedict and his way of life, he had wondered how he lived. Apart from his austerities, and his invariable choice of food that was least palatable, of late his body had begun to develop sores and ulcers. The priest had spoken to him on this last point, and had exhorted him at least to take more care of his sores, but Benedict had taken little notice. On his side, as the confessor could not but notice, and as is common with saints as death draws nearer, the love of God that was in him left him no desire to live any longer.

It came to Wednesday in Holy Week. Among the churches which Benedict frequented none saw him more than S. Maria dei Monti, not very far from the Coliseum. In this church he usually heard Mass every morning; in the neighborhood he was well known. On this day he had attended the morning services; as he went out of the door, about one in the afternoon, he was seen to fall on the steps. Neighbors ran toward him. He asked for a glass of water, but he could not lift himself up. A local butcher, who had often been kind to Benedict, offered to have him carried to his house, and Benedict agreed. They laid him on a bed, as they thought, to rest; but it soon became clear that he was dying. A priest was sent for; the Last Sacraments were administered; but Benedict was too weak to receive Viaticum. The prayers for the dying were said; at the words: "Holy Mary, pray for him", Benedict died, without a sigh or a convulsion. It was April 16, 1783; Benedict was thirty-five years of age.

And now some remarkable things happened. His confessor and first biographer writes:

> Scarcely had this poor follower of Christ breathed his last when all at once the little children from the houses hard by filled the whole street with their noise, crying out with one accord "The Saint is dead, the Saint is dead."—But presently after they were not only young children who published the sanctity of Benedict; all Rome soon joined in their cries, repeating the self-same words: "A Saint is dead." . . . Great numbers of persons who have been eminent for their holiness and famous for their miracles, have ended the days of their mortal life in this city; but the death of none of them ever excited so rapid and lively an emotion in the midst of the people as the death of this poor beggar. This stirred a kind of universal commotion; for in the streets scarcely anything could be heard but these few words: "There is a saint dead in Rome. Where is the house in which he has died?"

Nor does this description seem to have been exaggerated. Not only was it written within a year of the event, so that any one could bear witness to its truth; but we know that scarcely was Benedict dead before two churches were contending for the privilege of possessing his body. At length it was decided that it should be given to Santa Maria dei Monti, which he had most frequented; and thither, on the Wednesday night, it was carried. So great was the crowd that the guard of police had to be doubled; a line of soldiers accompanied the body to the church; more honor could scarcely have been paid to a royal corpse. From the moment that it was laid there the church was thronged with mourners; the next day, Maundy Thursday, and again throughout Good Friday, it almost lay in state during all the Holy Week services. The throng all the time went on increasing, so that the Cardinal Vicar was moved to allow the body to remain unburied for four days. People of every rank and condition gathered there; at the feet of Benedict the Beggar all were made one. They buried him in the church, close beside the altar, on Easter Sunday afternoon; when the body was placed in the coffin it was remarked that it was soft and flexible, as of one who had but just been dead.

But the enthusiasm did not end with the funeral. Crowds continued to flock to the church, soldiers were called out to keep order. At length the expedient was tried of closing the church altogether for some days. It was of no avail; as soon as the church was reopened the crowds came again, and continued coming for two months. Nothing like it had been seen before, even in Rome; if ever anyone was declared a saint by popular acclamation it was Benedict Joseph Labre, the beggar. Then the news spread abroad. Within a year the name of Benedict was known all over Europe. Lives of him began to appear, legends began to grow, miracles, true and false, were reported from all sides; it was to secure an authentic story, among many inventions, that his confessor was called upon to write the Life that we know.

Let us add one touching note. All this time the father and mother, brothers and sisters of Benedict were living in their home near Boulogne. For more than twelve years they had heard nothing of him; they had long since presumed that he was dead. Now, through these rumors, it dawned upon them very gradually that the saint of whom all the world was speaking was their son!

"My son was dead, and is come to life again; he was lost, and is found."

SAINT JOHN BAPTIST VIANNEY: THE CURE D'ARS

[*1786-1859*]

R. H. J. Steuart, S.J.

VERY NOW AND THEN the Spirit of Christianity seems suddenly to burst the bonds of convention and reveal itself in the life of some individual in all its untempered purity free of the modifying and relaxing effects of that progress in science and art and philosophy, and the rest of its component elements, which we call civilization. It shows itself as a thing entirely independent of human formulation, divine, eternal, sufficient in itself. Conjugately, it exposes the emptiness and unreality in themselves of all besides, making us realize in spite of our native prepossession to the contrary, that there is indeed nothing substantial in the very best and most satisfactory-seeming of them but what it lends to them. God is the truth in all that is true, the beauty in all that is beautiful, the goodness in all that is good, and only in Christ has he thus uttered himself to the fullness of the capacity that a created nature has for expressing him. Christianity, therefore, properly understood as the perfect "state of Christliness" (adapted, of course, to our use as a scheme of belief and of life) is in its own sole self all that there is possible of human truth and beauty and goodness: it is not only their one authentic standard, it is in fact the whole of their reality in no matter what medium they be expressed.

Art for art's sake, or wisdom for wisdom's sake, are no less delusive as ideals than those which the coarsest sensualist sets before himself, for art and knowledge and all that in our different ways we apprehend as good, are so for Christ's sake, or they are false goods. "He who is not with me is against me": we are against Christ, and the things that we love are against him, not only when we oppose him or when we ignore him, but always unless we are with and for and toward him. There is *no* other name given to us under heaven whereby we must be saved: no

401

ideals or ideas, no term of effort, no ultimate exemplar but such as is in him. It will, no doubt, sound overexacting to some if one says that the test of all excellence in all domains of human achievement is whether it "shows Christ" or does not; but what escape is there from that conclusion? For there are two camps only, Christs' and Antichrist's, and as between the two neutrality is impossible. By our reaction to that test is the quality of our truth and goodness assayed, and it is the task of the Christian to build his life upon that ideal.

The saints, the complete Christians, are indeed so few just because the task is so hard: but Christ has left us no alternative, for he has laid down that to follow him will and must mean to follow nothing else —"sell all whatsoever thou hast": and again and again, if we are to be loyal to that call, we shall have to set our teeth and say, It is *not* true, It is *not* beautiful, It is *not* good, because it is not Christ. Christianity is of its very nature challenging and intransigent, and our hold upon it will be defective and therefore unproductive in the proportion that our understanding of it admits of shades and qualifications and degrees. But in practice we do, nearly all of us, at least tacitly so understand it: and more and more as the evidence seems, through all our senses, to accumulate that there are other canons of truth and goodness besides his: and it is in aid of our weakness that these outbreaks of the sheer Spirit of Christ happen in the history of the Church and throw into confusion the orderly structure of accommodation between itself and its opposite by which we had unwittingly accustomed ourselves to live. When this happens some are frightened, some are incredulous and scornful, but the most are compeled to acknowledge the truth and value of what they see, and these are awestruck but grateful.

The life of St. John Baptist Vianney, Curé d'Ars, is just one of these "outbreaks" as we have called them. It was a life dedicated, with a wholeness which left nothing for any other object, to the service of God upon the model of him who said that his meat—what he lived on and lived by and lived for—was to do his Father's will who had sent him "to seek and to save", to give his flesh and blood and his life for his brethren: and who had laid down that by no other sign should his disciples be known than that they had the love for their brethren that he had shown for them. There is, perhaps, in all the story of the saints hardly a parallel to such self-immolation for the souls of others as we find here. It is no exaggeration to say of the Curé d'Ars that he gave to his own personal interests absolutely no care or consideration whatsoever: that he put all that he had to give of love and thought and health and strength and time entirely and without reserve at the service of all who needed him—and this for forty long years without respite or relaxation until, at the age of seventy-three, "I can do no more," he said, "it is my poor end."

Born of simple, laborious and devout peasant stock, John-Baptist was from his earliest years accustomed to the spectacle of goodness and piety, and no doubt too the open-air life that he was obliged to live during all his youth helped to build up a constitution able to support for so long the austerities and the unremitting strain that his priestly life was to involve. When he began his studies his only assets were his good will and his industry: power of assimilation, or even of memory, he seemed to have none, and under each successive test he failed completely, his final acceptance for the priesthood being grounded on the assurance given by his devoted and far-seeing teacher, the saintly Abbé Balley, that his pupil was thoroughly worthy and good and would continue his studies afterward under himself. But it would be a mistake to think that he was stupid or to make a miracle of the improvement in his intellectual powers that seemed to follow on his pilgrimage to the tomb of St. John Francis Regis in the Vivarais.

The bewildered student who appeared to be unable either to grasp or to retain even the elements of formal theology was later to be among the greatest of confessors and directors of souls, the wisest of counselors in the spiritual life, the surest of guides in the way of Faith that the Church has ever known. The question that was asked of Our Lord might have been asked of him, "How does this man know letters?" and have been answered in the same way, "My doctrine is not mine but his who sent me." "Letters" it may be true that he never knew, and perhaps the world would call that stupidity: but all that wisdom of which letters are only the outer form was his as ever more and more entirely he gave himself up to God. To such has Our Lord promised that he will give "a mouth and wisdom". It is related that during the first two years of his priesthood as *vicaire* to M. Balley his curé used to set him to unravel the most intricate cases of conscience and was amazed at the sureness of his judgment and the soundness of his solutions. But it seems to be true that with the majority of the people of Ecully as well as with the diocesan authorities, M. Vianney counted

during this period for very little, and that on the death of M. Balley
there was no thought of appointing him to be his successor. Instead,
he was sent off to an obscure village on the dreary flats of the Dombes
where the people were not indeed hostile to religion as they were in
so many other parts of France, but were for the most part practically
indifferent to it and very ignorant of its tenets.

On February 9, 1818, he set out on foot for Ars, a distance of about
twenty miles, accompanied by the Mère Bibost (an old woman who
was to act for a time as his housekeeper) and followed by his scanty
stock of furniture in a cart. Four days later he was inducted as curé (his
canonical title was really *vicaire-chapelain*, dependent on the parish of
Mizerieux): he was Parish Priest indeed, but of a parish so inconsiderable and undistinguished that there were none among his *confrères* who
envied him his promotion. It is known that the Department of the Ain,
in which Ars was situated, was regarded from an ecclesiastical point of
view as the most forsaken and unresponsive part of the diocese, and
for a priest to be sent to a parish in the Dombes was commonly held
to signify either that he was in disgrace or that he was useless. The
annual stipend was five hundred francs—perhaps £20 at that date: other
resources there were none. The village consisted of two streets lined
with yellow clay-and-wattle houses, windowless on their outward side
and facing round a courtyard of which the major part was taken up by
a midden.

In France farmers do not, as in England, live upon their farms but
gathered into villages, so that some of them have a considerable distance
to go to their fields. There were in addition three or four *estaminets*,
and in a kind of open Square the church, with a wooden steeple, plain
and poor and in very ill repair. The one-storeyed presbytery was next
door to the church, and possessed a garden containing a few fruit trees.
The surroundings could hardly have been more depressing for the new
curé or the prospects bleaker, and he must have realized on his first day
that he would have to build up everything from the beginning. There
were not more than fifty families in the parish, and of them barely half
a dozen really practiced their religion. It would, however, be unjust to
say that the people of Ars were entirely irreligious, much less positively
bad. Nearly all the women, it is said, and a proportion of the men,
went to Mass on Sundays, but also on the slightest excuse they went
to work in their fields instead: very few made their Easter duties: the

children received scarcely any schooling or religious instruction, and many could neither read nor write: the four *estaminets* were full every evening, Sundays and weekdays, and there was much drunkenness and rowdyism: and dancing, the favorite and constant recreation of the village, was often of a very unseemly type.

Another priest in M. Vianney's place might have given up in despair of doing any good, or at best have resigned himself to preserve, as he might, what little good there already was in the parish. But not so the new curé. He found himself in the midst of sin, which for him was the one and only evil in the world, and he could not tolerate that it should exist anywhere if at any cost to himself it could be averted. To sin is to oppose God—think of it, *to oppose God!*—it is to affront his goodness: he was frantic when he thought of it. That was the source of the reckless energy with which he flung himself—the whole of himself—into the life work for the sinners for whom he found himself responsible. He must bring them all to repentance and assure them of forgiveness, arm them against relapse and lead them on to holiness: for he had no less an aim than to convert all sinners into saints: it should not be enough for them to cease to ignore or hate or offend God, he would bring them to know him, to love him, and to serve him with all their heart and soul.

Nothing had power to stop him, neither man nor devil, and he had to fight with both. His own interests—health, comfort, peace of soul itself—he counted for nothing. In his own body he suffered for them what they deserved to suffer for themselves: he wore a rasping hairshirt and lashed himself nightly with a formidable discipline, he ate so little and such poor food that it seemed a continual miracle that he kept himself alive on it, he slept (or rather lay down, for often he was kept awake by a racking cough) not more than a couple of hours of the night, and he allowed his body no other rest during the day, no relief, no refreshment, no pause. More terrible still, he drank even of the bitter cup of their despair—he seemed to hear a chant of devils, "He is ours! We have him! We have him!" or at night a whisper in his ear, "Soon you must fall into hell!": all his life seemed to him a pretense and all his efforts wasted, he had perhaps saved the souls of others, but what had he made of his own? For a saint may feel all the agonies that accompany despair though he cannot yield to the thing itself: when such a cloud descends upon his soul he is like Christ in the Garden, crushed and exhausted but still with voice to say "Thy will be done!"

Yet never did he for one instant waver in the task that his consuming love for God urged upon him—"to seek and to save", to snatch back from eternal frustration the souls that their Creator had made to find their everlasting completeness in himself—he *could* not rest from it unless he could rest from the love of God itself.

But before all else it is as the saint—the martyr—of the confessional that the memory of the Curé d'Ars most vividly lives. What priest does not know that it is *there* that the test of his zeal for souls, of his love of God, of his likeness to Christ is applied—that it is in the administration of the Sacrament of Penance that the strain comes upon the genuineness of his vocation? To be patient and sympathetic, to sink one's own personality and convenience and curb the movements of repulsion or resentment or weariness that the tale of sin and folly and the hesitations and obstinacies of a penitent may arouse, to be temperate and just and gentle without harshness on the one hand or human-respect on the other, to remember that the priest is the servant, not the master, of those for whose sake he holds his sacred office, to understand that speaking and judging in the name and person of Christ —*binding* him, as it were, by one's words and decisions—it is a grave infidelity if one's bearing be not such as would befit him: to do all this well, is to draw heavily upon the best of the faith and charity that is in one, and one may rightly feel that it will demand something little short of heroism to sustain such an ideal faithfully for even an hour or two.

What then are we to think—how are we to picture it?—when we learn that the Curé d'Ars spent daily no less than *fifteen*, often *eighteen,* hours in his confessional, stifled in the summer-time, frozen in the winter, scarcely able to walk or even stand when at last he emerged from it, and that from the first moment to the last of those terrible sessions there was never a halt in the stream of penitents that beset him. Nor was there a halt, much less a change, in the attention, the patience, the gentleness, the zeal which he lavished upon all who thus approached him. And this not at Easter time only or at Christmas, but all the seasons through, year in year out, for over thirty years, up to within four days of his death. Indeed, though many were the other works that engaged his apostolic ardor it was in the confessional that

the inwardness of his spirit and spring of his sanctity most revealed itself. A simple enough thing in words—just fear and hatred of sin, the
obverse of his love of God. Yes, but a hatred of sin which proceeded
from a clear vision of what it really is—in itself, a destructive uncre-
ative thing because it is defiance of God's will which is the substance
of all created things: and in its import as a free human act, a shameful,
hateful thing because it is the denial and rejection of God's everlasting
love. "To be a saint", he once said, "one must be beside oneself, one
must lose one's head", and for his part he neither had nor intended
any restraint or moderation in his struggle with the evil wherever he
recognized it: he did not reason about it—God is love, sin is hate, there
is no more to be said.

It is this *sense of sin* that gives the Curé d'Ars his special value for us
who have to mix with a world in which it has almost ceased to have
any objective significance whatever. What would he have made of the
claim that right and wrong are convertible terms with the likes and
dislikes of each individual: or that sin is nothing but the liberation, under certain psychological conditions, from the repressive hold of habit
or convention, of primeval instincts in themselves no more moral or
immoral than are hunger or thirst? He would have seen at once that
underlying all such doctrines is the sheer denial of God, or at least of
a God who can have any care over us or we any duties toward him.

On which side of the argument should we expect to find Christ?

The Curé d'Ars knew nearly nothing about psychology but he knew
nearly everything about human nature because he knew so much about
God. A saint does not need learning as others do for the wisdom to
which, for all their learning, they will never attain. While others argue
about sin he sees it—tastes and touches and smells it: it is disease, it
is rottenness, it is a beginning of hell. And over against it he sets the
love of God for the souls that he made for himself, and being so near
to God, so tuned to him, he anguishes for the love thus scorned and
defeated. That was why he *could* not give himself rest in his war against
it. That was why in his sermons and instructions he beat and beat again
upon the topic, God's love for men on the one side, men's sin against
God on the other, and what came of it—"Cursed by God!" he sobbed
in his pulpit, "My children, do you understand? Cursed by God, by
God who loves only to bless!" That, too, was why day by day he tore
himself at one o'clock in the morning from the sleep which after the

scant two hours of uneasy rest that he allowed himself was just beginning to visit him, and stumbled down to his confessional in the church where already a throng of penitents was awaiting him, many perhaps since the afternoon before, and where as the hours passed by he raised his hand again and again in absolution of sin with an ever freshening joy of heart and soul that ended by mastering the mortal weariness and the almost continual internal pains that afflicted his body.

"Do only what you can offer to God" was one of his sayings. It was his antidote for sin, a homely rendering of Christ's own words, "I do always the things that please him."

It is well to remind ourselves that this wholly supernatural man lived, not as the story of his life might easily suggest in the heroic ages of Faith, but in the days of railways and steamboats and telegraphs—of at least the beginnings of that era of scientific advance which has since transformed the whole face of civilization—in an age, therefore, in which "the evidence of the senses" has increasingly developed into rivalry with "the evidence of things that appear not" and the faith which should be the life-stream of the "just man" is running thin. For thus we shall be the better able to focus to our sight the vision that inspired him.

Here was a man, then, practically of our own times, for whom, not speculatively alone but in ordinary circumstances of everyday actuality, the only good was the love of God and the only evil sin.

~

SAINT BERNADETTE SOUBIROUS

[1844–1879]

R. H. J. Steuart, S.J.

TAR DIFFERETH FROM STAR IN GLORY says St. Paul, and we are well accustomed to variations, amounting at times almost to contradictions, in style and type and expression of holiness as exhibited by the lives of those whom the Church has officially pronounced to be saints, to be persons, that is, who are proved to have practiced the Christian virtues —not on occasional impulse but with such regularity as fairly deserves to be called habitual—in a degree conspicuously above what is recognized as constituting a normally good life.

But in spite of this preparation one is scarcely ready to accept Bernadette of Lourdes as a saint, for at first sight (and perhaps even increasingly with further acquaintance) her life presents itself to us as so remarkably devoid of the features demonstrably common to all the other saints known to us that it is a real difficulty to associate her with them. A well-known authority on this subject, whose judgment and critical ability meet with respect in all quarters, has given it as his considered opinion that "in all the annals of sanctity it would be hard to find the counterpart of the history of Bernadette Soubirous" for, he continues,

> she did nothing out of the common, she said nothing memorable, she gathered no followers around her, she had in the ordinary sense no revelations, she did not prophesy or read man's thoughts, she was remarkable for no great austerities or striking renunciations or marvelous observance of rule or conspicuous zeal for souls . . . and yet she is to be proclaimed a saint . . . and for all future time, as long as this earth shall last, the Holy Sacrifice will be addressed to her to intercede with God, the common Father of us all, to bless the creatures who are the work of his hands.

Heroic virtue has always been associated in our minds with just such manifestations as here are truly stated to have had no place in her story, and one cannot help wondering how, then, she can have possessed what seems in no way to have revealed itself in her words or actions and therefore, as it appears, in no way to have influenced them.

But indeed, not with Bernadette alone but with other saints too, one suspects at times that these outward manifestations that seem to us to be the very stuff of their sanctity may in fact obscure rather than reveal the secret of it; may perhaps stand toward it in something of the same relation that the vocal or instrumental rendering of a musical theme does to the inner *motif* of which it is the only feasible, perhaps, but not really the inevitable and essential expression. Words are, as experience so often proves, but a clumsy vehicle of utterance of the "word" in one's mind: and it may be that audible music (even though we be unable to conceive of any other kind) is just as awkward a medium for the expression of musical reality. What if the circumstances of Bernadette's life were such that her humility, for instance, was already expressed and guaranteed by them? That her heroic readiness to do or to suffer whatsoever God might demand of her had no wider scope than the gentle bearing with such trivial occasions as occur to the most ordinary persons in daily life whether in the world or in the cloister: that her charity had no larger field for its exercise than in silence and obedience and cheerfulness under the irritating, but still not intolerable, curiosity of strangers or the nagging of a "commonsense" Reverend Mother: that her patience (the root of all virtue) had no greater strain put upon it than to bear with the importunities of well-meaning but inconsiderate admirers? It might be, then, that the essential sainthood, truly hers, had no more adequate instrument for its expression than these very narrow opportunities which though they detracted from its appearance did not affect its reality or its heroism. One might find a parallel in the case of an artist with nothing but inferior materials to work with, or of a statesman with only the affairs of a village to administer. It will be enough if we can find in her life evidence that this was indeed so, and that only by force of circumstances which were not her own responsibility did her reach so limit her grasp.

The life story of Bernadette (she was christened "Bernade", but from the first was always known by this affectionate diminutive) is short, and except for the great event of the Apparitions of Our Lady (the whole eighteen were comprised within a bare two months) was entirely devoid of unusual incident. She was born on January 8, 1844, when Louis-Philippe was on the throne of France, and the first Apparition took place on February 11, 1858, when she was fourteen, undersized, weakly, speaking the Lourdais *patois* and not yet able to read or write pure French. Her parents, feckless and incompetent by nature, but good Catholics according to their lights, rapidly muddled away the small property with which they had started their married life, and for several years before Bernadette had the first of her visions they had been living in the utmost poverty in a hut which had formerly been the jail of the little town. They had barely the necessary furniture and never a sufficiency of food. It is said that sometimes the children would pick wax from the church candles at funerals and other solemn functions and chew it to allay their hunger. They used to go about the town and the surrounding roadways and fields searching for bits of old iron, rags, bones and such like refuse, for which they would get a very few sous from a chiffonière of their acquaintance and so add a little to their miserably meager provision. Bernadette as the eldest, but also because she had that instinct for leadership which is so often the obverse of the talent for service, directed all these little expeditions, and in many ways supplied toward her sisters and her brothers for the neglect of their slatternly mother. But there were days when she was helpless under the agonizing suffocation of asthma, from which she suffered at intervals all her life through. She was no prodigy: indeed, the consensus of contemporary opinion is that, intellectually at least, she was more than ordinarily dull—she *could* not learn her Catechism, for instance! But all who knew her at that time were agreed that she was quite markedly *gentle*, with the brave pitiful gentleness of those who know suffering—the patient, helpless suffering of the very poor —from their own experience and are not embittered but rather sweetened and ennobled by it.

Still, to make her out to be a saint at this period of her life would surely be extravagant. She was a brave little girl doing her best, with everything against her: and her best was very small. Yet who may dare say that in God's eyes, with whom there is no boundary of big or little or time or number or space, *anything* can be small? It is within ordinary human experience that the bigger one is the less one is conscious of the distinctions that exist between things less than oneself, so that it is not difficult to understand that God reckons all things not by their size or importance (as we estimate these) but by their intention, within their limits: and that a thimble-full may be as vast as an ocean, and accomplishment be no more complete than effort.

Then came the Apparitions. One is conscious of an impression of incongruity and more than ordinary strangeness when one reads of them. For, first, the circumstances of the original appearance were entirely unfavorable to the expectation of any such thing, and Bernadette herself did not so much as suspect that it was Our Lady whom she saw —she said "a girl, not bigger than myself": further, in her account of what she saw, repeated again and again to a host of questioners, she never varied from her primitive statements, though her descriptions of Our Lady's features, dress, and attitude were quite out of harmony with what must have seemed most natural to her from the type of "pious picture" then (and, alas, now too!) in popular vogue. It will be remembered that when a number of images of Our Lady (some of them accepted as unquestionably "good") were shown to her for recognition she rejected them all, sometimes with exclamations of horror, but gave a distinct measure of approval to a copy of the very ancient Byzantine Madonna attributed by legend to St. Luke, which no doubt the good people who were examining her thought at best "quaint" even if not altogether repulsive. This quite uncultured village child knew, without knowing how she knew or anything else about it, that true art does not mean the accurate presentment of the body of a thing but the faithful interpretation of its soul! And here one may fancy that one sees the earliest indication in her of the heroism to which her canonization has testified—heroism, at least in the philosophical sense of being conspicuously beyond the ordinary.

Again, heroism is most nobly exhibited in constancy, and the constancy of this poor little half-starved, ailing, defenseless child, standing up to the alternate threats and cajolery, the menaces and flattery of civil and ecclesiastical authorities, and to the stupid if well-meaning efforts of pious sensationalists to get her to elaborate her simple narrative of what she had seen into something more consonant with their conception of what she *ought* to have seen, profoundly stirs one's admiration. She would not concede a point to such insinuations, nor on the other hand would she go back upon any of her original statements, and she clearly preferred to say nothing at all about her experiences and in fact never did so except under question. Nor, for all her poverty and the hardness of the life which she had to endure, would she ever accept the smallest gift of money or anything else, and her determination in this matter influenced her family to follow her inflexible example.

One is bewildered by the spectacle on the one hand of the commotion occasioned by the recent events, and on the other by the perfect balance and calmness of her who was the center of it all. The townspeople, the clergy, the police, the legislature, the army itself were set in motion all because Bernadette Soubirous, aged fourteen, had said, and stood by it, that she had seen "a white girl, not bigger than myself", in a cave on the rocky bank of the Gave, and that later, when at the command of the Curé she had asked the Apparition to say who she was, the answer had been "I am the Immaculate Conception"—words adapted to the comprehension of the child who, no doubt, had heard without very much understanding of the Definition of December 8, 1854.

Then she was sent to school, where she learned next to nothing, not because she did not want to but because she simply could not. One remembers that the Curé d'Ars was ordained priest though the extent of his knowledge of theology was little more than that he loved God. In 1859 she was sent by the doctors to take the waters at Cauterets, and then returned to Lourdes, to the Convent of the Sisters of Nevers, as a sort of boarder under observation, until in 1866 the petition which two years earlier she had made to be received into their Community was granted, and she left her home for ever on July 29. On April 16, 1879, she died, being then three months over thirty-five years of age.

It will be seen that Bernadette's life, apart from the Apparitions which occupied such a small fraction of it, presents none of the features which custom has led us to expect in the lives of the saints. Yet, in fact, the one essential element of all sanctity reveals itself, on examination, in every detail of it. For heroism is not dependent upon, or specified by, the magnitude of the occasions in which it manifests itself, and, studied closely, her life assumes no less than veritably heroic proportions. There can have been little flaw, and little that was merely ordinary, in the character of one who without any gifts of nature or of training was able by sheer heroic truth and simplicity to escape the multiple snares and pitfalls that beset her. The most famous shrine in the Christian world, an outstanding witness to the supernatural in an age of materialism, is founded upon her simple word. Nobody saw the Apparitions but she: upon no other authority than hers (now guaranteed by the

Church) is grounded the faith of these unaccountable thousands who year after year flock to the grotto of Massabieille: and it is because of this that they believe, and thereafter experience, that in visiting Lourdes they enlist on their behalf, in a very special way, her powerful advocacy whom Christ her Son commissioned from the throne of the Cross to be to all his brethren the mother that she had been to him.

Her sanctity was the sanctity of a child: but one remembers that Christ has said that only children are fit for the kingdom of heaven —"Whoever shall not receive the kingdom of God as a little child, shall not enter into it." All those tremendous things which we associate with canonized holiness she "received as a child". As we view them on the miniature stage of her life they look to us to be trifles, but they were great big real things to her: and rightly seen, in their true perspective, great big real things they should seem to us too. To be holy does not—cannot—mean to be extraordinary. Since Christ made his own (the choice of God) the ordinary life of man, and for thirty years of his life showed himself to be the Beloved Son of his Father by no greater thing than fidelity to the duties of ordinary human life, there is no excuse left us for lamenting our lack of opportunity. The canonization of Bernadette is like one of those occasional experiences which call us (uncomfortably, maybe) out of the unreal imaginings of our daydreams into the sharp reality of the waking day: we understand, then, that to serve God truly does not mean to try to be someone else than ourselves, nor even to be ourselves but in other circumstances than those that we have, but to aim at being the best that we can be as and where we are. One thinks of Bernadette, three hundred miles from her home and from all that life had held for her up till then (for she was younger than her age when at fourteen she saw Our Lady) yet peaceably content to finish the amazing story in the relatively trivial round of Convent life where nothing ministered to the recollection of her brief hour of splendor, and where in addition she had as Superior one who confessed afterward that whenever she had occasion to address her she found herself almost unconsciously speaking with "a certain asperity" as to *une paysanne grossière et sans instruction* who had no right to be on such intimate terms with the supernatural.

In the Process of her beatification the *Promotor Fidei* took exception to certain sharp sallies and other gestures of impatience which seemed to him to denote a lack of that perfect self-control which should be the mark of heroic perfection. One feels that he must have been no more than half-hearted in his objections, deferring perhaps unconsciously to the popular prepossession that the saint is a being not so much above as altogether outside normal humanity. But it is before all else important to look upon Bernadette as an intensely human person. From first to last she was just herself. She knew that she was ignorant, inexperienced, altogether undeserving of the high favors which had been granted to her, and she never by word or deed displayed the smallest satisfaction in the celebrity that was forced upon her. Indeed, the evidences of veneration which she could not fail to perceive, quite obviously revolted her. One regrets that among the chief offenders in this regard were the clergy. It is incredible what they made her suffer by their importunities, pestering and pursuing her with questions and demands and compliments in the worst possible bad taste. So, too, in the Convent, where often when she was summoned to the parlour for yet another interrogation by curious visitors, she would come to a standstill outside the door in an agony of repulsion for the coming ordeal, not seldom bursting into tears before she could bring herself to turn the handle. It all seemed so stupid to her, such a mistake: "Oh, why can't they leave me in peace!" she would cry. But she was always modest, courteous, patient with her visitors, showing obstinacy, gentle but unconquerable, only when they tried to force from her confirmation of one or other of the accretions to her story which popular imagination had been busy in supplying, or when they tried to press some gift, were it the very simplest, upon her.

She could speak up though at times, and could return a pointed repartee to a foolish or tactless question—as, too, could the Curé d'Ars. But it was remarked that she never did this when she thought that it might hurt or scandalize.

Much curiosity has been aroused by her statement that Our Lady had entrusted her with three secrets which she was never under any circumstances to reveal to anyone. She made it clear, over and over again, that these had nothing to do with the Church or with France or any other nation, nor with any question of civil or ecclesiastical politics. It seems to be quite certain that they were neither prophecies nor revelations but concerned herself alone, laying down, perhaps, the conditions upon which her sanctification was to be guaranteed. One who has very closely studied the history of Bernadette gives as his conclusion that these secrets were probably to some such effect as that she should never imagine that the privilege which she had had of converse with Our Lady was due to her own merits: that she should never consent to profit in any material way by what had happened: and that she should never do anything to attract notice to herself in connection with the renown that Lourdes was presently to acquire.

These, at any rate, seem to have been the principles upon which she ordered her conduct. She would not, though she was left free to do so, attend the consecration of the Basilica of Lourdes in 1876 except upon the impracticable condition that she might see without being seen, and all her life at Nevers was a testimony to the low esteem that quite unaffectedly she preserved of herself—Priez pour moi, pauvre pécheresse! were her last words.

To the end she was what she had been at the beginning, Bernadette, the poor child of Lourdes, doing always with her might what her hand found to do, little enough though that was. And now, by the infallible verdict of the Church, she is ranked as in her own right among the Shining Ones of the Company of Christ.

SAINT JOHN BOSCO

[1815–1888]

C. C. Martindale, S.J.

OHN BOSCO was born of very poor parents, in a tiny village near Turin. One hundred thousand persons came to his funeral. How was this?

Piedmont is a land of ancient history, wide plains gorgeous with vine and maize, and braced by keen breezes down from the Alps; its people are tough, genial, ambitious, hardworking. John's father, a small jobber, died all too soon, leaving his valiant wife to care for her stepson, Antonio, and her own two sons, Giovanni and Giuseppe. She brought them up rigorously and lovingly in the poor cottage; the small John, walking four times a day to school, covered thus twelve miles daily. Her stepson began to grow up a bully, and jealous of his half-brothers. He became better later on, but at first made life frankly miserable for his stepmother and half-brothers.

John, who had an astounding faculty for *dreaming*, decided at *nine*, on the strength of a dream in which he saw himself changing children from beasts into lambs, to become a priest and devote his life to *children*, and began at once. He haunted every caravan and fair; learned to walk tight-ropes, to become acrobat and conjuror at cost of often-broken nose . . . and provided fascinating entertainments, which he wound up with the rosary and a sermon. . . . Then this round-headed boy with tousled hair took to his books; he simply could not forget; between a Christmas and an Easter he learned the whole Latin grammar.

But Anthony was making life intolerable. His mother sent John away to work, and to learn. One experience he retained and used. The priests managing his elementary school were correct, aloof, chill. Bosco's temperament would never have allowed him to become that; but here he learned he *ought* not to become it. Nor ever did he. Yet, though he ate but maize and chestnuts, worked all day as houseboy and billiard marker; began to exercise his magnetism and became the center of a group; beat professional athletes and acrobats at their best performances; worked late into night with one tallow dip, it looked as if he had no future. He had to drop his studies, being too poor. Suddenly, all went right. Charity succored him; he won prizes. At twenty he entered the seminary at Chieri; after six years' study he was ordained. He had retained his irrepressible gaiety, despite his stiff, semi-Jansenized professors.

While finishing his training in another college he studied the Turin slums. Their degradation was then appalling. He could achieve no contact till one day a sacristan smacked the head of a big oaf who stood staring and had answered that he didn't know how to serve the Mass John was about to offer. "I won't have my friends treated like that", exclaimed the priest. "Your *friend*?" "The moment anyone is ill-used he becomes my friend." The lad was brought back; next Sunday he fetched others; in but a few months over a hundred were arriving. For three years this uproarious horde had for playground the courtyard of the college.

I wish I could mention the names of those who helped Don Bosco. Saints are among them. But in a quarter of an hour, impossible. Indeed, he soon met obstacles. An old priest put a thistle-grown field at his disposal—but the priest's housekeeper wouldn't have the noise, and she got the leave withdrawn. He obtained a chapel near some mills; the millers and their men said the lads were ruffians (so they were, half of them) and got *that* leave withdrawn. The clergy themselves objected to boys from their parishes hanging around Don Bosco. The Marquis of Cavour (father of the statesman) was told that Bosco was organizing a political conspiracy, and he was watched by the police. But it was the police who were converted, not Bosco arrested. When he visualized and announced what the future held they said he was a megalomaniac: two priests were sent to—literally—"take him for a ride". A drive to the asylum. Bosco guessed their errand, followed them to the carriage, and "After you", said he politely. They entered. Bosco slammed the door and called out: "To the asylum." Off the driver went, and took quite some time to get the poor men out. . . . Italians have a caustic sense of humor. Bosco had scored. After some setbacks he established himself, in 1846, in a slum center, obtained his mother's companionship, and started what he called his oratory, a group of four hundred lads of the roughest. Hitherto all this had been in the margin of his regular work; now he could devote himself to his true apostolate.

I cannot even outline his life, which was adventurous enough: Italy was in the throes of every sort of political and social upheaval; extreme disorder often prevailed. Half a dozen times Don Bosco was murderously set upon. Once a man shot at him through the window as he sat teaching. The bullet passed under his arm, ripping the cloth. "A pity," said he; "it is my best cassock." And he continued the lesson. More than once his terrific straight left sent the would-be garrotter flying; and a fascinating episode is that of the enormous dog Grigio, many-times-over-mongrel, who appeared intermittently from nowhere, refused a kennel, ate who knows how, hurled himself upon assailants, escorted the priest through dangerous patches, and once snarlingly refused so much as to allow him to go out. Had he done so, he would have fallen straight into an ambush.

Willingly I leave to one side his associations with great personages; enough to say that the most anticlerical officials were won by his frankness and forthrightness, and that twice when he was in Paris, Victor Hugo came, Nicodemus-like, by night, and made to him a profession of faith that his melodramatic will does not disannul. . . . I must concentrate on his educational work, and on his personality, and even these I must interweave. He began by realizing that today every religious enterprise on behalf of the young must have its educational aspect, just as no educational enterprise is of the slightest lasting value without being firmly based upon religion. The latter fact is proved by the whole of the last hundred and fifty years of European and American history; and experience forces the former one upon us. His groups of boys then at once included classes; the classes became schools—very simple schools developed others—others of a much higher grade. But to me his agricultural and professional schools have always been the most interesting: Italy and Spain herein may have more reason to be grateful to Bosco than to almost anyone else at any time, save perhaps the Spanish Jesuits.

His miraculous influence over the young enabled him definitely to exchange the almost prison-like existence in the schools of his day for something far more human. He gave liberty without loss of discipline; he was gentle without any softness; endlessly understanding without complaisancy; he shared in, and indeed initiated every sport, yet never lost his dignity. From Pope and prince down to gutter-snipe, he used the same free, dry, gay repartee. Only once, that I can remember, was he caught out. "What", said he to a rather talkative young ruffian, "is the most remarkable thing you've seen?" "Don Bosco." . . . The patron of all hikers, he was the first, maybe, in modern Europe to understand the virtues of sheer noise. But he made it musical. . . . Not even—well —the brass band of Rhodesian Chishawasha, shattering the silence of the veld, had so enchanted me as have the Salesian brass bands under the suave skies of Italy. "Salesian?" Bosco soon saw he must create an "Order" of men to support him. That Order, characteristically named after the witty, gentle, vigorous St. Francis de Sales, consists today of some nine thousand men. In Italy alone it has a hundred and fifty houses; in the rest of Europe about a hundred and seventy; in America two hundred and forty; in Asia, Africa, Australia about seventy. These enterprises range from seminaries and parishes, through colleges, all sorts of schools, but especially industrial and professional, to hostels, emigrant-institutions, and hospitals or leper-colonies. Parallel to this he founded the women's society of our Lady Help of Christians, with about six hundred houses, whose work again covers the whole civilizational and religious ground, from kindergartens through municipal schools to schools for domestic economy and the like.

Toward the end of his life Don Bosco developed two special interests: one was England, whither the Salesians came in 1887; there are thirteen of his houses now within the Empire, the latest opened being near Macclesfield, a training college for foreign missionaries especially for India, Thailand, and Palestine. And these Missions quite haunted his mind toward the last. Already in 1856 he had begun to think of England; in 1875 he sent his first missionary band to South America: Patagonia, Tierra del Fuego, the Isles of Magellan, then Ecuador; deep into Brazil, Paraguay, Bolivia. . . . I will not attempt to catalogue his missions today, the Salesians work all the world over.

Yet what, indeed, is all this exterior work, let alone the homage that surrounded his last years? When he was at Lyons the business of driving him through the crowds was such that the poor cabman lost his temper and cried out: "I had rather drag the devil than drive a Saint." And in Paris the church of our Lady of Victories was crammed two hours before he came to say Mass in that "refuge for sinners", and a poor woman exclaimed to a questioner: "You see, it is the Mass for sinners, and it is to be offered by a Saint. . . ." But what is all this, compared to, precisely, the man's sanctity? In a way Bosco lived simultaneously in four worlds—that exterior one, symbolizable by the absolute *town* that the Turin Oratory and its appurtenances are; the world of dreams—and believe me, an exact scientific study of his recorded dreams would be of infinitely more value to psychologists than that of diseased mentalities in Viennese hospitals; the world of souls, into which he read with an accuracy far beyond telepathy or second sight (whatever these may mean); and the world of God.

His purity, perfect to the very roots of his thought, enabled him, as our Lord promised, to "see God", and therefore, perhaps, to read so clearly within his fellow man; his total trust was such that literally he built up his entire work out of nothing; his lovable sarcasms that never hurt; his transparent simplicity; his bluff gaiety, despite terrific work (from youth he had promised never to sleep for more than five hours) and great physical pain and complete self-denial—all this was an affair not of temperament, not of talent merely, but from God. "God", says the Introit of the Mass said in his honor on April 26, "gave him wisdom and very great prudence, and a *breadth of heart* wide as the sea-sands". And later on: "He believed, hoping against hope, so that he became father of many peoples, as was said to him." And read its epistle, taken from St. Paul's letter to the Philippians, 4:4–7; it is, so to say, the essence of Don Bosco. Great men and their work cannot just be imitated. May God give to his successors a double portion of his spirit. I have, indeed, encountered that spirit, alike in his houses beneath the burning sky of Cape Town, and in the playgrounds more grim, but no less gay, of Battersea.

SAINT THERESE OF LISIEUX

[1873–1897]

R. H. J. Steuart, S.J.

HE STORY of St. Thérèse of Lisieux must be almost unique in the history of the saints. She was not quite twenty-five years old when she died, on September 30, 1897, having been a nun for just over nine years, and many who when she was born were already older than she was to be when she died, lived to see her name enrolled among the saints. Indeed, her whole history from her birth to her canonization lies well within the lifetime of countless persons now living [in 1949] who would by no means willingly consider themselves old. This, remembering the traditional slowness of the Church in according her official recognition to the heroic sanctity of the individual, would have been remarkable enough had the stage of Thérèse's life been set in public view: had she been a path-breaker in some region of active spiritual or social work: or had she been a martyr, an apostle or a foundress. But her life, as to three-fifths of it, was spent entirely within the narrow shelter of a provincial home of the *petite bourgeoisie*, and as to the remainder, in the virtual obliteration of a Carmelite cloister. Still more remarkable in these circumstances is the fact that canonization may verily be said to have been conferred upon her by public acclamation even before the Church had set her seal to it.

This inversion of the accustomed order of things has happened before, but then the subject of it has always been (as we should expect) one who in lifetime had already taken the public eye—one need go no further back for an example than to the Curé d'Ars or to St. Benedict Joseph Labre. But to her public, the little world of Lisieux, she was only known (and no doubt very soon forgotten) as the youngest of the five daughters of M. Martin the watchmaker, whose well-known piety seemed to have destined all his children to the religious life: while in

Carmel she was known just as the third of those children to enter the one convent, and probably to most of the nuns as, on the whole, the least distinguished of the three. In the very year of her death, when all the community knew that she was dying, she herself (with what satisfaction, one may imagine!) overheard one laysister say to another, "What *will* our Mother find to say about Sister Thérèse when she dies!" alluding to the Carmelite custom of sending brief appreciation of their deceased sisters to other communities of their Order. In fact, when the time came, the Prioress wrote nothing, or next to nothing. Instead, she printed and distributed Thérèse's own account of her life, written at the command of her sister Pauline (Sister Agnes of Jesus) who had held the office of Prioress between two periods of Mother Gonzaga's rule.

In this enchanting document, written in obvious if unconscious but finally triumphant, struggle with the traditional "common form" of such *journaux intimes,* is revealed the secret of that "Little Way" which has been by far the most important contribution to the spiritual science of our generation. The greater part of the *Récit d'une Âme* is autobiographical, and the "Secret" is rather implied by the course of her story than explicitly defined as a method of perfection. But in the last chapter, added by special request of Pauline some time after the rest had been completed, Thérèse lays bare without reserve the lines upon which she had ordered her life of heroic love and sacrifice. The theme is simple: it is abandonment of self into the hands of God, no new doctrine: yes, but an abandonment so thorough, so detailed, so consistent, so deep-reaching as to involve the smallest units of her volitional activity. Indeed, it is at its purest and sublimest in just those least observable matters wherein fidelity and resignation to the all-pervading, all controlling will of God has least external repercussion either upon the notice of others or upon the consciousness of the soul itself. It is the way of absolute giving, without limit or respite or reserve: a heroism of self-surrender commensurate with the very greatest occasions for it that could arise, and not in the least degree diminished in splendor because in fact no such occasion ever did arise. It is the *Little Way* because it lies always among little things, but in her it was of that quality which would have been adequate to the dizziest height and the fiercest strain.

Looked at from another point of view, it might be called the Way of

Perfect Acceptance. Everything, were it the tiniest trifle, was of God and from God directly for her. She accepted *everything*, without difference of distinction, as a holy thing, taking it reverently and delicately from his fingers into the center of her heart. The size or importance of the thing mattered to her not at all: she knew nothing of any "big" or "little", for the sufficing and inestimable worth of everything that she had to do or to endure was that all of it, greatest or least, first or last, was his Will, his personal Will for her. It was nothing less than Divine Wisdom itself that taught her how far more complete a sacrifice in God's eyes is the acceptance, as direct from him, of little troublesome teasing things, so easily avoided, than the offering of something perhaps much bigger to look at but chosen by oneself—"Sacrifice and oblation thou didst not desire . . . in the head of the book it is written of me that I should do thy will."

The more one studies Thérèse of Lisieux, whether in the records of those who knew her or in her own copious self-revelations, the more one realizes the profundity of their error who, misled no doubt by the simplicity and joyousness of the image thus evoked (powerfully aided by the insipid and conventionalized portraits of her now so much in vogue) think of her principally as something bright and pretty and facile like the pictures which she used to paint for festal occasions in the convent. Her "Little Way" becomes, so regarded, but a petty way after all: and she herself no more than a highly privileged child miraculously preserved from those struggles and agonies which one had been led to believe were of the essence of the life of sanctity. Devotion to the "Little Flower" (how one comes to dislike the title!) has been, to many such, a mere outlet for sentimentality and an argument for release from the uncomfortable implications of Christ's own warning that the way of perfection is hard and narrow and that consequently they are few who persevere therein. But no mistake could be more capital. The lesson of her life is actually the exact opposite of this. What it teaches—in words of one syllable, so to say—is that holiness is an achievement that costs one the full of one's resources in strength and courage. It is a goal to which there is no short cut, a Temple to which there is no back entrance. To it there is but one way, his who said of himself, "I am the Way": it is the way of self-renunciation, of burden-carrying and yoke-bearing, a way stretching for most of its length through darkness and the desert with no other star to guide one than the far-distant light of faith.

Holiness is the expression of the love of God possessing and actu-ating the soul throughout all its being, and the love of God is, as all true love is, realized in progressive self-giving. Love, whether of God or of the creature, is one and the self-same thing and it is expressed in one and the self-same way: but the foundations of the two differ in this, that the latter is born of the knowledge of an object similar to ourselves, ascertainable through the reason and the senses, whereas the former, being directed to the ineffable Being of God, needs be-sides this an infusion of supernatural grace transcending the scope of these faculties as its term transcends theirs, and proceeding, when the subject is fit to receive it, from the Holy Spirit, the Spirit of Love, who utters God's own immortal Love through us as our own. But in order to become such a channel of the Divine operation the soul has to make itself ready for it by doing all that can be done to that end in its own order. Little enough, indeed, but at the expenditure, none the less, of its whole substance—"If thou wilt be perfect go sell all whatever thou hast." This giving (for, after all, what have we to give?) comes in the end, by an apparent paradox, to *receiving*, for the act of entire renunciation of all right of ownership whatsoever is the obverse of an entire acceptance of everything as of God and from him, involving a voluntary and detailed recognition of him and his gift in every happening of life down to the most inconsiderable. Does one not realize what such an unbroken chain of acts of surrender as this will imply, and how in consequence her life, which was spent in forging and welding just such a chain, should have worn itself out in so short a space?

Her "Little Way", just because it meant the unremitting and minute implementing of this surrender in each and all of the little things that fill up the immensely greater portion of our lives, was in fact a Way of unlimited breadth and content: it meant not the fruit and the flower only, but the stock and the root too—the root first, and then of neces-sity all the rest with it. One understands how, to one bent as Thérèse was on missing no opportunity of giving whatever her hand found to give, such trifling irritations as the splashings of a too vigorous sister at the washtub or the bead rattling of a restless neighbor in Choir, were quite fit vehicles for that heroic abnegation which had the oc-casion been greater she would have practiced no less wholeheartedly. She could put *all* her holocaust of self into patient ministrations to a querulous invalid or smiling graciousness to a naturally antipathetic sister, and she could accept the exchange of a gracefully shaped and colored water jug in her cell for an ugly cracked one, or bear without seeking relief the heat and dust and discomfort of household work in the summertime, or grievously chapped and chilblained fingers in the winter, with no less heroism than she would (as in fact, at the end she did) accept agonies of pain and exhaustion.

Perhaps the chief difference between Thérèse and most other saints was that she did not ask for or *want* greater occasions of suffering or self-surrender: they were not in her way, and she knew well that they would have drawn no more exactingly upon her will than did these lesser ones that came to her unasked. Thus, though she practiced the regular corporal austerities of Rule with exactness, she never spontaneously added anything of the kind to what was already prescribed. Though no doubt she was well aware that such things may easily be made into an excuse for escape from bearing with the unsought disagreeables that offer themselves so readily in the course of ordinary convent life (and perhaps had had to recognize that those who did much in this way were not invariably the persons that she revered most) one feels that her real reason was her knowledge that to her they would afford no wider scope for the spirit of surrender and acceptance that animated her than did the humble-seeming opportunities of which she availed herself so greedily.

It might be, and indeed has been, urged in depreciation of the value of her "Little Way" for any but exceptional souls, that Thérèse had been, so to speak, in a Novitiate from her earliest days. Both her parents were persons of very saintly life, and their family of five girls (two sons and two daughters had died in infancy) was brought up in a singularly religious, almost conventual, atmosphere and sheltered with the utmost solicitude from all contact with dangerous worldly influences. She, in addition, was the object of adoring love on the part of a father whose dearest hope was that she might one day become a real saint, and who early initiated her in the life of good works and recollection. Yet on the other hand, the intense and unbroken happiness of her home life might just as well have proved an obstacle to her renunciation of the world, which nevertheless she made at the unusually early age of fifteen. But, in fact, whatever may have been her privileges by nature or by grace, so far from detracting from the value to us of the lesson that her manner of life affords, they were the very reason why we can read and learn that lesson so easily and feel its truth and attraction so strongly. God so fitted her, and so disposed her circumstances, that the secret of her holiness could not be missed. The lives of the saints are offered to us for our study in order that we may see therein at their finest and best the virtues, qualities, and motives that made them what they were. We are not called upon to imitate them in the personal details of their several lives, but to adapt to our own lives what theirs teach us. It is no part of favoritism (so to call it!) on God's part, far less any injustice to us but quite the contrary, that here and there he so endows a saint by nature or enriches him by grace that he is able to present to us an unflawed example of this or that Christian excellence to serve us for an ideal. The lives of some saints offer us the spectacle, in their most highly developed and therefore most authentic and intelligible form, of one or another of the virtues that should be the aim of all of us: others exhibit the perfect practical exercise of general spiritual principles in varying circumstances. The life of St. Thérèse of Lisieux is one of those which from time to time, as the world needs it, present a fundamental scheme of readjustment or reinterpretation of our attitude toward God particularly in regard of the pursuit of holiness, opening for us a fresh vista of the Way of Perfection.

It is the same journey to the same City, but with a new map to travel by.

~